Understanding Jihad

UNDERSTANDING JIHAD

David Cook

UNIVERSITY OF CALIFORNIA PRESS
BERKELEY   LOS ANGELES   LONDON

University of California Press
Berkeley and Los Angeles, California

University of California Press, Ltd.
London, England

© 2005 by The Regents of the University of California

Library of Congress Cataloging-in-Publication Data

Cook, David
    Understanding Jihad / David Cook
        p. cm.
    Includes bibliographical references and index.
    ISBN-13 978-0-520-24448-1 (pbk. : alk. paper)
    ISBN-10 0-520-24448-6 (pbk. : alk. paper)
    1. Jihad. 2. War—Religious aspects—Islam. 3. Islamic
    fundamentalism. 4. Islam—21st century. I. Title.
    BP182.C66 2005
    297.7′2—dc22

                                        2004026561

Manufactured in the United States of America
14   13   12   11   10   09   08   07   06
10   9   8   7   6   5   4

To Deborah Gerber Tor:
Who could hope for a better friend?

CONTENTS

Acknowledgments   ix

Introduction   1
1. Qur'an and Conquest   5
2. The "Greater Jihad" and the "Lesser Jihad"   32
3. The Crystallization of Jihad Theory: Crusade and
   Counter-Crusade   49
4. Jihad during the Nineteenth Century: Renewal
   and Resistance   73
5. Radical Islam and Contemporary Jihad Theory   93
6. Globalist Radical Islam and Martyrdom Operations   128
   Afterword   163

Appendix: Some Translated Documents   169
Communiqué from the Armed Islamic Group
(Algeria; September 8, 1995)   169

World Islamic Front for Jihad against Zionists and
Crusaders: Declaration of War (February 23, 1998)   173

A Communiqué from Qa 'Idat Al-Jihad Concerning the
Testaments of the Heroes and the Legality of the Washington
and New York Operations (April 24, 2002)   175

The Importance of Jihad, on the Goals of Jihad (by 'Ali al-'Aliyani)   181

Under the Shadow of the Spears (by Sulayman Abu Ghayth)   189

Translation of "The Last Night"   195

"Moments before the Crash, by the Lord of the 19"
(by Louis Atiyat Allah)   202

Timeline   209

Glossary   211

Notes   213

Bibliography   237

Index   253

ACKNOWLEDGMENTS

This book is a solicited work, and I probably would not have thought of writing it had it not been for Reed Malcolm of the University of California Press. Thus, I owe him my thanks. Many others have helped me along the way with my study of Islam, encouraging me to write and publish. For my intellectual development in the field of Islam, I owe an eternal debt of gratitude to the teaching of Yohanan Friedmann of the Hebrew University, Jerusalem, a uniquely gifted and patient man, who has encouraged me immensely over the years and persuaded me to persist in the field of Islamic studies. I owe an equal debt to Fred M. Donner of the University of Chicago, a man of amazing teaching skills, to whom I (like all of his students) look as one of the exemplary scholars in our field.

For helping me with this manuscript, I would like to thank my parents, W. Robert and Elaine Cook, who read successive drafts and offered valuable suggestions. My closest friend, Deborah Tor, made numerous changes and emendations on every page. I would also like to thank Elizabeth Urban, my student, who read the manuscript with meticulous attention, as well as Richard Haeder, who discussed a number of the problems and issues with me. Ellen Chang corrected a huge number of grammatical and syntactical errors. Thanks are also due to Martha Brill Olcott of the Carnegie Endowment for International Peace, who supplied me with citations concerning Central Asian radical Islam, and Richard Landes of the Center for Millennial Studies at Boston University, who offered valuable advice on many points of history and doctrine. The index was prepared by my graduate student Stephen Finley with exceptional diligence.

Thanks are also due to the Jon R. and Paula Mosle Fund for providing me with the wherewithal to buy Arabic and Persian texts, and to the Junior Research Fellowship Fund at Rice University for the ability to travel to the Middle East a number of times in order to collect materials. "The Last Night" translation (in the appendix) has been reproduced from my article in *Nova Religio,* for which I am indebted to the University of California Press. Thanks also to numerous friends in the Middle East, Africa, and Pakistan with whom I have discussed this subject. As always, errors and misstatements are my responsibility alone.

INTRODUCTION

Jihad. The word has entered into common usage in the United States in the wake of September 11, 2001. Politicians use it to conjure up terrifying images of irrational foreigners coming to destroy American freedoms; religious figures use it to define Islam. *Jihad* has even entered our everyday vocabulary, associated (by most non-Muslims) with unrestrained, unreasoning, total warfare. But what *does* it really mean?

Jihad, like other words taken from a religious context, has a long history and a complex set of meanings. Conventionally it is translated as "holy war," but this definition, associated with the medieval Crusades, is usually rejected by Muslims as too narrowly Christian. In Arabic, the word's literal meaning is "striving" or "exerting oneself," with the implication, on the basis of its usage in the Qur'an, "with regard to one's religion." Many contemporary Muslim writers, recognizing the negative connotations that *jihad* has acquired in European languages, maintain that the word means nothing more than "striving." Yet this position, predominant among Muslim apologists writing in non-Muslim (primarily Western) languages, is disingenuous. To gain a sense of the word's true meaning, one must begin by looking at its usage in classical Muslim literature, primarily in Arabic, but also in other Muslim languages, as well as at its function in Muslim history and historiography.

To complicate matters further, there are different types of jihad. The term's complexity is not surprising given the centrality of the concept of jihad for Islam and the length of time—fourteen centuries—that Muslims have had to work with it. "Warfare with spiritual significance" is the primary and root meaning of the term as it has been defined by classical Muslim jurists and legal scholars and as it was practiced by Muslims during the premodern period. This meaning is sustained in the standard definition given in the new edition of the *Encyclopedia of Islam*: "In law, according to general doctrine and in historical tradition, the *jihad* consists of military action with the object of the expansion of Islam and, if need be, of its defense."[1] This terse summary of Muslim law and history is the standard, scholarly one.

Nonetheless, many Muslims, seeking to distance themselves and their religion from associations with violence and conquest, maintain that the word's significance is exclusively spiritual. According to some of the most prominent Muslim leaders in the United States, jihad is entirely peaceable and represents the exertion of spiritual warfare waged by the faithful against the lower, or evil, soul.[2] This definition of jihad has considerable precedent in classical sources, although it is not the word's primary meaning.

Given the complexity and sensitivity of jihad's associations—the term is at once at the heart of polemics against Islam and of apologetics for Islam—it is easy to slip away from the facts and fall into polemics oneself. Therefore, I will attempt to base this study completely upon original sources, grounding the analysis in Muslim history, and clearly label any analysis or speculation on my part as such. The differences between what is written in theological and legal treatises and what a believer may practice in any religion, moreover, are often substantial. Therefore, the definition of jihad must be based both on what Muslims have written concerning the subject and on the historical record of how they have practiced it.

Using the above definition as a point of departure, one must also ask: how does one distinguish between a jihad and a conventional, purely secular war? That question is as fraught as the term's definition. The Prophet Muhammad never formally declared a jihad—not, at least, using that term—yet the many campaigns that he undertook on behalf of his faith are the prototypical jihad wars. In the same way, the label of jihad has been attached to the great Islamic conquests of the seventh and eighth centuries, but only long after the fact; we do not know what the Muslim participants called these wars. For centuries Muslims have fought each other, sometimes describing the conflicts as jihad, sometimes not. On some occasions the use of the term to describe warfare against other Muslims was rejected by the community as a whole, by a part of the community, or by the historians recording these conflicts. In other instances, such as the Ottoman conquests of southeastern Europe from the fourteenth to the sixteenth century, there is no secure evidence that the dynasty called for a jihad, and yet from an outsider's point of view, the conquests were unambiguously grounded in religion.[3] In principle, wars waged by Muslims against non-Muslims are more readily accepted by members of the faith as legitimate jihads than are wars against other Muslims. But even here, the nomenclature is slippery: the Ottoman call for jihad against the Allied powers during World War I—when the Muslim Ottoman state was allied with the Christian Austro-Hungarian and Hohenzollern German empires—was widely rejected by Muslims.

Among Muslims who acknowledge the associations of jihad with warfare, most would define the term as warfare authorized by a legitimate representative of the Muslim community for the sake of an issue that is universally, or nearly universally, acknowledged to be of critical importance for the entire community against an admitted enemy of Islam. Frequently regulations concerning its conduct are adduced to differentiate jihad from other types of warfare: these include formal announcement of the jihad and its causes; terms for its resolution prior to the commencement of hostilities; careful regard for noncombatants and their property; respect for the enemy dead; and restrictions on the type of warfare allowed. These issues are regularly treated—and at considerable length—in the legal and religious literature advocating jihad and discussing its meaning.

Because of the sacred nature of the combat, the jihad should benefit from divine support; some authors describe it as a sacrament for the community of Muslims.[4] Such boundaries place jihad squarely within the ideal of a "just war" familiar to Christian theologians, as distinct from the concept of "holy war."[5] Nonetheless, these idealized boundaries raise questions of their own: Were they ever followed exactly? To what degree would a Muslim soldier have been cognizant of these ideals? Does the abandonment or disregard of the ideals of jihad in the heat of battle, even temporarily, moot the conduct of the jihad? Have there been instances when Muslims, either individually or collectively, disavowed a jihad because of revulsion at the tactics used? Would such revisionism be associated with defeat or could it happen after a victory?

These questions and apparent inconsistencies make it exceedingly difficult for Muslims, let alone outsiders, to articulate authoritatively what constitutes a jihad. A good example is the present-day "jihad" that has been launched by globalist radical Muslims such as Usama b. Ladin against the United States and its allies. The movement's literature invokes the legal, religious, and military vocabulary of traditional jihad and situates the actions of the movement's adherents within the traditional parameters of Islamic jihad. Yet many Muslims reject the globalist radical Muslim claim to wage jihad, citing the movement's (apparent) lack of legitimate authority to wage war: declaring jihad, they argue, is solely the prerogative of a Muslim leader (such as a legitimate *imam* or a caliph). Jihad cannot legitimately be undertaken in the absence of a pronouncement by a recognized authority. Of course, radical Muslims have their own answers to this critique.

Present usage notwithstanding, one can neither deny the validity of an exclusively spiritual notion of jihad nor discount the possibility that Muslims may in time amend their interpretation of the concept to exclude militant aggression. One consequence of the present-day upsurge in jihad and visibility of the manner in which radical Muslims, and especially globalist radical Muslims (al-Qaʿida and its associates), practice it may be a decisive rejection of militant jihad by a majority of Muslims. If that were to happen, Muslim apologists would likely seek to ground the concept of nonviolent jihad as inherent in the religion, rather than as an amendment of the term's definition. (Historians of religion have often noted that the greatest changes in a given religion are sometimes masked by elaborate "proofs" of doctrinal consistency.) There is as yet no indication that such a redefinition of jihad has in fact been undertaken—outside of apologetics intended for "external consumption"—but it is still a possibility.

With these issues in mind, the life and teachings of the Prophet Muhammad must be examined first, and then the ramifications of the great Islamic conquests of the seventh and eighth centuries.

ONE

QUR'AN AND CONQUEST

MUHAMMAD, THE QUR'AN, AND JIHAD

Islam did not begin with violence. Rather, it began as the peaceful proclamation of the absolute unity of God by the Prophet Muhammad (ca. 610 C.E.) in the pagan-dominated town of Mecca. The early *suras* (chapters) of the Qur'an proclaim this basic message: "Say: He is Allah, the only One, Allah, the Everlasting. He did not beget and is not begotten, and none is His equal" (Qur'an 112). Initially, Muhammad was instructed merely to communicate this message to his immediate family and close friends, who, together with a number of social outcasts and slaves, formed the original community of Muslims. Within a few years, the Prophet and his adherents found themselves increasingly persecuted for their beliefs by the elite of the Quraysh (the tribe that dominated Mecca). Muhammad proselytized among the tribesmen of the oasis of Yathrib, about 150 miles to the north of Mecca, who accepted his message. In 622 he, together with the other Muslims, emigrated to this oasis, which was subsequently called Medina.

Muslim history begins with the *hijira*—Muhammad's emigration to Medina (although there continue to be major, unresolved problems with the historicity of the events narrated below concerning the life of the Prophet Muhammad and the first conquests). Medina was not a town in the conventional sense but rather a collection of small villages and forts spread over the oasis, divided politically among two pagan Arab tribes—the Aws and the Khazraj—and three smaller Jewish tribes: the Banu

Qaynuqa, the Banu al-Nadir, and the Banu Qurayza. Muhammad and the Muslims based their community within Medina, and over a period of five years they converted the Arab tribesmen that occupied the territory.

It was in this context that jihad arose, and the campaigns to gain adherents and control territory constituted the focus of the community's activity during the last nine years of the Prophet's life. Muhammad is recorded as having participated in at least twenty-seven campaigns and deputized some fifty-nine others—an average of no fewer than nine campaigns annually.[1] These campaigns can be divided into four groups:

1.   The five "thematic" battles of Badr (624), Uhud (625), Khandaq (627), Mecca (630) and Hunayn (630), undertaken with the goal of dominating the three principal settled areas of the Hijaz: Mecca, Medina, and al-Ta'if

2.   Raids against the Bedouin, undertaken to force local tribesmen to support—or at least not to attack—the Muslims

3.   Attacks against Jewish tribes to secure the oases in which they resided

4.   Two raids against the Byzantines at al-Mu'ta (629) and Tabuk (631) and the campaign led by Usama b. Zayd (632) against Syria, which, though less than successful at best, heralded the direction of Muslim conquests during the years following the Prophet's death in 632.

This evidence demonstrates categorically the importance of jihad to the early Muslim community. It is no coincidence that a number of the Prophet Muhammad's early biographers refer to the last ten years of his life as *al-maghazi* (the raids).[2]

The raids were a mixed success. Unexpectedly, the Muslims emerged victorious from the first of their battles—the Battle of Badr—but campaigns undertaken during the three years following ended in losses or stalemates, compensated in some instances by attacks on poorly defended Jewish tribes, first in Medina and later in the oases to the north. After the Battle of the Khandaq in 627, which was a stalemate, the tide turned for the Muslims, as a result of the Meccans' political weaknesses. By 629 Muhammad controlled the region to the north of Medina almost to the border with the Byzantine Empire, and in 630 he conquered Mecca and its allied town of al-Ta'if.

This mixed bag of victories, half-victories, Pyrrhic victories, and defeats associated with Islam's origins figured prominently in how the community defined itself. The revelations that constitute the Qur'an coincide with military activity, and many address issues related to the conduct of jihad; one of the earliest of these defines just causes for waging jihad, emphasizing the essential component of justice:

> Permission is given to those who fight because they are wronged. Surely Allah is capable of giving them victory. Those who were driven out of their homes unjustly, merely for their saying: "Our Lord is Allah." Had Allah not repelled some people by others, surely monasteries, churches, synagogues and mosques, wherein the name of Allah is mentioned frequently, would have been demolished. Indeed, Allah will support whoever supports Him. Allah is surely Strong and Mighty. (22:39–40)

This verse emphasizes the basic component of justice in the waging of jihad. The persecutions of the pagan Quraysh forced the Muslims to emigrate to Medina. During the course of this migration, many of the Muslims lost most or all of their worldly goods and were unable to adjust to life in the agricultural oasis of Medina (as Mecca lacked any agriculture [see 14:37]). Since Medina lay close to the route between Mecca and Syria, through which the Meccans had to pass in order to continue their trading activities, the Muslims sought recompense for their losses by attacking the caravans of the Quraysh. These attacks precipitated the first round of "thematic battles" leading to the eventual conquest of Mecca by Muhammad and the Muslims. In 624 a Meccan caravan was passing by Medina en route from Syria, and its commander, Abu Sufyan, realizing the danger, sent for reinforcements to assist him. Muhammad, who was leading the Muslims, intercepted the caravan, but Abu Sufyan managed to escape. The subsequent battle at Badr between the Muslims and Meccan reinforcements constituted the first of Muhammad's victories.

Much of *sura* 8 (the Spoils) deals with this event, which was important to early Islam for a number of reasons. The victory was unexpected because of the fact that the Muslims were outnumbered, necessary because the Muslims needed it in order to build up prestige, and sweet because of the number of prominent members of the Quraysh who were slain, for they had figured prominently in the persecution of the Muslims in Mecca. The battle was important for Islam in the long run as well. The Qur'an identifies God as the agent of the battle and the sole cause of the Muslim's victory. According to *sura* 8, it was God who induced the believers to march forward (8:5), compelled the Muslims to attack the Meccan reinforcements instead of the caravan (8:6), and supplied angels to assist the Muslims (8:9):

> It was not you [the Muslims] who slew them, but Allah; and when you
> threw it was actually Allah who threw, so that He might generously
> reward the believers. Allah is Hearing, Knowing. (8:17)

The Qur'an, moreover, directs the community of Muslims to preserve the memory of the event: "whoever turns his back on that day, unless preparing to resume fighting, or joining another group, incurs Allah's wrath and his refuge is Hell; and what an evil fate!" (8:16). All of this will be accomplished "so that He may cause the Truth to triumph and nullify falsehood, even though the wicked sinners dislike it" (8:8). Although Christian and Jewish bibles and apocalyptic literature, like the Qur'an, often describe God fighting on the side of believers (see, for example, Joshua 10:14), associating the will of the deity with victory is theologically problematic, and particularly so in the wake of a defeat.

The Battle of Badr was not taken advantage of by the Muslim community, which was too small to follow up on its unexpected victory. A year later, the Meccans sought revenge for their defeat and obtained it at the Battle of Uhud, fought just to the north of Medina. The Muslims took positions at the foot of Mount Uhud (a small butte), while the Meccans held a key strategic location between them and the entrance to Medina. Just before the battle, a number of Muslims, led by 'Abdallah b. Ubayy (the leader of the lukewarm, or uncommitted, Muslims, usually called "the Hypocrites" in the Qur'an), abandoned the Muslim force in full view of the Meccans. When the Muslims advanced from their base on Mount Uhud, the Meccan cavalry encircled them from behind; the Prophet Muhammad only narrowly made his escape, while many of his adherents, thinking he had been killed, fled the battle. Several prominent Muslims, including Muhammad's uncle Hamza (often called "the Prince of Martyrs" in the jihad literature), were killed in the trap. To a large extent, Muhammad and the Muslims could count themselves lucky that the Meccans did not take advantage of their victory and finish off the defenseless Muslim families in Medina.

Because of the theological weight placed upon the victory at Badr the previous year, the defeat at Uhud proved difficult to explain. Muslims asked: if God was on our side then, why did He allow this disastrous defeat? Answers are forthcoming in the Qur'an, especially in the last half of *sura* 3 (The Family of 'Imran), which introduces the idea that "Islam" needs to be divorced from the person of Muhammad (3:144); the death of the religion's prophet will not signal the end of the religion itself. The defeat at Uhud is explained in terms of God's alternating victories between people in order to test them (3:140–42, 152), and the

Prophet is commended for having forgiven those whose impetuousness caused the disaster (3:155–59). Thus, an event that could have divided the still small Muslim community was used to reinforce its unity.

This unity was tested yet again during the Battle of the Khandaq (627). By this time, the pagan Meccans had decided that the Muslim community must be decisively defeated, and so they gathered a large number of tribal allies—referred to in the Qur'an as *al-ahzab,* the Confederates—and laid siege to the oasis of Medina. Within Medina, the Prophet Muhammad's authority was challenged by the Hypocrites, who discounted the threat and refused to fight (33:12–20). The true believers are characterized as "men who fulfilled what they pledged to Allah; some of them have died, some are still waiting, without changing in the least" (33:23).

The Battle of Khandaq was not a battle of weapons, but rather a challenge to the disunity among Muslims first manifested in the Battle of Uhud (by 'Abdallah b. Ubayy's last-minute abandonment of the other Muslims). These problems were resolved by the massacre of the Jewish tribe of Banu Qurayza (33:26), God's causing a wind to arise and sending unseen hosts to defeat the Meccan besiegers (33:9), and the ultimate capitulation of the Hypocrites and their integration within the community loyal to Muhammad. These factors were decisive in the ultimate victory of the Muslims over their Meccan opponents three years later.

The conquest of Mecca (630) is treated only briefly in the Qur'an, although most of *sura* 48 is devoted to this subject. Of much greater importance for the study of jihad is the penultimate *sura* in the Qur'an, *surat al-Tawba* (Repentance). This *sura* is the only chapter of the Qur'an that is not preceded by the phrase "In the Name of Allah, the Compassionate, the Merciful," which in itself indicates the martial nature of the text. It was most likely revealed in 631.[3] *Sura* 9 contains the account of the salvific covenant between God and the Muslims that helps define the nature of jihad:

> Allah has bought from the believers their lives and their wealth in return for Paradise; they fight in the way of Allah, kill and get killed. That is a true promise from Him in the Torah, the Gospel, and the Qur'an; and who fulfills His promise better than Allah? Rejoice, then, at the bargain you have made with Him; for that is the great triumph. (9:111)

Like much of the language of the Qur'an, this covenant is presented in contractual terms. The exchange is clear: the Muslims' lives and wealth are given to Allah in return for an assurance of Paradise. Given the verse's unique power and relevance to the subject, it is no wonder that this verse is prominently cited in collections on the subject of jihad (for example, that of al-Bukhari).

However, *sura* 9 has many more important verses to offer concerning jihad. The *sura*'s main subject is the revocation of the immunity granted by God and Muhammad to those tribes that had not converted to Islam prior to this revelation. After the lifting of the immunity, the Muslims must fight the unbelievers:

> Then, when the sacred months are over, kill the idolaters wherever you find them, take them [captive], besiege them, and lie in wait for them at every point of observation. If they repent afterwards, perform the prayer and pay the alms, then release them. Allah is truly All-Forgiving, Merciful. (9:5)

This verse, together with the salvific covenant, is one of the most important verses on the subject of jihad. It is usually called the "Verse of the Sword" and is said to abrogate all other verses in the Qur'an on the subject of war and peace. While its immediate subject is the pagan Arabs—a narrow application sustained by early commentators—later Muslim jurists would use the verse to proclaim a universal jihad against all non-Muslims.

Sura 9 also deals extensively with social relations between believers and nonbelievers—again of decisive importance for the later development of Islam. According to 9:23–24, a Muslim should distance himself from his kin and friends if they persist in unbelief (see also 3:28, 4:139, 5:51, 57). This *sura* also establishes the paradigm of Muslim dominance over Jews and Christians that would dictate the social system of Islam for centuries to come:

> Fight those among the People of the Book [Jews and Christians] who do not believe in God and the Last Day, do not forbid what God and His Apostle have forbidden, and do not profess the true religion [Islam] until they pay the poll-tax out of hand and submissively. (9:29)

One of the goals of jihad was to conquer and dominate non-Muslims. Reading through *sura* 9, and understanding that this *sura* was probably revealed toward the end of Muhammad's life, just a few years before the conquests (making the final revelation a declaration of war), explains the aggressiveness of the early Muslims.

In summarizing the teachings of the Qur'an with regard to the subject of jihad, it is important to emphasize that we have a very martial and well-developed teaching here. Although it not an exhaustive treatment of jihad—many of the *hadith* and subsequent jurisprudence are devoted to annotating topics only adumbrated in the *suras*—the Qur'an nonetheless presents a well-developed religious justification for waging war against Islam's enemies. It covers questions concerning prisoners, the fate and rewards of martyrs, disunity and doubt within the Muslim ranks, and a number of other issues as well. The Qur'an even reveals that many Muslims were reluctant to fight (2:216, 9:38). The text provides the religious basis for the doctrine of jihad that would result in the great Muslim conquests of the seventh and eighth centuries.

THE EARLY ISLAMIC CONQUESTS: THEORY TO PRACTICE

The early Islamic conquests are one of the great bursts of military achievement known to history and arguably one of those with the longest-lasting effects. After Muhammad's death, the Muslim armies embarked upon a series of campaigns in the ancient Fertile Crescent (present-day Syria and Iraq) and quickly conquered the territory. The conquest of Egypt soon followed, and by 650 the heartlands of Islam— the area between Egypt on the west and the Iranian plateau on the east, and the Arabian Peninsula—were ruled by the Muslims.[4]

After a five-year hiatus (the civil war of 656–61), the Muslims, now centered in Syria under the Umayyad dynasty (661–749), embarked on a further surge of conquest in all directions. To the northeast, the regions of Central Asia and Afghanistan were conquered, albeit with great difficulty, while to the southeast, the Muslims mounted attacks in the area of the Indus River valley (present-day Pakistan) and parts of northern India. To the north, Armenia and the Caucasus were conquered, while two major unsuccessful attempts to take Constantinople—the seat of the Byzantine Empire—were undertaken in 676–80 and 715–17. To the south, the Muslims of Egypt launched unsuccessful attacks upon the Christian kingdom of Nubia (what is today the northern Sudan). To the west, the Muslims conquered and pacified North Africa and converted the native Berber population to Islam (by 699). By 701 the Muslim armies, using Berbers as reinforcements, had conquered the Iberian Peninsula and in the early 730s entered France, where they were defeated in 732 by Charles Martel at Poitiers.

One might legitimately ask how exactly these conquests were achieved, since previously (and thereafter) the peoples of the Arabian Peninsula had not demonstrated the capacity to control the neighboring settled regions, much less distant territories. Part of the reason was the unifying force of Islam. Another element of the conquests' success was a shrewd military strategy. The early Muslims adopted innovative tactics involving the extensive use of light cavalry to move quickly and target enemies at their weak points.[5] Some of these innovations are described in the *hadith* on the subject of jihad. The weakness of the Byzantine and Sasanian empires also aided the early Muslims immensely. With the exception of the Sasanians, not a single major powerful state fell to the early Muslims. Rather, the Muslims advanced through politically unstable regions or regions controlled by nomads, many of whom converted to Islam and joined the conquest. These auxiliary forces, by supplementing the manpower from which the Muslims could draw their armies, proved crucial in obtaining the ultimate victory.[6]

The Islamic conquests wrested control of an enormous territory from Christian and Zoroastrian religious domination (with local populations of Jews, Manicheans, Gnostic sects, and pagans) and resulted in a linguistic shift in the entire region from Aramaic (and its dialects) and Greek to Arabic. The changes engendered by the conquests culminated in the civilization known to historians as the high Islamic civilization, which lasted roughly until the thirteenth century. The speed at which the Muslims conquered is reminiscent of the campaigns of Genghis Khan, Napoleon, or Hitler, but none of these conquerors was able to sustain his conquests. The geographic scope of the Muslim conquest, the resultant advanced civilization, and religious and linguistic shifts could be compared to those of the Romans, the Spanish, or the British, but these empires expanded much more slowly in order to consolidate their gains. The most apt comparison is the conquests undertaken by Alexander the Great, whose victories over the Persian Achmenaeid Empire (330s B.C.E.) similarly heralded long-term religious and linguistic shifts (the spread of Hellenistic culture and the Greek language) in the territories he conquered at lightning speed.

For many Muslims, the conquests constitute a miracle from God attesting to the veracity of the revelation of Islam. During preparations for the Battle of the Khandaq, the following scene is said to have taken place:

> [Salman al-Farisi] said: I was striking [with a pick while digging the trench] on one part of the Khandaq, when there was a stone that was too tough for me. The Messenger of Allah [Muhammad] was close to me, and when he saw me and how difficult the place was for me, he descended [into the trench] and took the pick from my hands. He struck the rock with force that caused lightning to flash from the pick . . . then he struck again, and lightning flashed from beneath the pick . . . and then struck a third time and again lightning flashed from beneath it. I

said: "May my father and mother [be a redemption for you], O Messenger of Allah, what was that I saw beneath the pick when you struck?" He said: "Did you see that, O Salman?" I said: "Yes." He said: "With the first [flash] Allah gave me the Yemen, with the second Allah gave me Syria and the Maghrib [Morocco] and with the third, Allah gave me the East."[7]

Thus Muhammad, like Moses (Deut. 34:1–4), was granted a legitimizing vision of the lands his community was to conquer shortly after his death; the vision's meaning is explicated in the verse immediately following the account of promised territories:

> Abu Hurayra would say after these *amsar* [cities founded by the Muslims] were conquered during the time of 'Umar, 'Uthman and afterwards, "Conquer whatever you wish, because by the One who holds the soul of Abu Hurayra in His hands, you have never conquered nor will you ever conquer any city until the Day of Resurrection without Allah having already given its keys into the hands of Muhammad previously."[8]

Because of the miracle of the conquests, jihad emerged as one of the core elements of Islam. Without the conquests, the religion would not have had the opportunity to spread in the way that it did, nor would it have been the attractant that it was. Islam was not in fact "spread by the sword"—conversion was not forced on the occupants of conquered territories—but the conquests created the necessary preconditions for the spread of Islam. With only a few exceptions (East Africa, Southeast Asia, and to some extent Central Asia beyond Transoxiana), Islam has become the majority faith only in territories that were conquered by force. Thus, the conquests and the doctrine that motivated these conquests—jihad—were crucial to the development of Islam.

While the Qur'an provides the basis for the doctrine of jihad, it is the tradition literature of Islam that describes how Muslims perceived it as they were fighting and what they were fighting for.

ACCOUNTS OF THE JIHAD: THE *HADITH* LITERATURE

Such remarkable conquests could not have been achieved had they not been backed up by the developing Islamic tradition. The tradition literature, or *hadith*—sayings attributed to the Prophet Muhammad and accounts of events in his life recounted by his close companions—is in part a record of the warfare during this early period. These traditions cover a broad range of subjects, in some instances supplementing accounts in the Qur'an, in others treating events and issues not addressed therein. Scholars analyzing this material have concluded that few, if any, of the *hadith* are contemporaneous with the events that they describe; the earliest extant parts of the corpus likely date to the end of the seventh century (about seventy years after the Prophet's death). For Sunni Muslims the *hadith* literature is of central importance in deciding how to live one's life.

These early collections of tradition literature, although small compared to the genre's vast growth during the eighth and probably ninth centuries, record the living and developing religion of Islam at the time of its origins. The earliest *hadith* compilations that have come down to us are as random as the subjects they address. By the mid-eighth century, and especially by the ninth century, however, the collections become much more sophisticated, organized topically for the purpose of reference. These annotated *hadith* contain extensive discussions of jihad, which in most collections are located immediately after the sections devoted to the "five pillars of Islam."

Some of the earliest collections are devoted entirely to jihad, and with the aid of these books we can reconstruct to some extent the beliefs of the early Muslim conquerors. The earliest known writer is 'Abdallah b. al-Mubarak (d. 797), who was originally from the region of Central Asia and emigrated to Syria in order to fight the Byzantines. He was well known as a warrior-ascetic (see chapter 2), and his *Kitab al-jihad* complements his much larger book on asceticism. The *Kitab al-jihad* documents the evolution of the Muslim conception of warfare during the period of the conquests after Muhammad's death. The spiritual conception of warfare is much more detailed than it is in the Qur'an:

> The slain [in jihad] are three [types of] men: a believer, who struggles with himself and his possessions in the path of God, such that when he meets the enemy [in battle] he fights them until he is killed. This martyr *(shahid)* is tested, [and is] in the camp of God under His throne; the prophets do not exceed him [in merit] except by the level of prophecy. [Then] a believer, committing offenses and sins against himself, who struggles with himself and his possessions in the path of God, such that when he meets the enemy [in battle] he fights until he is killed. This cleansing wipes away his offenses and his sins—behold the sword wipes [away] sins!—and he will be let into heaven from whatever gate he wishes. . . . [Then] a hypocrite, who struggles with himself and his possessions in the path of God, such that when he meets the enemy [in battle] he fights until he is killed. This [man] is in hell since the sword does not wipe away hypocrisy.[9]

This tradition could be taken as a representative example of the numerous (262) traditions contained within this book on the subject of jihad. It presents jihad as spiritualized warfare in the same spirit as Qur'an 9:111. Of the three figures mentioned—the True Believer, the Sinning but Repentant Believer, and the Hypocritical Believer—the second is clearly the most interesting. This Sinning but Repentant Believer seeks to expiate his sins on the field of battle. According to the tradition, the sword, together with the pure intention of the fighter, wipes away the believer's sins.

Thus, there is a redemptive aspect to jihad that is crucial to understanding its development. We have already noted Qur'an 9:111, where this salvific contract is spelled out. In 'Abdallah b. al-Mubarak's *Kitab al-jihad* we see similar attitudes. In the above *hadith*, "the sword wipes away sins" in a manner similar to the Christian tradition, which places redemption in the Cross: "Being killed in the path of Allah washes away impurity; killing is two things: atonement and rank [in heaven]."[10] Fighters were encouraged to wear white so that the blood of their sacrifice would be apparent.[11] Later traditions distinguish several types of fighters:

> There is a man who fights in the path of Allah and does not want to kill or be killed, but is struck by an arrow. The first drop of blood [dripping] from him is atonement for every sin he has committed; for every drop he sheds he gains levels in paradise. The second type of man is one who fights desiring to kill but not to be killed, and is struck by an arrow. The first drop of blood [dripping] from him is atonement for every sin; for every drop he sheds he gains a level in paradise until he bumps Abraham's knee [on the top level]. The third type of man is one who fights in the path of Allah desiring to kill and be killed, and is struck by an arrow. The first drop of blood [dripping] from him is atonement for every sin; he will come to the Day of Resurrection with a drawn sword, [able to] intercede.[12]

These traditions are very powerful and descriptive, reflecting a belief system capable of inspiring the conquest of so much territory and achieving what the early Muslims achieved.

Much of the extensive tradition literature on the subject of jihad concerns broad themes: defining fighters and fighting, distinguishing classes of prohibitions in fighting, determining the equitable division of spoils and the fate of prisoners. Among the authoritative collections, those of Malik b. Anas (d. 795) and al-Awza'i (d. 773), although not included in the "six canonical collections" of Sunni Islam, are important because of the early date of their composition, their preservation by communities located close to the borders of Islam (Spain, in the case of Malik; North Africa and Syria, in the case of al-Awza'i), and the extent to which both authors capture much of the spirit of the early conquests. Malik encourages jihad, albeit without Ibn al-Mubarak's heavenly incentives for martyrdom. Rather, his emphasis is on defining the parameters of waging jihad: the prohibition on the killing of women and children, the division of spoils, and sanctions for illegal looting. It is only at the end of his discussion, in the context of a discussion of martyrs, that Malik treats the spiritual merit of fighting.

Al-Awza'i's presentation attests to the circumstances of Syrian Muslim communities, who were regularly subject to Byzantine naval incursions and shared the territory with a large Christian population of uncertain allegiances; for al-Awza'i, jihad is linked to the protection of Islam's frontiers (*ribat*). He does not glorify jihad, devoting considerably more attention to the merit of the fighter than does Malik, and he deals extensively with the weapons and tactics of the border warrior, as well as the problem of assimilation with the local population.[13] Other early precanonical collections, such as those of Ibn Abi Shayba (d. 849) and 'Abd al-Razzaq (d. 826) similarly reflect the particularities of the locations in which they were written. 'Abd al-Razzaq, who wrote in the Yemen, where there was little fighting, begins his discussion of jihad with a lengthy (eighty-page) explication of the equitable division of spoils. Only then does he treat the merit of the fighter and the other aspects of aggressive jihad common to the collections cited so far. The placement of a discussion of guarding the borders at the very end of the collection suggests that it was not as high a priority for him as it was for al-Awza'i. Ibn Abi Shayba, writing in Iraq, in contrast, begins his treatment of jihad with much of the same material cited by Ibn al-Mubarak, and the two collections share a similar emphasis on themes of descriptions of heavenly pleasures, conquest and victory, and forgiveness of sins for the martyr. However, Ibn Abi Shayba segregates administrative and legal materials into another chapter (as do a number of later collections).

The six canonical collections of Sunni Islam—those of al-Bukhari, Muslim, al-Tirmidhi, Abu Da'ud, al-Nasa'i, and Ibn Maja—are more important for the development of Islamic practice than these earlier collections (although the early works are more directly infused with the spirit of the first conquests). These canonical collections, in contrast to those discussed above, were written by Muslims from the eastern part of the empire—more specifically, eastern Iran. All six of the collections accord a prominent place to jihad, and they contain more elaborated discussions of the term's meaning than do the eighth-century collections.

Al-Bukhari (d. 870), whose collection is accorded a rank in Sunni Islam just below that of the Qur'an, starts his discussion of jihad with the citation of the salvific contract from the Qur'an (9:110) and repeatedly refers to the Qur'an, either by interspersing verses or by undertaking their exegesis in order to illustrate a point of law. (This sets him apart from the precanonical authors, who rarely cite the Qur'an.) Many traditions that he cites paint a vivid visual picture of jihad: angels' wings overshadow the fighters, feet that become dusty while fighting in the path of God will not enter hell, and martyrs are led into paradise smelling of musk, with their clothes the color of blood. The fighter who takes good care of his horse will find that the horse's feed-bucket, his bowl, his excrement, and his urine will be added to the balance of the fighter's good deeds on the Scales on the Day of Judgment. A light shines from the graves of the martyrs who die in battle.[14]

It should already be clear from this description how important the fighter's mount was to the success of his campaign. Each of the canonical collections (and most of the other collections as well) devote an extensive discussion to the merits of horses, donkeys, and other animals used in fighting, and to their upkeep, good treatment, and ultimate reward.

The canonical collections devote considerable attention as well to the question of whether women can fight in the jihad, although there is little unanimity among authors. In several isolated traditions women are said either to have fought during the time of the Prophet or to have received assurances from Muhammad that they would be allowed to fight in the future. There does not seem to have been any question that women could accompany fighters (Muhammad himself regularly allowed this) and serve as "inciters" or as nurses after the battle.[15]

Incitement and psychological fear are both important components of jihad, as is recognized in the Qur'an 3:151: "We will cast terror into the hearts of the unbelievers on account of their associating with Allah that for which He sent down no authority." The Prophet Muhammad further amplified this idea by noting that God had helped him with a fear *(ru'b* or *mahaba)* that He had sent before the Muslim armies to a distance of a month's journey.[16] According to this idea, all who lived at this distance from the Muslims would feel this fear and be defeated by it even before meeting the Muslims in battle.[17] The psychological preparation for victory or defeat is also a theme of the *hadith* literature, in which we find a great many references to poetry,[18] flags, and slogans

intended to aid the fighters.[19] Probably the most popular slogan—
Allahu akbar! (God is greater!)—is usually said to precede Muslim
advance into battle. There are also examples of curses to incapacitate
the unbelievers; among these, the best known is the Prophet's ritual
curse of the Confederates (during the Battle of the Khandaq in 627): "O
Allah! Revealer of the Book [the Qur'an], hasty in judgment (variant:
mover of the clouds), O Allah, defeat the Confederates; O Allah, defeat
them and shake them!"[20]

Other collections address the problems of continuous fighting. The
wives and children of the fighters at the battlefront have to be protected.
Traitors and spies are a constant danger. As always, dividing the spoils
and preventing battlefield looting, unruly behavior, and mistreatment of
prisoners are major issues. Other social problems are addressed, such as
those who pay others to go out and fight,[21] as well as those who take
money for fighting, but do not go. In almost every collection, there is a
section devoted to extolling bravery and excoriating cowardice. Advice
is given for the upkeep of horses (do not geld them, do not cut their
tails). Issues concerning treaties, redemption of prisoners, social relations with conquered peoples, and traveling in hostile lands are also covered. We also can see how closely interrelated Islam and fighting were
when the *hadith* on jihad allow mosques to be put to use as prisons for
enemy captives or as storehouses for weapons.[22]

Certain traditions demonstrate a grasp of the social and economic
realities of warfare:

> Allah causes three people to enter Paradise because of an arrow: the
> maker of the arrow who because of his manufacturing expects a reward,
> the one who shoots the arrow, and the one who collects it. So, [practice]
> shooting and riding, but it is better to shoot than to ride.[23]

No doubt this aided Muslims in seeing that an entire economy produces
a fighter and that the front-line fighters could not exist without the pro-
duction capabilities of the society supporting them. However, the dominant attitude in the jihad literature toward society and the sedentary
life—especially farmers and merchants—is a negative one. One example
of the negative attitude toward the sedentary life is the following tradition: "The Messenger of Allah said: One of the prophets [before me]
raided, and he said: No one who has built a house and has not lived in
it, who has married a woman and not had intercourse with her or who
has any desire to return should accompany me" (compare Deut.
20:5–7).[24] This is understandable because fighting the jihad necessitated

constant movement (probably the secret to the success of the early Muslim conquests) and exposed the fighters to constant danger. For this reason, the spiritual component to jihad is accorded high importance: the constancy of fighting divorced the Muslims from this world and increased their desire to inhabit the next.

Previously we had noted that the Qur'an was a powerful exponent of an aggressive jihad doctrine. The *hadith* literature follows in its footsteps. Whereas the Qur'an suffices with generalities and encouragement to fight, the *hadith* materials take us into a full-blown description of warfare with a heavy spiritual content. It is clear from even the cursory overview above that the subject of militant jihad was of critical concern to Muslims during the formative first three centuries of Islam, and there is no indication from any of this material that the jihad being described is anything other than military. However, while the legal component of the *hadith* literature describing the jihad is preponderant, it required codification.

LIMITS TO JIHAD: THE EARLY LEGAL DEFINITIONS AND RESTRICTIONS

Out of the disorganized mass of *hadith* a coherent body of law was produced. By the early ninth century, Muslim jurists had begun to codify the basic materials of the tradition to form the *shari'a*, sometimes translated as the "Divine Law." Although this was never a unified body of law, and is essentially the sum total of all the jurists' discussions and commentaries on the subject, it provides a focus for legal and definitional aspects of jihad that are not addressed in the Qur'an or the *hadith* literature. It also seems clear that the jurists of Islam wanted to regulate the nature of the warfare, as they did other aspects of social intercourse.

One of the bases for this type of regulation was defining the manner in which war should be declared and what its limits were.

> The Messenger of Allah, when he would send a commander with a raid or an army would enjoin upon him the fear of Allah, especially with regard to himself, but also with regard to the Muslims, and say: When you meet your polytheist enemy, call to him [to choose] between three possibilities—accept whichever one they accept, and desist from them:
>
> 1. Call them to Islam; if they accept, then accept it from them and desist from them. Then [if they accept Islam] call them to move from their homes to the home of the *muhajirun* [immigrants]; if they do this, then they will have the rights and the responsibilities of the *muhajirun*. If

they refuse, then designate their home, and inform them that they will be like the Muslim Bedouin—Allah's law, which is incumbent upon the believers, will be incumbent upon them, but they will not have any right to the movable or nonmovable spoils, except when they fight at the side of the Muslims.

2. If they refuse, then call them to pay the *jizya* [poll tax]. If they accept, then accept it from them and desist from them.

3. If they refuse, then ask Allah for aid against them, and fight them. If you besiege the people of a fortress, and they desire to surrender unconditionally (*'ala hukm Allah*), do not accept this from them, but let them surrender according to your judgment, and do with them what you wish afterwards.[25]

With these statements jihad is made into a legal process, regulated, and defined. While the Muslim history books leave us with the impression that Muslims always acted in accordance with the above regulations, this is difficult to accept and is not backed up by non-Muslim sources. But the mere establishment of such regulations, albeit with the goal of augmenting the Islamic polity, was a step toward systematizing warfare.

Already in the Qur'an and the *hadith* literature there is a sense of codification of rules. Some rules, such as those governing the division of spoils, hardly needed to be clarified after what was revealed concerning them in the Qur'an. For example,

And know that whatever booty you take, the fifth thereof is for Allah, the Apostle, the near of kin, the orphan, and the wayfarer, if you really believe in Allah and in what We revealed to Our servant on the day of decision [the Battle of Badr]. (Qur'an 8:41)

The principle of the *khums,* the fifth portion of the spoils that was to be designated for the above purposes, remains a constant in Muslim law down to the present time.

The previously cited tradition is foundational for answering an important question of law: against whom were the Muslims permitted to fight? Some of the Qur'anic verses cited seem to indicate that the Muslims were entitled to fight against everyone who fought them (e.g., 9:36). However, legal definitions based upon the above *hadith* distinguished several categories of territories: Dar al-Islam, the sum of the territory in which Islam and the *shari'a* was supreme; Dar al-Harb, the sum of the territory in which it was *possible* (not necessary) to fight, because this area had not submitted to Islam or was in an active state of war against it; and the Dar al-Sulh, that area with which Muslims had some type of treaty or cease-fire.

These categories clearly represent a refinement of the above *hadith* in that they presuppose that Muslims will not be in a permanent state of universal war but that there are stages to an inevitable God-ordained Muslim victory at the end of the world It was possible to live in peace over an extended period with non-Muslim neighbors because of the length of time granted to the non-Muslim to convert and because of the presumed inevitability of the process. The above *hadith* also distinguishes the process by which Muslims are entitled to declare war. Although the choices usually given—convert to Islam, agree to pay the *jizya*, or fight until one of the two sides gains the victory—are absolute and presuppose that Muslims are taking the initiative and have a generally victorious record of warfare, they present both sides with the stakes of warfare and the consequences of victory or defeat. The terms also presuppose that the wars that the Muslims and their opponents are fighting are wars of religion. The side that wins has received the affirmation of God.

Muslim legal literature is divided among four schools *(madhahib)*: Maliki (preeminent in North and West Africa), Hanafi (throughout the Muslim world), Shafi'i, and Hanbali. One of the earliest legal compendia to deal with the questions of jihad was that of al-Shafi'i (d. 820), who played a foundational role in the development of Muslim law. Like the *hadith* collections, he presents jihad as an ordinance of God essential for the continuation of the Muslim community, but his concern is to establish the legal foundations of the Muslim society that benefits from the victories obtained by means of jihad rather than to define the legal limits on the actual waging of war. For example, his first category, after the sections encouraging the waging of jihad, addresses the payment of the *jizya* by non-Muslims (Jews, Christians, Sabeans, and others) and the manner in which this tax should be levied and collected (see chapter 3). Sections on truces, cease-fires, dealing with rebels, safe-conducts, and disposition of spoils all follow, together with sections describing relations with captured women. All of these discussions presuppose a victorious polity and reflect the confidence of the early Muslims that God would give them the victory.[26] Other early legal compendia, such as the *Mudawwina* of Sakhnun (d. 854), do not detail the subject of jihad more than does al-Shafi'i (however, Maliki compendia such as al-Qayrawani's [d. 997] *al-Nawadir wa-l-ziyadat*, which is a supplement to Sakhnun, do).[27]

Al-Mabsut, a massive legal compendium attributed to the Hanafi eleventh-century jurist al-Sarakhsi, deals with jihad in greater depth than do those of other legal schools. Al-Sarakhsi begins with a discussion of the significance of jihad, and the reasons behind it, and he then proceeds to discuss the relative legal validity of tactics, including the process of surrender, the manner in which a siege is to be carried out, and dealing with captives—which ones can be killed, which enslaved. He describes many of the Prophet Muhammad's battles and extracts basic legal principles from each one. In summary, al-Sarakhsi completes the process begun by al-Shafi'i and covers the entire process of waging jihad in law. From this point forward, although individual points continued to be debated, the Muslim method of warfare was set.

One of the expressions of the codification of jihad is the listing of sins that are associated with fighting. The early list of al-Hakim al-Tirmidhi (d. 930) proscribes single combat with an enemy without the permission of the *imam* and prohibits asking for help from polytheists in battle, killing young boys, and hamstringing horses during battle.[28] The comparatively late treatise of al-Haythami (d. 1565) lists sins in considerably more detail: listed under the title of jihad we find the sins of leaving jihad, the failure to enjoin the good and forbid the evil, not responding to the *salam* greeting, love that begets the sin of pride, cowardice on the battlefield and desertion (Qur'an 8:15), fleeing from a plague, taking illegal booty, betraying a safe-conduct or an assurance of protection, spying on the Muslims, or taking horses for the purposes of personal gain or for racing rather than fighting.[29] Not all of these sins are directly connected with the process of fighting jihad, although all are connected to the social process. The reference pertaining to the waging of jihad in lists of grave sins implies that fighting was of crucial importance for Muslims, but it does not detail for us the ultimate goal of the warfare.

GOALS OF JIHAD: APOCALYPSE AND CONVERSION

The Muslim conquests of the seventh through the ninth century were by no means easy victories. In certain cases natural boundaries (mountains, impassable deserts, bodies of water) prevented the Muslims from advancing; in other cases they were defeated on the battlefield (Constantinople in 717, Poitiers in 732). After a century of warfare, the early Muslims suffered from a severe lack of manpower, and the logistical challenge of supporting conquests in an empire stretching several thousand miles from end to end was insurmountable. Was the goal merely to conquer as much as could be conquered while the going was good? Or was there a deeper religious goal driving the conquests?

One explanation is that the conquests were sustained by a strong belief in the imminent end of the world. This attitude could have been strengthened by the events of the late sixth and early seventh centuries, marked by plagues (the Plague of Justinian in 541, for example), wars (such as that between Byzantium and the Sasanian Empire, 602–28), and appearances of comets and other celestial phenomena. Both the war and various celestial phenomena are alluded to in the Qur'an (30:1–6, 53:1, 54:1),[30] and much of the holy book is written in an apocalyptic vein. However, there is little explicit prognostication, since in 7:187, 31:34, 33:63, 79:42 it is said that the knowledge of the future is with God alone. Other verses speak of the nearness of the Hour (42:17, 54:1), that there is no doubt that it will appear (22:7, 40:54, 45:32), and that when it does, it will appear suddenly (12:107, 22:55, 43:66, 47:18). But was this belief sufficient to fuel mass conquests?

While the texts that comprise the Qur'an do not answer this question, the *hadith* literature, especially the apocalyptic predictions, does. In this literature there is a strong connection between the fighting process and the imminent end of the world:

> Behold! God sent me [= Muhammad] with a sword, just before the Hour [of Judgment], and placed my daily sustenance beneath the shadow of my spear, and humiliation and contempt on those who oppose me.[31]

The Prophet Muhammad is portrayed, as Patricia Crone has stated, as a doomsday prophet, sent just before the end of the world to warn those who would heed a warning and to punish those who would not. Here, the process of jihad, as in the traditions cited above, is one in which the hold of worldly things over the believer is diluted. Because of the impermanence of the soldier's life, and the difficulties of establishing a stable family or gathering substantial possessions, many of the ties that bind people to this world are weakened or even dissolved entirely. When this is taken into consideration, the spiritual significance of jihad becomes even more pronounced.

It is clear why the connection with the end of the world had to be maintained in the jihad literature. Without this final date in mind, it would have been difficult for Muslim fighters to summon up the necessary energy to achieve the conquests. Dates of the end of the world are to be found in great numbers in the *hadith* and apocalyptic literature.[32] In Abu Da'ud's *Sunan* (one of the six canonical *hadith* collections), "jihad is in force until the Day of Resurrection."[33] Not only that, but a further tradition indicates that one specific group will be continually victorious until that time: "A group *(ta'ifa)* of my community will continue fighting for the Truth, victorious over those who oppose them, until the last of them fights the Antichrist."[34] This assurance provides a basis in Sunni Islam for deciding which sect or group will ultimately be the one saved, as is indicated by the books discussing it within the context of creedal statements, theological polemics, and heresiography.[35]

Jihad plays a major role in Muslim apocalyptic literature as well. Since the early Muslims' existence was largely dominated by fighting and conquest, it is hardly surprising to find that their vision of the future just before the end of the world, as well as their vision of the messianic future, was characterized by a state of continuous war. Apocalyptic traditions focus on the wars with the Byzantines, who were the early Muslims' only serious opponents. The early Muslims entertained hopes of conquering the Byzantine capital of Constantinople (besieged by them in 676–80 and 715–17) and completing their conquest of the territories historically controlled by the Roman Empire—the entire Mediterranean basin. This enterprise, cut short by the failures of the Muslim armies during the first half of the eighth century, remained a dream of the future in the apocalyptic literature.

For all the certainties associated with the "end of days," early Muslims were driven by fears that are reflected in the apocalyptic literature. The possibility that their families, surrounded by subject populations of infidels, could be violated while the men were away fighting is a major theme in these traditions. There was also a widespread fear of betrayal by Arab or converted nomadic tribes, whose allegiance to Islam was sometimes less than certain. Often these tribes are portrayed as apostatizing and joining the Christians in the event of a Byzantine victory. The Muslim Arabs had largely come from the Arabian Peninsula and were afraid that military defeat would force them to return to it. Having tasted the pleasures of the fertile settled communities in Egypt, Syria-Palestine, and Iraq, Muslims were naturally reluctant to abandon these places.

Muslim messianic traditions are a reflection of these realities. The Sunni Muslim messianic figure, the *mahdi,* will complete those conquests left undone by the early Muslims. He will conquer Constantinople, Rome, and Europe, as well as finishing the conquest of Central Asia, India, and Ethiopia. All of these places were precisely those that the early Muslims were unable to dominate. However, according to most accounts, the *mahdi* will not convert the subject populations to Islam, but will rule them justly according to their own laws. The Muslims will be required to give up their settled ways—their farms and houses—and return to fighting the jihad together with the *mahdi*, re-creating the warrior caste of early Islam where the Muslims were the fighters and the non-Muslims tilled the soil.[36]

In addition to the apocalyptic and messianic goals of the jihad, there are also the goals of spreading Islam. Although Islam was not spread by the sword, as is commonly imagined, conquest and jihad created the preconditions for conversion, and conversion or proclamation was one of the goals of the jihad. An early tradition describes the limits of fighting:

> I was ordered to fight people until they say: "There is no god but Allah." When they have said that, then their blood and their property is protected from me, solely by reason [of saying it], and judgment upon them is in the hands of Allah.[37]

As M. J. Kister has pointed out, this tradition was most likely one of the earliest to describe the radical change implicated by conversion, most probably with the intent of nipping the issue of questionable conversions in the bud, since according to the text, judgment is in the hands of God. If a person converted for less than pure motives—to save his life, for example—the conversion was still legitimate and he would be judged accordingly on the Day of Resurrection. However, the tradition also demonstrates the connection between fighting and conversion. The fighting will persist until conversion occurs, the only exceptions to this rule being the "protected peoples": the Jews, the Christians and the Sabeans (2:62, 5:69, 22:17).

Both the jihad literature and the apocalyptic literature are very frank in their assessment of the economic reasons that drew the early Muslims to conquest. Fantastic amounts of booty and slaves are described in the sources. In describing the eventual conquest of Constantinople, the apocalyptic sources speak of gold, jewels, and virgins, saying fighters "will ravish 70,000 as long as they wish in the Royal Palace."[38] These baser motives are acknowledged in the jihad literature, at the same time that they are dismissed as ancillary to the spiritual goals of jihad:

> A man came to the Prophet and said: "Some men fight for spoils, some for fame, some to show off; who is fighting in the way of Allah?" He said: "The one who fights to lift the Word of Allah to the highest, he is fighting in the path of Allah."[39]

Clearly the spiritual rewards of the martyr had to be defined more carefully; the first step in this process was the definition of who a martyr was.

DEFINITIONS OF "MARTYR"

Defining the Muslim martyr (in Arabic, *shahid*) is not an easy task. Originally the word "martyr" (from Greek) meant "witness": those who bear testimony as to the truth of their beliefs and are willing to attest to its veracity with their lives. Judaism and Christianity popularized the concept of martyrdom throughout the classical world.[40] Many followers of these faiths refused to compromise their beliefs and were willing to undergo torture or even death in order to prove their faith. The early Muslims in Mecca were also willing to suffer for their faith when persecuted by the pagan Meccans. However, after the *hijra* (the Prophet Muhammad's emigration to Medina in 622) there are comparatively few instances recorded in the literature when Muslims were persecuted on a large scale *specifically* because they were Muslims. Islam, in contrast to other religions, became closely identified with power.

Thus, the concept of martyrdom developed differently in Islam than it did in either Judaism or Christianity. Martyrdom in Islam has a much more active sense: the prospective martyr is called to seek out situations in which martyrdom might be achieved. For example, in 'Abdallah b. al-Mubarak's *Kitab al-jihad,* we find Nawf al-Bikali praying: "O, God! Make my wife a widow, make my child an orphan, and ennoble Nawf with martyrdom!"[41] Most often in early Islam, martyrdom meant dying in battle.

Other categories of martyrdom were established fairly quickly. An important tradition in the *Kitab al-jihad* lists seven:

> . . . the Messenger of Allah [Muhammad] said: God Most High has established [the martyr's] reward according to his intention. What do you count as the circumstances of martyrdom? They said: Dying in the path of Allah. The Messenger of Allah said: There are seven categories of martyr other than being killed in the path of Allah. The one who dies of a stomach complaint is a martyr, the one who drowns is a martyr, the one who dies of plague is a martyr, the one who dies of pleursy is a martyr, the one who dies in a structural collapse is a martyr, the one who dies in a fire is a martyr, and the woman who dies in childbirth is a martyr.[42]

This tradition is quite common, and one should note the absence of intention among all of these categories, which describe inadvertent or unavoidable circumstances that have nothing (necessarily) to do with war or violence.

The definition of "martyr" expanded greatly over the centuries. By the sixteenth century, an authoritative pamphlet on the circumstances of martyrdom included among the categories of *shahid* a merchant who dies defending his goods, a man who dies defending his wife and children, a person who dies in a strange land; martyrs include those who die of fever, snakebite, attacks by wild animals, or falling from their mount, in addition to those who die of seasickness or hypothermia.[43] This vast expansion of the term *shahid* rendered it almost meaningless by this time and probably facilitated the transition between the paradigm of aggressive jihad and "internal" spiritual jihad (the so-called lesser jihad and the greater jihad discussed in the next chapter). However, the tradition literature was most concerned to return the definition of "martyr" to its original sense of dying after fighting for the cause of Allah:

> A Bedouin came to the Messenger of Allah and said: "A man can fight for fame, another can fight in order to receive praise, yet another to receive spoils, and another in order to show off." The Messenger of Allah said: "Whoever fights in order to make the Word of Allah the highest [see Qur'an 9:40], that person is [fighting] in the way of Allah."[44]

This is the definition that was most widely accepted by the jurists of Islam, who had always been suspicious of the expansive categories that tended to displace the respect accorded to martyrs who died in battle. It is clear that the spiritual prestige of being a martyr contributed greatly to the expansion of the term. Part of that positive attitude derives from the rewards attached to being a martyr in the next world.

THE REWARDS OF A MARTYR

Paradise is extensively described in the Qur'an. In the early verses, the marvels described in heaven are promised to those who believe in God. In the later sections of the Qur'an, these descriptions are closely associated with being a martyr or dying in battle. For example,

> There surely was a sign for you in the two armies that confronted each other [at the Battle of Badr, 624], the one side fighting for the cause of Allah, and the other consisting of unbelievers . . . attractive to mankind is made the love of the pleasures of women, children, heaps of gold and silver, thoroughbred horses, cattle and cultivable land. . . . Say: "Shall I tell you about something better than all that?" For those who are God-fearing, from their Lord are gardens beneath which rivers flow, and in which they abide forever [along with] purified spouses and Allah's good pleasure. (3:13–15)

Comparisons of earthly, transient pleasures with the rich and permanent ones available in the next world are abundant both in the Qur'an and in the *hadith* literature, especially in those sections dealing with jihad. These descriptions fall into several major categories. One is the assurance of life after death and an immediate entry into Paradise. This is already available in the often quoted Qur'anic verse: "And do not think those who have been killed in the way of Allah as dead; they are rather living with their Lord, well-provided for" (3:169). It is clear that this assurance was of major importance in inducing believers to seek out martyrdom or to undertake acts of bravery. As we already noted, a number of the traditions included in the *Kitab al-jihad* and other books on the subject portray heaven as an army camp. This description, however, does not seem to have been a very popular one; understandably soldiers, having endured the privations of army camps for extensive periods of time, did not want to visualize heaven in this way.

Heaven is described in a sensual manner. Many of those things that were forbidden to the Muslim during life, such as drinking wine or wearing gold and silk, are not only permitted in Paradise, but are a major feature of the pleasures in store for the blessed. However, without a doubt, the literature concentrates on the women of paradise. Already in the Qur'an there is mention of the *hur al-'in,* those women with black-and-white eyes (44:54, 52:20, 56:22); although, if one can place credence on the dates accorded to these verses by Muslim scholars, none of them belongs to the Medinan phase of the Prophet's ministry and thus cannot have been exclusively directed at martyrs. In the later *hadith* literature, especially the *Kitab al-jihad,* the connection between the Muslim martyr and the women of Paradise is made more explicitly:

> The earth will not be dry from his [the martyr's] blood before two of his wives catch him—as if they were two nurses who had lost their young one in a desert—in the hand of each one of them is a garment better than the world and everything that is in it.[45]

During the course of the battle, the women of Paradise (the *houris*) are said to encourage the fighters in the following manner:

> Yazid b. Shajara said: O people, remember the grace of Allah toward you—what is better than the mark of Allah upon you! If you were only able to see what I see of yellow, red, white, and black, when on the saddles there is what there is! When the prayers are fulfilled, the gates of heaven, of Paradise and of Hell open; when the two lines meet [in battle] the gates of heaven, of Paradise and of Hell open [also], and the *hur al-'in* (*houris*) are decorated and descend. When a man advances, they say: "O Allah, make him steadfast, help him." When he retreats, they hide from him, and say: "O Allah, forgive him, make him charge the opposing side." May my father and mother be your ransom, do not dis-

appoint the *hur al-'in.* When he is killed, the first bubble of his blood causes his sins to fall off, like a leaf falls off of the branch of a tree. Two [*houris*] descend to him, and they wipe his face, saying: "We are ready for you" and he says to them: "I am ready for you." They will dress him in one hundred garments—if he put them between his fingers they would expand. They are not of human weaving, but are the fruit of Paradise.[46]

Although sexual imagery is absent from these particular traditions, a number are far more explicit, describing the promised seventy-two virgins and the pleasures they will provide.[47] Many collections cite examples of near-death or out-of-body experiences during which Muslim fighters view or experience the pleasures in store for them before they die—no doubt proving to the skeptical the truth of the traditions described above.[48]

Martyrs also have earthly rewards, although naturally they are subordinated to heavenly rewards. Fame and honor, important attributes in a tribal society, are conferred upon the martyrs and their families. One should note that although ordinarily bodies of Muslims are washed after death and before burial, the bodies of martyrs are buried as they are found, unwashed. Most probably this is the result of the presumed purity of their sacrifice and the evidence of the violent death they suffered as a result of it. All these outward manifestations of honor are worthy of a martyr's death.

Despite the attention given to the women of paradise, there are other spiritual privileges that seem to have been either of equal or greater importance to the martyr. One of these is the relative rank the martyr receives in Paradise. It is said that there are one hundred ranks in Paradise, and that the martyr will achieve the highest among them (ranking only below prophets and other righteous men of God in the hierarchy of Paradise). One of the most important reflections of this spiritual rank is the ability of the martyr to intercede on behalf of Muslims at the Day of Judgment. This intercession has been a subject of controversy in Islam, since, in principle, it might be construed to relieve the faithful of their obligations as set forth in basic Muslim teachings. A number of Qur'anic verses seem to indicate that each person will stand alone before God and not be able to receive help from other sources (e.g. 6:51, 9:116, 32:4), but this severe attitude was not accepted by all Muslims, and soon all manner of "intercessors" began to appear in the Muslim literature. For the most part these are prophets, descendants of the Prophet Muhammad, or Sufi holy men and women, but there are a substantial number of traditions concerning martyrs and those who lived in the border towns as well. For example, the early Syrian ascetic Abu al-Darda' is quoted as saying: "I heard the Messenger of Allah say: The martyr will intercede for seventy of his family."[49] On other occasions, this number is extended to encompass broader categories or left to the discretion of the martyr in question.

Cities are also associated with privileges of this nature—for the most part, cities in dangerous locations, such as those close to the Byzantine border, along the Mediterranean Sea (subject to regular Byzantine raids), in northern Persia facing the mountainous and unconquered area of Tabaristan, and in Central Asia. In all cases, those Muslims who guard the frontiers are assured either the rank of martyrs or the privileges of intercession after their deaths. It seems clear that the issue of intercession was a very powerful incentive for people to live in what would otherwise be undesirable locations.

Summing up the early material, one can say that during the first several centuries of Islam the interpretation of jihad was unabashedly aggressive and expansive. The Qur'anic material provides a core of teachings that leads the believer to assume that God is on the side of the Muslims, giving them victory over their enemies, and supporting them in every way possible. One cannot reasonably doubt that this Qur'anic material was instrumental in the great Muslim conquests. These conquests, however, created a whole additional genre of literature available today in the *hadith* collections Chapters devoted to jihad, as well as books and pamphlets on jihad surviving from this early period, flesh out the Qur'anic materials, and deal with many practical problems arising from the exigencies of battle in distant locations. This *hadith* literature was subsequently codified into law.

All these sources are to be found in great abundance, and it seems that comparatively little of the vivid jihad material was lost over the centuries. Judging from the frequency with which this material was cited by later authors, it has an important place in Islam overall. Most Muslim historians devote a good deal of attention to the conquests, and they are alluded to on a regular basis in almost every genre of literature. For this reason, we can state confidently that the conquests constitute a confirmatory miracle for Islam; because of the close identification between this miraculous event and the jihad ideology that enabled it to come about, jihad has remained of crucial importance in Islamic culture. This does not mean necessarily that there is always an aggressive aspect to the importance of jihad—in many cases the feeling is more nostalgic, alluding to this period of Muslim history as the ideal. But the importance of classical jihad is latent and can be brought to the fore in Islam at any time.

However, as the conquests died down after the middle of the eighth century, other versions of jihad began to become more prominent. It was no longer practical for all Muslims to live at the frontiers, and there were many converts to the new faith. Because of the attractive spiritual prestige of the martyr, many must have asked: is this spiritual rank to be confined solely to those who can die in battle? (answered partially by the expansion in the definition of "martyr" covered above).

TWO

THE "GREATER JIHAD"
AND THE "LESSER JIHAD"

As might be expected from the *hadith* literature, and especially from the definitions of "martyr" in early Islam, jihad did not necessarily entail actual fighting. As the conquests began to move to more distant regions, many Muslims were unable (or probably in some cases unwilling) to abandon their homes and families to go and fight. It is likely that the Islamic definition of "jihad" was expanded as a result from its original meaning to encompass "struggle" or "striving." Although most verses in the Qur'an are unambiguous as to the nature of the jihad prescribed— the vast majority of them referring to "those who believe, emigrate, and fight in the path of Allah" (see 2:218, 8:72, 9:20, 49:15)—some appear to describe a purely spiritual striving. The most obvious of these is 22:78:

> And strive *(jahidu)* for Allah as you ought to strive *(haqq jihadihi)*. He elected you and did not impose upon you any hardship in religion—the faith of your father Abraham. He called you Muslims before and in this [the Qur'an] that the Apostle may bear witness against you and you may be witnesses against mankind. So, perform the prayer, give the alms and hold fast to Allah. He is your Master; and what a blessed Master and a blessed Supporter!

In this verse the word *jihad* is presented in its original Arabic meaning of "striving," and some of the commentators cite traditions indicating a nonviolent attitude of internal spiritual warfare or opposing evil by speaking out against it. Nonetheless, however much weight is put on this verse, the Qur'an cannot support a reading that would make fighters and noncombatants spiritual equals, as a number of verses make clear:

> Those of the believers who stay at home while suffering from no injury are not equal to those who fight for the cause of Allah with their posessions and persons. Allah has raised those who fight with their posessions and persons one degree over those who stay at home; and to each Allah has promised the fairest good. Yet Allah has granted a great reward to those who fight and not to those who stay behind. (4:95)[1]

This idea appears extensively in 9:46, 81–83 as well, but the Qur'an does not support a completely nonviolent interpretation of jihad. Nonetheless, as the conquests ceased in the eighth and ninth centuries, we begin to find evidence for a somewhat demilitarized conception of jihad. It is most likely that those who first began to explore the possibilities of jihad's spiritual interpretation were the early Muslim ascetics.

THE ASCETIC AND HIS JIHAD

Ascetics were among the earliest converts to Islam and among the most enthusiastic fighters in the jihad. Probably the best known is 'Abdallah b. al-Mubarak, who wrote the early *Kitab al-jihad* cited extensively in the previous chapter. Ibn al-Mubarak was originally from the region of eastern Iran; he immigrated to Syria in order to fight the Byzantines, whom he viewed as Islam's most dangerous enemies.[2] During the course of his career, he became known as a popular figure who could (and did on occasion) challenge the caliph for not applying himself energetically enough to waging jihad.

In a tradition cited in the *Kitab al-jihad,* Ibn al-Mubarak makes it clear that he saw no contradiction between being a warrior and being an ascetic: "Every community has a form of asceticism *(rahbaniyya),* and the asceticism of this community is jihad in the path of Allah."[3] With this tradition in mind, he sought to present fighting as a spiritual activity. Ascetism, according to Ibn al-Mubarak, carries moral authority precisely because the ascetic is outside of society and can judge it:

> A Bedouin came to the Prophet, and said: O Messenger of Allah, which of the people is best? He said: A man who fights with himself and his wealth, and a man upon one of the mountain paths, worshiping his Lord and calling the people from their evil.[4]

Other traditions indicate that the best type of jihad was to speak openly and honestly to a ruler: "The best type of jihad is the word of justice in the presence of an iniquitous ruler."[5] This conception of jihad is not found in any of the collections grouped with those traditions describing militant jihad; it usually appears in chapters dealing with conduct or with the disintegration of society during the apocalyptic future. In the latter case, jihad is portrayed as a state of conflict because it is assumed that the ruler would be *non*-Muslim; rebuking him would most likely cost the life of the person performing the deed.

However, the tradition does not necessarily entail such an extreme and specific set of circumstances. One could interpret it in a larger context, as encouraging the pursuit of justice in an iniquitous society led by rulers with an at best tenuous connection to Islam. Such an interpretation ties the peaceful waging of jihad to the fundamental Muslim axiom of "enjoining the good and forbidding the evil."[6] This axiom is the ideal of Muslim society, requiring the religion's adherents to adopt a proactive attitude toward public morality. If at all possible, this should lead to individuals and groups of Muslims responding to broader social needs (such as charity or performing good actions) as well as punishing violations of Muslim norms. Including moral suasion under the rubric of jihad removes the term from a narrow association with violence and expansionism.

Other passages in the Qur'an similarly lend themselves to a non-violent—or at least not exclusively violent—interpretation of jihad. For example, in 25:52 we read: "So, do not obey the unbelievers and strive *(jahidhum)* against them with it [the Qur'an] mightily." The exegetes unanimously appear to interpret this verse within the context of the proclamation of the Qur'an. In other words, Muhammad is being enjoined to preach the holy text to the nonbelievers, and through this process to warn them of their impending doom and make them aware of the emptiness of their lives. Such an interpretation suggests that proselytizing might fall under the rubric of jihad as well. This is not inconsistent with the predominant militant interpretation of the word: as noted in chapter 1, part of the responsibility of the fighter is to proclaim the truth.

The verse's exclusive focus on jihad as proclamation, however, cannot be used to infer that this constitutes the exclusive meaning of jihad. Most traditions that elucidate jihad combine the two meanings; for example: "Combat *(jahidu)* the polytheists with your possessions, your selves, and your tongues."[7] Sometimes the idea behind the two types of jihad is cited as "the believer combats with his sword and his tongue," which conveys the duality of the activity. Because of the difficulties of ascertaining the original meaning, and given the ambiguity of the activity described, in certain cases, such as the Qur'anic verse 25:52 and these two traditions (and their variants), the better translation of the verb *jahada* would be the word "combat."

Therefore, some Qur'anic verses and certain traditions do appear to allow for construing jihad as a nonviolent activity—or at least as an activity that does not necessarily entail violence. This nonviolent warfare clearly was known to early jihad fighters such as Ibn al-Mubarak, who states in the *Kitab al-jihad:* "The fighter is one who fights his [lower] soul."[8] This doctrine is best expressed in the tradition that distinguishes the nonviolent and the violent jihads as, respectively, "greater jihad" and "lesser jihad."

DISTINGUISHING THE "GREATER JIHAD" FROM THE "LESSER JIHAD"

Among the traditions indicating that jihad might have a nonviolent meaning, the most commonly cited is the following:

> A number of fighters came to the Messenger of Allah, and he said: "You have done well in coming from the 'lesser jihad' to the 'greater jihad.'" They said: "What is the 'greater jihad'?" He said: "For the servant [of God] to fight his passions."[9]

Clearly this tradition is an attempt to radically reinterpret the originally aggressive intent of the Qur'an and the *hadith* literature in order to focus on the waging of spiritual warfare.

The tradition can be dated to the first half of the ninth century, when the ascetic movement in Islam was beginning to coalesce into Sufism, the mystical interpretation of Islam. Traditions indicating that jihad meant spiritual warfare, however, are entirely absent from any of the official, canonical collections (with the exception of that of al-Tirmidhi, who cites "the fighter is one who fights his passions");[10] they appear most often in the collections of ascetic material or proverbs.[11] One might reasonably infer from this that the *hadith* collectors construed as illegitimate the entire line of thought leading to the conclusion that spiritual warfare is part of or equivalent to aggressive jihad. Therefore, they did not include these traditions in their collections or rate them as "sound" (meaning that a Muslim can rely upon them as authority).

The substitution of the idea of fighting the lower self for aggressive jihad was probably first developed by the early moralists al-Muhasibi

(d. 857) and Ibn Abi al-Dunya (d. 894). That neither author cites the tradition of the "greater jihad" suggests that it postdates their writings. Al-Muhasibi's work concentrates on the idea of combating one's passions and desires in order to achieve worldly success. To accomplish this, the believer is directed to eradicate negative emotions and qualities such as fear (or anxiety), sorrow, and lust. However, al-Muhasibi's presentation contemplates aggressive fighting as well, and he seems to be aware that the battlefield is a location where one may fight this type of jihad. Nonetheless, he does not maintain that the act of fighting is a panacea for worldly desires; on the contrary, he points out that the desires to show off, to gain spoils, and to achieve fame through victory persist even in a state of physical danger.[12]

Ibn Abi al-Dunya, who wrote many books and pamphlets on moral and ethical issues, also explored the possibilities of spiritual warfare. His book on the subject, *Muhasibat al-nafs wa-l-izra 'alayha (Holding the Soul Accountable and Blaming It)*, contains doctrines that would later become the basis for Sufi teachings. Ibn Abi al-Dunya's concern, like that of al-Muhasibi, is moral self-examination. Neither writer, however, describes precisely how this should be accomplished. Ibn Abi al-Dunya speaks of the soul as an enemy, but he does not employ the tradition of "I returned from the lesser jihad to the greater jihad" even in the chapter entitled "The jihad of the soul, and forbidding it its desires," which seems to indicate that the tradition—even during the late ninth century—had not yet been formulated. The presence of the words *jihad* and *ghazw* (raiding) in Ibn Abi al-Dunya's account makes it difficult to believe that Ibn Abi al-Dunya would not have used this tradition had he known of it.[13]

Other famous proto-Sufi and early Sufi writers such as Abu Talib al-Makki (d. 996) are silent on the tradition of the "greater jihad," even though the latter's famous *Qut al-qulub (The Food of Hearts)* has several lengthy sections on combating the evil tendencies of the soul. Nor do such roughly contemporaneous authors as al-Qushayri (d. 1073), al-Sulami (d. 1021), and al-Hakim al-Tirmidhi (d. 930) invoke a specific doctrine of the "greater jihad." In common with the early ascetics, it is clear that they saw the settled life, with its progressive dulling of the believer's willingness to take spiritual risks, as the primary enemy:

> It is not your enemy who kills you so that Allah can cause you to enter Paradise—[though] if you kill him it will be a light for you—but the worst of enemies is your soul that is between the two sides [of your body], and the woman whom you bed.[14]

A variant adds one's children to the list of one's worst enemies. Traditions of this type have a great deal in common with jihad traditions cited in chapter 1: the factors in a man's life that tie him to normalcy—that prevent him from taking the risks of spiritual advancement and denial—are his worst enemies to the same extent that they would be if that man were on a battlefield. In both cases, his ties to this world incapacitate the individual and render him unable to make the sacrifices he needs to make in order to achieve perfection (al-insan al-kamil) or victory over the enemy.

For the true beginnings of the "greater jihad" we must go to the great theologian and Sufi al-Ghazali (d. 1111). It is to his formulations that we owe the success of this doctrine. In his great work *Ihya 'ulum al-din (Revival of the Religious Sciences)*, al-Ghazali presents the lusts and passions of the soul as an invading army trying to conquer the body and to keep it from following the path of mysticism. In an interesting reinterpretation, he strips a passage from Qur'an 4:95 from its context (indicated in bracketed text) to argue that Muslims must fight not *by means* of their possessions and "persons" (the word being the plural of *nafs*, soul), but *against* their possessions and their souls:

[Those of the believers who stay at home while suffering from no injury are not equal to] those who fight in the cause of Allah with their possessions and persons. Allah has raised those who fight with their possessions and persons one degree [over those who stay at home; and to each Allah has promised the fairest good. Yet Allah has granted a great reward to those who fight and not to those who stay behind].[15]

This creative reinterpretation of the Qur'anic verse turns the focus radically away from the original intent to concentrate on the battle against one's lower passions, especially the soul.

Al-Ghazali takes this argument further when he deals with the subject of exercising the soul. Throughout the *Ihya*, he uses military, and especially jihad, imagery to describe this battle.[16] However, al-Ghazali nowhere indicates that he sees the jihad against the soul as a substitute for militant jihad (he in fact rarely deals with militant jihad in the *Ihya*). But in the section on enjoining the good and forbidding the evil (al-amr bi-l-ma'ruf wa-l-nahi 'an al-munkar, one of the most fundamental principles of Islamic social law), al-Ghazali adduces the example of the jihad fighter who sacrifices himself for the greater good and leads a charge against a large number of the enemy in an attempt to cause them distress (this would later become the legal basis for the suicide attack or martyrdom operation of contemporary times).[17] Therefore, al-Ghazali does not entirely abandon militant interpretations of jihad, but rather sidelines them to a greater extent than had the predecessor ascetics and Sufis. Unlike them, al-Ghazali does not appear to have had close connections with fighters, even though he lived during the period of the Crusades.

Al-Ghazali's Sufi successors went a good deal further than he was willing to go. Chief among these was Muhyi al-Din Ibn al-ʿArabi (d. 1240), a Spanish Muslim mystic who developed a number of later Sufi doctrines, such as the belief in pantheistic monism *(wahdat al-wujud)* considered to be heretical or at least problematic by many Muslims. Like al-Ghazali, Ibn al-ʿArabi cites the tradition of the "greater jihad" in the context of combating the soul's lower passions while explicating Qur'anic verse 9:60:

> The alms are for the poor, the needy, their collectors, and those whose hearts are bound together, as well as for the freeing of the slaves, [repaying] the debtors, spending in Allah's path, and for the wayfarer. Thus Allah commands. Allah is All-Knowing, Wise.

As we have seen in chapter 1, the phrase "in the path of Allah" invariably means "jihad." Ibn al-ʿArabi recognizes this as the exoteric meaning of the phrase but maintains that warfare is but "one of the sum total of good paths that bring one closer to God."[18] "Fighters" *(mujahidin)* in the path of God are known for their good deeds, according to Ibn al-ʿArabi, and therefore are reinterpreted as those who engage in working for the common good, as well as engaging their passions in battle.

This interpretation is a bold one, and it goes beyond what al-Ghazali had stated earlier. Ibn al-ʿArabi appears to see the *mujahid* as one who improves society and provides for the welfare of God's creatures—in contradistinction to al-Ghazali's emphasis on inner spiritual battles that do not necessarily affect anyone other than the person fighting them. Unlike al-Ghazali, Ibn al-ʿArabi does not avoid citing militant traditions concerning jihad, although his primary purpose does not appear to have been to emphasize their militant aspects. For example, he uses the famous tradition "I was ordered to fight people until they bear witness that there is only one God . . ."[19] to underscore the awesomeness of the Muslim confession of faith (the *shahada*) contained within it, rather than focusing upon the (probable) original purpose of the tradition.[20]

In other definitions of *jihad*, Ibn al-ʿArabi does not preclude fighting, but merely seems to place it at a lower rank. William Chittick in his study of Ibn al-ʿArabi's thought cites a categorization of four types of "strugglers" *(mujahidin)*; his first two categories are clearly taken from the Qur'anic jihad passages (4:95).[21] In other passages Ibn al-ʿArabi notes with approval that there are two events in Islam that take place in rows: prayer and fighting (citing Qur'an 61:4).[22] In this citation there is no reinterpretation away from literal fighting; in yet other citations his definition of the word *shahid* (martyr) focuses solely upon those who have died in battle.[23] Thus, Ibn al-'Arabi's interpretations are much more nuanced and open to reinterpretation than are al-Ghazali's. Ibn al-'Arabi strongly preferred the spiritualization of jihad, but he did not go so far as to ignore or deny any validity to militant warfare within Islam. Many other Sufi writers describe the "greater jihad," but to a large extent follow in the footsteps of these great thinkers.

Although few books have been entirely devoted to the subject of the "greater jihad," we should note the one writer—Ayatullah Ruhallah al-Khumayni (d. 1989)—who did write on the subject, even though his work is contemporary and takes us away from the premodern period. Al-Khumayni sees the issue of the "greater jihad" as a call to radical social transformation that is divorced from a quietistic interpretation of the concept. He describes it as a battle against the ego, and as a preparation for any type of militant jihad:

> Those who engaged in *jihad* in the first age of Islam advanced and pushed forward without any regard for themselves or their personal desires, for they had earlier waged a *jihad* against their selves. Without the inner *jihad,* the outer *jihad* is impossible. *Jihad* is inconceivable unless a person turns his back on his own desires and the world. For what we mean here by "world" is the aggregate of man's aspirations that effectively constitute his world . . . it is the world in this narrow, individual sense that prevents man from drawing near to the realm of sanctity and perfection.[24]

These comments are very much in the spirit of early ascetic and Sufi doctrines, but Khumayni's comments do not preclude the possibility of overlap between the "greater jihad" and the "lesser jihad"; in fact, they seem to promote an identity between the two types of jihad. How have scholars dealt with this difficulty?

CONTEMPORARY SCHOLARS AND THE "GREATER JIHAD"

"Greater jihad" has been a subject of particular interest among contemporary non-Muslim scholars. Although scholars devote more attention to greater jihad than is warranted by its treatment in classical Islamic texts, and although the concept would appear to have little relevance for jihad as a whole (let alone for Islam as a faith in its relationship toward other peoples and faiths), the notion of "greater jihad" occupies a prominent place in Western scholarly discussion of jihad. The most eminent of these scholars is Alfred Morabia, whose *Le gihad dans l'Islam medieval* is the most thorough and reliable treatment of the subject. (The preceding treatment of "internal jihad" is heavily indebted to his discussion, especially his highlighting of Qur'anic verses that might be construed to accord with to the nonviolent practice of jihad.) To his credit, Morabia notes that the "greater jihad / lesser jihad" dichotomy is a fiction devised to ease the acceptance of jihad into Muslim society. Similarly he recognizes that Sufis worked together with jihad fighters in many different areas of the Muslim world. But, in the final analysis, Morabia's discussion of the place of the internal jihad in the classical Muslim tradition[25] dances around the basic point that the internal jihad has no reality whatsoever—that it is a theoretical, scholarly construct for which we have little to no practical evidence. Morabia lacks the courage to go where the evidence is leading him. Throughout his book he carefully compares jihad theory to practice. But with internal jihad there is no practice, just theory.

Others have fallen into this error as well. They comprise two basic groups: Western scholars who want to present Islam in the most innocuous terms possible, and Muslim apologists, who rediscovered the internal jihad in the nineteenth century and have been emphasizing it ever since that time as the normative expression of jihad—in defiance of all the religious and historical evidence to the contrary. The motives of the first group are well intentioned, probably undertaken with the goal of furthering interreligious dialogue and skirting an issue that has long been used by polemicists as a vehicle for attacking Islam. For example, Ahmad Rashid, in his *Jihad: The Rise of Militant Islam in Central Asia,* a fascinating journalistic treatment of the radical Muslim and globalist radical Muslim groups in Central Asia, especially Uzbekistan, says:

> In Western thought, heavily influenced by the medieval Christian Crusaders—with their ideas about "holy war"—*jihad* has always been portrayed as an Islamic war against unbelievers. Westerners point to the conquest of Spain in the eighth century by the Moors and the vast Ottoman Empire of the thirteen through twentieth centuries, and focus on the bloodshed, ignoring not only the enormous achievements in science and art and the basic tolerance of these empires, but also the true idea of *jihad* that spread peacefully throughout these realms. Militancy is not the essence of *jihad*.[26]

Rashid goes on to describe the internal jihad in glowing terms (albeit without presenting any evidence that the doctrine of the internal jihad was ever present in Muslim Spain or the Ottoman Empire), but let us concentrate upon the above statement. Aside from the fact that Westerners have hardly ignored the achievements of the Spanish Muslims or the Ottomans—it was after all Western scholars such as Reinhart Dozy who first publicized these historical facts—this entire statement is an attempt to sidestep the basic issue. There is no question that the Spanish Muslims and the Ottomans built glorious empires. The question is: what was the ideology behind their conquest? That ideology was clearly militant jihad in the case of Spain, and while there are questions as to the jihad ideology of the earliest Ottoman conquerors,[27] later rulers clearly utilized militant jihad, as is demonstrated by countless contemporary historical and religious documents. The above statement in essence maintains that the ends justify the means. Rashid's denial of the essential militancy of jihad is simply the logical conclusion of an entirely illogical paragraph.

Such discussions of radical Muslims and their practice of jihad are also basically attempts to delegitimize the beliefs of these groups at the very outset. This is fundamentally wrong, in addition to being judgmental to an extent that is, at the very least, open to debate on the basis of the available evidence. Statements like Rashid's lead to further confusion among Westerners who know nothing about Islam and who logically ask: why, if it has no validity, is the doctrine of militant jihad so influential in the Muslim world? Maintaining that the internal jihad is a major doctrine in Islam makes this entirely reasonable question unanswerable.

Another writer, Carole Hillenbrand, whose excellent book *The Crusades: Islamic Perspectives* is probably the best and most objective book on the subject, says with regard to jihad:

> It should be emphasized that from the earliest period the notion of *jihad* (struggle) as a spiritual concept for individual Muslims was paramount. Two kinds of *jihad* were identified: the greater *jihad (al-jihad al-akbar)* and the lesser *jihad (al-jihad al-asghar)*. The greater *jihad* is the struggle which man has to wage against his lower self and is, indeed, more meritorious than the military struggle conducted against infidels.[28]

At the very least, such a broad statement calls out for documentation—which Hillenbrand supplies abundantly in other instances—but her conclusion is essentially dogmatic and unsupportable. The flat statement is the refuge of scholars who believe in the essentially irenic nature of jihad, while the footnote is the response of those who do not.

Similar statements can be found in the works of John Esposito, whose writings on the subject of jihad border between the scholarly and the apologetic. For example, in *The Islamic Threat*, he states:

> The term *jihad* has a number of meanings, which include the effort to lead a good life, to make society more moral and just, and to spread Islam through preaching, teaching, or armed struggle.[29]

This definition has virtually no validity in Islam and is derived almost entirely from the apologetic works of nineteenth- and twentieth-century Muslim modernists. To maintain that *jihad* means "the effort to lead a good life" is bathetic and laughable in any case. In all the literature concerning jihad—whether militant or internal jihad—the fundamental idea is to disconnect oneself from the world, to die to the world, whether bodily (as in battle) or spiritually (as in the internal jihad). The priorities of jihad in Islam here are exactly reversed from the historical and religious realities: the armed struggle—aggressive conquest—came first, and then additional meanings became attached to the term. Esposito goes on to say:

> In its most generic meaning, "jihad" signifies the battle against evil and the devil, the self-discipline (common to the three Abrahamic faiths) in which believers seek to follow God's will, to be better Muslims. It is the lifelong struggle to be virtuous, to be true to the straight path of God. This is the primary way in which the observant Muslim gives witness to or actualizes the truth of the first pillar of Islam in everyday life.[30]

Again, Esposito apparently deliberately spiritualizes what is an unambiguously concrete and militant doctrine, without a shred of evidence from the Qur'an or any of the classical sources, in which the jihad and fighting is against real human enemies, and not the devil (although, as discussed below, 'Abd al-Qadir al-Jilani, a later Sufi, includes Satan in his list of enemies against whom one can wage jihad). To his credit, Esposito includes the doctrine of "enjoining the good and forbidding the evil" under the rubric of jihad—as did al-Ghazali—although because he does not define what that means, one might conclude that, unlike the reality, no coercion is involved. But then Esposito loses his way again, maintaining that Islam expanded during the early stage by "preaching, diplomacy and warfare," and once again inverts the actual order. He seems to have an extreme aversion to dealing with Islamic history as it really was.

In his more recent *Unholy War*, while discussing the many meanings of jihad, Esposito continues to avoid all historical context for his discussion and simply repeats what contemporary Muslim apologists say about this doctrine. Since he has already decided that radical Muslims are terrorists, Esposito is able to avoid dealing with the fact that they have extensive support in the central texts and doctrines of Islam. This

is the most common fallacy of those scholars and apologists who promote the irenic interpretation of jihad.

The second group—Muslim apologists—is far more ideological and
pointed in its defensiveness concerning the subject of jihad. Robert
Crane, of the Center for Understanding Islam, for example, says:

> The Qur'an refers to *jihad* only in terms of intellectual effort to apply
> divine revelation in promoting peace through justice "[so, do not obey
> the unbelievers] and strive against them with it [the Qur'an]" (25:52);
> and "The word of your Lord has been completed in truth and justice."
> (6:115)[31]

This is a disingenuous attempt to highlight the fact that strictly speaking
in the Qur'an the word *jihad* is used comparatively rarely for actual fighting (it appears only four times; other words such as *qital*, fighting, are
more common). But Crane's statement that *jihad* never means "fighting"
is incorrect, since it appears in that sense in 9:24 and 60:1. Crane's treatment of the subject becomes more strained in avoiding the fact that the
root (the verbal derivatives) of the word *jihad* appears quite frequently
with regard to fighting (e.g., 2:218, 3:143, 8:72, 74–75, 9:16, 20, 41, 86,
61:11) or fighters (*mujahidin,* 4:95, 47:31). It goes without saying that
either Crane is ignoring the entirety of Muslim history and law with
regard to jihad, which cites dozens of militant verses from the Qur'an, or
he is attempting to present the material in an apologetic fashion. It is far
from clear that Muslim apologetics are well served by statements that
are so blatantly transparent and call the credibility of the writer into
question.

Attempts to rewrite history occur solely in Western-authored presentations of jihad, or those with Western audiences as the primary focus.[32]
It is ironic, but the fact remains that few Muslim scholars or even apologists writing in non-European languages have ever made the exagger-
ated claims seen above. Perhaps because early Muslim history is heavily
emphasized in the Islamic educational curriculum, those who write in
Arabic or other Muslim majority languages realize that it is pointless to
present jihad as anything other than militant warfare.[33]

The common denominator of the above citations is the flat statement
unsupported by any evidence. In relying upon the most theoretical and
arcane teachings of Sufi thinkers, one must ask whether there is any way
to test the real importance of the "greater jihad" in the history and experience of Islam. Here the question a scholar must ask is: was the "greater
jihad" and "lesser jihad" dichotomy a practical reality in Muslim history? Did Muslims actually distinguish between the two types of jihad

in their conduct, and if so, which of the two was the more prevalent and influential?

SUFI WARRIORS

Like ʿAbdallah b. al-Mubarak, a great many of the proto-Sufi ascetics and early Sufi mystics participated in militant jihad. Ibn al-Mubarak demonstrated the manner in which this was accomplished in two works that have come down to us: the *Kitab al-jihad* and the *Kitab al-zuhd wa-l-raqaʾiq* (his collection of ascetic traditions and admonitions). These two books are the two faces of the Muslim ascetic, who is not necessarily a man of peace. (My comments here do not imply the opposite conclusion; not all ascetics or Sufis are necessarily militant.) The ideal ascetic practices both types of jihad—internal and external—and does not deny either.

From the time of al-Muhasibi and previously as well, ascetics and fighters inhabited the same niche. Many of the early ascetic-fighters avoided the centers of the Muslim empire, preferring the outlying areas where there were enemies to fight, such as Cilicia from the eighth through the eleventh century where the Byzantines were a menace, or Qazwin, close to the border with the then-wild and un-Islamized region of Tabaristan. These areas—coastlands or border regions—also provided opportunities to preach Islam to the as-yet unconverted locals. Fighting in these border regions was frequently a magnet for groups known in the sources as *muttatawiʿa,* or volunteer fighters. These "volunteer fighters" were usually Sufis or ascetics, who would join Muslim armies in order to increase their own spiritual reward.[34] Only toward the end of the thirteenth century, with the rise of regular armies in the Muslim world, do these formations begin to disappear.

Looking through the biographies of ascetics and Sufis, we find no separation between militancy and asceticism. A good example is Abu Muʿawiya al-Aswad, an ascetic who lived in the border city of Tarsus during the eighth century. His actions of self-denial included continual weeping, spending the night in prayer, living in the local garbage heap, as well as other expressions of devotion to God. Among the latter was his participation in numerous raids against the Byzantines and keeping watch over the fortress of Tarsus.[35] Hagiographical collections such as those of Abu Nuʿaym al-Isfahani (d. 1039) and Ibn al-Jawzi (d. 1200) are filled with stories of Sufis and ascetics who spent part of their lives in self-denial and another part fighting the enemies of Islam. How could this be otherwise, when the paradigms of the early Sufis—the Prophet Muhammad's Companions—had initiated and participated fully in the great conquests? It would be entirely unexpected if this spiritual example was not emulated by later devotees.

This paradigm persisted into medieval times, where we often find the Sufi groups fighting the enemies of Islam. For example, after defeating the Crusaders under Guy de Lusignan at the Battle of the Horns of Hittin (1187), the Muslim leader Salah al-Din al-Ayyubi (1169–91) gave the captive Crusaders to several of his Sufi regiments to slaughter.[36] A few years later, when the Crusaders of the Fifth Crusade attacked Egypt in 1249–50 and tried to conquer the Nile Delta (in order to use it as currency to trade for Jerusalem), we find Sufis listed among the prominent fighters. For example, one 'Abd al-Rahman al-Nuwayri, described as one of the greatest Sufis, "would regularly go out to battle"[37] and was killed by the Crusaders at the Battle of Damietta.

Important Sufis such as 'Abd al-Qadir al-Jilani (d. 1166, the founder of the early and widespread Sufi brotherhood of the Qadiriyya) cited the tradition of the "greater jihad" versus the "lesser jihad,"[38] but he also proclaimed the need for actual fighting and demonstrated the connection between the two:

> [There are] two types of jihad: the outer and the inner. The inner is the jihad of the soul, the passion, the nature, and Satan. It involves repentance from rebelliousness and errors, being steadfast about it, and abandoning the forbidden passions. The outer is the jihad of the infidels who resist Him and His Messenger [Muhammad] and to be pitiless with their swords, their spears, and their arrows—killing and being killed. The inner jihad is more difficult than the outer jihad because it involves cutting the forbidden customs of the soul, and exiling them, so as to have as one's example the Divine commands and to cease from what it forbids. Whoever takes God's command as his example with regard to the two types of jihad will gain a reward in this world and the next. Bodily wounds on the martyr are just like someone cutting their hand—there is no real pain in it—and death with regard to the soul of a *mujahid* who repents from his sins is like a thirsty man drinking cold water.[39]

Wherever Sufi groups went, they took both aspects of jihad with them.

In North Africa and Muslim Spain the revivalist Murabitun (1091–1145, about whom see chapter 3) was clearly a militant Sufi dynasty that used motifs of both asceticism and jihad in order to further its legitimacy. Other dynasties, such as the Safavids (ruling in Persia, ca. 1500–1700) followed this same idea. In other areas, local missionaries led the way. Many of the Sufi holy men of South Asia (today India and

Pakistan) were both ascetics and warriors. Throughout the South Asian Subcontinent, the Sufi order of the Naqshbandiyya-Mujaddidiyya was closely associated with Muslim revivalism and conquest. Simon Digby's translation of the *Malfuzat-i Naqshbandiyya,* aptly titled *Sufis and Soldiers in Awrangzeb's Deccan,* illustrates this trend. The major figure of the work, Baba Palangposh, is a local holy man who joins the army of the Moghul ruler Awrangzeb (1657–1707) and participates in the campaign to subdue the region of southern India. He witnesses a vision of the Prophet Muhammad's uncle Hamza (slain at the Battle of Uhud in 627, and usually called "the Prince of Martyrs") in which Hamza gives Baba Palangposh a sword and says: "Take this sword . . . and go to the army of Mir Shihab al-Din in the land of the Deccan [southern India]."[40] Just as in African Islam during the following centuries, prayer and piety are mixed with military activity.[41]

Many of the resistance movements fighting European incursions during the eighteenth and nineteenth centuries were derived from Sufi orders—the Qadiris and Tijanis who supported Usaman Dan Fodio in West Africa, the movement of Imam Shamil in the Caucasus, the Mahdist movement in the Sudan and Somalia, and the Sanusis in Libya.[42] Although some of these jihad activities, such as those undertaken in response to the Crusader attacks, were clearly defensive, others were not. These Sufi warriors participated in offensive jihads as well; for example, Awrangzeb's invasion of southern India was hardly defensive. One has to wonder: did anybody really consider the difference? All of this material—treated here only briefly—raises the question of whether those who practiced both types of jihad distinguished between the two. It is difficult to isolate a single historical instance of either an individual or a group using the idea of the "greater jihad" in order to reject the possibility of aggressive warfare.[43]

In conclusion, several important points need to be made about the "greater jihad." The spiritual, internal jihad is the derivative form, and not the contrary. This is clear from the absence of any mention of the "greater jihad" in the earliest *hadith* books on the subject of jihad (it is entirely absent from the canonical collections and appears only in the genre of *zuhd,* asceticism, and then in comparatively later collections). Nor does the "greater jihad" find any mention in the later literature on jihad, except occasionally in the most perfunctory form. It is also apparent that anyone who studies the subject of jihad has to wonder about the focus placed upon the spiritual warfare among contemporary Muslim apologists. This focus does not seem warranted when considering the classical (or the contemporary Arabic, Persian or Urdu language) sources. There are, after all, literally hundreds of sources for militant jihad in classical Islam. With books and pamphlets devoted to the subject,[44] as well as sections of every *hadith* and law book, along with most commentaries on the Qur'an and historical materials, as well as anecdotal snippets in the literary sources, and martial poetry, the Muslim who wishes to practice aggressive jihad has an abundance of literary material upon which to base his actions and derive his precedents. But with the exception of Ayatullah al-Khumayni's contemporary book on the "greater jihad," there do not seem to have ever been *any* works devoted exclusively to the subject of the spiritual jihad. Works such as that by Eric Geoffroy, *Jihad et contemplation,* which is a thoughtful study on the subject, are written, like virtually all the literature on the subject, in a European language for non-Muslims.[45]

While this fact still leaves room for the descriptions and studies that we find in ascetic and Sufi literature, it raises the question of whether the "greater jihad" has ever indeed been "greater" than the militant version in the collective consciousness of Muslims, or whether its very title—the "greater jihad"—is an attempt to arrogate to a purely spiritual activity the prestige that is usually accorded to fighting. It seems to the outside observer a patently apologetic device designed to promote a doctrine that has little historical depth in Islam, is not well attested in the *hadith* literature, has few practical examples to illustrate precisely how it was practiced, and was adduced in order to overcome a resistance to the acceptance and legitimacy of jihad. The name is nothing more than false advertisement designed to pull the wool over the eyes of the audience. While this method of advertisement is as acceptable as any others that promote radical change within a tradition, citation of the doctrine of the "greater jihad" should not be used today by scholars of Islam as "proof" that nonviolent jihad has historical depth or universal acceptance in classical or even in contemporary Islam (see chapter 5).

It should be further noted that although the possibility remains that over the coming centuries Islam may decisively reject all forms of militant jihad in favor of spiritual, internal warfare, there is nothing in the tradition up to the present day that precludes the mixture of the two. In fact, it seems that the ascetic and Sufi groups who first pushed spiritual warfare and promoted it within the Islamic tradition did so as a supplement to the waging of aggressive warfare. This is persuasively indicated by the original tradition that distinguishes the two: "You returned from the 'lesser jihad' to the 'greater jihad.'" The implication of this tradition is that one form of jihad is complementary to the other, and that the ideal Muslim practices both, as can be seen from the citations of militant ascetics and Sufis above. This is evident as well in the literature penned by contemporary radical Muslims (although many attack the irenic aspects of the internal jihad) and globalist radical Muslims. For example, the document left by the attackers of September 11, 2001, "The Last Night," mixes spiritual jihad together with militant jihad in a manner completely in accord with the citation from 'Abd al-Qadir al-Jilani above.[46]

It seems clear that the appearance of purely internal, nonviolent jihad never fully took hold because of the inherent ambiguities of the doctrine, as well as the events that occurred in the Muslim world while the doctrine was being formulated. As long as the high Muslim civilization was not in any peril from the outside world, a spirit of nonviolent jihad could be cultivated. What happened when non-Muslims began to challenge the Muslim world aggressively and tried to reverse the conquests?

THREE

THE CRYSTALLIZATION OF JIHAD THEORY

Crusade and Counter-Crusade

Islam enjoyed a large degree of success during the conquests of the seventh and eighth centuries, and it continued to prevail during the periodic local invasions that followed during the ninth and tenth centuries (the conquest of Sicily and southern Italy, for example, and the conquest of Crete). However, many of the initial Muslim victories were achieved because no strong states other than the Byzantine Empire (and more distantly, the Chinese Empire) stood in the path of the Muslims. In fact, the Muslim conquests to a large degree facilitated the development of strong states, especially in Europe, as loosely ruled regions began to oppose the Muslims collectively. In the Iberian Peninsula, southern France, and Italy, the resurgence of European Christian civilization during the High Middle Ages began with the systematic expulsion of the Muslims. Muslims in southern France had never been particularly strong and were the first to be attacked.[1] In the tenth century, the papacy encouraged the Normans in southern Italy to attack their Muslim neighbors, and gradually, over a period of nearly a hundred years, they conquered that region, as well as the island of Sicily.[2]

The most prominent example of Christian reconquest was in Spain, where several small Christian kingdoms continued to control the northern mountainous region after the Muslim conquest. For centuries these kingdoms coexisted more or less peacefully with the Spanish Muslims, but starting in the middle of the tenth century they initiated extensive raids upon the disintegrating Umayyad caliphate of Cordova (finally abolished in 1031). These raids galvanized the Muslims, led by al-Mansur b. Abi al-ʿAmir, who ruled *de facto* from 978 to 1002 and attempted to conquer (or at least subordinate) the Christian kingdoms. During the course of his rule, al-Mansur directed and in many instances personally led no fewer than fifty-seven campaigns against the Christian northern kingdoms and prevailed (as his name, *al-Mansur*, the Victorious, implies) in the vast majority of them.[3] However, with the collapse of the Umayyad caliphate a short time after his death and the renewal of Christian offensives against the divided Muslim states, the strategic situation changed rapidly.

For a period of approximately one hundred and fifty years, starting with the capture of the city of Toledo by Alfonso VI of Leon in 1085, there was a general stalemate in the wars between the Muslims and the Christians. Faced with irresolvable disunity, the Spanish Muslims increasingly sought the protection of powerful African Muslim dynasties, first the al-Murabitun (usually referred to as Almoravids, 1091–1145), then the al-Muwahhidun (usually referred to as the Almohads, 1171–1212). Although leaders of these dynasties provided the support required, they also deprived the Spanish Muslims of political independence and caused the latter to become dependent upon them for survival.[4] Victories over the Christian invaders (in 1086 and 1195) were not decisive, nor would it have been in the best interest of either dynasty to win the war against the Christian kingdoms decisively, for it was the continual threat of Christian attack that kept the squabbling Spanish Muslims loyal to their African Muslim overlords.

By the beginning of the thirteenth century, however, the Christian kingdoms had built up a critical mass of power, and in 1212 they overwhelmed the al-Muwahhidun at Las Navas de Tolosa. This victory proved to be decisive, and with the exception of the kingdom of Grenada, located in the southeastern mountainous region of the Iberian Peninsula, all previously Muslim-dominated regions came under Christian control. This situation persisted until the 1480s, when the marriage between Ferdinand of Aragon and Isabel of Leon-Castile, coupled with the heightened fear of Muslim domination engendered by the fall of Constantinople to the Ottoman Turks in 1453 and increased religious intolerance, led, in 1492, to the extinction of the kingdom of Grenada.[5]

The Spanish *reconquista* constituted one of the few successful attempts by non-Muslims to secure a significant territory previously controlled by Muslims—with either a sizeable or a dominant Muslim population—and to end entirely its Muslim presence. Although the

Muslims suffered some significant territorial losses during the eighteenth and nineteenth centuries (in the Indian Subcontinent, southeastern Europe, and the region of the Ukraine), for the most part these territories had been held by Muslims from a minority position and were not supported by large, exclusively Muslim civilizations. Other Muslim territories that were controlled, dominated, or conquered by non-Muslims usually reverted to Muslim control within a fairly short period.

THE CRUSADES

In contrast to the Spanish *reconquista*—which had something of the character of a liberation movement—European Christians also sought to conquer territory in the core lands of Islam. The most significant of these wars of conquest were the Crusades—a series of semipopular, religiously inspired invasions, with strong economic motives, that took place over a period of several hundred years.[6] For the Muslims, the Crusades, which lasted from 1096 until the fall of the last major Crusader fortresses on the Levantine coast in 1291, were a very traumatic period. Nominally the Crusaders came at the behest of the Byzantine emperor, Alexios I Komnenos (1081–1118), who sought help from the pope to defeat the Turkish tribesmen who had dominated the Anatolian Peninsula since the Battle of Manzikert in 1071. In actuality, many of the Crusaders were either uninterested or only marginally interested in saving the Byzantines. Many of them wanted to "liberate" Jerusalem from the Muslims and establish petty kingdoms in the Levant for themselves.

During the course of more than thirty tumultuous years (1098–1131), the Crusaders managed to establish four quarreling polities along the Levantine coast, the most important of which were the Latin kingdom of Jerusalem (covering most of the historical region of Palestine and Lebanon) and the principality of Antioch (centered around northern Syria). Although the Fatimid rulers of Egypt made periodic attempts to defeat the invaders, there was little popular support for a jihad to expel them,[7] and many local Muslim rulers either allied themselves with the Crusaders or did little to defeat, let alone expel, them.[8]

This mutual accommodation gradually came to an end during the 1140s with the rise of Zangi, the ruler of the region of the Jazira (today northern Iraq), who conquered one of the Crusader states, Edessa, in 1144. This event triggered the Second Crusade (1147–48), which accomplished nothing, and it led to a forty-year stalemate between the Muslim and the Christian states. However, this time was also characterized by a heightened awareness of jihad and by the publication of a number of fundamental treatises on the subject, as well as the formulation of legal definitions that remain important to this day. This stalemate was broken by the victory of Salah al-Din al-Ayyubi (d. 1193) over the combined forces of the Latin kingdom of Jerusalem at the Horns of Hattin in 1187. For the Muslims, this was a decisive victory—although the Christians eventually recovered some of their lost territory—that enabled them to reconquer Jerusalem and to limit the Crusader presence to the coastal regions of the Levant.

There the Crusaders remained for the following century, their existence prolonged by the Italian domination of the sea, by repeated Crusades (many of which did more to hurt than help them), and, after 1258, by the threat the Mongol invasions posed to the Muslims and the possibility that the Crusaders or their allies in Europe might cement an alliance with the Mongols.

MONGOL INVASIONS

The Mongol invasions are the sole instance, other than the European colonialist ventures of the eighteenth and nineteenth centuries (and those states founded by them, which continue to this day), during which the core lands of Islam have come under the control of non-Muslims. These invasions, conducted between 1220 and 1300, led to the devastation of the eastern part of the Muslim world, the end of the ʿAbbasid caliphate (747–1258), and the foundation of an initially non-Muslim state to the east of the Euphrates River. Although previous nomadic invasions originating in Central Asia had also devastated the core lands of Islam—for example, the Seljuq Turks during the eleventh century— these nomads had already converted to Islam prior to their invasion or did so quickly afterwards; their presence served as a catalyst for further Muslim conquest directed against the Byzantine Empire and India. The Mongols, however, did not fit into this pattern. Although they converted to Islam after several generations, they never actively worked to expand the territory of Islam; indeed their attacks were directed not against "infidels" but against the Muslim Mamluks of Egypt and their Muslim kinsmen in the Golden Horde (today the area of southern Russia and the Ukraine). Even after their conversion, the Mongols maintained a form of Islam considerably laxer and more tolerant of non-Muslims than that practiced in the Middle East.

Muslims might have been forgiven for believing that the first Mongol invasions of 1219–23, although catastrophic, would not persist. Ghenghis Khan (d. 1227) used the massacre of a number of Muslim merchants, who were either his ambassadors or spies—and perhaps both—by one of the governors of the Khwarazm-Shah, the ruler of Central Asia, as a pretext for attack. His incursion was distinguished by its thoroughness and cruelty, and many of the major Muslim cities of Central Asia and eastern Persia—which had been among the principal centers of high Muslim culture for centuries—were destroyed or seriously damaged. However, the Mongols did not establish an occupying presence in the region, although they continued to control Central Asia.[9]

They returned in the middle of the 1250s. Hulagu, the younger brother of the famed Kublai Khan, had received a mandate to establish Mongol rule in the area of Iran and Iraq and to wipe out the Isma'ili Assassins (based in northern Persia), whom the Mongols hated and feared. Between 1254 and 1256 the Mongols carried out the latter goal, which many Muslims, both Sunnis and Shi'ites, were happy to see completed, since the Assassins were universally loathed. However, Hulagu also sought the subordination of the caliph, viewed by the Mongols as just another potentate subject to the authority of the Great Khan. In 1258 Hulagu besieged Baghdad, captured the 'Abbasid caliph, and had him murdered. For Sunni Muslims, this action deprived the Muslim community of a legitimate caliph. According to many prophetic traditions, the presence of a caliph was a both a prerequisite for Sunni Muslim political stability and a unifying force. Although eventually a subsidiary line of the 'Abbasid family was established in Egypt as "caliphs," they never achieved the universal recognition that the Baghdadi caliphs had received.

Even worse for all Muslims, the Mongols were clearly "infidels" and sought to attack and subjugate the entire Muslim world. Only the fervently Sunni Mamluk Empire in Egypt, which had been forged in the resistance to the Fifth Crusade in 1249–50 and based its power on the same nomadic slave-soldier groups as did the Mongols, stood between them and that goal. In 1259 the Mongols and the Mamluks met in battle at 'Ayn Jalut (a short distance to the south of Nazareth, in Israel), and the Mongols were defeated. The defeat confined the Mongols' core territory to the region east of the Euphrates River.[10] However, periodically during the following forty-some years, even after their conversion to Islam in 1295, the Mongols continued to attack the Mamluks in attempts to secure territory; the most sustained and ambitious attack was the invasion of Ghazan Khan in 1299, during the course of which he tried and failed to conquer Syria. The Mongol Empire suffered from serious structural weaknesses, and its unity was already compromised by the end of the thirteenth century. But while it existed, the Mongol threat consumed Sunni Muslims, during the period when the laws of jihad were being formulated and codified, in a way that no previous threat had done. For Sunni Muslims, the absolute, Manichean nature of the conflict, the terrible destruction wrought by the Mongols in Central Asia, Persia, and Iraq, and the challenge to Islam posed by military success achieved by infidels heightened the perception that there needed to be a shift in thinking about warfare. No previous foe other than the Byzantines receives such attention in the sources.

THE MUSLIM RESPONSE TO THE CRUSADES
AND THE MONGOL INVASIONS

Structurally, the major response of the Muslim world to the Crusaders and the Mongols was the full flower of the *mamluk* system for the defense of Islam. The system was unique to Islam, which was dependent upon the importation of slaves, usually from Central Asia but also from Africa.[11] These slaves were then converted to Islam, trained extensively in warfare, and allowed to advance in the military through a rude and frequently violent meritocracy. The system was nonhereditary and limited to a single generation: the children of a *mamluk* could not inherit their father's position. Every *mamluk* started out as a slave, but many climbed to positions of great power and wealth through their achievements and personal alliances with other *mamluk*s.[12]

This system became prominent in Islam during the ninth century under the ʿAbbasid dynasty, which began the large-scale importation of Turkish slave-soldiers to serve as personal bodyguards to members of the court. Later on the Turks came to control their nominal masters and exported the *mamluk* system to many other parts of the Muslim world. The two most notable *mamluk* dynasties were the Egyptian Mamluks, who ruled from 1250 to 1517, and the Slave Dynasty of Delhi (in India), which ruled during the thirteenth and fourteenth centuries. But the *mamluk* system persisted under the Ottoman Turkish Dynasty (ca. 1300–1924) as the *yenicheri* (called the Janissaries by Westerners), who were taken from Christian families, primarily in the Balkans, converted to Islam, and trained as soldiers. The Janissary system continued until its suppression in 1828.

At the time of the Crusader and Mongol invasions, the *mamluk* system was in its prime. Until that time, the Muslim world had lacked permanent standing armies, but the threats posed by these incursions made permanent armies necessary. Because of the outstanding military qualities of the Turks and other nomadic peoples, the *mamluk* system provided the Muslim world with a bulwark against the nomadic Mongols. Only with the rise of firearms in the fifteenth and sixteenth centuries was there a force that was capable of defeating the *mamluks*.

The latter part of the Zangid-Ayyubid period (1144–1250) into the early Mamluk period (1250–1318) was marked by an upsurge in writings concerning jihad. Probably the best known among these is that of al-ʿIzz b. ʿAbd al-Salam al-Sulami (d. 1262), who also wrote a number of influential legal opinions. His booklet, however, did little to advance the formulation of a law of jihad, merely recapitulating the material previously discussed in chapter 1, and it does not mention any of the momentous events of his time. From this period we have one of the largest and most significant books on jihad ever written (until the present day): the *Mashariʿ al-ashwaq ila masariʿ al-ʿushshaq* by Ibn al-Nahhas al-Dumyati (d. 1411).[13] Ibn al-Nahhas was a fighter who lived along the Egyptian coastlands and tried to defend them against periodic raids from the Crusaders (by whom he was ultimately killed) during the early fifteenth century. (Although the Crusaders were expelled from Syria in 1291, they continued to rule Cyprus and periodically raided Egypt, launching a major attack on Alexandria in 1365. The Muslims of Egypt devastated Cyprus in 1426 in retaliation.) This substantial work, containing 1,289 traditions (compared to Ibn al-Mubarak's paltry 262), is a summary of medieval Muslim teachings on jihad. It covers the traditional topics of the encouragement of jihad, delineation of the rank of martyrs, and discussions of legal issues associated with jihad, as well as copious notes documenting Muslim history up to the time of Alp Arslan (d. 1072), who defeated the Byzantines at the Battle of Manzikert in 1071. Although many of these issues were already standard elements of *hadith* literature and legal compendia, Ibn al-Nahhas adds a number of discussion points, including the practicalities of dividing the spoils of war, how an *imam* calls Muslims forth to battle, the permissibility of allowing infidels to fight on the side of the Muslims, dealing with human shields, as well as the tangled question of the use of mangonels.

Although the mangonel—a spring-powered device designed to lob large payloads of either rock or explosive at a fortified target—was supposedly known during the time of the Prophet Muhammad,[14] it seems likely that it did not come into general use until the time of the Crusades. Since the weapon is indiscriminate and can inflict extensive casualties upon noncombatants, Muslim treatises on jihad and warfare regularly treated questions regarding its moral legitimacy, in particular questions of "collateral damage" and a military force's responsibility to avoid civilian casualties. Ibn al-Nahhas takes a practical view of the subject, typical of Crusader and post-Crusader Muslim jihad theorists:

> It is permitted to place mangonels against them, and to cast fire and/or water against them, even if there are women and children among them [the enemy], even if there are Muslim prisoners, merchants, or those who have been granted a safe-conduct.[15]

These principles are noteworthy for the extent to which they reverse those of Muslim writers active during the period previous to the Crusades. For example, Ibn Abi Zaminayn, a Moroccan Muslim jihad writer (cited in chapter 1), disallowed the use of mangonels, stating that they were indiscriminate killing machines.[16] The question of whether to permit the use of mangonels persisted in jihad literature for many centuries, and it seems to have been answered more on the basis of exigency rather than strong legal precedent.

Ibn al-Nahhas is an intensely engaging writer, and unlike many other commentators on jihad, he does not content himself with mere citation of traditions. In many cases he anticipates the possible objections of his readers and answers them directly, on such issues as whether jihad is obligatory at all times. Ibn al-Nahhas argues strongly in favor of the perpetuity of the obligation.

> Know that jihad of the infidels is *fard kifaya* (obligatory upon the entire community, not upon every single member of it) in their lands by general agreement of the *'ulama'* . . . the least number of jihad raids [that should be accomplished] each year is one, and more is better without any doubt. A year without raids is not permissible, other than as a result of necessity, such as the weakness of the Muslims, the superiority of the enemy, fear of complete annihilation if they [Muslims] attack them first, or because of a lack of provisions or fodder for the mounts.[17]

His misogyny is evident in his polemic against Muslims who use marriage as a pretext to avoid jihad:

> If you say [wanting to avoid jihad]: My heart is not comfortable parting from my wife and her beauty, the companionship I have close to her and my happiness in touching her—even if your wife is the most beautiful of women and the loveliest of the people of the time, her beginning is a small drop [of sperm] and her end is a filthy corpse. Between those two times, she carries excrement, her menstruation denies her to you for part of her life, and her disobedience to you is usually more than her obedience. If she does not apply kohl to her eyes, they become bleary, if she

does not adorn herself she becomes ugly, if she does not comb her hair it is disheveled, if she does not anoint herself her light will be extinguished, if she does not put on perfume she will smell bad and if she does not clean her pubes she will stink. Her defects will multiply, she will become weary, when she grows old she will become depressed, when she is old she will be incapacitated—even if you treat her well, she will be contemptuous toward you.[18]

Just as with Ibn al-Mubarak, and as we will see in chapter 6 with respect to globalist radical Muslims, the act of following jihad often seems to have been associated with a rejection of women and the earthly ties that they represent.

A further interesting development during this period was the assimilation of poetry into the corpus of jihad writings.[19] Traditionally poetry had been viewed with some suspicion by pious Muslims because of the negative comments about poets in the Qur'an (e.g., 26:224, 36:69). Poetry has always been an important part of Arabic culture. Although poetry was viewed as suspect by pious Muslims on the basis of passages in the Qur'an that critique poets (e.g., 25.224, 36:69), jihad fighters made substantial contributions to the tradition. Large collections of war poems are associated with the wars against the Byzantines in the tenth and eleventh centuries in the east and the wars against the Spanish Christians in the west during that same period.[20] For the most part, these poems are not part of the truly magnificent poetic heritage of the Arabs; they are either semidescriptive—accounts of various battles in poetic form—or ditties designed to encourage the fighters.

The only other writer of significance during the post-Mongol period is Jalal al-Din al-Suyuti (d. 1505), who contributed several pamphlets to the subject of jihad, among other voluminous works. The most original of these—his treatise on martyrdom—covers all known traditions on the subject, although al-Suyuti offers little direction as to which of the sixty-five traditions are significant.[21] By the sixteenth century, the definition of "martyr" in Islam had lost all meaning and was essentially accorded to anyone who wanted to claim the title.

THE DEVELOPMENT OF CLASSICAL MUSLIM JIHAD THEORY

One of the hallmarks of the middle Islamic period (ca. CE 1000–1500) was the organization of the legal theory behind jihad into a coherent framework. This material falls into two categories: the Spanish Muslim and North African legal compendia, and the Mamluk Egyptian and Syrian works. Faced with the loss of their territories to the *reconquista*, Spanish Muslims sought to codify the legal literature and to establish Islamic parameters with regard to warfare. Whereas Muslim jurists had previously assumed that their armies would be victorious and that Islam would be the ruling faith, that assumption was no longer sustainable for the Spanish Muslims; their jurisprudence, as a consequence, had to take into account that large numbers of Muslims were living under the rule of Christians.

Among the most prominent of Spanish Muslim scholars was Ibn Hazm (d. 1064). He is best known for his polemical work against Jews and Christians, *al-Fasl fi al-milal wa-l-ahwaʿ wa-l-nihal (The Distinction concerning Religions, Heresies, and Sects)*, in which he examined and refuted both the Hebrew Bible and the New Testament at length, and for his touching collection of personal romantic anecdotes, *Tawq al-hamama (The Dove's Neck-Ring)*, in which the fierce theologian reveals his more human side. Ibn Hazm also published an extensive commentary on the *hadith* literature, formulated by posing questions of law and reviewing the possible solutions to these questions. Although his categories with regard to jihad start out with the standard mandate of the necessity of fighting—Ibn Hazm himself is not known to have participated in jihad—he quickly moves to the tougher issues. Problems such as the question of destruction of an enemy's property are addressed, with the recognition that what the Muslims did to their enemies could be done to them as well. Ibn Hazm categorically rejects the killing of women and children, but he condones the killing of any male: "combatant or noncombatant, merchant, hireling . . . elderly man . . . peasant, bishop, priest, monk, blind man . . ."[22] or, equally, sparing their lives, subject to the discretion of the Muslim fighters. During the course of his discussion, Ibn Hazm adduces a number of traditions that admonish fighters to avoid killing any individuals other than combatants; his systematic refutation of these traditions indicates a hardening of attitudes toward opponents of Islam.

Ibn Hazm also addresses other interesting questions with regard to jihad. He asks, for example, whether a Muslim can fight under the command of a sinning *(fasiq)* Muslim leader. Citing Qurʾan 9:41 ("March forth, on foot or mounted") he answers in the affirmative but then, complicating his conclusion, asks, given that jihad is supposed to be an advertisement for Islam, how can non-Muslims be expected to see the truth if Muslims are led by an individual who does not exemplify Islam?[23] Unfortunately, Ibn Hazm does not answer this follow-up question, leaving the relationship between jihad as fighting and jihad as proclamation and proselytizing unresolved. He also covers the question of safe-conducts and protection given to merchants and travelers; such protections were absolutely essential in Muslim Spain, where Muslims and Christians frequently traveled back and forth between the different states. In all of his discussions, Ibn Hazm demonstrates himself to be fair and balanced.

Another major Spanish Muslim writer who discussed jihad was the jurist Ibn al-ʿArabi (d. 1148/9)—not to be confused with the Sufi mystic Muhyi al-Din Ibn al-ʿArabi discussed in chapter 2. Ibn al-ʿArabi, like Ibn Hazm, was concerned with formulating law to cover issues that had been left unaddressed in the classical literature. While the latter concentrated upon the standard *hadith* literature, the former concentrated upon the Qurʾan. (This was a characteristic of Spanish Muslims during this period.) Like Ibn Hazm, Ibn al-ʿArabi also discusses the question of who is permitted to be killed in jihad on the basis of Qurʾan 9:5; however, in contrast to Ibn Hazm, Ibn al-ʿArabi does not allow the killing of any parties other than those who are fighting the Muslims.[24] He then goes on to ask: "Where can they be killed?" and answers: "Any place other than the Holy Mosque [in Mecca]." Continuing with his exegesis of 9:5, "lie in wait for them at every point of observation," he states that this verse permits the use of assassination or treacherous killing, but only of confirmed opponents.

Ibn al-ʿArabi also details the issues connected with the payment of the *jizya* (poll tax) imposed upon non-Muslims as part of their submission to Muslims (based on Qurʾan 9:29). Although the *jizya* had been a tenet of Islamic law from the earliest period, by the tenth century the concept had become much more refined. Until this time, the Muslims, although always politically dominant, had been themselves numerically a minority. But after some five hundred years of Muslim rule, Christians and Jews were reduced to minority status and were feeling the weight of the social discrimination mandated by the Covenant of ʿUmar.[25] Scholars debate the extent to which these discriminatory measures were applied—since clearly there were differences between given rulers and dynasties concerning the manner in which they chose to impose them—but in Muslim Spain and North Africa they were regularly enforced. (In other areas, farther from conflict with Christian states, these regulations were sometimes ignored.) Thus, Ibn al-ʿArabi's discussion of the *jizya* reflects the collective humiliation of Spanish Christians during this time. According to him, this tax is paid with fifteen different conditions:

1. Paid by the person standing, while the payee is sitting, 2. Given for themselves individually, 3. Paid hand to hand, 4. Paid on the basis of their power, 5. Paid on the basis of their presence, 6. Paid without their being complimented or having been requested to do so, 7. Paid with a bent neck, 8. Paid with humiliation, 9. Paid from [their own] sufficiency, 10. Paid as a result of the Covenant, 11. Paid with cash, 12. Paid with the admission that the Muslims are above them, 13. Paid by compulsion, 14. Paid with their acceptance of it [the *jizya*], 15. Paid promptly not as an equal.[26]

This list leaves no doubt that the primary focus of the *jizya* from the religious point of view was to humiliate.

Moving from Spanish Islam to the heartlands of Islam, it is important to discuss Abu Bakr al-Kasani (d. 1191) who was one of the great codifiers of Muslim law. He starts off with a clear definition of jihad:

> *Jihad* linguistically means to devote exertion—meaning energy and ability, or an exaggerated amount of work in striving—and in the legal realm it is used for the devotion of energy and ability in fighting in the path of God with one's self, wealth, and tongue, anything else or an exaggerated amount of that.[27]

As one might expect, al-Kasani constructs an entirely logical treatment of the subject. Like al-Shafi'i and others discussed in chapter 1 and above, al-Kasani sees jihad as part of a process leading to a call directed to infidels by the Muslims. This leads inevitably to fighting between the two sides, whereupon the Muslims will eventually win and establish a society with Islam in a dominant position. Al-Kasani cautions against the killing of noncombatants and shows a higher regard for human life than do his predecessors and contemporaries. For example, when he discusses the issue of what to do when Muslims are located in the region where jihad is to be fought, he says that the Muslim fighters should be careful to avoid targeting Muslims if at all possible. When speaking of the possibility of infidels using Muslim children as "human shields," he says:

> In the same manner, if they shield themselves using Muslim children, there is nothing wrong with targeting them because of necessity, but they should target the infidels and not the children. But if one of the Muslim [children] is hit, then there is no blood-price or expiation [necessary for the one who is guilty].[28]

This attitude, which was the norm for Muslims prior to the Mongol invasions, changed when Muslims were faced with Mongol armies who used human shields on a large scale.

Ibn Qudama al-Maqdisi, a Hanbali jurist who took part in the Battle of the Horns of Hattin against the Crusaders in 1187, was another major writer on legal issues from this period. Like Ibn Hazm, Ibn Qudama deals with problematic issues, although he is not necessarily as exhaustive in his choice of topics as al-Kasani. However, he more than makes up for this by dealing with *each topic* exhaustively. One of the first subjects he covers is the question of who can participate in jihad; he lists seven essential characteristics of the *mujahid*: Islam (that the person is a Muslim), maturity (post-puberty), intelligent (not insane), free (not a slave), male, free from bodily defects, and able to support himself. Ibn Qudama states that the first three characteristics are absolute, but that the last four are subject to some discussion, since there are historical examples of exceptions to these rules, most of them dating from the time of the Prophet Muhammad.[29]

Another key question for Ibn Qudama is the identity of the enemy. Qur'an 9:123 says, "O you who believe, fight those of the unbelievers who are near to you." This seems straightforward enough, but Ibn Qudama is puzzled by examples of prominent Muslims who appeared to deliberately ignore this commandment, in particular Ibn al-Mubarak, who was originally from Khurasan (eastern Iran) but moved to Syria to fight the Byzantines. Ibn Qudama opposes the idea that people should migrate long distances just to fight a given enemy when an enemy is close at hand.[30] He also makes an interesting pronouncement with regard to the Islamic declaration of faith. Whereas previous Muslim scholars point out that it is important to declare war openly upon Christians and to invite them to Islam prior to the commencement of hostilities, Ibn Qudama maintains that this proclamation has by now been made sufficiently and that there is no further need to make it.[31] For Ibn Qudama, it is self-evident that Muslims are in a permanent state of war with Christians.

Several of Ibn Qudama's categories and questions are important in considering the present status of jihad. He discusses in some detail the treatment of prisoners of war, dividing them into three categories:

1. Women and children, who may not be killed, because the Prophet [Muhammad] forbade the killing of women and children, but may be enslaved.

2. Christian, Jewish, and Zoroastrian males who accept the (possible) payment of the *jizya*. The *imam* of the Muslims may decide with regard to them among four possibilities: killing

them, freeing them without receiving compensation, allowing them to be ransomed, or enslaving them.

3. Pagan males from whom the *jizya* cannot be accepted. The *imam* of the Muslims may decide with regard to them among three possibilities: killing them, freeing them without receiving compensation, or allowing them to be redeemed. There is no possibility of enslaving pagan males.[32]

Like most of the Muslim jurists (with the notable exception of Ibn Hazm), Ibn Qudama does not allow women and children to be killed. Ibn Qudama's discussion is far and away the most exhaustive of the premodern Muslim jurists, and it demonstrates the extent to which jihad—treated in almost three hundred pages of text—was elaborated during this time.

In many cases the most interesting and unusual materials appear in the responsa *(fatwa)* literature, in which an acclaimed and authoritative jurist was asked questions concerning many different issues and pronounced opinions on the subject. However, it should be noted that in Islam these legal opinions are not necessarily binding either upon the individual who solicited the answer or upon the larger Muslim community, and scholars are divided as to their relevance for the study of Islam. Some maintain that the *fatwa* literature is merely academic; others see it as an expression of Islam at its most vital point. For the purposes of studying jihad, the *fatwa* literature brings out a number of issues that other jurists had ignored and therefore is of interest.

Probably the most interesting collections of *fatawa* for the discussion of jihad are those originating in North Africa after the fifteenth century. *Fatawa* of the Tunisian jurist al-Burzuli (d. 1438) reveal the extent to which circumstances had complicated traditional paradigms for Muslims in North Africa and the Mediterranean littoral: abductions by both Christians and Muslims, endless frauds, problems with apostates, traitors, and renegades on both sides, and questionable battle tactics figure prominently in al-Burzuli's *fatawa*.[33] Since the Muslims were gradually losing their position of strength in the western Mediterranean during this period, and given the occasional occupations or raids on the Muslim towns of North Africa, al-Burzuli does not have much difficulty in allowing for legal stratagems that would help the Muslims' cause.

A collection of *fatawa* by al-Wansharisi (d. 1508), another important North African jurist, became authoritative for Moroccan and West African Islam during the following centuries. Al-Wansharisi was writing during what was probably the most desperate time for Moroccan Islam:

the period immediately after the fall of Grenada to the Spanish Christians in 1492, and the large-scale migration of Muslim refugees to the region, followed almost immediately by continual Spanish and Portuguese attacks upon Morocco and North Africa until the end of the sixteenth century. These desperate times are reflected in the types of questions he is asked: is it permissible for Muslims to buy a truce from the infidels? (under certain circumstances, yes); is it permissible to kill women and children of the infidels when they are fighting the Muslims? (no); is it permissible to take a woman or a copy of the Qur'an into a combat zone? (respectively: probably not, and no); should a Muslim country respect a contract made with infidels? (yes, if they signed it knowingly); and is it permissible to finish off enemy wounded who are helpless after a battle? (no).[34]

It is clear from reading al-Wansharisi that a great many of the Muslim communities in North Africa were paying ransom to Spanish and Portuguese raiders and uncertain as to the legality of such payments. Just as with al-Burzuli some eighty years previously, the exchange of prisoners was a subject of particular concern: the obligation arising if person who is to be exchanged or ransomed dies or escapes, and the legal implications of raids on towns by treacherous merchants to carry off captives. But the big question after the fall of Muslim Spain in 1492 was whether Muslims should stay in Spain or emigrate (make *hijra*) to a Muslim land (i.e., North Africa). This question was to bedevil Muslim jurists until the nineteenth century, by which point Europeans had conquered so much Muslim land that there were few places left for Muslims to emigrate. Al-Wansharisi reviews the requirements of Muslim law in answer to this question and details those that cannot be fulfilled under non-Muslim rule; he concludes that it is impossible for a Muslim to live under these circumstances, and that it would be humiliating to try.[35] Ultimately it took more than a century of Christian persecution, forced conversions, and expulsions before Spanish Muslims left Spain.

Al-Wansharisi, like most Muslim jurists, was often quite willing to bend the rules for the good of the Muslim community and creatively reinterpret Muslim law. This is closely in accord with the crystallization of Muslim law during this period. All of the writers to some extent fit into the jihad tradition. One, however, requires separate attention.

IBN TAYMIYYA

The iconoclastic Muslim theologian and polemicist Ibn Taymiyya (d. 1328) occupies a unique position in Muslim jurisprudence. Ibn Taymiyya was a refugee from the Muslim East, fleeing the Mongol invasions with his family and settling in Egypt. The seat of the Mamluk Empire, Egypt was the last powerful bastion of Sunni Islam. As Ibn Taymiyya saw it, the disasters and defeats suffered by the Muslim community had to be confronted both militarily—in which the Mamluks achieved success—and religiously. Therefore, his writings present a bleaker and more black-and-white view of Islam and its relations with the non-Muslim world than do other writings on the subject of jihad, reflecting Ibn Taymiyya's direct and emotional engagement with jihad. Even Spanish Muslims, who were gradually losing their homeland to the resurgent Christians, do not convey such an absolute sense of urgency in their writings. The issues were not academic for Ibn Taymiyya; they represented an immediate reality.

Although Ibn Taymiyya wrote extensively on the issue of encouraging jihad and explaining its laws,[36] his most significant work concerns the tangled issues of Muslim ethics in warfare. This was especially critical with regard to the Mongols, who prior to 1259 employed or coerced large numbers of Muslims to fight for them, and subsequently themselves adopted Islam as their religion. These situations were unlike any that Muslims had faced previously. (Although the Spanish Christians and Crusaders also occasionally employed Muslims as mercenaries, they did not do so on the scale of the Mongols.) Since such large tracts of territory had fallen to the Mongols, it was not always possible for Muslims to leave the conquered regions and emigrate to Muslim territory, as had been the practice in the past. Questions of this nature had to be dealt with.

In 1256, when the city of Mardin (in present-day Turkey) fell to the Mongols, Ibn Taymiyya was asked whether the city was considered to be *Dar al-Harb* (abode of war) or *Dar al-Islam* (abode of Islam). He replied that the Muslims of Mardin were still Muslims and should not be accused of hypocrisy or condemned for residing in a city under non-Muslim rule, but by the same token maintained that they should not render any obvious aid to their Mongol overlords. As to the question of whether Mardin was Dar al-Harb or Dar al-Islam, Ibn Taymiyya answered:

> It is not accorded the status of Dar al-Islam in which the laws of Islam are in force, because its armies are Muslims, nor does it have the status of Dar al-Harb whose inhabitants are infidels, but it falls into a third category: the Muslim in it acts according to the level that he is able, and fights the outside [presumably the Mongols] on behalf of the *shari'a* of Islam according to what he is able.[37]

Clearly, in contemplating the possibility that Muslims and their rulers might not be in religious accord, this statement divorces the individual Muslim from the Muslim state, something that with the exception of Spanish Muslims, had not previously been addressed (not, at least, in the legal literature).

Ibn Taymiyya went much further than prior commentators in addressing the legal implications of the Syrian invasion of the Mongol ruler Ghazan Khan in 1299. Ghazan was among the first Mongol Il-Khanid rulers to convert to Islam, and so the battle-lines between his Mongol forces and those of the Mamluks were not so clearly drawn as they had been a generation previously at 'Ayn Jalut (1260). Nevertheless, Ibn Taymiyya made a distinction between the two sides in stating that the Muslim side is the one that upholds the laws of Islam and fights for the victory of Islam. Since the Mongols fought with the backing of a coalition of troops—including Christian Armenians, Georgians, still-pagan Mongols, and Shi'ites, in addition to Sunni Muslims—they could not be considered to be fighting for Islam.

But Ibn Taymiyya went even further than this in concluding that not only were the Mongols infidels and false Muslims; they were even more dangerous and must be fought on a more consistent basis than other obvious infidels (such as Christians).[38] This was a novel conclusion: traditionally Muslims did not judge the relative quality of other Muslims' Islam. If a person said that he or she was a Muslim, they were, unless their actions obviously and incontrovertibly put them outside of the community. As the tradition cited in chapter 1 states, the Prophet Muhammad was ordered to fight until people said that there was only one God. Judgment as to their motives and the depth of their conversion would be in the hands of God. Ibn Taymiyya went much further than this and was willing to identify the quality of a given person's Islam with that person's being willing to fight for Islam. Since the Mongol Muslims' primary loyalty was to the larger Mongol state, and not to any Islamic state, they were non-Muslims according to the formulation of Ibn Taymiyya. Although one might have expected this type of intense identification of Islam with the Mamluk state to have gained Ibn Taymiyya the favor of the rulers, in fact he spent a good deal of time in prison for his willingness to confront these rulers as well.

Several of Ibn Taymiyya's *fatawa* convey the atmosphere of fighting at the front. He describes the fighting against the Mongols as a re-creation of the Prophet Muhammad's battle against the Confederates (the *ahzab*), which is described in *sura* 33. Commenting almost verse by verse, he parallels the two battles. For example, the disparate coalition led by the Mongols is similar to the coalition of Bedouins and Jews led by the Quraysh to destroy the Prophet. Ibn Taymiyya emphasizes that both the *ahzab* and the Mongols are defined by their hatred of Islam and by their desire to uproot it completely. He also notes that like the Prophet's enemies, the Mongols suffered from bad weather, which he describes in picturesque terms.[39] From the time of 'Abdallah b. al-Mubarak until that of Ibn Taymiyya, there was probably no comparable example of a senior Muslim religious leader participating in the fighting and so emotionally and religiously involved in the outcome.

One cannot doubt Ibn Taymiyya's influence, especially during the present time. Because of his spiritual prestige, his willingness to confront and judge the established Muslim authorities, his unique and interesting analyses, and his direct and harsh indictments of all infidels and deviants from Islam, his writings have been extremely popular with contemporary radical Muslims (see chapters 5–6).[40]

MUSLIM TREATISES ON THE WAGING OF WAR

At approximately the same time as the Crusades and the Mongol invasions, we find the appearance of the first Muslim treatises specifically devoted to the art of warfare. For the most part, these were composed as elements of "mirrors for princes" (manuals of moral and practical instruction for rulers), but there are also a number of separate treatises devoted to the subject of warfare. As stated in chapter 1, the accounts of the first Muslim conquests are silent as to the military strategies used by the conquerors. We read of battles formed as two opposing lines and of the extensive use of light cavalry for outflanking the foe, or the use of heavy cavalry to overwhelm them,[41] but there is little discussion of more complicated battle tactics.[42] For the most part accounts of the Prophet Muhammad's battles—with the exception of Uhud, which employed the feigned retreat—involve a general rush without tactical maneuvers. Toward the end of Muhammad's life, at the siege of al-Ta'if, we read of mangonels being used to bring down the town's fortifications, but it remains an open question whether this is a historical invention: Medina's "fortifications" comprised a large surrounding ditch; how much more fortified could al-Ta'if have been? However, the appearance of the word "mangonel" in the text of the Prophet Muhammad's biography came to serve as a powerful legitimizing force for innovative military tactics and formed the basis for the discussion concerning weapons of mass destruction for al-Qaʿida and its ideological affiliates. The early books on jihad provide little information on tactics: they treat the ideology of jihad in great detail, but devote little attention to describing the process of fighting. At a later time, Turkish tactics involving light cavalry (once again), coupled with the use of the matchless archers that the Central Asian steppes produced, became the mainstay of Muslim fighting technique.[43] However, during the wars against the Crusaders these military tactics were less than efficacious.

It is apparent in reading these military treatises, which date from the tenth century onward, that we have moved from the realm of the romantically presented traditions on jihad in the *hadith* literature into the blood and gore of real warfare. Al-Tartushi (d. 1126) says:

> Know that the beginning of warfare is [characterized by] complaints, the middle of it is trying to save [one's life], and the end of it is sorrow. War is disorderly, frowning, ugly, [and] somber; an incision into the basins of death, an intractable horse in battle that feeds off souls. The first part of war is talking, the last part is death; war is bitter to taste as it is dispensed. Whoever remains constant during it knows [this], whoever is weakened by it perishes. The body of war is bravery, its heart is preparation, its eye caution, its arms [lit. wings] obedience, its tongue stratagem, its vanguard comradeship, and its rearguard victory. The Messenger said: War is deception. They [others] used to say: War is horrible.[44]

Far from the triumphalist tone of the early jihad literature, the later Muslim treatises on war demonstrate a considerable amount of respect for their (usually) Christian enemies. Al-Tartushi starts his section on the subject with the comment that one should be extremely cautious when going into battle. He warns of being overconfident and notes that many large armies have been overcome by smaller ones (citing Qurʾan 2:249, the Qurʾanic version of the story of David and Goliath) because they did not take their enemy seriously. He then speaks of the role of psychological terror in paving the way for victory and emphasizes that in order to win a battle, the general must gather accurate intelligence, maintain constant discipline, and keep in close contact with his soldiers.

Al-Tartushi was a North African, and most of the battles he describes to illustrate his points are from either Spain (those of al-Mansur b. Abi ʿAmir) or Sicily, but he includes a long description of the battles of Alp Arslan, the Turkish warlord who had defeated the Byzantines at Manzikert in 1071. A high percentage of the battles al-Tartushi recounts did not end in victory for the Muslim side. He analyzes the reasons for these losses, noting that even clear victories were not easily won. War is a deadly serious business for him. Most of the other "mirrors for princes" contain similar sections on warfare, but do not provide a concrete basis for discussing Muslim tactics during the middle Islamic period.

This situation clearly changes during the Mamluk period, which was the first time in Muslim history that there was a regular standing army (similar to the situation in Europe, where regular armies were appearing as well). For the most part, these are professional treatises detailing tactics, ruses that have historically been successful in battle, and new developments in battlefield technology. But there is a considerable time lag between the introduction of a given piece of technology into Muslim society and its appearance in the literary sources. For example, the mangonel appears (probably anachronistically) in the Prophet Muhammad's biography, but the first detailed treatise that we have on the subject is that of Ibn Arnabagh al-Zardakush (d. 1462), composed when this weapon was close to being replaced by far more deadly technologies. Muslim advances in the field of military technology are quite numerous and were attested to by the centuries of Muslim victory on the battlefield. But the late flowering of treatises on military matters was rendered moot by the appearance, in the fifteenth and sixteenth centuries, of European technologies that made most of these treatises irrelevant and obsolete.[45] Nonetheless, they fueled a second wave of Muslim conquests during the period immediately prior.

THE MUSLIM REVIVAL: THE SECOND WAVE OF CONQUESTS

After the defeat of the Crusaders (1291) and the conversion of the Mongols to Islam (ca. 1300), the Muslim world went through a second stage of conquests. The most deeply felt of these (at least by Europeans) was the Ottoman push toward Central Europe, which started about the time of the defeat of the Crusaders. The Ottoman state, originally located on the borders of the Christian Byzantine state centered at Constantinople (after 1261), expanded rapidly during the following two and a half centuries with important conquests, including that of Adrianople in 1361, the defeat of the Serbians at Kosovo in 1389, the taking of Constantinople in 1453, and the conquest of Hungary in the early sixteenth century. By the middle of the sixteenth century the Ottoman state controlled southeastern Europe (the Balkans) completely and menaced Austria, Italy, and Poland.[46]

Elsewhere in the Mediterranean, however, Muslims continued to lose ground with the final reconquest of Spain (1492), and the occupation of a number of Moroccan and Algerian seaports by the Spanish and Portuguese during the sixteenth and seventeenth centuries. The most obvious reflection of Christian naval superiority in the western Mediterranean was the Battle of Lepanto in 1570, during which a coalition of European naval powers defeated a massive Ottoman expedition. The Ottoman state also assumed responsibility for the protection of the Golden Horde state located in what is today the Ukraine. Starting from 1552 the Russian Empire, centered in Moscow, advanced through the region reaching the Black Sea at the end of the seventeenth century. After the failure of the second siege of Vienna in 1680–83, the Ottoman state began a long period of defeats and retreats in the face of the Austro-Hungarian and the Russian Empires.

The economy of the Ottoman state, including its matériel, was in effect dependent upon the economies of European states. From the middle of the seventeenth century until 1918 (the end of the Ottoman Empire), the Muslims' only effective countermeasure was to play the various European powers off against one another and try to reform their own state and economy as best they could. However, as demonstrated by the Ottoman resilience during World War I, during which the empire successfully launched offensives against the British in Egypt and inflicted defeats or delays upon the British on other fronts (Gallipoli, Iraq), the Ottoman state was far from being the "sick man" of Europe, as it was frequently called. Even at the end of their existence, the Ottomans maintained a surprising ability to recover from military setbacks and sometimes defeat their enemies.

On other fronts the Muslims were more successful, most notably in the Indian Subcontinent and in Central Asia, where the conversion of the Turks, Uzbeks, and Mongols added large territories. From the century prior to the First Crusade, Muslims under Mahmud of Ghazna (a Turkish ruler located in what is today Afghanistan) attacked northern India; by the thirteenth century, much of this region was under the domination of Turkish military adventurers. However, the culmination of the Indo-Islamic civilization was under the Moghul dynasty (ca. 1520–1750), which effectively ruled most of the subcontinent until the end of the seventeenth century.

Of all of these rulers, only Mahmud of Ghazna (d. 1031) and Awrangzeb (d. 1707), the last major Moghul ruler, can be said to have been enthusiastic jihad fighters who saw their mission as one of religious aggrandizement. Most of the Turkish rulers of the Slave Dynasty of Delhi (who were the other Mamluk dynasty) and the early Moghul rulers were quite tolerant toward the non-Muslim, predominantly Hindu, majority population of India. Mahmud, however, launched no fewer than thirty-one major campaigns against the Hindus and Buddhists of northern India, and he clearly saw himself as the champion of Islam. Although many of his campaigns had the goal of looting the riches of India, a striking number of them had a proselytizing intent: to demonstrate the power of Islam and the impotence of the Hindu gods. The best known of these was the campaign of Somnath (1025–26), which was a major Hindu temple located near the Indian Ocean in what is today Gujarat (western India). This temple had little strategic significance and was located at a considerable distance from Mahmud's capital in the mountains of Afghanistan. Its capture and destruction served only the purposes of jihad. Mahmud and his successors made no attempt to control the vast territories he raided.[47]

More than six hundred years later, the Moghul ruler Awrangzeb (1658–1707) also used jihad in an attempt to conquer the entire Indian Subcontinent. Awrangzeb's Moghul ancestors had been quite tolerant toward the region's Hindu majority population. At least one of them, Akbar (1556–1605), practiced a syncretistic religion and Akbar's son, Jahangir (1605–27), took a vow of nonviolence.[48] Awrangzeb, in contrast, based his rule squarely upon the Muslim minority of the Indian Subcontinent and imposed the shari'a (including the jizya) on the region's Hindu population in 1679. He also actively sought to complete the conquest of the entire subcontinent, in which he was successful—uniting it (if briefly) for the first time in almost two millennia.

Although it is difficult to know whether Awrangzeb considered these wars to be a jihad,[49] he was clearly intensely interested in the subject. The Fatawa al-Hindiyya, a collection of legal opinions that has served as a basis for normative Sunni Indian Islam, was composed under his supervision. The collection's treatment of jihad reflects Indian Islam's lack of unanimity on the issue. The Fatawa al-Hindiyya gives the following definition of jihad: "Jihad is the call to the true religion (al-din al-haqq), and combating (qital) all those who refuse or rebel against accepting it—whether with one's soul or possessions."[50]

The ambiguity of this definition is fairly obvious. It employs the same words that previous definitions of jihad had employed, including the word qital, which I have translated as "combat" because the author has carefully refrained from saying explicitly that jihad involves actual fighting. Note that of the usual three categories of jihad—with one's tongue, with one's possessions, and with one's sword—only two are present in this definition. However, the definition employs aggressive terminology as well. The words "refuse" and "rebel" in close proximity to the word "combat" seem to imply a military aspect to jihad that is seemingly denied by the beginning and the end of the definition. The *Fatawa* subsequently discuss military matters in depth, but oddly they contain hardly any citations from the Qur'an or the *hadith* literature concerning the subject. Although one would not want to be too categorical, the *Fatawa al-Hindiyya*, while recognizing the military provenance of jihad, betray an ambiguous attitude toward the subject that accords with the later apologetic Indian Muslim interpretations (see chapter 5).

The only region that saw large-scale Muslim expansion through military conquest during the period following the sixteenth century was Africa, especially West Africa. As a result of this region's isolation from European influence, Muslim kingdoms in West Africa and the Sudan had no obvious competition and continued to conquer and convert the pagan black Africans in the area until the arrival of the British and the French during the latter half of the nineteenth century.[51] In East Africa, European power stopped a jihad intended to conquer the ancient Christian kingdom of Ethiopia, led by Ahmad b. Ibrahim Grañ in the 1530s and 1540s.[52] Since Grañ had effectively overrun Ethiopia in its entirety during the period 1529–43, it seems reasonable to assume that without the aid rendered by the Portuguese during this time, Ethiopia would have become Muslim. During those decades, Grañ devastated the highlands of Ethiopia, forcibly converting almost the entire population to Islam. Although in the end he was repulsed, it took many years for Ethiopia to recover.

Fortunately, a detailed Muslim account of this group of attacks has survived, and it leaves no doubt that this jihad was designed to expand the frontiers of Islam against a state that had never posed any threat to Muslims. (Further to the north, during this time, the ancient Christian kingdom of Nubia was gradually being reduced under another jihad that resulted in the Islamization of the Sudan.) The author of the Muslim account of the Ethiopian invasion, Shihab al-Din (known as 'Arabfaqih), was one of Ahmad Grañ's close companions; it is reasonable to assume that despite the cheerleading nature of the history, it expresses what Grañ and his followers felt during the time. 'Arabfaqih presents the invasion as an apocalyptic jihad. He begins his account saying:

> In that manner it [Islam] has become the best of communities, and its best manner of worship has been its constancy for the truth, and its jihad against the infidels of all other peoples who oppose this religion—from

all directions: east, west, north and south. With the sword they have been victorious east and west, in rocky terrain and flat plains, and have spread the earth out, humbling the infidels with their swords, pounding in their tent-pegs and raising up [their tents]. It will continue . . . until the Resurrection comes with its blowing, as God said: "Thereupon your Lord made it known that He would send against them one who would inflict on them the worst punishment until the Day of Resurrection" [Qur'an 7:167], and [Muhammad] said: "A group of my community will continue standing [firmly] upon the truth without being harmed by those who abandon them or those who oppose them until the Will of God comes while they are in that situation."[53]

This introduction is a delicious example of the spirit of victorious jihad—even though the jihad in Ethiopia was ultimately unsuccessful and Ahmad Grañ was slain. Nonetheless, it is appropriate to conclude this discussion of the second wave of Muslim conquests with a writer like 'Arabfaqih. With the exception of the writings of Usuman Dan Fodio and the Sudanese Mahdi (see chapter 4), there is probably no better example of Muslim triumphalism until the globalist radical Islam of our own time.

In other regions bordering the Indian Ocean, such as Indonesia and East Africa south of Ethiopia, conversion to Islam proceeded more peaceably. Although Muslims were retreating from the north during this period—under pressure from Europeans—they were expanding to the south in Africa and gaining territory in Southeast Asia. By the beginning of the nineteenth century, Islam had assumed what might be called its natural borders (meaning the regions in which Muslims during or since that time have formed either a majority population or a strong and viable minority).

FOUR

JIHAD DURING THE NINETEENTH CENTURY: RENEWAL AND RESISTANCE

During the eighteenth and nineteenth centuries, Western domination of regions previously controlled or dominated by Muslims did not stop at the boundary between non-Muslim majority and Muslim majority territories. Nonetheless, many Muslim majority regions held out longer against Western domination than did regions in which other religions were dominant, though there are significant exceptions to this rule (among them: Algeria, Indonesia, the Muslim majority areas of India, and Central Asia). Muslim resistance to Western encroachments was intermittent. In areas where the majority of the Muslim population acknowledged a state—even from afar—they tended to either emigrate to that state or tried to induce its leadership, both political and religious, to liberate them from the European Christian rule. The most obvious example of this tendency is the Ottoman Empire, whose long retreat from southeastern Europe (the Balkans) left a wide variety of Muslim minorities in its wake. Many of these populations simply relocated to Ottoman territory. In other cases, further to the west, Muslims who resisted the French conquest of Algeria (starting in 1830) looked to the stronger Muslim state of Morocco close by to help them (which proved to be a mirage). However, each region reacted differently, and rarely in close accord with others.

Prior to major resistance jihads against European conquests, there were several significant "purification" jihads directed against other Muslims. It is not entirely clear whether these jihads, concentrated in Arabia and West Africa, were initiated in response to European encroachment, since both of these regions were located at a considerable distance from any territory conquered from Muslims. However, these jihads set the tone for later anti-European warfare in that they influenced most of the great *mujahid* fighters of the nineteenth and early twentieth centuries, who sought to use the process of their own jihad fighting to educate their people—both combatants and noncombatants—about what they would call a "purer" form of Islam (which involved removal of local cults of holy men and women).

IBN ʿABD AL-WAHHAB AND THE
CALL FOR PURIFICATION OF ISLAM

Probably the most radical of all the anti-Muslim jihad movements was that of Muhammad b. ʿAbd al-Wahhab (d. 1791), which became the state interpretation of Islam in the kingdom of Saudi Arabia, and stands at the heart of the present-day radical Islam movement. Ibn ʿAbd al-Wahhab preached a stark interpretation of Islam that characterized all elements deriving from Sufism—mystical interpretations of Islam—and Shiʿism as apostasy. The primary objects of his wrath were the veneration of Sufi holy men and women, visible adornments upon mosques and sacred structures, and ritual practices that detracted from a complete focus upon God alone, as one God (his interpretation of *tawhid*). Although Ibn ʿAbd al-Wahhab invoked tenets that are central to Islam, such as the emphasis on the absolute unity of God, there is good reason to believe that, as Hamid Algar has stated, Wahhabism is considerably different from any other form of Islam hitherto attested historically.[1] This is manifested by the extremely promiscuous use of *takfir*, the process of declaring someone (usually already known to be a Muslim) an infidel. Historically Sunnis maintained a rather "big tent" approach to the question of who was or was not a Muslim. Even those who fiercely criticized their religious or intellectual opponents generally avoided charging them with apostasy.[2]

Ibn ʿAbd al-Wahhab did not see himself or his movement as bound by this precedent; both he and his followers arrogated solely to themselves the name "Muslims" while using the classical Islamic terms for infidels to refer to their Muslim opponents. His ideology was politically bound to the family of one Ibn Saʿud, who proceeded during the late eighteenth century and early nineteenth century to establish a state in the Arabian Peninsula based upon Ibn ʿAbd al-Wahhab's principles. In 1746 the Wahhabi-Ibn Saʿud state openly declared jihad against other

Muslims. In 1802 the Wahhabis occupied and destroyed Karbala', one of the holy cities of the Shi'ites (the site of the murder of Husayn, the grandson of the Prophet Muhammad in 680). They then turned their attention toward the holy cities of Islam: Mecca and Medina, which they occupied at various times between 1803 and 1813. During the course of this occupation, virtually all the sacred shrines dedicated to the Prophet Muhammad and his Companions, as well as the Sufi holy places, were demolished—an act that incited the Muslim world. In the end, the Ottoman Empire, which nominally ruled the area of Mecca and Medina, deputized the son of Muhammad 'Ali Pasha (the ruler of Egypt), Ibrahim Pasha, to defend the holy places of Islam. He defeated the Wahhabis in 1813 and destroyed their state.

The Wahhabi attempt to "purify" Islam would be merely a footnote in history were it not for the fact that the Saudi Arabian state, revived in the early twentieth century after almost a hundred years of a shadowy existence, today again controls the holy cities of Islam. It has gained vast riches from its oil wealth. These factors, religious and economic, have enabled the Wahhabis to propagate their beliefs throughout the Sunni Muslim world, ultimately leading to the appearance of radical Islam. The initial Wahhabi jihad, however, was merely destructive and did not bring about a reform of Islam. Since the religious credentials of Ibn 'Abd al-Wahhab were slender—Algar remarks that his published works barely fill a pamphlet, and that none of them are intellectually deep, which is true—and his mass condemnation of virtually all other Muslims as infidels commanded no respect outside of his immediate circle of supporters, his jihad could be merely dismissed as one of the periodic eruptions of religious fervor that have swept the Arabian Peninsula. However, others who used jihad against their fellow Muslims gained more lasting results.

NIGERIA AND WEST AFRICA

As noted in chapter 3 the only major Islamic conquests achieved after the seventeenth century were in Africa (Indonesia, although it converted to Islam during this period, did not do so as the result of conquest, and the conquests in India did not result in a Muslim majority, nor did they persist for a lengthy period of time). Major Muslim empires, such as those of Ghana, Mali, and Songhai, were established in the area of the Sahel immediately to the south of the Sahara Desert. These empires were closely linked to trans-Saharan trade in salt, gold, and slaves; they grew wealthy as a result.[3] However, the Islamic roots of some of these states were weak, and feeding off the slave trade,[4] these states demonstrated little concern for the conversion of the pagan Africans to their south. In many cases conversion to Islam was limited to the ruling elites and did not penetrate to the common people.

In this atmosphere, it is easy to see why a jihad conducted by more devout Muslims against allegedly "nominal" Muslims was thought to be necessary. But the jihad conducted by Shehu Usaman Dan Fodio[5] during the years 1804–10 was considerably different in character from that waged by Ibn 'Abd al-Wahhab and the Wahhabis at almost the same time in the Arabian Peninsula. Dan Fodio and his followers stood squarely within the consensus of Sunni Islam and did not attack Sufism or issue blanket accusations of apostasy against their opponents. Instead, they sought to create an environment in which the *shari'a* was preeminent and Islam dominated the state so that it could expand further to the south. Located on the borders of Islam, Dan Fodio and his followers needed to establish clear and obvious demarcations between Islam and paganism.[6] Without that clarity, Islam was in serious danger of becoming syncretistic.

To accomplish this, Dan Fodio used two classic Muslim methods. The first one was *hijra,* emigration, following in the footsteps of the Prophet Muhammad and the Muslims who made the first conquests.[7] Together with other devout Muslims who felt as he did, he emigrated from the nominal Muslim environment of the Habe kingdom (present-day northwestern Nigeria) and, in 1795, established his own community immediately to the south. He quickly gained spiritual prestige and gathered a large number of followers. He made another *hijra* in February 1804, and after the community he had established was attacked by one of the nominal Muslim rulers, Dan Fodio commissioned fourteen flags to be given to trusted followers in order to fight the jihad. Over the next six years, Dan Fodio and the Muslims fought their Muslim opponents and defeated them one after the other, eventually establishing the Sokoto Caliphate (in what is today northern Nigeria).[8]

The second method that Dan Fodio used to wage jihad was to write. One hundred and fourteen books and pamphlets are attributed to him, many of which are still in print. For hundreds of years prior to the Sokoto jihad, Islam had been closely associated with education and literacy throughout West Africa. But it is from the time of Usaman Dan Fodio that documentary evidence appears detailing the practices against which the Muslims were fighting and the reasons why they were deemed non-Islamic. These practices are collectively referred as *bida',* innovations, and they are the subject of numerous classical Muslim treatises.

However, no Muslim prior to Dan Fodio had conducted a jihad against the *bidaʿ*. Probably the reason why it was so important for Dan Fodio to do so was to establish basic Islamic norms so that the faithful could differentiate between true Islam and "innovations."

Usaman Dan Fodio's most complete work on jihad, *Bayan wujub al-hijra ʿala al-ʿibad* (translated as *The Exposition of the Obligation of Emigration upon the Servants of God [and the Exposition of the Obligation of Appointing an* Imam *and Undertaking Jihad]*), written in 1806, is a complete manual on Muslim warfare. It is firmly grounded in Muslim law and history, attesting to Dan Fodio's excellent command of his sources. He explains the factors necessitating jihad, the obligation of appointing a leader and following him, and the legal limits on jihad. According to Dan Fodio's presentation, jihad is a process that starts with *hijra*, continues with the establishment of a pure Muslim community, and culminates with actual fighting. He places particular emphasis on the necessity of pure belief among Muslim soldiers—hence his concern with ridding the community of innovations—and counsels soldiers to avoid any actions that would compromise the spiritual value of their jihad. These include the wearing of silk in battle, embellishing weapons with gold and silver, and tying bells and cords to their mounts on the way to or during battle.[9] Throughout his presentation, Dan Fodio mixes the practical with the spiritual, and gives a great deal of advice as to how a campaign should be fought. His book is exemplary in this regard.

Usaman Dan Fodio's movement is unusual as well for its messianic and apocalyptic qualities.[10] This is evident in his "Sword of Truth" vision, dated to approximately 1794, during the course of which Dan Fodio saw the founder of the Qadiriyya Sufi order, ʿAbd al-Qadir al-Jilani, in a dream and received a sword from him. The vision, in Mervyn Hiskett's translation, is as follows:

> When I reached forty years, five months and some days, God drew me to Him, and I found the Lord of jinn and men, our Lord Muhammad. With him were the Companions, the prophets and the saints. Then they welcomed me, and sat me down in their midst. Then the Savior of jinn and men, our Lord ʿAbd al-Qadir al-Jilani, brought a green robe embroidered with the words "There is no god but God; Muhammad is the Messenger of God" and a turban embroidered with the words "He is God, the One." He handed them to the Messenger of God, and the Messenger of God clasped them to his bosom for a time; then he handed them to Abu Bakr al-Siddiq [the first caliph], he handed them to ʿUmar al-Faruq [the second caliph], he handed them to ʿUthman Dhu al-Nurayn [the third caliph], and he handed them to ʿAli [the fourth caliph], and then to Joseph, and Joseph gave them back to my Lord

'Abd al-Qadir al-Jilani; and they appointed him to act upon their behalf, and said: "Dress him and enturban him, and name him with a name that shall be attributed exclusively to him." He sat me down and clothed me and enturbaned me. Then he addressed me as "Imam of the saints" and commanded me to do what is approved of and forbade me to do what is disapproved of; and he girded me with the Sword of Truth, to unsheathe it against the enemies of God. Then they commanded me with what they commanded me; and at the same time gave me leave to make this litany that is written upon my ribs well-known, and promised me that whoever adhered to it, God would intercede for every one of his disciples.[11]

With such a powerful vision—preceded and followed by others of a similar nature—it is clear that Usaman Dan Fodio saw his mission as one of cosmic significance. The Sword of Truth that he had received would enable him to differentiate between good and evil and also had a messianic function.

Of Dan Fodio's numerous books and pamphlets,[12] ten deal with issues that are connected with the end of the world. Among these are pamphlets on the duration of the world, the signs of the Hour, the characteristics of the Mahdi (the messianic figure). When coupled with another dominant theme in Dan Fodio's writings—the necessity of differentiating Islam/ Muslims from apostasy/infidels—his conception of messianic jihad becomes quite clear. From the beginnings of Islam until the present day, there has been a close connection between the waging of jihad—whether in a violent or spiritual manner—and the expectation that the world will shortly end.

Usaman Dan Fodio's jihad was less than successful, since a great many of his Muslim comrades took advantage of their newfound power and abused it. This abuse led to a number of revolts against the purportedly ideal Muslim state that Dan Fodio had struggled to achieve.[13] Although the Sokoto jihad changed West African Islam radically, this change was not accomplished as quickly as its instigator had hoped. The West African jihad was nonetheless the only unambiguously successful nineteenth-century jihad, in part, perhaps, because it did not face a determined and technologically capable opponent. Other contemporaneous jihads did.

INDIA

Among all the Muslim resistance movements to Western hegemony, that of the Muslims of India was the most unfortunate.[14] Indian Muslims, having ruled or at least dominated India culturally for approximately seven hundred years, were in an unenviable position by the middle of the eighteenth century. During those centuries, the Muslim population had gradually grown, until it totaled approximately one quarter of the subcontinent's population. For the most part, the Muslim rulers of the Moghul dynasty had been tolerant toward their non-Muslim subjects, and, although the court resembled a military aristocracy—similar to the other Muslim dynasties in northern India prior to their time—religious revolts were rare until the time of Awrangzeb (1658–1707).

Basing the legitimacy of his rule solely upon his Muslim subjects, Awrangzeb sought to impose Islam upon the region's Hindu majority and to conquer the entire subcontinent—a feat unknown since the time of King Ashoka (d. 232 B.C.E.). The failure of his attempt to Islamicize India consigned the Muslims of India to a permanent minority status, but it also meant for the first time that there was a very good reason for the Hindu population to *fear* Muslim rule. With the subsequent collapse of Moghul rule, the failure of Awrangzeb's jihad left the Muslim population for the first time in the position of being subject to the British Raj that had filled the power vacuum and unable to expel the foreigners alone. The era of Muslim domination in India was over.

By the beginning of the nineteenth century, there were attempts to encourage a jihad against the British. In 1803, India was proclaimed Dar al-Harb by Shah 'Abd al-'Aziz Dihlawi.[15] Of those who responded to this call, the most fervent was probably Sayyid Ahmad Shahid (d. 1831), who had previously been exposed to Wahhabi teachings during a year that he spent in Mecca (1821).[16] Sayyid Ahmad founded a primitive organization, which, according to contemporary accounts, had support throughout the Muslim population of northern India. However, Sayyid Ahmad was much less successful in gaining the support of Muslims outside of India, which would have been critical to his success against the British and their allies. A number of his surviving letters, which document his belief that jihad was the means by which Muslims could regain their supremacy in India, have a defensive quality; they are as much an apology for his methods as a call to expel the British.[17]

Fundamentally, this was to remain a basic problem with the Muslims of India and their opposition to British rule. The call for jihad (or, anachronistically, "freedom," as some have called it[18]) was blunted by the fact that the goal of their struggle was unclear. Was it intended to "liberate" the Indian Subcontinent from the British or to renew the Muslims' domination of the Hindus? Sayyid Ahmad Shahid's message was abundantly clear—he sought the latter goal. For this reason he was killed by the Sikhs in 1831. Nonetheless, Indian Muslim writing—from this period until the present day—is dominated by apologetics concerning the role of jihad, the Muslim relationship toward the Hindus, and the repression of Muslims, whether by the British or by India's contemporary Hindu government. Of course, the most severe form of disconfirmation is when a previously despised group—as the British or the Hindus were from the Muslim perspective—gains an advantage over one that believes in its God-given right to rule. Scholars should not be taken in by propaganda produced by the losing side in order to compensate for their losses, but should maintain balance when dealing with problematic periods such as that of Western colonialism.

Although the issue of jihad remained alive in India during the next twenty years, it came into most evident prominence during the so-called Indian Mutiny of 1857–58.[19] This revolt against the rule of the British East India Company, which controlled the British possessions in India, was widespread in northern India, and it was embraced by both Muslims and Hindus. Indeed, many of the proclamations issued by the rebels are addressed to both groups. However, the proclamations themselves attest to a lasting inconsistency between the desire to wage jihad for the renewal of Muslim rule and the desire to win liberation for the inhabitants of the subcontinent. In January 1857, Ahmad Allah issued a *fatwa* calling for Muslims to fight the English.[20] This was followed by disturbances and massacres throughout the Ganges River Valley. Significantly this was the region with the highest percentage of Muslim inhabitants. Most of the other areas of British control were not affected by the mutiny.

Among the proclamations issued during the Indian Mutiny, that of the Royal Army in Delhi dated September 15, 1857, is the most important. Although it is directed at both Muslims and Hindus, it is striking that only Muslim grievances against the British are listed. The Qur'an and other Muslim holy works are cited, but no Hindu sayings or issues. Bizarrely, the proclamation directs Hindus (specifically mentioned) to recite the saying "O Allah, give victory to the religion of Muhammad" 360 times, along with other verses from the Qur'an, in order to protect themselves from any magic (and presumably other, technologically based attacks as well).[21] A similar proclamation by Firoz Shah (the former king of Delhi), dated February 18, 1858, calls for jihad and universal brotherhood between Hindus and Muslims, but then says that this is a purely religious war that should be waged for the sake of the faith (without specifying *which* faith).[22] As in so many cases with jihad, there were abundant messianic prophecies related to the mutiny. The one that appears to have had the widest circulation was that of Shah Niʿmat Allah Wali foretelling the defeat of the British in 1854–55 (dating from prior to the mutiny but then changed to 1862 in later editions). The relevant parts of this prophecy read as follows:

> Then the Nazarenes [Christians] will take the whole of Hindustan; they will reign one hundred years. There will be great oppression in this world in their reign, for their destruction there will be a King in the West. This King will proclaim a war against the Nazarenes, and in the war a great many people will be killed. The King of the West will be victorious by the force of the sword of jihad, and the followers of Christ will be defeated. Islam will prevail for forty years, and then a faithless tribe will come out of Isfahan [Persia]. To drive out these tyrants Jesus will come down from heaven and the expected Mahdi will appear.[23]

Such a prophecy, together with the other proclamations of a more official nature, clearly indicates that the Muslims were fighting for a renewal of Muslim domination, not for freedom for all Indians. Thus, their fight in 1857–58 was clearly conceived as a jihad.

By the end of the mutiny, Indian Muslims had largely moved away from the aggressive interpretation of jihad and were gradually inching toward the nonmilitant interpretations that would become so popular with Indian Muslim apologists during the latter half of the nineteenth century. This trend is exemplified in the writings of Sir Sayyid Ahmad Khan (d. 1898), who promoted a nonviolent interpretation of jihad. Those who still held to militant interpretations of jihad had largely been reduced to the role of cheerleaders for the Ottoman Empire in its many battles to retain its possessions. A good example is the Indian Muslim leader Siddiq Hasan Khan (d. 1890), the nawab of Bhopal, who wrote *al-ʿIbra mi-ma jaʾa fi al-ghazw wa-l-shahada wa-l-hijra* (*The Example concerning That Which Has Been Related of Raiding, Martyrdom, and Emigration*) on the occasion of the Russian-Ottoman War in 1875–76. Unlike the apologists, Khan does not deny that jihad means warfare,[24] and there is no mention of any spiritual aspect to it in his work. All the theoretical elements of jihad are present in his rendition, taken straight out of classical Muslim law books, along with relevant Qurʾanic citations and *hadith*s.

But Khan also recognizes the irrelevance of these precedents for Indian Muslims, and the best that he can do is hope that the Ottomans will win. The only section of the book that has any relevance for his environment is the question of whether British India is Dar al-Harb.

Even that is divorced from its connection to jihad—in other words, whether Muslims should actively fight the British. It is brought in only in relation to the issue of whether Indian Muslims should emigrate from India. Perhaps under other circumstances Khan might have supported this option, but clearly for the millions of Indian Muslims emigration was not a realistic strategy. He points out that the Prophet Muhammad lived for years in Mecca under the domination of infidel pagans—an example that proved to be very useful for Muslim Modernists shortly thereafter (chapter 5).[25]

For Indian Muslims the idea of jihad against the British was probably unfeasible from the beginning. Not only did Indian Muslims suffer from disunity and lack of focus, but their population was scattered over the huge subcontinent and had no geographic base from which jihad operations could conceivably be launched. Faced by a mighty foe armed with technology that the Muslims lacked, surrounded by a large majority of Hindus whose experience of Muslim rule had rendered them less than sympathetic toward any prospect of its resumption, Indian Muslims could only protest.

THE CAUCASUS

The Muslims of the Caucasus, located in Chechnya and Daghestan (to the north and east of the Caucasus Mountains and along the shores of the Caspian Sea), had all the advantages that the Indian Muslims lacked. The Caucasus Mountains constitute some of the most difficult terrain in the world for military operations—an assessment that has been pronounced by numerous (would-be) conquerors during the past three millennia, including the Arabs.[26] In many cases, the mountainous terrain is sliced by gorges containing deep rivers that are virtually impassable. Villages located close together on the map are separated by topographical obstructions that make journeys from one to the other extraordinarily difficult. For the most part, the inhabitants of the northern and eastern sides of the Caucasus Mountains were Muslims, while those on the southern and western sides were Christians (Georgians and Armenians). The mountaineers of the northern Caucasus, the Chechens and the Daghestanis, had been allowed considerable autonomy by their nominal overlords, the Ottomans and the Persians. But this changed by 1829. During the early part of the nineteenth century, the Russian Empire had gradually been advancing through the region between the Black and the Caspian Seas at the expense of the Ottoman and Persian (Qajar) Empires.

Russian rule was not welcomed for a variety of reasons. The Chechens and the Daghestanis were loath to cede control of their locally autonomous states to a large autocratic empire. For these Muslim mountaineers, the prospect of being ruled by Christian Russians, who aggressively promoted the superiority of Christianity and denigrated Islam, was unacceptable. The Russians compounded these difficulties by exercising petty tyrannies, such as humiliations and confiscations, upon the independent-minded locals. These issues, together with a terrain ideal for guerrilla warfare and the native toughness of the Chechen and Daghestani mountaineers, made it relatively easy for Ghazi Muhammad to proclaim himself *imam* of Daghestan in 1829 and to encourage a jihad against the Russians.[27] Ghazi Muhammad, like many of the Indian Muslim revivalists, was closely associated with the Sufi Naqshbandiyya order popular throughout Turkish- and Urdu-speaking lands. Thus, his jihad took on the characteristics of both a liberation movement and a revival-purification movement. He and his more prominent successor, Shamil, sought to establish an Islamic state and to encourage devotion to Islam.

Ghazi Muhammad was successful on a small scale and was able to carry out a number of raids on Russian and allied Muslim strongholds prior to his death in 1832. His successor Hamza Bek, known as the second *imam*, was assassinated by fellow Muslims in a blood-feud in 1834, whereupon Shamil, the most successful leader of the three, was proclaimed the third *imam*. Shamil had impressive military abilities and sought to revolutionize the military methods used by the Chechen and Daghestani mountaineers (he introduced the use of cannon, among other tactics), as well as to establish a Muslim state allied with the Ottoman Empire. Although he was successful in founding a ministate that lasted until his capture in September 1859, in the end his temporary success was due less to the strength of the state that he established than to Russian incompetence (court favorites had been appointed to lead the campaigns against him).

This was nowhere more evident than in Shamil's one very close escape. In 1839 he established headquarters at Akhulgoh, a castle surrounded on three sides by deep ravines and water, and at a considerable distance from Russian bases. Russian troops under the command of Pavel Grabbe managed to reach the fortress and by repeated direct assaults (at a heavy cost) overwhelmed it. Shamil and his closest associates were only barely able to escape, and his authority collapsed for a brief period. He quickly reinvented himself as a true guerrilla leader.

During the following ten years he carried out a series of brilliant campaigns, keeping the Russians off balance and periodically inflicting humiliating defeats upon them. However, from 1851 Shamil was increasingly on the defensive, and suffered from defections to the Russians by his senior lieutenants, as well as war-weariness among his subjects. With the coming of the Crimean War (waged by the Ottomans, the British, and the French against the Russians, from 1853 to 1856) Shamil's only real hope was to gain the support of one or more of the Russians' foes. This proved to be a pipe-dream, since Chechnya and Daghestan were simply too far away for the Ottomans or the British to help him; nor did his jihad ideology win him allies. After the end of the war, the Russians ground the mountaineers down, and Shamil's support collapsed very suddenly in 1858–59.

Shamil's letters attest to his very realistic and pragmatic approach toward jihad.[28] Some of his conceptions, such as the establishment of a larger Muslim Caucasian state or his efforts to obtain aid from the Ottomans, were visionary and unrealistic, but he sought to negotiate with the Russians whenever possible, and he does not appear to have demonized them overmuch in his letters, even though some of their actions might have warranted demonization.[29] In these letters Shamil appears mostly as a man of action: giving orders, asking for information, and sending condolences. His own letters, as well as surviving letters to Shamil by his supporters, contain virtually no citations of either the Qur'an or the *hadith,* nor is there much explanation of his militant beliefs. Usually Shamil was addressed as *amir al-mu'minin,* a caliphal title, and as *nasir al-sunna wa-l-din,* "the one who aids the Sunna and the Religion [Islam]," titles that indicate his reliance on jihad for his religious legitimacy. Overall, Shamil's state was completely dedicated to the waging of jihad; thus when the war ended, his attempts to revive Islam in the Caucasus were forgotten until the beginning of the present war in Chechnya in 1991.

Other jihad fighters in topographically favorable locations, such as the mountains of northern Morocco and Algeria, were able to maintain a continuous tradition of warfare against European invaders over a period of a century.

MOROCCO AND ALGERIA

Another location that favored defensive jihad was the Atlas Mountains of northern Morocco and Algeria. As the Muslims of Spain were gradually pushed out of the Iberian Peninsula during the *reconquista* (chapter 3), many took refuge in this region. This was to no avail, as the Spanish and Portuguese followed the Spanish Muslims to North Africa and conquered a great many of the port cities of the region. But by the end of the sixteenth century, this first wave of European conquest had largely dissipated, sometimes through military defeat (such as that of the Portuguese at Wad al-Makhazin in 1578, where the Portuguese king Sebastian was killed), but often simply through neglect. During this period, the Moroccan rulers, especially the 'Alawi dynasty (from the middle of the seventeenth century onward), were far from passive. They used the raids against European shipping and the general opposition to European expansionism as a means to legitimize their dynasty.[30]

Starting in the 1830s, the French began a second wave of European conquest in Algeria and were opposed by 'Abd al-Qadir, the hereditary amir of Mascara (to the west of Algiers). From 1832 until his defeat and imprisonment in 1847, he fought the French for control of Algeria and proclaimed a jihad to liberate it. As with Shamil, it took a good deal of time and several sharp reverses before the French were willing to take 'Abd al-Qadir seriously. But unlike the Russians, the French quickly learned from their setbacks, attacking 'Abd al-Qadir in two major campaigns (1835–36 and 1840–43), and eventually grinding his forces down through a combination of military and diplomatic maneuvers.[31]

'Abd al-Qadir's struggle would just be another list of victories and defeats were it not for the fact that he was intensely interested in the method of waging jihad and has left a series of exchanges on the subject between him and the Moroccan scholar 'Ali b. 'Abd al-Salam al-Tusulli (d. 1842). Examination of these questions and their answers reveals a great deal about the state of knowledge concerning jihad during the nineteenth century in North Africa.[32] Like other contemporaneous Muslim leaders—Shamil, Shehu Usaman Dan Fodio, and Ibn 'Abd al-Wahhab—'Abd al-Qadir, a leader of the Sufi Qadiriyya order, was concerned about the prevalence of innovations and other beliefs that he deemed non-Islamic. He had to confront the question of how to lead a Muslim army to fight a legitimate jihad against the infidel when a large percentage of his troops believed in or tacitly accepted practices that were non-Muslim.[33] Since 'Abd al-Qadir sought to found a Muslim state, as did Shamil, he used the process of fighting to educate his largely tribal followers.

Many of 'Abd al-Qadir's questions concern money and how to obtain it.[34] This is not surprising since although he was ruler of an emirate,

Mascara, its land was devastated early on by the French (1835) and thus could not provide him with revenues. Many of the other territories that he nominally ruled were not able to support the expenses of his continual fighting. Nor could 'Abd al-Qadir rely upon other Muslims; the major Muslim ruler in the area, Sultan Mawlay 'Abd al-Rahman of Morocco, had proved unreliable and ultimately denied him support altogether from 1844 onward. 'Abd al-Qadir's jihad had to adhere to a strict religious code, but it also needed financing. Those finances could be obtained only from the local Muslim population, who therefore had to supply both money and loyalty to the amir—a difficult combination under the best of circumstances.

'Abd al-Qadir was also concerned about discipline and the punishment of malefactors (including those who concealed them). This was an important issue in a tribal society, where the punishment of a given offender, even if his guilt was universally acknowledged, might be seen as an affront to the tribe's honor. In accord with the *hadith* literature and Muslim history, traitors and spies were clearly to be punished by death. (Indeed, 'Abd al-Qadir does not question the treatment of traitors and spies, only those who conceal them.)[35] But a successful guerrilla leader must not lose the confidence of his supporters, so 'Abd al-Qadir had to be very careful with this issue. A similar question was raised with regard to the punishment of those who refused to respond to a call to arms.[36] Many villagers and tribesmen would not see the refusal to fight as a criminal offense, yet to go without punishing this refusal might weaken discipline, thereby putting the success of the war at risk.

Even before he signed a truce with the French (between 1836 and 1840), 'Abd al-Qadir asked under what conditions a Muslim might make peace with infidels. Like Siddiq Hasan Khan, al-Tusulli gives the impractical answer that the Muslim is required to emigrate from the country controlled by the infidels and is not allowed to make peace with his enemy.[37] It would take the Muslim religious leadership much of the nineteenth century before they acknowledged that it was unfeasible for all of the Muslims in a given location to pack up and emigrate to another Muslim country when their homeland was conquered by infidels.

'Abd al-Qadir's questions reveal him to have been a thoughtful and ethical person, who saw jihad as warfare distinguished by its virtue and righteousness, rather than as warfare seeking to achieve victory at any cost.[38] Unfortunately, al-Tusulli's formulaic answers ignore the character of 'Abd al-Qadir and his genuine concern for his Muslim subjects. 'Abd al-Qadir's jihad was probably doomed from the beginning because

Algeria, while rugged and mountainous, was simply too close to France and too important to French national pride to be given up. France had the troops and technology to make its claim good, at least during the nineteenth century. Further to the south, in the Sudan and Somalia, Muslims could still hope, during the middle of the nineteenth century, to found successful jihad states that, located at distant margins, were not sufficiently economically attractive for the colonial powers to take any interest.

THE SUDAN AND EAST AFRICA

After the Egyptians defeated the Wahhabis in the Arabian Peninsula, Egypt went through a period of immense—albeit temporary—growth. Egyptian armies conquered the region of Syria-Palestine and challenged the Ottoman Empire during the 1830s and 1840s. Some observers feared that the newly powerful Egyptian state would topple the Ottomans, but this proved to be an illusion when Egyptian troops withdrew from their vast conquests almost without a fight after being faced down by Great Britain, Austria-Hungary, and other allies in 1840–41. Although Egyptian conquest was not welcome in Syria-Palestine, the European powers did not appear to object to Egyptian expansion toward the south, primarily along the Nile Valley and the Red Sea. Through the middle of the nineteenth century, Egypt embraced the "suppression of slavery" cause that enabled it to expand its influence. But many of the Sudanese were far from pleased to see slavery abolished, as it had been a lucrative livelihood for them. The Egyptian government's tendency to appoint Europeans as governors and sub-governors in the Sudan, on the grounds that suppressing the slave trade required officials that were truly dedicated to the task, caused resentment among both the Sudanese and the local Egyptian officials, who objected to foreigners and (mostly) Christians being in positions of power over them.

In 1881 Muhammad Ahmad from southern Egypt declared himself to be the Mahdi, the messianic figure, following visions that affirmed his divine appointment (similar to those manifested to Shehu Usaman Dan Fodio). Initially his goals were fairly modest, and together with his followers, he emigrated to a secure location from whence he could launch raids.[39] These were successful, and the Mahdi went from one victory to another during the following four years until he besieged Khartoum, the capital, in 1884–85. Khartoum had been the seat of General Charles Gordon, sent by the British government to salvage the Sudan. However,

Gordon did not have sufficient military backing at his disposal, and given his nature—some would later suspect him of desiring to be a martyr—he essentially came to Khartoum to die. This was granted him in January 1885 when the Mahdi and his forces stormed the city.

Ironically, the Mahdi lived for only four months after his greatest triumph, but his successor, the Khalifa ʿAbdallahi (of the Taʿishi tribe from the western Sudan), continued his policies of aggressive expansionism and militant jihad against all the neighboring states (Egypt, controlled by the British from 1882, Ethiopia, and Eritrea, controlled by the Italians). With the exception of the defeats suffered by the Ethiopians in 1888 and 1889—who were the only possible allies the Mahdist state had among its neighbors—none of these enemies were in any danger. Indeed, the British administered two sharp defeats to the Mahdist movement in 1886 and 1889 without taking advantage of either one to reconquer the Sudan.[40] Indeed, it is difficult to read the history of the Mahdist movement without concluding that its ultimate demise in 1898 was the result of its own belligerent policies and that the British and Italian colonial powers had little interest in fighting the Mahdist state.

The Mahdi's policies and proclamations reveal him to have believed that God had chosen him to reunite the Muslim world and to liberate it from Christian imperialist rule. One of his first proclamations was:

> From the servant of his Lord, Muhammad al-Mahdi son of the Sayyid ʿAbdallah to the Hukmdariyya [Muhammad Raʾuf Pasha]: in accordance with correspondence, it must be revealed that I call everyone to straighten the Sunna and to emigrate with the Religion [of Islam] from the disposition of these times—a directive from the Lord of Existence [Muhammad]. [Also] telling [you] that I am the Expected Mahdi from the Lord of Existence many times, together with divine communications and signs, through which the Lord of Existence informed [me]. Whoever follows will be among the close ones, the successful ones, and whoever disobeys God will cause him to be among the losers in both places [this world and the next], and will block him through His power against which all creation is helpless. As for the counsel to the believers, it is clear—whoever does not believe will be purified by the sword.
>
> It should be known that from the two visits—that of the Prophet and that of the Poles[41]—I received a sword, and that as long as it is with me, no one will be victorious against me. [Muhammad] informed me that whoever comes against me in enmity God will have the earth swallow him up or be drowned. That is information from [Muhammad]. In all of this I do nothing for myself or for my own purposes, but it is all from God and for God. His verse is well-known: "If you support Allah, He will support you." (Qurʾan 47:7)[42]

Clearly the Mahdi's vision was very similar to that of Usaman Dan Fodio: both received visitations from the Prophet Muhammad and prominent Sufi holy men, and both received mystical gifts of swords with instructions to purify the world. The Mahdi had a strongly universalistic view of his mission. Until the abortive invasion of Egypt in 1889, many of his followers believed that they would be welcomed as liberators. This expectation led to their defeat and ultimate annihilation at the hands of the British that year.

Fundamentally, the Mahdi's movement was messianic and suffused with the spirit of jihad, but both the Mahdi and the Khalifa 'Abdallahi were prisoners of their beliefs, which rendered them helpless in the face of advancing colonial forces. Even as the British were advancing to finish off the Mahdist state in 1898, the Ethiopian emperor Menelik II sent an embassy to the Khalifa offering him an alliance and aid. This was refused in the most contemptuous terms possible.[43] Reading the Khalifa's reply, one is amazed at his arrogance and inability to see that Menelik—one of the few African rulers to maintain independence from European powers at the end of the nineteenth century—was actually offering him a lifeline.

In Somalia, on the Horn of Africa, British rule also came under attack between 1899 and 1920 from yet another jihad movement, led by Mohammed Abdulle Hassan, popularly known as the "Mad" Mullah of Somalia.[44] The Mullah is the only the major jihad figure of the nineteenth and early twentieth centuries who was clearly influenced by Wahhabism, and possibly also by the Mahdist movement in the Sudan just a few years before his own revolt. All of the others described above were *mujahid* fighters, messianic figures, or revivalists. Just as with the Mahdist state in the Sudan, the Mullah was able to fight for a number of years because Somalia was not essential to the British, and because of his matchless knowledge of the local terrain. Even so, his lengthy revolt was punctuated by a ten-year truce between 1905 and 1915 when he was allowed to live in peace.

British interests in Somalia during this time were concentrated along the seacoast of the north side of the Horn of Africa; Britain's activities in the interior of the country were limited to keeping Somali tribes in check. The Mullah, whose exposure to the outside world included a *hajj* to Mecca undertaken between 1886 and 1890, was able to use imaginative tactics against the British troops sent to defeat him, and he led them on a merry chase for four years until his defeat in 1904. Although he was abandoned by a great number of his followers and compelled to take refuge in the Italian part of Somalia, the Mullah did not give up the fight. It is clear from his writings and poems that the Mullah was fundamentally opposed to any foreign presence in Somalia and viewed the only legitimate response to occupation as jihad. However, there is still a debate as to whether this opposition to foreigners and use of jihad stemmed from religious causes or constituted a nascent form of nationalism. Having read the Mullah's works (available to me only in translation), I would place him clearly within the overall tradition of religious jihad and argue that nationalism was a secondary consideration.[45]

Like Shamil, but unlike Sayyid Ahmad and the Khalifa Abdullahi, the Mullah was willing to make compromises with foreign powers, which undoubtedly prolonged his revolt. The fact that their truce with the Mullah coincided with the beginning of World War I (1914–18) also made it difficult for the British to act against him. In 1915, he sent diplomatic feelers to the Ottoman Empire (then fighting the British) offering his aid. Finally, in 1919–20, the British decided to finish him off completely, and using airplanes and unrelenting ground pursuit, they succeeded.

All of the jihad movements of the nineteenth and early twentieth centuries were failures (with the possible exception of that of Usaman Dan Fodio). Fundamentally they were all pitted against foes against whose superior weaponry and better-organized armies they could do nothing. By the end of the nineteenth century, with the exception of Somalia, resistance to Western hegemony had died out. It is noteworthy that all of the jihad efforts described in this chapter took place in the peripheral areas of Islam. The intellectual and popular centers of Islam are entirely unrepresented in Muslim opposition to European conquest and domination during the nineteenth century.[46] All of the above movements were essentially anticentral as well as anti-European (some were influenced by proto-nationalism). They represented a powerful and negative assessment of the intellectual and military capacities of the Muslim world of the center and called for reform. In essence the Muslim periphery was judging the center and finding it lacking.

THE PERSIAN AND OTTOMAN CALLS FOR JIHAD

At the beginning and again toward the end of this period of resistance, Muslim governments called for jihad on two occasions. The Persian religious leadership declared a jihad during the Russo-Persian Wars (1808–13, 1826–28); the Ottoman religious leadership issued a similar call during World War I (1914–18). Both need to be examined in order to understand why theories of jihad would need to be radically reworked for the contemporary period. These calls, although using language that had been effective for hundreds of years since the Mongol invasions, did not carry the weight of religious authority, and few Muslims responded to them.

The Persian calls for jihad demonstrate a considerable deviation from the classical Shiʿite teachings on jihad, as Kohlberg has demonstrated in his article on the subject.[47] He notes that traditionally Shiʿites had been reluctant to authorize jihad without an *imam*—since the Shiʿite twelfth *imam* had been in occultation since 874—and had usually tried to defer any consideration of resuming jihad until the time when he would be revealed and usher in the messianic age.

The Persian calls for jihad themselves are fairly restrained when compared to the types of radical Muslim materials that have become common during the twentieth century. Kohlberg details the intellectual discussion in the one *fatwa* that was available to him and lists twelve differences between offensive and defensive jihad. These differences describe the various measures that might be taken legally to repel the enemy, which laws might be amended or modified in extreme circumstances, how funds could be obtained, and how spoils should be distributed. Other *fatawa* carry no more fire than did the one Kohlberg examined. For example, in 1813 Aga Sayyid ʿAli Tabaʿtabaʿi, a leading Shiʿite cleric, issued a similar *fatwa* against the Russians.[48] Readers of the *fatwa* are encouraged to spare no effort in order to repel the enemy, and the religious reasons for this are given. A number of historical examples, mostly from the life of ʿAli b. Abi Talib (fourth caliph and first *imam* of the Twelver Shiʿites), are mentioned, prayers are cited, and legal issues similar to those already discussed by Kohlberg are discussed. But the *fatwa* and others like it show no awareness of any of the larger issues behind the Russian invasion. It seems that the writer is merely arguing that repelling the Russians will cause the problem to go away. Practically speaking, there is not very much that the reader of the *fatwa* can do (or is directed to do) other than render assistance in whatever way possible.

Another Persian *fatwa* from that same year, which is anonymous, declares outright that the Russians want to conquer Persia and that Persians must fight this goal.[49] This at least puts the stakes of the battle into perspective and gives the fighters a powerful incentive to defend their homes. But it is clear from reading these *fatawa*, as Kohlberg states, that the religious leaders issuing them were unpracticed at this type of writing. The style is that of a theological tract, and few of the rousing verses of the Qur'an—although more in the second *fatwa*—are cited to encourage the fighters. Nor is the history of the Prophet Muhammad invoked very much. The Shi'ite religious leadership simply lacked practice in writing aggressive *fatawa*, but they would make up for that during the twentieth century.

One could argue that the Ottoman Empire's declaration of jihad against the Allies (Britain, France, Russia, and the United States) in 1914 was problematic not because of lack of practice, but because of lack of intellectual clarity. Jihad traditionally was a means by which Muslims fought non-Muslims for the sake of Islam either offensively or defensively. But in 1914, Muslim Ottoman Turkey was allied with Christian Germany and Austria-Hungary, and for some time previously, various European Christians—British, French and German—had held powerful positions in the caliphate at the request of the Ottoman government. Count Rudiger von der Goltz (a serving German officer and a Christian) had even been commander of the Turkish army for a time during the nineteenth century. Therefore, the call for jihad in 1914 was clouded by the fact that the Ottomans were fighting with Christians against other Christians.

The *fatwa* itself is a series of five questions addressed to the Shaykh al-Islam (the highest figure in the Ottoman Muslim religious structure), asking whether the jihad was incumbent upon all Muslims, whether the Muslims living in the countries of the Allies, Russia, Britain and France, should rise up against them, whether those Muslims who refrain from fighting are committing a sin, whether Muslims who are compelled to fight against the Ottomans should resist to the death, and whether Muslims should avoid fighting Germany and Austria-Hungary.[50] All of these questions are answered with a simple affirmative, without any illustration or citation from the Qur'an, Muslim law, or history. Again, there is little fire in this *fatwa,* and it is not difficult to see why this dry series of questions and answers did not inspire Muslims worldwide to rise up against the Allies—quite aside from the fact that the *fatwa* offers no practical advice for those who heed its instructions.

Clearly new thinking was needed on jihad by the early twentieth century. Although the doctrine itself was a dynamic one, it did not seem to command as much attention from the masses of Muslims as the Persian or Ottoman leaders had hoped—or as the British, Russian, and French governments had feared. One might have prematurely come to the conclusion that there was no future for jihad because of this. But it was about to experience a revival.

FIVE

RADICAL ISLAM AND CONTEMPORARY JIHAD THEORY

Contemporary jihad theory begins from the time that overt military resistance to Western incursions ceased and the need arose to radically redefine the meaning of jihad, either for apologetic reasons or because the definition was no longer relevant to new circumstances. By the early twentieth century, most of the Muslim world was ruled by Europeans, who imposed their laws and norms upon the Muslim societies. In some cases the Europeans ruled directly (as they did in India and Algeria); in others they ruled through proxies (as in Morocco, Tunisia, and Iran) or through local elites that were clearly subservient to their dictates. By 1920 the only areas of the Muslim world not directly or indirectly controlled by Europeans were those that no one wanted. No Muslim army or opposition stood in their way, other than the residual revolts or pockets of resistance discussed in chapter 4. After 1924, with the extinction of the Ottoman Empire, there was no caliph who could authorize the proclamation of jihad for Sunni Muslims.

For Muslims, all of this was a major shock. Islam mandates that Muslims be in an obviously dominant position in this world so as to manifest the truth.[1] By the beginning of the twentieth century, not only were most Muslims not in a ruling or a dominant position vis-à-vis the world; they were not even in a dominant position within their own nations. New elites appeared in Muslim countries, often composed of precisely those groups previously accorded the least respect. These included foreigners (or carpetbaggers) who flocked to Muslim countries in large numbers and often established local colonies, Christians and Jews who had lived in Muslim countries for centuries but had never been allowed to rise above the level established for them in the Pact of 'Umar, Hindus in India, and heterodox Muslim groups (such as the Nusayris and the Ahmadis).

All of these changes required a redefinition of jihad. Muslims could not count on being in positions of authority to proclaim jihad or even to defend Islam; for the most part the *shari'a* was no longer the source of law, and in some cases it was no longer even *a* source of law. Clearly all of the assumptions laid down thus far by Muslim writers on the subject were no longer relevant. New thinking was necessary. To a large extent, the Modernist Muslims concentrated in the great centers of contemporary Muslim thought, primarily Egypt and India, filled this intellectual gap.

MUHAMMAD 'ABDUH, RASHID RIDA, AND THE MODERNISTS

In Egypt, Muhammad 'Abduh (d. 1905) and his more conservative disciple Rashid Rida (d. 1935) had developed new paradigms for jihad. This is clear from their *fatawa*. In the journal *al-Manar*, which was their principal outlet, Rida responded in 1913 to a question from one Muhammad Hadi al-Birjundi, who asked the following:

> The obvious meaning of "defense" is not appropriate [for jihad], nor the division of jihad into defensive and offensive [parts] . . . if the meaning of "defensive" were to be true—being conditional upon the opponent's [entering into] the dispute first—then how can we say that the Persians and the Byzantines disputed with Muhammad and his Companions, when they were in the Hijaz, so that he was compelled to push them to the borders of China in the east and Africa in the west?
>
> One is amazed at those who count the Europeans [al-Ifranj] in their occupation of the lands of Islam, the captivity of its men, the humiliation of its women, and the slaughter of its children for the smallest economic benefit that comes to them, without any reason, as a civilized and even religious right, and do not count the striking of the sword or the choice, upon the religiously obligated person, between Islam and the attainment of its eternal happiness for his descendants, or accepting the lowest *jizya* [tax] with its maintenance of human rights among his progeny as a religious, Islamic right.[2]

This is a clear-headed question, although the author's verbiage makes it more complicated than it needs to be. Essentially he is asking: if jihad is only waged defensively, then how could the first Muslim conquests be interpreted as defensive actions? Even if only some the conquests were defensive, how was it that the early Muslims were able to conquer all the territory they did "defensively"? Even more boldly, he asks: is there a similarity between the manner in which European colonialists and imperialists treated their subjects during the nineteenth and twentieth centuries and rationalized their harsh and cruel actions in the name of economic gain and "civilization," and the manner in which the early Muslims acted?

This is a line of critical thinking that was entirely absent from classical Islamic literature and is still very rare in Muslim discourse to this day. Because the first conquests were as much of a confirmatory miracle for the truth of Islam as the Qur'an was, Muslims have never subjected them to critical scrutiny. For the most part, even today historians in the Muslim world, and especially in the Arabic-speaking Muslim world, avoid the question of whether the early Muslims were imperialists and colonialists. Al-Birjundi, the questioner, is of course also trying to establish some of the absolute boundaries and definitions of warfare—not merely with regard to Muslims, but with regard to Europeans as well. In this endeavor he is clearly attracted by Rashid Rida's attempt to divide jihad into two categories: one defensive (to repel enemies of Islam who attack it) and the other internal, the "greater jihad" discussed in chapter 2.

Of these two categories the first is the more important for our purposes. Defining jihad as purely defensive would challenge Christian missionaries' claims that Islam was a religion of the sword, and thus benefit Islam as a whole. However, al-Birjundi is confronted with a problem in his interpretation: if jihad is only defensive, then that definition needs be sustained historically, which means that it should be applicable to the Prophet Muhammad and the first conquests. A Muslim could legitimately argue that many of Muhammad's battles against the Quraysh and the pagan Arabs were either defensive in nature or justified because of the wrong that was done to the Muslims (Qur'an 22:39, for example). However, this argument is undermined by the Muslims' attacks on the Byzantines, who had themselves been victims of attacks by the Sasanian Empire (602–28). When the Muslims attacked them, first during the time of the Prophet Muhammad (629–32), and then under the second caliph, 'Umar b. al-Khattab (634–44), the Byzantines had recently reoccupied Syria and Palestine, from which they had been absent for a generation. The notion of a purely "defensive" jihad is stretched thin by the claim that all the conquests of the entire region between Central Asia and Spain were undertaken "defensively."

Clearly Rashid Rida is uncomfortable with these questions. He notes the defensive character of the Prophet Muhammad's early battles (a fact not in serious dispute), but he then takes a new turn by maintaining that war was the common state of the time, and that in such a state, there is no issue of "aggression" because war is continuous. Muhammad's wars after this initial phase were fought in order to protect the right of Muslims to proclaim the truth of Islam. As for the "defensive" character of the war against the non-Arabs, Rida claims that the war was provoked by the Byzantines massing against the local Arabs in order to expel them into the desert so that they would die of famine (there is not a shred of evidence for this in the historical literature; in fact the Byzantines had always maintained good relations with the Syrian Arab tribes, and it is doubtful that nomads would have necessarily died of famine in the desert).

Since, according to Rida, the Muslims' neighbors had prevented the proclamation of the truth, the Muslims were obligated to fight them:

> But they only used force when in need or when it was absolutely neces-
> sary, since they would offer the [conquered] peoples Islam—and if they
> accepted, they would assimilate—if they avoided, then they took a little
> *jizya* [poll tax] from them . . . and left them their personal freedom,
> their possessions, and their religion that they [the Muslims] were not
> required to judge between them.[3]

After this gloss of Islamic history, Rida makes the character of "defense" clear. "Our religion is not like others that defend themselves . . . but our defense of our religion is the proclamation of truth and the removal of the distortion and misrepresentation of it."[4] This definition of defense blurs the lines between "defense" and "offense" to the point where there is no real distinction between the terms and reduces the question to a semantic game. Whereas al-Birjundi was seeking some absolutes in order to define what constitutes legitimate and illegitimate warfare, Rida was merely shuffling the cards.

'Abduh and Rida do not achieve deeper intellectual clarity in their commentary on the Qur'an in *al-Manar*. They are confronted with the unambiguously aggressive character of several verses in the holy book and their lack of congruence with the picture of Islam they wish to paint. This is most evident in their commentary on *sura* 9, the locus for a great deal of authoritative teaching concerning jihad. For example, 'Abduh and Rida advance a unique interpretation of 9:5, the "Verse of the

Sword," and 9:36 "fight the polytheists all together just as they fight you all together," both of which seem to encourage fighting on a universal scale until the entire world is converted to Islam. They distinguish several *hadith*s that command Muslims to avoid fighting specific groups, such as the Turks and the Ethiopians, and conclude from this that the verse cannot be interpreted to have universal applicability. Since the Turks were pagans at the time of the *hadith*s' composition and the Ethiopians were Christians, the *hadith*s seem to render the Qur'anic verse moot or at least amend it to mean that jihad is permitted only against those Arab pagans of the time of Muhammad.[5]

This interpretation of the Qur'an is unprecedented, as are many of 'Abduh and Rida's other interpretations. From a Muslim point of view, it is a bit of a stretch to say that a comparatively obscure pair of *hadith*s on Turks and Ethiopians nullify a major Qur'anic doctrine. Nonetheless, 'Abduh and Rida do not place too much weight upon this point and work it in with their other teachings on the subject of jihad. For example, they entirely reframe the language of 9:111, the salvific contract between God and Muslims to fight in the path of God to preclude waging war, defining its exclusive subject as a form of self-sacrificing proclamation of Islam. Their commentary on the verse entirely excludes fighting or bloodshed from the purview of jihad.[6] Furthermore, they present war for its own sake as abhorrent (in accordance with Qur'an 2:216, although this verse was never interpreted thus in classical times), and the *shahada* (martyrdom or bearing witness) described in the Qur'an—for example, 3:140—as meaning the proclamation of Islam.[7]

All in all 'Abduh and Rida manage to spiritualize warfare in a considerably different direction than did the Sufis with the doctrine of the "greater jihad." For them, jihad is to be understood almost entirely as a proclamation of the truth (which is a classical doctrine as well) and as warfare only in the most limited, defensive manner possible. Clearly these conclusions were at odds with most earlier Muslim teachings about jihad, but they resonated with some Muslims. Others, however, such as the Muslim Brotherhood, took exception to this vision of jihad.

HASAN AL-BANNA' AND THE MUSLIM BROTHERHOOD

Hasan al-Banna' is one of the more complicated and interesting Muslim leaders of the early twentieth century. Born into a fairly conservative family and interested in Sufism from a young age, he founded the Muslim Brotherhood in 1928 when he was just twenty-two years old. The organization has been dedicated since its founding to promoting a revival of Islam and a return to the study of its primary texts. Although today its influence has clearly diminished, and a great many of its teachings have become gradually amalgamated with Wahhabism (which, as noted in chapter 4, is based on considerably different premises), the movement remains at the core of the growth of revivalist and radical Islam. Al-Banna' preached Muslim revival in Egypt during the 1930s and 1940s and achieved a good deal of success in transforming Egyptian society; his assassination in 1949 was probably revenge for the assassination of Egyptian prime minister Nokrashy Pasha in 1948.

Al-Banna' wrote his twenty-page pamphlet in the spirit of apologetics that were common during the second quarter of the twentieth century. He begins by saying that jihad is strictly defensive and then cites a wide range of Qur'anic selections, following each quotation with his commentary in order to prove that the verse supports his general thesis. Al-Banna' cites a long list of *hadith*s in this same manner, as well as quotations from jurists who support his position. The scholarship that he cites is a bit thin, given the huge number of classical Muslim jurists who wrote on the subject. Perhaps al-Banna' felt that additional citations might bring to light statements that would reveal the considerably different attitudes common in classical Islam and reflect unfavorably on his presentation of the subject.

His major point is reached late in the pamphlet, when al-Banna' asks "What do Muslims fight for?" and answers:

> God obligated the Muslims with jihad not as a means of aggression nor as a vehicle for their personal desires, but in order to protect the proclamation [of Islam], as a surety for peace, and as a means to fulfill the great mission whose burden has been taken up by the Muslims, which is the mission to guide people to truth and justice. Islam, just as fighting was made obligatory, celebrates peace, as "and if they incline to peace, incline to it too, and put your trust in Allah." (Qur'an 8:61)[8]

Clearly, with his language of "taking up" great missions, al-Banna' has been influenced by Rudyard Kipling, and it is difficult not to see these words in an apologetic light. However, al-Banna' was far from being an advocate of worldwide peace. He is well aware of prevailing apologetic arguments about the "greater jihad," which had become quite popular among Muslims during his time, and he devotes several pages to pointing out the problems with the tradition of "I returned from the 'lesser jihad' to fight the 'greater jihad.'" Al-Banna' does not want Muslims to avoid fighting simply because it is fighting, but rather advises them to make certain that when they fight, they fight for the right reason. He is also concerned that Muslims are losing their desire for the next world because of their fear of death (a common theme among popular medieval Muslim preachers) and their interest in the good life of the modern world.

ABU AL-'ALA AL-MAWDUDI

This latter concern also weighed heavily upon the dominant and influential Indo-Pakistani Muslim thinker Abu al-'Ala al-Mawdudi (d. 1979). Mawdudi to a large extent provided the intellectual framework for the "Muslim revival" of the latter half of the twentieth century. His book on jihad, written early in his career (1930), was only one part of his considerable intellectual output. However, it is valuable since many of the ideas conveyed in it form the basis for apologetic thought concerning jihad among South Asian Muslims, along with the synthesis that would later be put to use by radical Islam.

Though many of Mawdudi's works are apologetic in nature, *al-Jihad fi al-Islam* stands out as a work of a different character. English words are frequently cited in the text—such mistaken definitions of *jihad* as "holy war" or "fanaticism"—and Mawdudi parodies the visual images of jihad common in the West: the thundering hoofbeats of horse-riding conquerors, wielding the sword and demanding conversion to Islam or the death of all in their wake. It is clear that Mawdudi was deeply troubled and resentful of the image of jihad popularized by missionaries and other Westerners in order to convert Muslims to Christianity and (as Mawdudi saw it) to stir up dissension between Muslims and Hindus in British India. The first third of the booklet does not contain any Qur'anic citations or *hadith*s whatsoever; it is devoted solely to presenting definitions, mostly of concepts connected with jihad. Mawdudi does not hesitate to turn the tables on European polemicists, saying that it is hypocritical of them to associate such terms as "holy war" exclusively with Islam when their own history is replete with holy wars and fanatical movements. The Qur'anic verses that traditionally are associated with jihad are ignored throughout the booklet, and Muslim history is hardly touched upon until the last apologetic note, which concerns the question of whether the first Muslims were colonialists.

Mawdudi's most evident apologetics are expressed in his radical redefinition of what constitutes jihad in Islam. According to him, jihad has nothing whatsoever to do with fighting:

What do we have to do with fighting, sirs? We are simply missionaries proclaiming, and we invite [people] to the religion of Allah, the religion of security and peace . . . what do we have to do with the sword or with fighting with it? God forbid that we have any connection with it what-soever! Other than that we protect ourselves when we are attacked by someone.[9]

Mawdudi is at pains to point out that jihad is considerably different from other types of warfare; it is founded, he argues, on the true mean-ing of Islam: a revolutionary call to worship God alone. Therefore, the purpose of jihad is to confront man's tyranny over man and to make it possible, through liberation, for man to assume his proper role in cre-ation. Mawdudi sees tyranny as the result of man's unwillingness to acknowledge the truth of who God is: we have created unjust social and belief systems to give ourselves purpose in life.

Islam represents a challenge to this man-made tyranny and is in es-sence a call of freedom and liberation to the entire world:

"O people, worship your Lord who created you . . ." [Qur'an 2:21] is the core of this message, the revolutionary message of Islam, and its very essence. It does not speak to the inhabitants of this globe in the name of workers or peasants or landowners or capitalists who are owners of fac-tories and industrial plants, and does not call them by the names of their parties or classes, but Islam speaks to all humanity together, and does not refer to them in any other way than as individuals of the human race.[10]

It is the right and the responsibility of Muslims to proclaim and to expose the corruption in the present world system. Jihad is basically designed to confront those illegitimate and tyrannical rulers and their supporters who prevent the actualization of the world's unity and equal-ity. Mawdudi calls upon Muslims to continue with this world-changing revolution and to realize the Muslim state in order to protect the weak (see Qur'an 4:75). This vision, as stated previously, is a dramatic depar-ture from classical jihad, where justice is rarely stated to be a goal in and of itself. More commonly the goal is Muslim supremacy or "to raise the Word of Allah to the highest" (see Qur'an 9:41). It seems clear that a great deal of Mawdudi's presentation of jihad owes an intellectual debt to socialist and communist dogma.

Although nominally Mawdudi was writing on jihad, most of the booklet does not deal specifically with how jihad should be waged, given his premise that it is not military in nature. However, in the last ten pages of the booklet, he describes some of the history (or perhaps one should say his reinterpretation of the history) of Muslim warfare. This is not his most successful presentation, and he was wise to leave it till the end, because it is here that he has to confront the same question that al-Birjundi asked: if jihad is defensive in nature, then how did the great Muslim conquests occur? Within the context of Mawdudi's own anti-colonialist polemic, he is obligated to confront the question of whether the first Muslims were colonialists. With some honesty, he divides his analysis of the conquests into two segments: the perception of the non-Muslims and the purpose of the Muslims. Mawdudi recognizes that the conquered non-Muslim peoples at least initially saw their conquerors as imperialists. They fought the Muslims only until "it was clear to them the purpose of the Muslims, and the reason why they had come out of their homeland [the Arabian Peninsula]; then they knew the completely revolutionary way of life that was their [the Muslims'] desire to spread and to propagate its belief-system to the corners of the earth."[11]

Since this was the case, the early Muslims were not colonialists or imperialists. Rather, they were liberators and freedom-fighters. Mawdudi does not devote much argument to this theme, nor does he provide specific examples to explain how he arrives at this highly dubious conclusion. Finally, Mawdudi has to confront the question of whether jihad is done offensively or defensively. Given that his definition of what constitutes jihad is considerably different from the classical definition and entirely divorced from any historical context, and that he is writing in the spirit of apologetics, it is not surprising that he maintains that jihad is simultaneously on both the offensive and the defensive.

> If you want the truth, Islamic jihad is both offensive and defensive at the same time. It is offensive because the Islamic party opposes and confronts the systems founded upon the principles that are contrary to Islam, and desires to destroy their power—and does not shrink from the use of force in order to do so—and defensive because it is compelled to construct the building of the kingdom and to reinforce its foundations so as to make possible the work in accordance with its established program and plan.[12]

Mawdudi's description does not appear to really answer the question, and it is difficult to escape the impression that his apologetic presentation of jihad would satisfy only an audience already receptive to his arguments. Were it subject to any Islamic or historical critique, it would collapse immediately.

To a large degree all the thinkers discussed thus far take a strongly apologetic position with regard to the subject of jihad. For them jihad is entirely defensive in nature and purpose, even if they allow for some degree of offensive attacks in order to account for the first conquests; for that reason, they try to de-emphasize (for the first time in Muslim history) the character of the early Muslim conquests, presenting them as, a "liberation" of oppressed peoples instead of an imperialistic venture. Undoubtedly this tone was a response to Christian missionary polemic, as well as the uncomfortable realization that the early Muslim conquests were easily comparable to the contemporary European imperialist and colonialist ventures. Without the element of "liberation," there might be the distinct possibility that the two types of conquest and colonization would be indistinguishable. A considerably different attitude appears with the rise of radical Islam in Egypt.[13]

SAYYID QUTB

Although Mawdudi was a important intellectual influence upon radical Islam, Sayyid Qutb (executed 1966) could be said to have founded the actual movement. Mawdudi, writing from the fringes of the Muslim world, mostly in Urdu rather than in Arabic, and very conscious of the Muslim minority position in British India, was not in a position to initiate a large-scale movement in the core lands of Islam. On the other hand, Sayyid Qutb was from Egypt, the very center of Arab Muslim political, intellectual, and religious debate, and his life and achievements parallel and exemplify the rise of radical Islam.

Qutb was a literary critic during the 1930s and 1940s and was from a semisecular background. In 1949, he visited the United States and stayed for two years; the nation's capitalist, consumer society, and its influence on Egypt, horrified him and transformed his politics. During the following years, he joined the Muslim Brotherhood (then in a state of flux as a result of the assassination of Hasan al-Banna') and quickly became its dominant intellectual figure. Most of the Brotherhood's leadership—Qutb included—was arrested by Gamal 'Abd al-Nasir's regime in 1954 and sentenced to long prison terms, accompanied by torture and degradations.

This experience was the anvil upon which radical Islam in Egypt was forged. Qutb wrote many of his important works in prison, including his commentary on the Qur'an, *Fi Zilal al-Qur'an (In the Shadow of the Qur'an)*, which was published in serial form. In 1965 he was released from prison, only to be re-arrested after the publication of his most famous work, *Ma'alim fi al-tariq (Milestones along the Way)*—which is largely composed of selections from the Qur'anic commentary. Charged, spuriously, with attempting to assassinate Nasir, he was executed the following year. For most radical Muslims, especially Egyptians, Sayyid Qutb was a martyr who spoke the truth and was killed for it. His works have been cited by radical Muslims from the 1960s until the present, and his influence upon the movement is significant.

Unlike the previous writers, Qutb is not an apologist. His formative experiences in developing the major doctrines of radical Islam were his persecution by the Egyptian government and the knowledge that large numbers of fellow Muslims had been similarly imprisoned, tortured, and sometimes executed or murdered by the authorities (Mawdudi, although imprisoned several times, was never treated harshly). Therefore, Qutb had an absolute view of the problems facing the Muslim world, arguing that these problems stemmed from the fact that Muslim societies were no longer ruled by Muslim norms and laws (the *shari'a*) and had become apostate. Since (true) Muslims were visibly in the minority, they must concentrate upon (re)making society Muslim.

He begins *Milestones* with his fundamental point: all ideologies other than Islam, whether associated with the West (capitalism) or the East (communism or socialism) have failed and have demonstrated their bankruptcy. Islam, Qutb argues, is nowhere present on the contemporary stage other than in the hearts of believers—it has been abandoned by the rulers and the elites. This situation is analogous to that of the Prophet Muhammad, and thus we are living in a re-creation of the pre-Islamic period of *Jahiliyya* (ignorance or barbarism). Therefore, it is necessary for Muslims to revive Islam and fight the *Jahiliyya* of the present day. As a preliminary to this revival, Islam rid itself of the accretions of tradition and custom that distract people's attention from recognizing it as the cure for humanity's ills. Qutb focuses upon what he calls the "unique Qur'anic generation"—in other words, the experiences of the first Muslim generation that knew only the Qur'an.

Given his focus upon the Qur'an, it is hardly surprising that a substantial part of Qutb's doctrine deals with the question of jihad, which he analyzes in the following terms: First, the entire religious and social system of Islam is a realistic one and makes realistic demands on its followers. Therefore, it follows that the system of jihad is also a realistic one. Second, jihad is a progressive program, leading from one stage to another in a rational manner. By this, Qutb means that in the progression of teachings about jihad derived from the Qur'an (as rearranged by Muslim exegetes), there is a logical progression from peaceful proclamation, to warfare on a limited scale, to revenge for wrongs done to the Muslims, to the final stage of unlimited warfare.

It is easy to see the reasons why Qutb was not an apologist. His chapter on the subject of jihad does not avoid the citation of the militant Qur'anic verses, nor does it avoid the subject of early Muslim history in the way that Mawdudi did. Perhaps also the fact of writing for an Arabic-speaking audience, steeped in Muslim history, would have made it harder for Qutb to avoid or reinterpret widely known facts and traditions. Qutb states fairly early in the chapter on jihad in the *Milestones* that, contrary to what "defeatists" have said, jihad in Islam is not merely defensive.[14] However, he does show some sensitivity toward the outside (non-Muslim) world by adding that even though jihad can be offensive, it is not coercive in its goals. Qutb basically sees jihad as the means by which Muslims ensure that the proclamation of the message of Islam can be heard—ridding the world of structures or powers that stand in the way of peacefully and noncoercively proclaiming the truth. Like Mawdudi, Qutb says that jihad is not precisely warfare, but unlike Mawdudi, he does not avoid the subject of violence or military action.

Jihad and proclamation are closely connected:

> Jihad is necessary for proclamation, since its goals are to announce the liberation of man in a manner that will confront the present reality with equivalent means in every aspect, and it does not suffice with hypothetical or theoretical proclamation, whether the Islamic lands are safe or threatened by their neighbors.[15]

He hastily defines the word "peace" as "when the religion is entirely Allah's" (Qur'an 8:39) and maintains that a true state of peace can occur only when people do not have any lords other than Allah. Qutb sees this progression as inherent in the very fabric of Islam:

> The Islamic jihad is a different reality and has no relationship whatsoever with modern warfare—neither with regard to the causes of war or with its apparent conduct. The causes of Islamic jihad have their roots within the very temperament of Islam and its true role in the world, and the very high principles that God has laid down for it.[16]

Jihad does not detract from the fundamental goals of the religion, nor does it in any way contradict Islam. It regulates the relationship between Muslims and non-Muslims. Qutb is clearly indebted to Mawdudi for seeing jihad as a radical and revolutionary proclamation to mankind, and the terms he uses to describe it are identical to those of Mawdudi. Like Mawdudi, Qutb cites few Qur'anic passages in the first half of his treatise. However, the treatise's second half is amply documented with citations to the Qur'an.

Qutb is not an apologist for jihad, nor is he uncomfortable with its implications or with the historical materials that demonstrate the offensive use of war. He states clearly:

> It is the right of Islam to move first, because Islam is not the belief of a [single] group, nor the system of a state, but the way of life of God and a system for the world. Thus it has the right to move to destroy impediments, whether systems or circumstances, that rob the person of the freedom to choose. It does not attack individuals in order to compel them to embrace its creed, but it attacks systems and circumstances in order to liberate the individuals from false influences that corrupt the innate nature [of man] and prevent freedom of choice.[17]

With this understanding of jihad, Qutb clearly arrogates the right to interfere anywhere in the world in which Muslims are not allowed to proclaim Islam freely; the traditional elements of jihad, such as expanding the territory of Islam or even defending its borders, do not seem to interest him. This may stem from the difficulties that he acknowledges in defining "Islam." When so many nominal Muslims are apostate or being ruled by apostate rulers, there are no obvious borders to defend. Radical Muslims during the 1950s, 1960s, and 1970s did not participate in the struggle against Israel, for example, which was of crucial importance to most Arabs (and many non-Arab Muslims as well), nor were they particularly prominent in the struggle against European colonialism. For them, the more pressing issue was the nature of the society that was to be liberated from foreign rule.

Qutb is quite unperturbed by the history of Islam that Mawdudi carefully sidestepped and glossed over. As Qutb states in his *Milestones,* Islam is a general declaration of mankind's freedom. Therefore, the question of whether the Arabs actually "conquered" non-Muslim peoples is irrelevant. By its very nature jihad must be world-wide and aggressive because the stakes are global: either the world hears the message of Islam and is able to freely choose to accept it or reject it, or it does not. Without jihad, the fundamentally anti-God institutions of this world will deny humanity the right to make that choice. Only under Muslim rule can humanity be truly free to choose between Islam and infidelity. Thus Qutb interprets the important verse "there is no compulsion in religion" (2:256) to redefine the issue of compulsion, as well as defensive and offensive war, to the point where these concepts no longer mean what they do in the West.[18]

Qutb does not avoid mentioning the internal jihad or the "greater jihad." He clearly sees the internal jihad as valuable for personal piety, but promoting it to take the place of militant jihad degrades the meaning of Islam by not embracing the militancy that is integral to it. Clearly Qutb is aware that this is a point at which his readers might disagree with him; he preempts such objections with a lengthy discussion of why the Prophet Muhammad did not wage militant jihad when he was in Mecca. This is a key point, frequently brought up by radical Muslims in their writings during the 1970s, 1980s, and 1990s. Qutb anachronistically presents the Meccan milieu as a democracy in which there was freedom to preach. Therefore jihad did not serve an obvious purpose. He lists other reasons why there was no mandate for fighting, none of which, other than the fact of the Muslim minority position at the time, are convincing.

In all of his works Qutb demonstrates himself to be a highly original and courageous thinker. Virtually the only works he cites are the Qur'an and the Prophet Muhammad's biography. In that, he lives up to his message of focusing—protestant-like—upon the "first Qur'anic generation" and largely ignores the *hadith* literature. Nor does Qutb cite Ibn Taymiyya as radical Muslims following him were to do. Because his ideas are simple and simply expressed, it is easy to see why his presentation is a popular one. That *Milestones* was the basis for the charges that led to his execution gives the work an added poignancy: it is his final testament, for which he was willing to die.

SUNNI ANTIGOVERNMENTAL RADICAL ISLAMIC THOUGHT: EGYPT

To a large extent Sayyid Qutb formulated radical Islam as it eventually came to be known throughout the Muslim world. It was not an immediate success. Radical Islam's prominence during the 1980s and 1990s was partly the result of the Muslim leadership's failure to modernize; a more decisive factor, however, was the perception that both secular and religious leaders had failed Islam in regard to Israel. The decisive moment came in June 1967 during the Six Day War between Israel and the neighboring Arab states of Egypt, Jordan, and Syria, during the course of which the three Arab states were defeated and large chunks of their territories appropriated by Israel. Many Arabs had hoped that experiments in Arab socialism and military rule of the 1950s and 1960s, in breaking with the past, would renew their societies by propelling them into modernity. But as a result of the Six Day War, the regimes' promises were revealed to be insubstantial and, more important, unable to fulfill the expectations of their constituencies. There was clearly something fundamentally wrong with Arab Muslim societies.

Radical Muslims argued that the "something wrong" was the neglect of Islam by these semisecular regimes. Many of these radical Muslims had spent years in prison or being hounded by the security apparatus; as a result, they could paint themselves as "out of the office" when the disaster of 1967 happened. This made them attractive to many Arab Muslims, who were frustrated by the turn of events. After the 1977–79 peace negotiations between Anwar al-Sadat of Egypt and Menachem Begin of Israel, it was comparatively easy for radical Muslims to demonize the Egyptian regime and the clerics who supported it as non-Muslims.

Sadat was assassinated by an Egyptian radical group led by Khalid al-Istambuli on October 6, 1981. After the assassination, the Egyptian police found a document titled *al-Farida al-gha'iba (The Neglected Duty)*, penned by 'Abd al-Salam Farag (or Faraj), which was published serially after its discovery. The contents of this document are of the utmost importance in tracing the ideological changes that had been happening in Egyptian radical Islam during the fifteen years since the execution of Sayyid Qutb; they need to be examined in full in order to understand which elements of Qutb's teaching were accepted and amplified and which ones were not. In contradistinction to Qutb, Farag uses the *hadith* literature extensively (as well as Qutb's preferred sources: the Qur'an and the Prophet Muhammad's life) as a source for his deliberations, an indication that Qutb's exclusive focus on the texts associated with the "unique Qur'anic generation" was not acceptable to later radical Muslims. Farag has a much more ambitious conception of why Islam needs jihad. Whereas Qutb felt that jihad was a proclamation of liberation for humanity, Farag maintains with absolute certainty that jihad will enable Muslims to rule the world and to reestablish the caliphate. Probably much of the difference between the two authors has to do with the falling prestige of socialism and communism during the late 1970s, which made Qutb's evocation of these movements' sloganistic invective seem anachronistic to radical Muslims.

Farag presents jihad as a global imperative designed to ensure Islam's conversion of the world. Unlike Qutb, he is not entranced with the notion of free choice for humanity (between Islam and infidelity) that would result from this situation; rather, he speaks of restoring the glory of the Muslim community and combating infidelity directly. There is no indication in Farag's work that he believes that conversion to Islam would be freely chosen after a conquest; people would be attracted to Islam because of its victorious mandate from God.

Basically Farag's message is that jihad has been willfully ignored by Muslim religious leaders (the 'ulama') because of their sycophantic relationship with the apostate "Muslim" political leadership. (As one can see from the actual number of books and tracts on jihad written by 'ulama' during the 1970s and 1980s, Farag's criticism is not necessarily fair.)[19] As far as Farag is concerned, the ultimate triumph of Islam has been prophesied, and all that remains is for Muslims to fulfill this prophecy. He quickly gets to the crux: present-day Muslims are living in states that are ruled by apostates, governing according to laws that are not based upon the *shari'a*. It is imperative for Muslims to establish a Muslim state. No other goal can be allowed to distract the believers from this purpose. Any excuse, such as seeking political power to spread Islam, emigrating from apostate lands, proselytizing, or educating peacefully, is invalid from the beginning.

For many radical Muslims this absolute position was rendered problematic by the struggle against the state of Israel, which could be said to have priority. Farag confronts this issue directly: it is more important to fight the enemy that is near (the apostate regime) than the enemy that is far (Israel). Furthermore,

> Muslim blood will be shed in order to realize this victory [over Israel]. Now it must be asked whether this victory will benefit the interests of an Islamic state? Or will this victory benefit the interests of Infidel rule? It will mean the strengthening of a state which rebels against the Laws of God [the *shari'a*]. . . . These rulers will take advantage of the nationalist ideas of these Muslims in order to realize their un-Islamic aims, even though at the surface [these aims] look Islamic. Fighting has to be done [only] under the Banner of Islam and under Islamic leadership.[20]

This equation between Israel and the apostate rulers of Muslim countries is a bold one, placing Farag and his group well outside the mainstream in the Arabic-speaking Muslim world.

Another seriously problematic issue is whether it is permissible for radical Muslims to wage jihad against forces fighting under the compulsion of an apostate ruler. To deal with this question, Farag places a great deal of weight upon the opinions of Ibn Taymiyya with regard to the Mongols. Since many of the Mongols and their supporters were nominal Muslims (according to Ibn Taymiyya's presentation), the present-day situation, Farag argues, is a re-creation of conditions during the latter half of the thirteenth century. The apostate rulers are only nominally Muslim and are supported by large numbers of people who could be either true Muslims or apostates—there is no way to distinguish among them with certainty (from the perspective of the radical Muslims). Violence against those who support the apostate regime could very well kill "true" Muslims. Ibn Taymiyya's legal ordinances give support to the idea that it is the responsibility of "true" Muslims to prove themselves; anyone who is not making this effort is probably a false Muslim. According to Farag's interpretation, this gives Muslim radicals the freedom to fight and to kill nominal Muslims with the excuse that they should know better than to support the apostate regime.

This raises another difficult question that radical Muslims such as Farag and his followers have had to confront: what is "true" Islam, and how can one define when precisely the boundary between it and "false" Islam is crossed? Gradually the issue coalesced around whether a given regime or elite has openly manifested unbelief (in Islam), refused to implement the *shari'a,* or refused to fight for Islam. If all of these elements are present, then the regime is an infidel regime, although there has continued to be a great deal of discussion about the subject. For Farag and his immediate followers, the issues were more clear-cut; he does not seem to have devoted much time to analyzing whether the regime of al-Sadat was infidel, for the answer to this question was self-evident to him and his group.

Since *al-Farida al-gha'iba* was intended solely for internal consumption, Farag does not have to persuade any serious opponents. Instead, he has to persuade his followers that alternate and religiously mandated methods of living a pious Muslim life are no longer valid given the status of Islam in the society. It is no longer acceptable to be a quietist, to conduct private proclamation and proselytizing under such circumstances. As does Qutb, he also spends some time refuting the idea that present-day Muslims live under the same circumstances as the Prophet Muhammad did in Mecca and are not therefore obligated to fight. But Farag has far less patience with this approach than did Qutb. Unlike almost all radical Muslims, Farag does not avoid addressing the issue of the "greater jihad," which he characterizes as nothing more than a distraction from the actual waging of jihad. Essentially it is the Muslim's responsibility to fight. Ultimately, Farag argues (commenting on Qur'an 9:14), God will intervene and provide the victory:

> This means that a Muslim has first of all the duty to execute the command to fight with his own hands. [Once he has done so] God will then

intervene [and change] the laws of nature. In this way victory will be achieved through the hands of the believers by means of God's [intervention].[21]

Much of the rest of the pamphlet is taken up with discussions concerning Islamically legitimate methods of fighting. Among these are deceiving the enemy, lying to him, attacking by night (even if it leads to accidentally killing innocents), and felling and burning trees of the infidel. Farag confronts questions such as whether one should surrender if the cause is hopeless (no), whether one can use nonbelievers who offer their aid in the battle (yes), the optimal time for going out to fight (on Thursday), and whether it is permissible to attack superior forces with little hope of survival. Farag's affirmative answer to the latter question has given rise to the martyrdom operations or suicide attacks (see chapter 6).

Farag conceives of jihad as a panacea for the Muslim world. According to his analysis, the abandonment of jihad is the principal reason for "the lowness, humiliation, division, and fragmentation in which the Muslims live today."[22] There appears to be no question in his mind that fighting is the only solution to the Muslims' problems; of all the writers surveyed up until this point he comes the closest to seeing jihad as a salvific action, even to the point of reducing Islam to the question of whether or not Muslims fight. Qutb, in his presentation of jihad, spoke of the benefits of Muslim culture, and he appears to have promoted the idea that Muslims have responsibilities toward the world as well as the right to rule (though not to coerce). Farag merely speaks of Muslims' rights and the responsibility of the believers to claim these rights by force.

Therefore, Farag constitutes a transitional figure who founded a completely different type of movement of radical Islam. No longer is the apologetic tone of 'Abduh and Rida acceptable, nor the avoidance of the issues promoted by Mawdudi and even to some extent by Qutb. Farag embraces the whole militant aspect of Muslim history and religious teaching but ignores any part of the Muslim tradition that does not lead him on the path of militant jihad. In a narrow sense he is truer to the first century of conquest than any other Muslim writer, but at the same time he, no less than Mawdudi, he chooses to gloss over and ignore large parts of it.

SHI'ITE ANTIGOVERNMENTAL AND RESISTANCE JIHAD: IRAN AND LEBANON

At the same time as Qutb and Farag were synthesizing their analyses of Sunni Muslim society, Shi'ite religious culture in both Iran and Lebanon was undergoing a transformation. In general, classical Shi'ite doctrines of jihad have been directed not so much against the encroaching outside world as against the Sunni oppressor *(ahl al-baghi)*,[23] and for the most part they are analogous to Sunni Islam's teachings concerning the jihad against the unjust ruler or non-Muslim features of society. However, this attitude has changed dramatically in the recent past. Beginning in the mid-1960s, opposition to Shah Reza Pahlavi (1941–78) in Iran had coalesced around the person of Ayatullah Ruhullah al-Khumayni, who was exiled in 1963. Khumayni incited the Iranian people to reject the shah's attempts to modernize and secularize Iranian society, and these exhortations culminated in the overthrow of the shah in 1978 and Khumayni's triumphal return the next year. Ultimately, Khumayni was successful in establishing an Islamic republic in Iran, and waged a successful—although costly—war against Iraq (1980–88), dying the year after the war's end.

We have already seen, in chapter 2, that Khumayni developed a theory of internal jihad. He also had the distinction of developing Shi'ite doctrines concerning militant jihad. For the most part in his *Vilayat-i Faqih* Khumayni maintains the traditional Shi'ite teachings of jihad against oppressive rulers, usually citing the Prophet Muhammad's grandson, al-Husayn, who was martyred at Karbala' in 680 during what was probably the prelude to an uprising. However, Khumayni expands the term to include liberation from economic exploitation as well as to convey the struggle that Iranian Shi'ites were then waging to establish and develop an independent and powerful Islamic state.[24]

A significant change in jihad doctrine took place after Khumayni came to power and the Islamic Republic of Iran was threatened by the United States (because of the Iranian taking of American diplomats in Tehran as hostages in 1979) and attacked by Iraq in September 1980. On September 13, 1980, Khumayni gave a speech in which he stated:

> The armed forces, the Revolutionary Guards, the gendarmerie, and the police stand ready to defend the country and uphold order, and they are prepared to offer their lives in jihad for the sake of Islam. In addition, a general mobilization of the entire nation is under way, with the nation equipping itself to fight for the sake of Islam and the country.[25]

Clearly under this interpretation jihad was coming to approximate the meaning of the Sunni term, and Khumayni continued to speak of self-sacrifice and militant jihad during the years to come, as did other Shi'ite clerics.[26] The mass mobilization of the population in the Iran-Iraq war served to solidify support for the Islamic republic, and the glorification of the numerous martyrs produced by the war until its end in 1988 created a whole galaxy of new martyrologies.

In Lebanon, the civil war (1975–90) was at its peak during this time. After some thirty years of domination, the Christian (former) majority was gradually losing its grip over the country due to a combined challenge from Sunni Muslims and Palestinian refugees located in the southern part of the country. These groups fought one another in various combinations, until Israel invaded southern Lebanon in 1982 in an apparent attempt to divide authority in the country with the Christians based in northern Lebanon. While Israel had little difficulty defeating and expelling the Palestinians, most of the inhabitants of southern Lebanon were Shi'ites who had long been ignored by the Sunni elite in Beirut. Between 1983 and 1986, the Shi'ites formed a number of militant organizations to attack and expel the Israelis, as well as the international peacekeeping forces (comprising U.S., French, and Italian soldiers) in Beirut. Eventually the Shi'ites pushed the Israelis back to a security zone that they periodically attacked between 1986 and 2000, after which Israel withdrew from Lebanese territory altogether.

These dramatic changes in the Lebanese Shi'ite community—which effectively altered it from a passive, nonpolitical group into a militant and triumphalist one—were brought about by radical modifications to Shi'ite teachings on jihad. Starting in 1983, the Shi'ites, probably led by the Hizbullah or one of its many offshoots, pioneered the extensive use of suicide attacks among radical Muslims (secular Marxist groups such as the Kurdish PKK and the Syrian Social Nationalist Party had been using suicide attacks as a weapon for some time previously).[27] On the morning of October 23, 1983, a truck loaded with explosives killed 241 U.S. Marines, and another attack was launched simultaneously against French troops, killing 56. Between 1983 and 1985, Israeli targets were hit by a succession of suicide attackers, until the Israeli army withdrew to a "security zone," which it continued to occupy until the summer of 2000.

Many prominent Iranian and Lebanese Shi'ite leaders encouraged the suicide attackers and praised them as embodying the ideal of jihad. Apparently Khumayni himself was the first to do so (according to his successor 'Ali Khamenei). Among others who encouraged this type of jihad were the ayatullahs Nasir Makarim al-Shirazi, Husayn Nuri al-Hamdani, Muhammad Fadil al-Lankarani, and Shaykh Muhammad Yazdi. In Lebanon, Ayatullah Muhammad Husayn Fadlallah, the spiritual leader of the Hizbullah, stated: "Martyrdom operations are legal and constitute one of the [legitimate] types of jihad in order to expel the occupier, especially when the occupation began with genocide against the Palestinian people."[28] There is no small irony in the fact that eventually the Hizbullah found suicide attacks to be ineffective against the Israeli army; by 1989, it had abandoned suicide attacks entirely, transforming itself into a guerrilla group that specialized in low-level but imaginative warfare that ultimately brought about an Israeli withdrawal from Lebanon. However, the view of many Muslims, especially Arabic-speaking Muslims, was that the Hizbullah's victory had been achieved by jihad and the application of Islamic principles to the war against Israel. Radical Islam was (and continues to be) a profoundly satisfying synthesis for many Muslims. Although it attracted followers in Egypt throughout the 1980s and 1990s, it first manifested itself powerfully in disputed regions such as Israel and the occupied areas of Gaza and the West Bank, and the Indian province of Kashmir.

RESISTANCE MOVEMENTS: PALESTINE AND KASHMIR

Among all the unresolved problems in the Muslim world, two geopolitical and religious issues stand out: Palestine and Kashmir. The disputes concerning both territories are geographical, religious, and political, and, with regard to Israel at least, economic and cultural as well. Both trace their origins to botched attempts by British colonial authorities to divide lands in order to accommodate irreconcilable claims of their inhabitants. For Arabic-speaking Muslims, the conflict between the state of Israel and the Palestinians has been a continuous focus for the neighboring states of Egypt, Syria, Jordan, and Lebanon, and it has played a major role in the politics of other Arab states as well. Of the numerous wars fought between Israel and the Arab states (1948–49, 1956, 1967, 1973, 1982–84), most resulted in outright Israeli victories. This pattern of defeat led to major social tensions in the defeated Arab countries and ultimately helped persuade Egypt and Jordan to sign peace treaties with Israel so that the ruling elites could concentrate on addressing those tensions.

For the most part, the Palestinians were passive combatants in these wars. After April 1948, the Palestinians played no significant role in the struggle against Israel until the Six Day War of 1967, after which the Palestine Liberation Organization (PLO) came into prominence. During the late 1960s and the 1970s, the PLO carried out a number of violent operations against Israel and Israeli interests in Europe and elsewhere.

For the most part these operations were militarily valueless, directed against noncombatants and intended to attract worldwide attention to the PLO's cause. In all of these operations, Muslims played virtually no part. Indeed, the PLO made a point of representing itself as a progressive secular organization, composed of Christians and Muslims without regard to sectarian affiliation. This posture was unacceptable to Muslims, especially the budding radical Muslim movement in Gaza and the West Bank (occupied by Israel since 1967).

During the fall of 1987, radical Muslims, led by the small Islamic Jihad organization (founded by Fathi al-Shiqaqi), launched several small-scale operations against the Israeli army in Gaza, including some daring prison escapes and attacks. These culminated in the outbreak of the first Intifada on December 3, 1987, which apparently took both the PLO and the radical Muslims (who would later coalesce into Hamas) by surprise. Over the years following, popular Palestinian anger against the occupation was channeled into protests, confrontations with Israeli troops, and nonviolent resistance (including boycotts of Israeli products and refusals to pay taxes to the occupation government) until the beginnings of the negotiations between Israel and the PLO in the early 1990s.

Ironically, the Islamic Jihad organization did not benefit much from all of this. It remained a small organization that did not place much premium upon its own existence and was periodically depleted during the course of fighting. Although nominally the most extreme of the radical Muslim organizations fighting Israel, it has a curiously underplayed religiosity, evident in the group's communiqués. During the weeks prior to the outbreak of the first Intifada, for example, Islamic Jihad suggested a decidedly secular slogan for the people of Gaza: "What do you [Israelis] want with us? Why don't you go to hell!"[29] Religious slogans, Muslim motifs, and citations from the Qur'an or the *hadith* appear only rarely in the collected works of Islamic Jihad's founder, Fathi al-Shiqaqi (assassinated in 1995). Virtually all of the material is revolutionary and semisecular—quite unlike that of other radical Muslim organizations.[30] The Islamic Jihad remains (probably for this reason) a small and experimental organization, having frequently pioneered new tactics in the Palestinian context (such as suicide attacks), but never attempting to attract a mass following.

The much larger radical Muslim organization Hamas (Harakat al-Muqawama al-Islamiyya) was unprepared for the beginning of the Intifada in December 1987. Not only had its members been largely passive (with regard to Israel) during the decade of the 1980s—when many

Israeli leaders had seen them as a counterbalance to the nationalism of the PLO—but the organization was widely viewed as conforming to the stereotypical fatalistic Muslim acceptance of the occupation. This image was so strong that the parent organization of Hamas, al-Mujamma‘ al-Islamiyya (itself closely connected to the Muslim Brotherhood), issued a pamphlet during October 1987 intended to refute the charge that devout Muslims had never played a part in the resistance against Israel,[31] and a substantial part of the Hamas Charter (issued on August 18, 1988, almost nine months after the beginning of the Intifada) deals with this question (e.g., article 7).

To overcome these difficulties, Hamas focused upon the several strengths that it did have. One of the most important of these was the ideological closeness between Palestinian (Hamas) and Egyptian radical Muslims. Since Egypt has always been one of the primary, if not *the* primary, intellectual centers for Arabic-speaking Muslims, this axis gave Hamas access to a vast intellectual underpinning, including the writings of Qutb and Farag, as well as many others. These influences are easily discernible in the Hamas Charter, as well as in its many subsequent communiqués and publications. This connection makes the ideology more securely rooted in the movement of radical Islam, which, in contrast to the socialist-nationalist ideology of the PLO, was on the rise during the late 1980s and early 1990s.

Hamas also acquired for itself some historical depth in several different ways. First, it adopted the figure of ‘Izz al-Din al-Qassam, a rebel against the British mandate in Palestine, who was killed in November 1935 in a shootout with the British authorities. Qassam's "rebellion" (which never exceeded thirty men) can be read in several different ways: the PLO had consistently represented Qassam as a proto-nationalist who pointed the way to the great Palestinian rebellion of 1936–39 that laid the foundations for Palestinian nationalism. Because of its greater need to ground itself historically, Hamas has been much more successful in adopting Qassam, finding resonances in his religious attitude toward fighting the British and the Jews of Palestine, as well as in his pan-Islamism (Qassam was himself a Syrian).[32]

The Hamas Charter contrasts with the semisecular publications of the PLO in that it regularly cites Qur'anic verses as well as *hadith*s that support the message the writers are attempting to communicate.[33] This is a distinguishing feature of the Hamas "style"; it is rare that a paragraph in the communiqués or other publications passes without a citation from traditional Islamic sources. However, these citations are not always taken from the militant literature of classical Islam; in fact, not a single jihad-oriented verse is cited in the Hamas Charter, although jihad is a common theme in the organization's communiqués. The Charter itself is the constitution of an organization that seeks to establish a complete Islamic society and does not focus specifically upon jihad. Article 15 addresses methods to be employed in order to defeat Israel, but its specific provisions with regard to jihad state only that it has become an obligation of all Muslims at the present time. This article and other provisions of the Charter (especially article 34) demonstrate a grasp of history from the Muslim perspective and trace the roots of the conflict back to the time of the Prophet Muhammad.

Twenty-five leaflets published by Hamas between January 1988 and May 1991 (out of seventy-four issued, according to the Hamas numbering system), collected by Shaul Mishal and Reuven Aharoni, expand on these themes, calling (with Islamic slogans) for repeated confrontations with the Israelis and adducing numerous historical precedents of Muslims who fought the Crusaders (Salah al-Din) or the Jews (such as Muhammad at Khaybar). These works emphasize the importance of Palestine (and particularly Jerusalem) for Islam. Frequently they praise the religious steadfastness of the Palestinians; they encourage the Palestinians to be *murabitun*—Muslim guardians of the borders (as opposed to the secular PLO doctrine of *sumud*, steadfastness)—and deal with issues such as the PLO's negotiations with Israel or the question of Palestinian (and especially Hamas) prisoners in Israel.[34]

During the first Intifada, Hamas was insufficiently large to play a substantial role in the confrontation with Israel. Increasingly during the 1990s, it played another role, attracting those disaffected by the negotiations between Israel and the Palestinian National Authority (PNA) under Yasser Arafat (1992–2000). Arafat has clearly used Hamas in something of a "good cop, bad cop" routine with Israel, since there is some plausible deniability as to his responsibility for its actions. Suffice it to say, that since the first signature of peace between Israel and the PNA in September 1993—an agreement that was fundamentally, and on principle, unacceptable to Hamas—Hamas has continued the struggle with Israel as a means by which to eventually take power and establish an Islamic state in Palestine. It has carefully avoided violence against the PNA and acquired great spiritual prestige among Palestinians and Muslims worldwide by constantly attacking Israel and responding to what Palestinians perceive as Israeli aggression or oppression.

These responses have two distinct phases: the period between 1993 and 2000 when Hamas conducted operations that were inimical to the PNA's stated goals (although arguably in line with its overall strategy), and a second, ongoing phase that began in 2000 comprising operations conducted in tandem with the PNA. During the first period, on several occasions Hamas's attacks upon Israel brought down upon it the wrath of the PNA (in 1994 and 1996), and as a result its operations were fairly minimal between 1997 and 2000. With the beginning of the second Intifada in September 2000, the PNA has progressively lost control over both territory and supporters to Hamas. For the first time in the organization's history, it is poised to take control of the Palestinian leadership. Between December 2000 and July 2003 Hamas and Islamic Jihad conducted a large number of suicide attacks against Israeli targets, usually civilians (approximately ninety of these were successful; a somewhat larger number of attempts were thwarted). The al-Aqsa Martyrs Brigade (associated with the PNA) has adopted the tactic,[35] a disturbing trend for the PNA, since it highlights the organization's comparative loss of leadership and obligates the PNA to follow the Islamic organizations it had previously scorned.

Fundamentally, Palestinian radical Muslims suffer from several strategic weaknesses, one of which is that they tend to fight atomistically, so it is not difficult for the Israeli army to grind them down over the long run. Another major problem is fine-tuning their actions to fit their ideological and propaganda needs. Since 1994, Islamic Jihad and Hamas's primary violent expression has been the suicide attack or martyrdom operation (about which see chapter 6), which creates a number of problems for the Palestinians' image abroad. Although one might conclude that world opinion means nothing to Hamas, and that the organization is fighting exclusively for an Arab or a Muslim audience, in the long term Hamas must consider what individual and cumulative operations do to and for the Palestinian cause. Since Palestinian radical Muslims look to the martyrdom operations as a means of evening out the dramatic military and economic disparity with Israel, they have come to depend upon it excessively. The extensive use of military or paramilitary operations is one of the features that distinguishes the second Intifada from the first, and it has to a large extent denied the Palestinians their most potent weapon against Israel: perceived moral superiority. This has led Palestinians to openly question their own choice of tactics.[36]

For many Muslims of the Indian Subcontinent—India and Pakistan primarily, but large expatriate communities in Europe and North America as well—the issue of the independence—or at least the self-determination—of the Indian province of Kashmir (in northern India, close to the Himalayan Mountains) is of considerable importance. At the time of the Indian partition in 1947, the region had a Muslim majority; its ruler, who was Hindu, made the decision to join the territory to India rather than to Pakistan. It is no longer possible to judge objectively whether this decision was against the will of his subjects, nor whether decisions about the Kashmir's figure were more appropriately vested in the ruler or in his subjects: these questions now are buried under an avalanche of polemics on both sides. Part of the province was subsequently invaded and occupied by Pakistan; this area (usually called by Pakistanis "Free Kashmir") is sparsely inhabited, and the remainder of Kashmir (and the bulk of its population), concentrated in the Valley of Kashmir, was controlled by India.

This issue has remained a sore point between India and Pakistan. Pro-self-determination riots began in 1989 (note the similarities to the outbreak of the Intifada among Palestinians two years previously), and many Muslim Kashmiris were even sympathetic to an independence movement. Throughout the 1990s Pakistani groups gathered in "Free Kashmir" to launch raids in the Indian-ruled part of the province, and these activities took the character of a jihad. The precise goals of this jihad are unclear since a number of Pakistani radical Muslim groups have called for the union of all Muslims in the subcontinent into one state (India itself is between 11 and 12 percent Muslim, although the Muslim population is not concentrated geographically, and it is doubtful that more than a tiny minority is in accord with the goals of radical Islam).

Radical Pakistani and international Muslim groups (for the most part), throughout the 1990s, united in the Harakat al-Mujahidin led by Fazl al-Rahman Khalil, conducted guerrilla operations against the Indian army and against India's civilian population. Moderate Muslim leaders have been assassinated and threatened with assassination so that the differences between the indigenous Kashmiri movement and global radical Islam have become blurred (Khalil, for example, signed a number of Usama b. Ladin's declarations). Since the year 2000, two other organizations have largely taken the place of the Harakat al-Mujahidin: Lashkar-i Tayba and Jaysh-i Muhammad. Lashkar is led by Mohammed Masood Azhar (imprisoned in India from 1994 to 1999), who has written on jihad extensively, although these documents are not very original and do not add very much to our understanding of the issues.[37]

Usually the conflict in Kashmir is presented by Muslim advocates in terms of justice, with globalist ramifications. (As I stated earlier, it is not clear whether the cause of Kashmiri self-determination or independence is served by the close link with globalist radical Islam.)[38] This is revealed by 'Abd al-Rahman Makki, another leader of the Lashkar, who sees the liberation of Kashmir first as an Islamic imperative, but also as a means to ensure the Muslim future of Pakistan. Without this process of constant fighting, Makki fears that the Muslims will become too settled and sedentary and will never advance toward the greater goal: the Islamization of all India. His rhetoric raises the question of whether victory in Kashmir would be beneficial for the radical Muslims. It may very well be that they have deliberately prolonged the conflict in order to highlight and promote their larger goals.[39] Ultimately the Kashmiri cause has merged with globalist radical Islam in a way that the Palestinians have thus far sought to avoid.

ALGERIA: THE CONTINUATION OF RADICAL MUSLIM ANTIGOVERNMENTAL JIHAD

The Gulf War of 1990–91 had a number of unintended effects, one of the most long-lasting of which has been the Algerian civil war. Huge antigovernment demonstrations arose in Algeria during the Gulf War, although they were peripheral to the fighting going on and clearly focused upon the government. For years there had been a profound gap between the governmental elite, still largely secular and heavily influenced by French law and social policy almost thirty years after independence, and the nation's conservative, Muslim population. The regime had failed to deliver on promises of a developed society, and Algeria's oil wealth of the 1970s and early 1980s had disappeared, most probably into the corrupt and inefficient bureaucracy. With heavy population growth and little prospect of employment in Algeria, many young people went to Europe, especially to France, to find work. But by the late 1980s, emigration was curtailed as France drifted to the right politically and began to restrict immigration, especially Muslim immigrants.

These tensions came to a head in 1992, when the first round of the Algerian national elections gave a decisive victory to the Islamic National Salvation Front. The secular Algerian army (supported by France) responded with a military coup and called off the second round of elections scheduled for that year. This touched off a civil war that still dominates Algeria and shows little sign of abating. Initially, the radical Muslim group, al-Jabha al-Islamiyya li-l-Inqadh (the Islamic Salvation Front), demonstrated itself to be a radical social movement whose politics (and capacities) stopped short of full-fledged warfare.[40] However, a splinter group, al-Jama'a al-Islamiyya al-Musallaha (the Armed Islamic Group, usually known as the GIA), quickly demonstrated its mastery of war. It began to root out any and all foreign influences (according to its interpretation) from Algeria with a series of murders—usually of unarmed civilians such as monks, sailors, and journalists—designed to spread terror.

This spiral of terror quickly spread to secular Algerians, especially intellectuals and Westernized women, who were particular targets. In 1994 the GIA hijacked a plane to Marseilles, where it was captured by French commandos. It is clear that the hijackers had intended to crash the plane into the middle of Paris in order to protest French support for the Algerian government. During the late 1990s, there were repeated instances of massacres in areas supportive of the GIA—massacres that were often difficult for outside observers to interpret. Were they conducted by the radical Muslim rebels in an attempt to solidify their rule or by the government trying to extirpate and terrorize populations sympathetic to the rebels? The question remains unresolved. However, the proclamation of September 1995 by the GIA (see appendix) made the matter academic for many, since the group proclaimed that it would slaughter and rape anyone who opposed it. Such a fierce and uncompromising stand brought about a split in the GIA and ultimately led to the formation of other groups.

In 1998, the GIA collapsed and began to negotiate with the Algerian government. Its military position had been weakening for some time previously, and that of the government—with international support—had become considerably stronger. Dissidents from the GIA then founded al-Jama'a al-Salafiyya li-Da'wa wa-l-Qital (the Salafiyya Group for Proclamation and Fighting), which since that time has been the primary expression of radical Islam in Algeria. Its first communiqué tells the tale:

> The glory of this Islamic community is concealed within its holding fast to its religion, and its jihad against its enemies, according to the word: "When you sell with *'ina* [an illegal financial transaction], grasp the tails of cattle, are satisfied with farming, and have left jihad, then God will cause humiliation to overtake you that will not leave you until you return to your religion." The fact that enemies have overpowered us, owning the power over the Muslims and their possessions is nothing

more than the result of their shunning the straight path of God and their ignoring fighting *(jihad)* of their enemies.[41]

This is the standard radical Muslim explanation of the wrongs suffered by contemporary Muslim society along the lines that Qutb and Farag had already laid down.

Frequently the Jamaʿa has issued proclamations of innocence with regard to slaughters and rapes; these statements are clearly attempts by the radical Muslims to regain their credibility. In 2002 the group issued a statement criticizing the well-known Palestinian radical Abu Qatada, who had issued a legal ruling *(fatwa)* entitled "Allowing the killing of the children of the apostates [i.e., the secular Muslims] in order to lift the torment of the children of the *mujahidin*."[42] Clearly the endorsement of such a *fatwa* would have been politically disastrous for the *mujahidin,* similar to what happened to the GIA in 1995, but the fact that other radical Muslims were thinking along these lines demonstrates the difficulty of maintaining balance and public trust during civil war. Just as with the Kashmiris' failure against India, the Jamaʿa's failure in Algeria has brought it closer to globalist radical Islam during recent years.

Fundamentally, the Algerian radical Muslims made the mistake of targeting foreigners at the beginning of their insurrection. By deliberately striking at these soft targets and murdering them in gruesome ways, they lost all non-Muslim (and a great deal of Muslim) sympathy for their cause and allowed the Algerian government to paint them as barbaric. Protests by foreign governments of these actions have little effect, either on the violence or on bringing those responsible to justice, and it may be years before truth and falsehood are sorted out with regard to the ultimate responsibility for the many massacres. Both the GIA and the Jamaʿa al-Salafiyya have maintained that they are not responsible for many of the massacres. This claim may be partly true, yet the groups' tactic of murdering foreigners during the early 1990s and continuing to threaten outsiders effectively destroyed the credibility of their case even before it was made. The fact is that those foreigners were the radical Muslims' only real protection against the oppression of the Algerian government. Strikes against foreigners afforded the regime wide latitude in its treatment of the radical organizations.

CONTEMPORARY JIHAD THEORY

Not all contemporary Muslim thinkers who have written about jihad have been radical Muslims, nor would all associate themselves with antigovernmental jihad—let alone the globalist radical jihad to be described in chapter 6. Despite Farag's complaint that the Muslim religious leadership has largely ignored the issue of jihad, a large number of major works about the subject have been composed over the past several decades. In general, these works continue the two major lines of thought dealt with in this chapter: either jihad is defensive and concerned primarily with the proclamation of Islam, or it is militant and aggressive, intended to revive the fortunes of Islam and take it to new heights.

Professor Muhammad Sa'id al-Buti of Damascus University best exemplifies the first trend. He clearly emphasizes the role of positive proclamation in jihad, and although he does not negate the role of fighting altogether, his emphasis is on jihad as a defensive measure:

> It becomes axiomatic that the responsibility for guarding and defending these two possessions [Islam's territorial abode, and the Islamic society] cannot be fulfilled by peaceful jihad, by tongue or da'wa [proclamation]. It is a task that can only be achieved by driving back aggressors, repelling them and foiling any dangers likely to be caused by them.[43]

For al-Buti, belligerent jihad or jihad without an obviously defensive purpose is an oxymoron, so he describes it by using a comparatively uncommon word, *hiraba* (belligerency), that does not appear very often in the classical legal texts. *Hiraba* communicates for al-Buti that state when Muslims are aware of the obviously aggressive intentions of a foreign power or state and reserve the right for themselves to strike preemptively against this enemy. According to him, this was the dominant feature of the last years of the Prophet Muhammad's warfare against the Jews and pagan Arab tribes.

Al-Buti also has to deal with the discriminatory social system against non-Muslims (exemplified by the payment of the *jizya*) that is upheld by waging jihad. Again, his treatment of the subject is highly apologetic; Muslims do not compel non-Muslims to take a lower social position. Even in these instances, al-Buti makes it clear that the needs of the Islamic state are paramount:

> What is *logically* [emphasis in original] required is that the Islamic country must establish its foundations firmly and its structure forcibly in order to become strong, mighty, dignified and awe-inspiring lest it become liable to attack and aggression . . . includ[ing] among many other things, arousing sectarian tendencies, creating religious differences between Muslim and non-Muslim citizens with the ultimate aim of creating chaos and anarchy in the Islamic state.[44]

Al-Buti does not seriously address the historical questions that his analysis of Muslim and non-Muslim relations raises.[45] The English translation of al-Buti's book omits a significant portion of his work, notably the chapters in which he addresses the permissibility of jihad against a regime, following the arguments of Qutb and Farag. Together with other Syrian Muslim leaders, such as Nasir al-Din al-Albani, al-Buti opposes such a jihad. (Al-Buti is not, however completely in accord with al-Albani, taking issue with al-Albani's well-known call for all Palestinians to leave Israel, the West Bank, and Gaza so that these territories could be declared *dar al-kufr,* an infidel land.)[46]

The responses of al-Buti to his critics, published in the third edition of *al-Jihad fi al-Islam,* give some indication of the extent to which some readers have found his theories problematic. Whereas earlier non-Arab writers such as Mawdudi could get away with a radical reinterpretation of the Qur'an and Muslim history, al-Buti's comparatively tolerant and defensive approach to jihad has aroused considerable opposition. For example, one of his readers was troubled by al-Buti's definition of the territory of Islam, objecting to the omission of Spain: "isn't it necessary for all the Muslims to purify it from the rapacious aggressors, and to return it to the Islamic state?"[47] Al-Buti, in response, maintains that Spain must be re-Islamized (conquered?):

> Al-Andalus [Spain] remains part of the territory of Islam *(dar al-Islam)* legally, and Muslims bear the responsibility, according to the jurists, of returning it back to the fold of Islam. The Muslims' neglect of their responsibility during all of these centuries does not change this obligation one bit.[48]

Clearly al-Buti's tolerant approach has limits. For the most part, his critics have focused upon his prioritizing of the jihad of proclamation over the jihad of fighting. Al-Buti framed the discourse concerning the question of legitimate fighting in order to conform with present-day standards: jihad, he argues, can be declared only to deal with aggressive behavior on the part of another non-Muslim group or state. For radical Muslims, this entirely misses the point.

Al-Ghunaymi, one of al-Buti's critics, focuses on this issue. Muslims do not fight to repel aggression; they fight to put an end to infidelity. In order to support this position, al-Ghunaymi adduces a host of Qur'anic and legal citations from the classical sources. Since al-Ghunaymi sees a pattern of non-Muslim aggression against Muslims throughout history, it is not surprising that he feels that jihad is justified any place and any time Muslims feel it to be justified.[49]

This position is also taken by the Saudi writer al-Qadiri, who is very truimphalist in his description of the purpose and scope of jihad. However, al-Qadiri demonstrates some interesting developments. Almost alone among writers sympathetic to radical Islam, he does not hesitate to include a discussion of the "greater jihad"—although he does not cite the conventional traditions probably because they do not appear in the canonical collections—and tries to assimilate this doctrine into his overall description of warfare. For al-Qadiri, spiritual warfare is an integral part of military warfare, and he believes that one of the reasons why Muslims repeatedly fail on the battlefield is precisely because they do not arrive upon it spiritually prepared. Although other radical Muslims stress this spiritual preparation for warfare as well, for most of these writers the issue of the "greater jihad" raises the uncomfortable fact of Sufism—the mystical interpretation of Islam—to which most of them are quite hostile. Only al-Qadiri seems to feel that the "greater jihad" is a necessary component of warfare. For al-Qadiri, like most radical Muslims, the reasons for jihad are clear: to glorify the believers and to humiliate the unbelievers. Once jihad is proclaimed, there is no question that the Muslims will be victorious and that infidels will freely convert to Islam in waves. Jihad will unify the Muslim world and cause the broader community of Muslims to be more connected to Islam. Finally, it will enlighten the world with the light of Islam.[50]

The most impressive work on the subject of jihad written during the 1990s was the three-volume summary and discussion of the subject by Muhammad Khayr Haykal entitled *al-Jihad wa-l-qital fi al-siyasa al-shara'iyya (Jihad and Fighting according to the Shar'i Policy).* Among the many unusual subjects Haykal discusses—only rarely addressed in jihad literature—are whether or not women can be fighters in a jihad, whether it is Islamically legitimate to use weapons of mass destruction, and whether and under what circumstances it would be permissible for a Muslim army to surrender. The following summary of Haykal's research and discussion cannot do him justice, and only a few of the more unusual issues he raises can be dealt with.

For the most part, mainstream Muslim writers on jihad avoid the favorite radical Muslim topic: can jihad be declared against an unjust Muslim ruler? (This is primarily the realm of Qutb, Farag, and their radical Muslim followers.) Haykal, however, confronts this issue squarely, maintaining that under certain circumstances fighting the unjust Muslim ruler must be considered to be legitimate jihad. In defining jihad, Haykal, very conscious of Muslim history and consistently relating all of his discussions to the Prophet Muhammad's life, he asks whether the Prophet's wars were defensive or offensive. Haykal is perfectly aware of the apologetic strain of thought represented by Mawdudi and others.

He points out that their opinions are directly contradictory to those held by classical Muslim scholars (such as Ibn Kathir), who consistently define jihad as offensive war. In the end, Haykal himself takes a fence-sitting position, calling the early Muslim conquests "offensive defense," and citing, unusually, the experience of the United States in fighting Japan during World War II. He interprets the Pacific Campaign as an "offensive defense": although the United States was attacked first and without provocation, it responded with such overwhelming power as to totally destroy the Japanese.[51] He neglects, however, to cite a comparable example that would apply to documented conflicts between Muslims and non-Muslims.

Haykal lists the possible reasons for declaring jihad, after summarizing all the classical and contemporary viewpoints. He states that all authors concur that aggression against Muslims is a reason for jihad, as is (for most scholars), attacking non-Muslims under the protection of Muslims (*dhimmi*s). Many, but not all, of the writers he surveys maintain that the propagation of Islam and protection of Muslim missionaries is a legitimate reason for jihad, but he notes few dissenters who argue that modern communications technology (radio, television, and the Internet) have mooted the declaration of jihad in order to proclaim the truth. Few of the authors consider that adding land to the lands of Islam constitutes a legitimate reason for jihad.[52] Haykal demonstrates himself willing to ask tough questions when he says: Can we say that jihad constitutes interference in the internal affairs of non-Muslim countries? He answers:

> The answer is unequivocally yes! May Allah be praised and thanked for this, that in the name of humanity that comprehends its true interests, the interference of Muslims in the internal affairs of others is not like the foxes and wolves in the affairs of the weak of Allah's creation—in order to satisfy their craving for prey—but it is like the interference of fathers and mothers in the affairs of their children with the purpose of establishing truth and justice between them, and to sow love and mercy in their hearts.[53]

This is one of the rare occasions where Haykal drifts into apologetics.

On a more serious note, he asks other tough questions. Are there occasions when jihad is disapproved of or even forbidden? He then names them: it is disapproved of when it is undertaken without the permission of the *imam* (legitimate authority), when using weapons of mass destruction, and (according to some authorities) when attacks are mounted at night; forbidden when parents forbid it (except when jihad is considered to be *fard ʿayn*, incumbent upon all Muslims), or when it would cause harm to the Muslims. Haykal also spends a good deal of time discussing whether women can take part in jihad (he allows it under some circumstances), and the types of deception that are permissible in war. What are the outer limits of the trickery and lying that the *shariʿa* permits under these circumstances? In general, the answer to this last question is that the limits are removed according to the exigency of the situation. Haykal also raises the issue of the use of human shields, especially civilians. Since he considers it unlikely that Muslims would use human shields, his principal focus is on whether Muslims should attack if an enemy uses non-Muslim or Muslim civilians to protect themselves. In general, Haykal opposes attacking an enemy that uses human shields.

Almost alone among the contemporary jihad thinkers, Haykal discusses weapons of mass destruction and their legality in jihad. Just as the radical Muslims (in chapter 6) made use of the analogy of the mangonel in battle, Haykal argues that the fact that the Prophet Muhammad was known to have approved the mangonel, even though its destructive power is indiscriminate, constitutes a legitimization of the contemporary use of weapons of mass destruction. He states:

> Yes, these two are connected one to another, despite the great difference between them with regard to the range of danger and the scope of influence . . . this is because the contemporary weaponry is within the definition of the legal texts which allow the use of any and every military weapon or tactic against an enemy during combat. . . . Thus, building upon this foundation, it is permitted to use contemporary weaponry such as the atomic bomb.[54]

Haykal supplements this ruling by saying that if possible the land(s) targeted by weapons of mass destruction should be free of Muslims, but he recognizes that this stipulation is not very realistic in the modern world.

All in all, Haykal writes in a factual tone and addresses most of the toughest questions that need to be faced by someone who writes on jihad. It is clear that his mastery of the subject is nearly total, and I have been unable to find any major writer or trend in classical jihad and legal literature that he does not summarize or address in some way. For the most part, his judgments are fair, pragmatic, and free from any apologetics, and his basic doctrines can be summed up by saying that jihad is regulated warfare, but that the regulation of jihad is subject to the needs of the Muslim community on a case-by-case basis. Haykal's discussions have much in common with radical Muslim, especially globalist radical Muslim, thinking on the subject of jihad. Like Haykal, these writers have sought to shed apologetics from discussions of jihad; unlike Haykal, they have practical command of followers who are willing to die for their causes.

SIX

GLOBALIST RADICAL ISLAM AND MARTYRDOM OPERATIONS

To a large extent the agent of the transition from contemporary jihad theorists and local Muslim resistance movements to globalist radical Islam was the Palestinian radical ʿAbdallah ʿAzzam. ʿAzzam's method of fighting for the sake of Islam, rather than for the sake of Palestinian nationalism, against Israel found little support among Palestinians during the 1970s (the heyday of the leftist and secularist Palestine Liberation Organization and its many associates). When the Soviet Union invaded Afghanistan in 1979, ʿAzzam moved to Peshawar (Pakistan), where he began to preach a globalist and salvific variety of jihad to audiences that, over time, comprised volunteers from all over the Muslim world.

For many, this equation of jihad with the war in Afghanistan was powerful and liberating. Although the largely Arab Muslim volunteers probably played only a small part in the eventual defeat of the Soviet forces in Afghanistan, the campaign was the first time in centuries that people from all over the Muslim world had gathered together—irrespective of their ethnic and sometimes doctrinal differences—to fight exclusively *for the sake of Islam*. Thus, the battlefield of Afghanistan was the religious and social incubator for globalist radical Islam in that it established contacts among a wide variety of radicals from Muslim antigovernmental and resistance movements and fused them together.

ʿAzzam's writings have been published extensively (although today they are banned most in Arabic-speaking countries),[1] and they are frequently cited by contemporary radical Muslims. First and foremost,

ʿAzzam emphasized that jihad, and jihad *alone* would resurrect the Muslim world, re-create the primal Muslim society from the time of the Prophet Muhammad, unify world Muslims, and establish a state that would encompass all Muslims and be a world-wide power for the proclamation of Islam. ʿAzzam had a strong belief in the power of martyrdom to persuade and move people—a belief that probably has not been equaled in Sunni Islam since the conquests of the seventh and eighth centuries. His statements in this regard are extremely frank:

> The life of the Muslim *umma* [community] is solely dependent on the ink of its scholars and the blood of its martyrs. What is more beautiful than the writing of the *umma*'s history with both the ink of a scholar and his blood, such that the map of Islamic history becomes colored with two lines: one of them black—that is what the scholar wrote with the ink of his pen—and the other one red—what the martyr wrote with his blood. And something more beautiful than this is when the blood is one and the pen is one, so that the hand of the scholar, which expends and moves the pen, is the same as the hand that expends its blood and moves the *umma*. The extent to which the number of martyred scholars increases is the extent to which nations are delivered from their slumber, rescued from their decline and awoken from their sleep.[2]

The alliance that ʿAzzam sought to create united scholars and warriors—ideally in the same person—and he hoped to utilize their sacrificial example in order to liberate the Muslim world, and re-create its glory.

ʿAzzam was not under any illusions as to the likely cost of this endeavor, since he writes immediately following the above statement:

> History does not write its lines except with blood. Glory does not build its lofty edifices except with skulls. Honor and respect cannot be established except on a foundation of cripples and corpses. Empires, distinguished peoples, states, and societies cannot be established except with examples. Indeed, those who think that they can change reality or change societies without blood, sacrifices, and invalids—without pure innocent souls—do not understand the essence of this *din* [Islam] and they do not know the method of the best of Messengers [Muhammad].[3]

No other Muslim writer prior to ʿAzzam had been quite so explicit about the nature of martyrdom and the consequences of fighting. Muslim jihad literature often tends to idealize warfare, concentrating upon the glories of the charge, the noble rank of the martyr, and the spiritual significance of fighting. Nowhere in the literature, until the time of ʿAzzam, is there mention of war's human consequences: cripples, suffering, corpses, and the like. To his credit, ʿAzzam does not flinch from acknowledging the inevitable results of the salvific warfare he preaches.

'Azzam has to a large degree practiced what he preached, and he provides the Muslim world with an obvious example of a capable man who did not spend his life in the pursuit of wealth or status, but lived for the sake of Islam and jihad. In what is probably his most popular call to battle, *Ilhaq bi-l-qafila (Join the Caravan)*, 'Azzam called for Muslims everywhere to come to Afghanistan and fight. His tremendous spiritual prestige made him a magnet for many, and he frequently proclaimed that jihad was incumbent upon all Muslims while Afghanistan and Palestine were occupied by non-Muslims. 'Azzam did not forget his homeland. Instead he saw Afghanistan as a place where jihad could be established, far away from strong secular governments bent upon suppressing radical Islam. After the jihad in Afghanistan was successful, then the *mujahidin* could fight Israel.[4]

'Azzam's call to battle was based on the hope that warfare would revolutionize Muslim society and turn it away from failure and impotence. He maintained that jihad was a sacrament on the level of the five pillars of Islam (the *shahada,* the five prayers, charity, fasting during Ramadan, and the *hajj* to Mecca), and that every Muslim who did not participate in jihad was living in a state of sin. He stated:

> I believe that every Muslim on earth bears the responsibility of abandoning jihad and the sin of abandoning the gun. Every Muslim who passes away without a gun in his hand faces Allah with the sin of abandoning fighting. Now, jihad is compulsory upon each and every Muslim on earth except those who are exempted [he lists the blind, the terminally ill, the lame, the oppressed, and those who cannot find their way to the battlefield], and by definition a compulsory act is an act that brings reward or punishment.[5]

This is a revolutionary restatement of the nature of jihad. Although prior authors had noted that sinful acts might accompany jihad (such as cowardice or fleeing from the battlefield), 'Azzam defines the avoidance of jihad in a contemporary context as a sin in itself. However, 'Azzam goes even further and unambiguously accuses the entire Muslim world of complicity in the war:

> I believe that the Muslim *umma* is responsible for the honor of every Muslim woman that is being violated in Afghanistan and is responsible for every drop of Muslim blood that is being shed unjustly—therefore they are an accessory to these crimes.[6]

This is a more personal indictment of the Muslim world for abandoning jihad than had been previously (or has since) been issued: Jihad is the sole operative criterion on which a Muslim should judge his faith, according to ʿAzzam.

In addition to these ringing statements, ʿAzzam also wrote a great many other works, including a study of *sura* 9 (al-Tawba), which is a locus for most of the important teachings concerning jihad in the Qurʾan. He established martyrologies for the fighters (see below), gave legal opinions on subjects such as killing the elderly, women, and children during warfare, and the execution of prisoners, and wrote some very vivid accounts of fighting on the front line. Like Ibn Taymiyya before him, ʿAbdallah ʿAzzam has come to exemplify globalist radical Islam.

ʿAzzam, assassinated in 1989, did not live to witness the Soviet withdrawal from Afghanistan. But success for the *mujahidin* was not precisely what they had expected. After the heady experience of working with groups from all over the Muslim world to "defeat" the Soviet Union—one of the world's two superpowers—the allies of the *mujahidin* were shocked by the experience of returning to their own countries in the early 1990s. In these countries they saw Islam dominated by government appointees, who often failed to adhere to what radical Muslims saw as core Islamic values. Throughout the 1990s there were periodic peace negotiations between various Arab and Muslim governments and Israel—a process that was fundamentally unacceptable to radical Muslims (and many other Muslims as well).

GLOBALIST RADICAL ISLAM:
THE EMERGENCE OF USAMA B. LADIN

Many of the groups discussed in chapter 5 fall under the category of radical Islam. Here we will discuss the characteristics of globalist radical Islam as developed during the 1990s. This development had several different axes that eventually merged. First among them was the unifying figure of Usama b. Ladin, a Saudi radical who had fought in Afghanistan, studied with ʿAzzam, and eventually served as a rallying point for the Arab "Afghani" volunteers after the liberation of Afghanistan. After the victory of the *mujahidin* in the early 1990s, Bin Ladin sought to unify the fighters under the banner of globalist radical Islam in an organization called Qaʿidat al-Jihad (the Base, or Foundation, of Jihad) founded in 1988. This attempt at unification was a failure, as was Bin Ladin's proposal to gather his *mujahidin* in 1990–91 to defend Saudi Arabia against Iraqi invasion. The Saudi Arabian government did not take this proposal seriously and instead invited the United States to take up positions in the region.

In 1991 Bin Ladin left Saudi Arabia for the Sudan, which had been ruled since 1989 by the radical Muslim regime of General 'Umar Bashir, and sought to provide refuge and work for the "Afghani" Arabs who were viewed with deep suspicion by their own governments and often put under surveillance or detained.[7] This interlude ended with Bin Ladin's expulsion from the Sudan in 1996, whereupon he went to Afghanistan and began working in earnest for the cause of globalist radical Islam.

One of the most surprising events of the 1990s was the transformation of the major Egyptian radical Muslim group, the Gama'at al-Islamiyya, from an antigovernmental movement into part of the globalist coalition. Egyptian radical Islam, as one might gather from chapter 5, had always been at the forefront of leadership and innovative ideas, just as Egypt is one of the principal intellectual centers for contemporary Arabic culture. During the middle 1990s, the Gama'at fought a campaign to overthrow the semisecular Egyptian government of Husni Mubarak. Basing themselves in Middle Egypt (a region heavily populated by Coptic Christians) and Cairo, radical Egyptian Muslims used terror and assassination to accomplish their goals.

Probably their most impressive document is the much-published section of *al-Qawl al-Qati'* *(The Decisive Word)* entitled "Seven Misconceptions in Fighting the Apostate Ruler and His Regime."[8] Although the logic of the argument has not advanced significantly beyond that of Farag (see chapter 5), the authoritative manner of its communication makes it a significant statement, especially when it is compared to the activities of the Gama'at during the same period. This document sought to deflect criticism of the group as it transformed itself from a radical Muslim antigovernment movement into one that was willing to kill its opponents and their supporters more or less indiscriminately in the manner of the Algerian Jama'a al-Islamiyya al-Musalliha. Each of the "Seven Misconceptions" deals with the ethical problems of killing Muslims and fighting armed units that keep the Muslims from attaining power, including those who assist the regime voluntarily (e.g., the police), and those who are compelled to assist the regime (e.g., soldiers). The final two "Misconceptions" address the question of legitimate jihad; should it not be proclaimed by a righteous *imam* alone? Classical jurists made it clear that one should not rebel against a ruler who prays (the five prayers). "Seven Misconceptions" goes a long way to alleviate the fears of radical Muslims and provides a link with globalist radical

Islam by maintaining that the above questions can be resolved only when one believes that the goal of an Islamic state justifies the means to attain it. Certainly throughout the 1990s, the Gama'at provided good reason to believe that it would be successful in the long run.

Given the assured tone of the document, one might have been astonished to find that in early 1998 Ayman al-Zawahiri, the *amir* (leader) of the Gama'at, had placed himself under the authority of Usama b. Ladin. That an Egyptian who is a highly qualified doctor and a reasonably effective leader should subordinate his group (and eventually amalgamate it) to al-Qa'ida was surprising. This clearly represents an abrupt turn from the hitherto antigovernmental aspect of al-Gama'at to the globalist radical Muslim ideology of al-Qa'ida; it also demonstrates an admission of failure with regard to Egypt. What could have caused such a shift?

Beginning in 1995, the Gama'at launched a series of terrorist operations in Egypt intended to bring down the government. These included an assassination attempt on President Mubarak on June 26, 1995, and the murder of thirty Greek tourists on April 28, 1996. (The Gama'at had intended to attack Israeli tourists, but the Greeks had switched buses with the Israeli group at the last moment.) The campaign culminated in the murder of fifty-eight tourists (most of them Swiss) at the Temple of Queen Hatshepsut in Luxor on November 17, 1997. The Gama'at had previously warned tourists to stay away from Egypt in an attempt to damage the country's tourist industry, which was (and remains) fundamental to the nation's economy. The Luxor operation was clearly intended to make good this threat, and it in fact led to the collapse of tourism in Egypt between 1998 and 1999. But these acts, intended drive a wedge between the government and the Egyptian people, exposed the Gama'at to the full wrath of virtually all of Egyptian society, as everyone sought to distance themselves from those who committed the murders at Luxor. The communiqués of the Gama'at themselves tell the tale.[9]

On November 17, 1997, the group issued a communiqué claiming responsibility for the attack. Three days later, on November 20, the group issued another communiqué stating that it would never deliberately attack foreigners and placing responsibility for the murders on the Egyptian government. This was a marked change in tone and about as close as the group ever came to admitting a mistake. Over the next few months, the Gama'at issued several additional communiqués, saying that it would abandon the strategy of targeting tourists. It is not surprising that in the wake of the Gama'at's failure to defeat the Egyptian government or to spark a popular revolt against it, the group subordinated itself to al-Qaʿida in early 1998. What other choice did it really have? Al-Zawahiri later wrote that the topography of Egypt is unsuited to guerrilla campaigns, and therefore it was necessary to abandon them, although this analysis does not explain why the Gamaʿat had failed to attract widespread popular support.

Other important threads in the tapestry of globalist radical Islam were being woven at the same time in Bosnia and Herzegovina. During the period 1992–95, the Bosnian Muslims fought the local Serbian Christians, sometimes with the aid of the Croatian Catholics, sometimes against them. Large numbers of "Afghan" Arab fighters came to Bosnia in order to fight what they perceived as a continuation of a war against the Muslim world. As is well documented by the ongoing trials of various Serbian militia and political leaders for human rights violations, the Serbians committed massive slaughters and rapes against the Muslim population. The fact that the European Union, the United States, and the United Nations were all very slow to respond to these horrors—and in some cases stood by while they were occurring—was widely interpreted by many Muslims as a deliberate campaign of genocide, not merely among the Serbians, but among the entire non-Muslim world. When the conflict ended with the Dayton Peace Accord of 1995, many foreigners fighting on behalf of the Bosnian Muslims were expelled; others made their way to Chechnya.

After the breakup of the Soviet Union in 1991, the Chechens in the Caucasus Mountains received *de facto* independence from Russia. Given the long history of Chechen revolts and passive resistance to imperial and Communist rule (detailed in chapter 4), this was hardly surprising. However, by 1994 the fact of Chechen "independence" had come to gall the Russians, who decided to do something about it, although their actions were fraught with bumblings, mishaps, and misunderstandings.[10] The first phase of the Chechen revolt against Russia ended in 1996 with large numbers of Russian casualties. The revolt drew an influx of foreign fighters, largely from Bosnia, but also from radical Muslim groups in Saudi Arabia and other places in the Muslim world. The most prominent among these fighters was a Saudi national known as Khattab (his real name was Sami al-Suwaylim),[11] who promoted a radical Muslim agenda but insisted that he was not part of the globalist radical Muslim movement of al-Qaʿida.

In both Bosnia and Chechnya, there was a strong tension between the local populations and the radical Muslim fighters who allied themselves with the Muslim cause. The Muslim populations of both territories had been heavily influenced by Sufism (a doctrine abhorrent to radical Muslims); having been dominated by Communist rule for several generations prior to their wars of independence, Bosnian and Chechen Muslims had little knowledge of trends in the larger Muslim world. Therefore, most of the Muslims in Bosnia and Chechnya were not prepared to accept the radical Muslim interpretation of Islam and resisted the association of their struggles for independence with the globalist vision of universal fighting against the enemies of Islam.

Central Asia was also a focus for radical Muslims during this period. Like Bosnia and Chechnya, the five "independent" countries of Central Asia—Uzbekistan, Kazakhstan, Tajikistan, Kirghizstan and Turkmenistan—had all been under imperial or Communist rule for generations; when independence came in 1991, they were ill prepared handle it. All of these countries, to one degree or another, remain under totalitarian rule. In Uzbekistan and Kirghizistan, home-grown radical Islamic movements arose, and from the middle of the 1990s onward they conducted periodic guerrilla raids in both countries, but especially in Uzbekistan. Of the five formerly Soviet Central Asian nations, Uzbekistan, prior to its occupation by Russia in the nineteenth century, was the region with the deepest Islamic roots and the most settled and literate culture. In the search for identity after the liberation from Communist rule, some Uzbeks turned to radical Islam. As in both Bosnia and Chechnya (and in Afghanistan as well), the primary expression of Islam in Central Asia had always been the Sufi orders—unacceptable to radical Muslims, and especially to globalist radical Muslims such as those to the south in Afghanistan during the rule of the Taliban.[12]

The unifying point for all of these groups was Afghanistan once more. Bin Ladin and the foreign *mujahidin* had tried to capitalize on the sense of Muslim unity in the immediate wake of the liberation of Afghanistan from Soviet control. The ethnic rivalries in Afghanistan, however, were deep-rooted, and there could be no compromise between the numerous warlords and petty chieftains who tore the country apart between 1989 and 1996. In 1994, a movement known as the Taliban (the students) rose in the area of Kandahar (southwestern Afghanistan) and began to assume control of Afghanistan. The Taliban took Kabul in 1996, and by 2000 it controlled the entire country, with the exception of the province of Badakhshan, held by Ahmad Shah Mas'ud, close to the former border with the Soviet Union

The Taliban were originally composed of war orphans educated in schools largely run by mullahs who preached a form of radical Islam.

Led by Mullah Muhammad ʿUmar Mujahid, who in 1996 proclaimed himself to be the *amir al-muʾminin* (a caliphal title), the Taliban were not, strictly speaking, part of the globalist radical Muslim movement. However, they were highly sympathetic to the movement, remembering the aid that pan-Islamic volunteers had rendered during the Soviet occupation, and allowed Usama b. Ladin to take refuge in Afghanistan after his expulsion from the Sudan in 1996.

Although it did not happen overnight, eventually all of these groups either fused together or came to a working arrangement concerning ideology and operations. Many of them, such as the Chechens and the Taliban, have had strong reservations about joining or being affiliated with a globalist radical Muslim movement because of the negative attention such an affiliation would bring. The Egyptian Gamaʿat al-Islamiyya has split over the issue, and many in the Kashmir have wondered whether associating themselves with a world-wide struggle has made the non-Muslim world turn a blind eye to their plight.

One must note the key role of Usama b. Ladin in this fusion. Bin Ladin as a leader is far from being understood at first glance. Bin Ladin hardly stands out in this regard. His educational achievements are unremarkable, which is clearly reflected in his statements, poetry, and communiqués, and although many respected his exploits against the Soviets during the 1980s, there are other radical Muslims who did just as much or more and would have a better claim to leadership of a globalist movement. Nor is his wealth the key to his appeal; numerous attempts to document his supposed wealth have revealed that his fortune is not great.

However, Bin Ladin has several points in his favor. First of all, he has a simple message, and a political agenda that constitutes a single demand: the Muslim world needs to expel the United States from the Arabian Peninsula (or, as he would put it, "from occupying the two holy places" of Mecca and Medina).[13] As we will see, all of Bin Ladin's other core beliefs proceed from a very simple idea. There is no question that his vision is global in nature because of the universal assault he sees leveled against Muslims because of the fact that they are Muslims.

THE CONSPIRACY TO DESTROY ISLAM

One of the factors binding globalist radical Muslims together is the shared belief that the entire world is united in a concerted effort to destroy Islam. The numerous conflicts in which Muslims were pitted against non-Muslims throughout the 1980s and 1990s have been adduced as evidence to support this belief: among them, Palestine, Chechnya, Bosnia-Herzegovina, Kashmir, the Sudan, Somalia, the Central Asian states, Xianjaing, the Philippines, East Timor, and Nigeria. One of the most popular traditions that supposedly prophesies this reality is the so-called Tradition of Thawban:

> The Messenger of God said: The nations are about to flock against you [the Muslims] from every horizon, just as hungry people flock to a kettle. We said: O Messenger of God, will we be few on that day? He said: No, you will be many in number, but you will be scum, like the scum of a flash-flood, without any weight, since fear will be removed from the hearts of your enemies, and weakness *(wahn)* will be placed in your hearts. We said: O Messenger of God, what does the word *wahn* mean? He said: Love of this world, and fear of death.[14]

This tradition was rarely cited in classical Muslim literature (principally in collections dating from the Crusades and the Mongol invasions), if only because it describes a time when Islam would suffer defeat on a grand scale. During our own time, that attitude has changed significantly—with good reason. It is difficult to imagine a tradition that is more ideally suited to the purposes of globalist radical Islam. According to the tradition, the world will be united against the weakened Muslims and fall upon them like starving vultures on a carcass. This tradition implies that most Muslims, in spite of their numbers, will be unwilling to devote themselves to the active waging of jihad demanded by the situation, and it goes to the heart of the reason for the Muslims' weakness (according to the globalist radical interpretation): they no longer cultivate the pursuit of jihad, they are soft, and they love this world instead of the next.

There is an immediacy and a paranoia to this tradition and the way it is interpreted among radical Muslims. For many of them, the outside world is actively seeking to destroy Islam and annihilate all the Muslims. Beginning with the 1977 book by Jalal 'Alam, *Qadat al-gharb yaquluna: dammiru al-Islam, ubidu ahlahu (Western Leaders Are Saying: Destroy Islam, Annihilate All of Its People)*, this paranoid aspect has been in the background of many conspiracy theories. Mohammed Masood Azhar, the leader of the radical group Lashkar-i Tayba (in Pakistan and Kashmir) says:

> Fellow Muslims! We cannot appeal to the unbelievers to assist us, we have to understand that the annihilation of Muslims is their main purpose and mission; they are overjoyed upon seeing the free flow of Muslim blood.[15]

Although it is tempting to dismiss such statements as hyperbole on the basis of their constant repetition in the literature of radical Muslims—and especially the literature of globalist radical Muslims—they clearly resonate among a certain constituency. The "fight or be killed" attitude lends a great deal of immediacy to the call for jihad, and it enables radical Muslims to characterize those who deny this Manichean picture as part of the problem.

These accusations in fact stand at the heart of the radical Muslim (and especially the globalist radical Muslim) indictment of their own societies. Jihad for the radicals is not merely a defensive measure (as they interpret it) or even a proselytizing strategy, although it is of course necessary for both. Rather, it reinforces a certain type of Muslim society, one that is not focused on how to gain the easy life, how to best emulate the United States or Europe, and gain the pleasures of this world. A jihad-based society will enforce boundaries between belief and infidelity. It will create an environment in which faith can be maximized and in which any and all victories automatically highlight the truth of Islam (rather than personal qualities, good fortune, or abilities of someone in a nonviolent society), where the Muslim will stand proud and dominant rather than weak and submissive.[16]

Since, according to the tradition, the fear that once was characteristic of the enemies of Islam is now present in the hearts of the Muslims, it is important to create situations in which bravery will be apparent and universally extolled by the Muslim world. Fighters—not scientists, entertainment stars, or even charismatic religious figures—should be the models for Muslim youth. Only those who spend themselves sacrificially upon the battlefield can communicate true Islam.

The necessity to differentiate between "true" Muslims and "false" Muslims is one of the most important points for contemporary radical Muslims. To illustrate, they have fixated upon one of the Prophet Muhammad's battles, the Battle of the Khandaq (627). The situation (as portrayed in the Prophet's biography) was that the Quraysh, the Prophet's tribe and foremost enemy, had made a concerted effort to destroy the Muslim community. In order to do so, they gathered a coalition of tribes and mercenaries to attack the Muslims in Medina. Within Medina, there were many nominal Muslims who were not entirely loyal to the Prophet Muhammad. These "lukewarm" Muslims *(munafiqun)* are described as follows in the Qur'an

> Allah would surely know those of you who hinder the others and those who say to their brothers: "Come over to us"; and they do not partake

of the fighting, except a little. They are ever niggardly towards you, but if fear overtakes them, you will see them look at you, with their eyes rolling like one who is in the throes of death. But when fear subsides, they cut you with sharp tongues. (Qur'an 33:19)

To a large degree, the Battle of the Khandaq spiritually differentiated the "true" believers from the "false" or "hypocritical" believers.

Today radical Muslims seek a similar criterion to differentiate between "true" and "false" Muslims. Although a mechanism of declaring a Muslim to be an infidel *(takfir)* was available throughout Muslim history, it was little used, and examples of "heresy trials" in classical Islam are rare (as noted in chapter 4). This situation has changed completely in recent decades as radical Muslims have increasingly sought to "unmask" supposed heretics or dissidents. However, even these types of "heresy trials" (such as the Nasr Abu Zayd case in Egypt in the early 1990s) pale before the general accusation of infidelity leveled by globalist radical Muslims against substantial parts of the Islamic world. Radical Muslims in general, following in the wake of the teachings of Sayyid Qutb (chapter 5), do not hesitate to condemn large numbers of apparent Muslims as apostates if they are unwilling to support a *shari'a*-based society or fight for the sake of Islam. Globalist radical Muslims go even further, maintaining that *every* Muslim who does not actively participate in jihad against non-Muslims is himself a non-Muslim, and some—the true extremists among them—declare that these apostate Muslims, together with their families, must be killed.[17]

FIGHTING APOSTATE OR HYPOCRITICAL MUSLIMS

Usama b. Ladin has a second point in his favor, which is his personal, unifying charismatic appeal. Just as his message is a simple and direct one, so is his ability to unify disparate radical Muslim elements and get them to work together. In order to achieve this, Bin Ladin has identified the enemy as collaborationist or corrupt Muslim governments and elites. Again, this message has a powerful resonance with the larger Muslim population, which is grimly conscious of the collective failure of the Muslim world to modernize either in competition with the (Christian) West or even with respect to local non-Western powers such as Israel, Turkey, and India.

Whereas non-globalist radical Muslims in the wake of Sayyid Qutb and others had advocated revolt against pseudo-Muslim governments that resisted calls to reimpose the *shari'a*, globalist radical Muslims adopted a more sophisticated strategy. Although they come from the same mindset as these non-globalist radical Muslims, the globalists have for the most been loath to shed Muslim blood in order to accomplish their goals. Instead, they have worked to establish a spiritual criterion by which "true" and "false" Muslims can be distinguished. This criterion is the willingness to wage militant jihad and to defend Islam.

Globalists continue to indict specific regimes as collaborationist, including religious elites that they view as subservient to these regimes, but they do not usually violently attack either of these groups. It is clear that in this regard globalists have learned a lesson from the failures of radical Muslim groups in Algeria and Egypt (and other places as well), who fought these regimes and were demonized because of their propensity to shed Muslim blood. Documents such as the "Seven Misconceptions" cited above discuss this problem in depth. In retrospect, it is clear that the decision taken by radical Muslims to allow the killings of Muslims who supported the so-called apostate regime (either willingly or through coercion) led directly to the failure of the Algerian and Egyptian radical Muslim movements.

Instead, globalists focus their violence on non-Muslim enemies of Islam (Russia, India, Israel, the United States, and others) and seek to use their position as "defenders of Islam" in order to hammer home their propaganda points. Since their so-called apostate Muslim opponents within the Muslim world are not willing to fight in an obvious and self-sacrificial manner, this method of isolating them and exposing them is much more effective than violence. In the long run it will most probably have the effect of creating the differentiation that radical Muslims crave.

This does not mean that globalist radical Muslims are always successful in their endeavors. They appear to thrive on their ambivalent status, as being part of Islam yet above the petty issues of governments and elites. For them, it is most painful (and damning of their Muslim opponents) when they are expelled after the fight is over (as in Bosnia) or handed over to foreign enemies of Islam, such as the United States (as Pakistan did after September 11, 2001). The radical Muslim news service www.azzam.com had this to say when the government of Pakistan handed over Ramzi Ben-al-Shibh—one of the key planners of the September 11 attacks—to the United States on September 17, 2002:

> The whole nation of Pakistan is guilty before the Lord of the Worlds for betraying those *mujahidin*. It is incorrect to blame only the leaders and government, for the armed forces, police, intelligence, and media all comprise ordinary Pakistanis from ordinary walks of life. Those who tipped off the Pakistani authorities were . . . ordinary Pakistanis. When

a nation allows its leaders to fight Islam, it is only a matter of time before Allah's punishment comes to that nation, either in the form of natural disasters, or worse, by Allah taking away Islam from that country as He did with Turkey after the people of Turkey supported Kamal Ataturk in destroying Islam in Turkey.

This attack is far more damning than if it were accompanied by violence. Like 'Abdallah 'Azzam's condemnation of the Muslim world for the Soviet occupation of Afghanistan, the personal tone of the attack is unmistakable (and sustained in many other examples).

One cannot understand radical Islam, let alone globalist radical Islam, until one comprehends the importance of the doctrine known as *al-wala' wa-l-bara'* (loyalty or fealty and disloyalty or disassociation). Basically, this is a polarizing doctrine by which radicals—and this idea is emphasized almost exclusively by radicals, so virtually any book or pamphlet on the subject will be written by radicals—maintain their control over what constitutes the definition of "Islam." Islam is defined according to this doctrine not only by the willingness to fight, but also by the polarities of love and hatred: love for anything or anybody defined as Islam or Muslim, and hatred for their opposites or opponents. In other words, anybody who demonstrates what radicals define as "love" for what is a non- or an anti-Muslim position, or associates closely (or sometimes in any way) with non-Muslims, must be a non-Muslim and is excluded, by definition, from the Muslim community.[18]

It is self-evident that this doctrine is of crucial importance for radical Muslims, not only in their war with the outside world, but also in their attempts to gain spiritual prestige and power within the Muslim world. One of the principal reasons for the ineffectiveness of moderate or anti-radical Muslims is the power of the doctrine of *al-wala' wa-l-bara'* over even those Muslims who do not accept the radical Muslim vision of the present or the future. *Al-wala' wa-l-bara'* enables radical Muslims to assert control over the definitions of who is and who is not a Muslim and it forces those who would wish to challenge that control into silence or into being categorized as "non-Muslims." Thus, it is not a question of whether a minority or a majority of Muslims support or oppose the actions and agenda of radical Islam or globalist radical Islam. It is impossible to know in many cases what Muslims really think or feel concerning a given operation. The crucial fact is that Muslims in the vast majority, whatever they truly believe, are unwilling to disassociate themselves publicly from radical Islam. This passivity is the work of the doctrine of *al-wala' wa-l-bara'*.

In all of their actions, radical Muslims seek criteria to differentiate between the true and the false, and then to expose the latter.[19] One of the most effective methods by which this is accomplished is suicide attacks or "martyrdom operations."

RESPONSE: MARTYRDOM OPERATIONS

Martyrdom operations are a comparatively recent phenomenon in Sunni Islam—so recent in fact that Muhammad Khayr Haykal's exhaustive book on jihad written in 1993, summarized in chapter 5, does not even mention them. In other versions of Islam, such as Isma'ilism or Imami Shi'ism, self-sacrifice was well known and widely accepted as a means of promoting the teachings of the sect. But in Sunni Islam examples of suicidal attacks are rare prior to the early 1990s (there are some scattered reports of similar actions during the time of the "Indian Mutiny" in 1857). Suicide, of course, is strictly forbidden in Islam (Qur'an 2:195, 4:29), and traditionally Muslim countries have had the lowest suicide rates in the world. Even those facing torture or certain death rarely commit suicide.[20]

Contemporary radical Muslim authorities define the subject in this manner:

> Martyrdom or self-sacrifice operations are those performed by one or more people, against enemies far outstripping them in numbers and equipment, with prior knowledge that the operations will almost inevitably lead to death.[21]

The definition itself reveals the mindset leading to martyrdom operations. These operations are justified because the Muslims lack either the manpower or the advanced technology of their foes. Therefore, Muslims must make maximum use of the one advantage that they do have: the willingness of their fighters to die. The document from which the above is taken, "The Islamic Ruling on the Permissibility of Martyrdom Operations," continues:

> The form this usually takes nowadays is to wire up one's body, or a vehicle or suitcase with explosives, and then to enter among a conglomeration of the enemy or their vital facilities and to detonate in an appropriate place there in order to cause the maximum losses to the enemy ranks, taking advantage of the element of surprise and penetration. Naturally the enactor of the operation will usually be the first to die.[22]

At least there are no illusions in that matter.

But it is very important to distinguish the issue of martyrdom operations from any hint of similarity to suicide:

> The name "suicide operations" used by some is inaccurate, and in
> fact this name was chosen by the Jews to discourage people from such
> endeavors. How great is the difference between one who commits
> suicide—because of his unhappiness, lack of patience, and weakness
> or absence of *iman* [faith]—and the self-sacrificer who embarks on the
> operation out of strength of faith and conviction, and to bring victory
> to Islam by sacrificing his life for the uplifting of Allah's word.[23]

Numerous legal rulings address martyrdom operations. Most of the
ones available to this author are related to Palestinian suicide attacks
against Israeli civilians. Others, such as the one cited above, are either
related to the Chechen insurgency or are global in nature (applicable to
any perceived enemy of Islam).[24]

The logic behind the religious justification of martyrdom operations
follows much of the jihad material that we have seen up to this point.
But some unusual verses are cited in this regard. First of all, one should
note "And some people sell themselves for the sake of Allah's favor.
Allah is kind to His servants" (Qur'an 2:207). This verse is rarely cited
in the classical jihad literature. Taken out of its Qur'anic context, where
it is used to contrast the arrogant and hypocritical with true believers,
the verse seems to be describing people who are willing to die for the
sake of God. Moreover, according to the second part of the verse,
God accepts this type of sacrifice (although one should note that it
is Qur'anic style to add on various phrases such as the above, and
they do not necessarily have a connection with the main body of the
verse).

Another Qur'anic verse often cited in the context of martyrdom is:

> Indeed, you will find them [the evil-doers] of all people the most
> attached to life, even more than those who associated other gods with
> Allah. Every one of them wishes to live for one thousand years. This
> long life, however, will not spare them the punishment. (Qur'an 2:96)

This verse relates to the situation of the Muslim world as the radicals perceive it and as was illustrated by the first citation from the "Islamic Ruling." Non-Muslims are perceived to be far in advance of the Muslims
with regard to science and technology. The Muslims, however, have the
advantage in that they are willing to give up their lives for the sake of
God. Non-Muslims have something to live for, since they have invested
a great deal in bettering their lives here in this world. Muslims, by con-

trast, do not have much to live for. Therefore, it is important, in order to affirm God's truth in the world—lest people, including Muslims, be seduced by the happy life of the unbelievers—to deny the unbelievers their (long) life. This can be achieved through martyrdom operations.

Finally, we find that the verse from the David and Goliath story in the Qur'an (2:249–51) is cited: "How many a small band has defeated a larger one by Allah's leave. Allah is with the steadfast" (Qur'an 2:249). Clearly this verse affirms the radical Muslim perception that even though the numbers of Muslims in the contemporary world are large, there are few who are willing to fight. These fighters, despite their small number, are granted victory by the power of God. Martyrdom operations are one way in which small numbers can accomplish this task. The legal justifications of martyrdom operations then further connect them to the already established legal category of the "single soldier charging a superior enemy force" (see chapter 1), and state that as this single soldier was effectively involving himself in a suicidal operation, so the person who commits suicide by blowing himself or herself up in the midst of the enemy is doing something legitimate according to Muslim law.

Martyrdom operations have become widespread throughout the core Arabic- and Urdu-speaking Sunni Muslim countries. They are, in effect, one of radical Islam's most effective communication tools to the rest of the Muslim world and have done a great deal to promote its agenda. In addition to the advantages attached to conventional jihad, martyrdom operations are a clear strike against the authority of the establishment: government-supported Muslim leadership. Many of these leaders, such as al-Tantawi of al-Azhar University, al-Qaradawi, and others have responded to the popularity of martyrdom operations by issuing *fatawa* supporting them.[25] However, these "respectable" leaders regularly seek to control the target of the martyrdom operations and focus them upon Israel.[26] These efforts, however, have not been universally successful, for martyrdom operations are a popular expression of jihad tactics and cannot be controlled by the government-sponsored (or even independent) Muslim religious leadership.

This is illustrated by the fact that martyrdom operations are regularly used against civilians. The religious leadership of Islam that has "permitted" the use of martyrdom operations has usually stipulated that they should be used against military targets alone (with the exception of al-Qaradawi, who has stated that since all Israeli civilians are part of the military, they are all legitimate targets). Attacking civilians is a problem in Muslim religious law, but as we can see, al-Qa'ida and other globalist radical Muslim jihad organizations have overcome this difficulty (see appendix for their justification). Martyrdom operations *by their very nature* are really only useful (over the long run) against civilian targets. Military targets are usually prepared for infiltration attempts, even those where the attacker is prepared to die, and thus in general the level of terror cannot be achieved by a "martyrdom operation" either with the casualties necessary to justify the operation or over a long period of time (if an army could be penetrated with such ease by unconventional methods, it would be a failure).

However, such terror can be achieved with regard to a civilian population, at least in democratic countries where consciousness of civilian (and military) casualties is high. It seems clear that martyrdom operations are only useful in attacking civilians in democracies. Democracies in general cannot use the methods necessary to actually bring about effective retribution against the organizations perpetrating martyrdom operations. Nondemocratic countries, by contrast, are not bound by these ethical standards.

To some degree, the problems of attacking civilians are overcome by the reliance upon intention. We have noted in chapter 1 the importance of intention in fighting. But whereas in classical jihad intention was important to ensure that fighting was undertaken for the sake of God (and not for spoils or worldly status), in martyrdom operations intention is actually the method by which the operation is distinguishable from murder. In other words, if one *intends* that an action such as a martyrdom operation—which could kill a large number of civilians— achieve a permitted military purpose, then it is the same as if the action accomplished nothing more than the goal for which it was intended; all other consequences are ignored if the assessment was legitimate. "Collateral damage" is not to be taken into account if the overall intent was to achieve a military victory for the sake of God (in accordance with Qur'an 9:41).

A further problem has appeared that goes even deeper than the killing of infidel women and children as a by-product of martyrdom operations: the question of female "martyrs." Because of the prestige attached to martyrdom operations (and jihad as a whole), one finds that more and more women wish to participate. This is problematic in more than one sense for radical Muslims. On the one hand, radical Islam does allow for a greater level of female participation in general (within the confines of "Islamic feminism"), and there are examples of women fighting during the time of the Prophet Muhammad and the early conquests.[27] Thus, women cannot be denied the right to participate in jihad on the grounds of the *hadith* literature. In addition, self-sacrifice of women lends huge spiritual prestige to the movement. On the other hand, Muslim radicals, at least those in the Arabic-speaking world, clearly do not want women to participate in martyrdom operations for various reasons. However, it is significant that the Chechens have produced a number of female suicide attackers, and the "Islamic Ruling on the Permissibility of Martyrdom Operations" was in fact generated by questions regarding one of them (Hawa Barayev, concerning whom there is a great deal of hagiographic material).

There is also the question of rewards for the female martyr. Since men receive a fairly extensive harem of women in return for martyrdom, it would be reasonable to expect a woman to receive a comparable reward. It seems that the question took Hamas aback when it was asked on their website (on January 18, 2002):

> I wanted to ask: what is the reward of a female martyr who performs a martyrdom operation; does she marry 72 of the *houri*s?
> [Answer] . . . the female martyr gains the same reward as does the male, with the exception of this one aspect [the *houri*s], so that the female martyr will be with the same husband with whom she dies. "And those who have believed and their progeny, followed them in belief. We shall join their progeny to them. We shall not deprive them of any of their work; every man shall be bound by what he has earned" [52:21]. The one who is martyred and has no husband will be married to one of the people of Paradise.[28]

Clearly this answer reflects the novelty of the idea that a woman could be a martyr, because her reward does not seem equal to that of the man, and this is a question that has yet to be resolved. But it is far from being a moot question, since several Palestinian women (albeit those associated with the semisecular PLO rather than radical Islamic groups) and a number of Chechen women have carried out martyrdom operations.

Martyrdom operations bestow additional advantages on radical Islam. They not only promote a self-sacrificial version of Islam that is useful (and indicting) against the established Muslim religious leadership; they provide yet another criterion to divide "true" from "false" Muslims. They create a very powerful boundary between Islam (as radical Muslims interpret it) and the rest of the world and invite the revulsion of the non-Muslim world. This revulsion will often be general in nature, against all Muslims, again having the effect of driving Muslims into the fold of radical Islam. Revulsion against martyrdom operations will often be the strongest among precisely those non-Muslim groups (the media, liberals, human rights organizations) that radical Islam most despises, and so it has the intended effect of striking against them as well.

COMMUNICATION AND MISSIONIZATION

Jihad and *da'wa* (either communication or missionization) are closely connected in Islam, as was detailed in chapter 5. Therefore, it is legitimate to ask: what is the message communicated by contemporary jihad and martyrdom operations? How is this message being phrased and how is it being received? Every action that a contemporary violent radical Muslim group takes is intended to communicate its message. None of these groups is strong enough to expend time or energy on activities that do not represent its overall goals. These goals either represent direct attacks on the enemy chosen by the group (its *raison d'être*) or attempts to win converts—either to the group or to the Muslim religion. Ideally each action should fulfill all of these goals.

In order to communicate their message, radical Muslims regularly issue statements, communiqués, epistles, and books. The form of the communication is important. In almost all cases it begins with a Qur'anic verse or a *hadith* that illustrates or supports the subject of the message. Often the title is also taken from a Qur'anic verse or a *hadith,* and it is rare to find a paragraph without some citation from either of these two sources, even if it is just an exclamation and not germane to the subject. Radical Muslim writers do not avoid the use of poetry— common in Arab societies, but frowned upon by the Qur'an (see Qur'an 36:69)—to communicate their messages and to praise their heroes or curse their enemies.[29]

Al-Qa'ida and other globalist radical Muslims excel at manipulating the Arabic media and in many cases other Muslim-language medias (Urdu, Indonesian-Malay, etc.). However, they recognize their inability to speak to or to manipulate the worldwide media. To this end, they do not emphasize words or statements so much when speaking to the world, but rely upon simple images (such as those of September 11, 2001, and other operations). Usama b. Ladin said:

> Those young men . . . said in deeds, in New York and Washington, speeches that overshadowed all other speeches made everywhere else in the world. The speeches are understood by both Arabs and non-Arabs— even by the Chinese. It is above all the media said . . . this event made people think [about true Islam], which benefited Islam greatly.[30]

This was true in a certain way, although it is clear that the radical circle around Bin Ladin is mistaken with regard to several of these conclusions. On an individual or local level, it is true that people were impressed by the September 11 attacks, and one cannot reasonably doubt that some converted to Islam as a result of this publicity. But these individual or local conversions cannot be compared to the negative publicity that Islam as a whole received, and this demonstrates the difficulty that globalist radical Muslims have in communicating their message to a neutral or hostile world audience.

Frequently militant radical Muslims resent even the statements and conclusions made about them in the relatively friendly Arabic- or Urdu-language media (for example, al-Jazeera, which in the West is often perceived as al-Qaʿida's mouthpiece). A good example of this attitude surfaced during the occasions when al-Jazeera has discussed either Usama b. Ladin or al-Qaʿida; the station is often critical of the methods or priorities of both. When the testaments of the September 11 hijackers were presented and discussed on al-Jazeera, radical Muslims wrote a rejoinder to the presentation because they felt that the discussion did not properly emphasize the bravery of the action or treat the perpetrators with the respect they deserved.[31]

Overall, the major image problem that the globalist radical Muslims face with regard to their audience in the Muslim world is the question of why they have done so little to attack Israel.[32] Since for many Muslims, especially Arab Muslims, confronting Israel and defeating it (or at least weakening it) is a major priority, the spectacle of the September 11, 2001, attacks on New York and Washington, D.C., while emotionally satisfying to many, was problematic for many others. Even the *mujahidin* have asked whether such an attack was well timed and planned, since the net effect was to cement the relationship between the United States and Israel, and to create sympathy for the victims of September 11. After the radical Muslims' loss of Afghanistan in October–December 2001 these questions multiplied, and it is clear that globalist radical Islam was at pains to explain this apparent defeat and how it would ultimately be turned into a victory.

Probably the biggest difficulty of militant radical Islam is explaining the deaths of apparent innocents or Muslims who are killed accidentally during a given operation. We have already seen that the inability to explain this point properly destroyed the Egyptian Gamaʿat al-Islamiyya after the Luxor massacre of 1997. While the Gamaʿat argued that these tourists were only apparent innocents, the vast majority of Egyptians rejected this claim. Many Arab Muslims are willing to tolerate killings of Israeli civilians with the argument that the entire society of Israel is militarized and that most Israelis serve in the nation's army. According to this interpretation, true Israeli civilians are uncommon. However, even with the prevalence of this belief, there can be qualms concerning individual operations.

These problems multiply with regard to targeting other apparent opponents in the world. It is clear that globalist radical Muslims have had a great deal of difficulty justifying the legality (according to Islamic law) of the September 11 attacks (see the appendix, which deals with this issue).[33] Not only were virtually all of those killed civilians—although not at the Pentagon—but there were a large number of Muslims among the slain at the World Trade Center as well. Globalist radical Muslim groups rationalize such attacks by saying that everyone who participates in the economy of the United States and pays taxes to its government or votes in its elections contributes directly to a system that oppresses and kills Muslims worldwide and that they are therefore legitimate targets. This argument has not been entirely persuasive to Muslims worldwide, and a number have commented that Muslims in the United States pay taxes just the same as anyone else and do not deserve to be attacked. (One suspects that behind the globalist radical Muslim logic is the hidden accusation that true Muslims would not live in the United States at all.) Like the indictments of 'Azzam above, this one is global in its analysis of the nature of the society of the United States, and most Muslims who do not already subscribe to the beliefs of radical Islam are not willing to accept its logic.

There is also the problem of the unwillingness of globalist radical Muslims to find common ground with their enemies with regard to the conduct of war. Since they regularly denounce treaties such as the Geneva Convention and other basic human rights codes as non-Islamic,[34] it is difficult for them to find a legal basis to argue for the humane treatment of their own prisoners. This unwillingness to make even the smallest gesture toward the legitimacy of their opponents has cost globalist radical Muslims virtually all support outside of the Muslim community and has provoked internal controversy within the radical Muslim camp as to whether rejection of the Geneva Convention is wise at this time (especially given the fact that large numbers of radical Muslims are prisoners in various foreign countries).

In the end, the actions and strategies of radical Muslims in fighting jihad are buffered by an widespread belief in conspiracies. These conspiracy theories are ubiquitous in the Muslim world, and especially in the Arabic- and Urdu-speaking sections of it. They present to the Muslim audience a vision of powerlessness and innocence in relation to events in the world as a whole. Everything that happens is manipulated by outside powers. Nothing is the responsibility of the Muslims. Usually this attitude is expressed as a belief in a "worldwide Jewish (or Zionist) Conspiracy" to destroy Islam. This conspiracy is so vast in its scope, so satanic in its malevolence, so insidious in its nature that no one can hope to resist it—except for the conspiracy theorist who manages to see through all the subterfuge.

Conspiracy theories and violent actions by radical Muslims are closely linked. The former provide the necessary buffer of innocence required to maintain a distance from violent and gory attacks. The conspiracy theories enable Muslim audiences to feel pride in a given action—as many did on September 11—and at the same to time place responsibility for it upon the heads of someone else, usually the Jews. This was manifested by the idea that four thousand Jews did not show up for work at the World Trade Center on September 11, 2001, and proves conclusively to the Muslim world that the true responsibility belongs to the Jews.[35] Where there is an abundance of conspiracy theories involving world domination and passivity by the population, together with a sense of humiliation and a disconnect from participation in the world system, radical Islam flourishes. Perhaps for this reason, Turkey and Turkish-speaking and Turkish-influenced Islam have to a large degree been immune to radical Islam.

Conversion to Islam is a major focus for radical Muslims everywhere. Ideally, as Bin Ladin stated in his videotape, "when people see a strong horse and a weak horse, by nature they will like the strong horse."[36] This accords with one of radical Islam's major critiques of present-day Muslim societies: they are not demonstrating the truth of Islam by victory. The early Islamic conquests (detailed in chapter 1) suffused Islam with a strong need to be clearly and obviously superior in this world so as to attract people to convert and thereby to deter apostasy. One of the most commonly listed goals of jihad is "to raise the Word of Allah to the highest" (see Qur'an 9:41). Since the present-day status of Islam does not accomplish this goal, it is important to convey a message that does: strength, power, and retribution for (past and present) humiliation are vital to the missionizing method. However, pure manifestations of power are not always enough to make people want to convert.

TECHNIQUES AND TACTICS OF CONTEMPORARY JIHAD

Modern-day jihad is considerably different from classical jihad. Radical Muslims who wage jihad have spent a great deal of time analyzing changes in warfare techniques and regularly confront their own failures. In this regard—although sometimes their estimation of the military value of the *mujahidin* is considerably inflated—their attitude is much more mature than that of previous Muslim fighters.

In general, the *mujahidin* tactics noted above, like their communications, are designed to send a message. The basic goals may be to establish a Muslim state or at least take vengeance for perceived wrongs inflicted upon Muslims, but no radical Muslim group is strong enough to be able to accomplish either goal at this point. Therefore, radical Muslims favor attacking symbolic targets that will produce a high level of exposure, maximize casualties among their opponents, and generate both terror among the target population and admiration among the world-wide Muslim population. Since they know that the vast majority of potential targets (soft targets) cannot be adequately protected at any given time, let alone at all times, the initiative is on their side. However, in reality radical Muslims are severely constrained by difficulties in gathering intelligence, massing fighters in a given area, and securing retreat after an attack. Of course, one of the benefits of martyrdom operations is the fact that this latter consideration is moot.

Their choice of fighters is limited but most probably adequate for the task at hand. Since the basic cause is that of Islam, hypothetically speaking, any Muslim could be a potential recruit. But in fact, because of the limitations of the ideology of radical Islam, many Muslims are either hostile or indifferent to these concerns and are unwilling to be recruited. Radical Islam makes a very obvious point of declaring large numbers of apparent Muslims apostate, and it therefore sacrifices their aid in the overall struggle. In general, radical Islam has proved to be most effective among marginal Muslims—newly religious Muslims, especially second-generation immigrants or those originally from a semisecular background, converts, or those Muslims who have been compromised in their faith—and among Muslims who feel the humiliations of the modern world very strongly. This latter group often includes the well-educated, especially those who have come from a Muslim society to a Western country for the purposes of education or temporary employment. Often these people feel more keenly the dramatic disparity between their societies and Western societies and have a desire to do something about it. Of course a desire to change one's society does not necessarily imply of violence. Often such impulses are channeled into positive directions and do not aid in recruiting followers.

Radical Muslims also must consider issues of weapons. Although in many countries throughout the world—especially those that have undergone civil wars or have large regions given to lawlessness—weapons are easily obtainable; for the most part, however, these weapons are insufficient for the tasks globalist radical Muslims would like to accomplish. This limitation constitutes a major difficulty for globalists, as they usually lack access to a highly developed economy that can manufacture or develop the weaponry they desire. Even otherwise friendly governments are often reluctant to allow the *mujahidin* access to advanced weaponry because of the fact that they are not subject to any type of control or discipline, and can just as easily turn against the government as fight its enemies. These limitations have made radical Muslims masters of improvisation and innovation, but they also constrain their choice of targets.

As mentioned previously, targets are chosen for their symbolic and propaganda value: they are not chosen lightly. They *must* have the communicative importance or else the action will be wasted. The action also must be explicable to both the target audience and to the Muslim audience, so that the appropriate messages are brought home to both.

Radical Muslims regularly issue political and military analyses reflecting their interpretation of events. A good example of these interpretations is the war in Afghanistan between the so-called Northern Alliance and the United States against the Taliban and its globalist radical Muslim allies, al-Qa'ida and other volunteers during the latter part of 2001 and following. During the spring of 2002 and after a great number of articles appeared on globalist radical Muslim websites asking: what went wrong? Did we choose to fight an enemy that was too strong at the wrong time? The answers to these questions describe a change in tactics after the loss of the Islamic Emirate of Afghanistan, until then globalist radical Muslims' primary base, and a switch to guerrilla tactics that sought its precedents in the life of the Prophet Muhammad. Other more purely military analyses exist in abundance. It is true that in many of these instances the accomplishments of the *mujahidin* are played up considerably more than an outside observer would see as warranted, but these analyses are far from mere cheerleading. They represent a continual process in which the *mujahidin* seek to learn from their enemies and assimilate new tactics.[37]

Political consequences also might have military consequences, as radical Muslims discovered in the wake of September 11. For the most part, globalist radical Islam had a merely nuisance value to Western societies previous to that time. Although radical groups were present in a number of different areas—and were usually fought with the support or at least tacit approval of Western governments—no one had really engaged the *mujahidin* on their home ground in Afghanistan since the Russian withdrawal in 1989.

Probably the most difficult situation for radical Muslims, and especially globalist radical Muslims, is their lack of operational bases. Between 1996 and 2001 Afghanistan served as the primary base for the globalists, and many radical or separatist movements have safe locations to which they can withdraw or adjacent friendly countries that are willing to give them support and sanctuary. Although wresting control of Afghanistan from the Taliban will not finish off globalist radical Islam by any means, it was an important step in putting a great deal of governmental pressure on the movement's infrastructure and denying it a sanctuary for growth. This will probably continue to be a major problem for the globalists during the coming years, unless they are able to dominate another country to take the place of Afghanistan. Gradually the quality of their training will deteriorate as those who were trained in Afghanistan are either killed or lose their peak form. Stockpiling of supplies, accumulation of intelligence, and coherence of command will all become increasingly haphazard as the years progress, unless this situation is resolved.

All of this does not actually lessen the appeal of globalist radical Islam, but it does make its propaganda job more difficult. Fortunately for the movement, it has built up a myth for difficult times: its martyrologies.

MIRACLE STORIES AND MARTYROLOGIES

Miracle stories and martyrologies are a major component of globalist radical Islam. In this regard, as in so many others, 'Azzam paved the way. In his booklet *'Ibar wa-basa'ir li-jihad al-hadir (Lessons and Insights for Present-day Jihad)* written during the Soviet occupation of Afghanistan, there are numerous miracle stories.[38] These can be grouped into six categories:

1. The continuity and purity of the *mujahidin*'s bodies. Frequently the *mujahidin* when wounded heal quickly or are not hurt by wounds that would either kill or incapacitate others. They

emerge from battle looking like shining moons. But for the most part the manifestations of the pure body appear after the martyrdom of the *mujahid*. His beard occasionally grows after death; a sweet smell is frequently attested from his body, which is not subject to corruption. (By contrast, evil smells emanate from the bodies of dead Communists, and sometimes the very ground itself refuses to accept their bodies.) White light shines from the graves of the *mujahidin*, and on a number of occasions voices of dead martyrs have been heard to shout *Allahu akbar* when a fierce battle was raging.

2. Divine or angelic aid (attested in Qur'an 3:125, 8:9).[39] Many miracle stories involve the theme of angels, men dressed in white, or anonymous strangers helping small groups of *mujahidin* to defeat larger Communist units. Sometimes the *mujahidin* are puzzled as to why their foes have been defeated; on other occasions the Communists ask, "Who were those people fighting with you?" or other variations on this question. Occasionally fire from heaven will knock down enemy airplanes and helicopters.

3. Aid from animals or other nonhuman sources. Food is sometimes provided for the *mujahidin* from unknown sources (the implication being that it is supernatural), dogs do not bark at their passing, and rain falls to cover their tracks while returning from a mission.

4. Dreams and prognostications are very important among the martyrdom and miracle stories. For the most part these revolve around the theme of knowing when a successful operation is about to happen, or when a given fighter is going to attain martyrdom.

5. Confusion among the enemy. Frequently the enemy ends up killing each other, so that the *mujahidin* do not need to.

6. The protective role of the Qur'an. Oftentimes the Qur'an will be responsible for protecting a fighter's life or on occasion even guide him away from danger.

Afghanistan proved to be an important forge in the creation of the mythology of the *mujahid* as a special type of Muslim and in the spiritual prestige they gained from this experience.

Many other martyrologies have arisen out of conflicts that have occurred since the end of the Afghan war in 1989. The wars in Bosnia-

Herzegovina (1992–95) and Chechnya (1993–94, 1996–99) produced large numbers of martyrs. For the most part, the stories told about these martyrs do not deviate significantly from the themes mentioned above. In the Bosnian martyrologies, the fighter usually has to pass through some type of test in order to arrive at the battlefield; often he is said to have been tempted by, and resisted, the fleshpots of Europe before he can fight. Visions of the *houris* are common among the martyrs; for example, it is told of one Abu Zayd al-Qatari that he "even saw the Hoor al-ʿAyn not in his sleep, but while he was at his position on the mountain. Every day as he used to look in the sky, a woman would come to him, a most beautiful woman."[40] Another martyr, Abu Muaʿadh, was seen in a dream by a certain fighter, who was told what it was like to die. Abu Muʿadh said: "You don't feel a thing. As soon as you are killed, you see two beautiful blonde girls; they come and sit beside you in Paradise."[41] Visions of *houris* are ubiquitous in the martyrdom stories, and as counseled by ʿAbdallah b. al-Mubarak's *Kitab al-jihad* (chapter 1), there is a strong tendency to avoid marriage or relations with earthly women. Other themes, such as the pure scent of the bodies of the martyrs, as described above, are equally prominent.

Martyrology can also take the form of stories, idealizing the deaths of the martyrs. Louis Atiyat Allah wrote such a story about the September 11, 2001, hijackers (translated in the appendix), in which the emotions of the radical Muslim with regard to the self-sacrifice of the attacks are described. The story communicates the primary focus—for the radical Muslim—of the bravery of the action, its self-sacrificial nature, and the emotion of love and devotion that impelled it. These emotions might be difficult for a non-Muslim, especially an American, audience to understand because they see the attacks as mass murder. Nonetheless, it is important to understand that the acts of September 11 were not conceived by their perpetrators as acts of hatred (although that might have been present in the hearts of some of the hijackers), but as an act of love for Islam.[42] The martyrology can be open to the accusation that it is romanticizing events and simplifying emotions to the point of absurdity, but its power over the imagination cannot be dismissed. Whether one accepts the historical truth of the presentation is irrelevant. This is a successful spin that interprets the September 11 attacks in a manner acceptable to certain people.

News reports issued by www.azzam.com and other radical Muslim news websites (www.qoqaz.com, www.markazdawa.net, etc.) have supplied a great many of the martyrologies for the *mujahidin* in Afghanistan since October 2001. A great many of the themes are predictable.[43] The *mujahidin* attack "ferociously" (January 19 and February 8, 2003) or "pounce" upon the enemy (December 23, 2002, and February 8, 2003), their planning is "careful" (October 15 and December 23, 2002), and they always make a safe exit. Extensive lists of American and coalition (Afghani) forces are given; these are always described as "terrified" (November 3, 2002, and January 18 and February 8, 2003) by the tactics of the enemy, or "horrified" (January 30, 2003) by their own technological or intelligence failures. For the radical news websites, it is of paramount importance to note that the American or Afghani coalition dead are "rotten" (February 8, 2003) or "stinking" (December 3, 2003), while the fallen *mujahidin* are pure and untainted (January 11, 2002). Coalition (Muslim) forces who die in battle are refused burial by the Afghani religious leadership because they are clearly fighting against Islam (January 31, 2003).[44] Frequently the reports point out that the same military commanders who fought the Soviet Union during the 1980s are fighting the new Afghani government and the United States today.

At every point, a David and Goliath picture is painted of the warfare: the American forces rely on their superior technology and weaponry; when this fails them—as it apparently does with regularity—they are at a loss as to what to do (December 25, 2002, and February 7, 2003). Then they have to face the *mujahidin* on equal terms, which invariably leads to disaster for the American or coalition forces. Frequently, the American and coalition forces die in friendly fire. Many civilians are killed in these news reports, but the *mujahidin* are never responsible for any of these acts (e.g., February 2, 2003). The *mujahidin*'s plans always go right, and they regularly win immense victories.

Since the Taliban regime was often held to be repressive toward women, a number of the martyrdom operations or revenge stories cited by radical Muslims involve women. Various accounts exist of women using deception in order to kill American soldiers by blowing themselves up.[45] However, an even more popular idea involves Afghani women taking vengeance upon Americans for having taken liberties with their honor (January 11, 2002), or in revenge for intrusions into their homes (September 23, 2002). These stories are all the more successful because they depict the Afghani women as supportive of the Taliban and of the standards of radical Islam, and wishing for their quick return.

Often the stories are "spun" in such a way as to make clear what the *mujahidin* are fighting for (from www.azzam.com, September 26, 2002):

. . . a convoy of 150 *mujahidin* had been captured after running out of ammunition in Takhar . . . after they were captured, U.S. troops using chains hung one *mujahid* by his arms for six days questioning him about Usama Ben Laden. After six days of the *mujahid* not saying a word the U.S. troops gave up and asked him about his faith. The *mujahid* replied that he trusted in Allah, the Prophet Muhammad, and the Holy Qur'an. Upon receiving this answer, the U.S. troops replied that "Your Allah and Muhammad are not here, but the Qur'an is, so let's see what it will do to us." After this, one U.S. soldier brought a Holy Qur'an and began urinating over it, only to be joined by other US and Northern Alliance troops who did the same. A little while after this incident, the *mujahid* was brought down out of the chains and given some water to drink and some flour with which to make bread. The *mujahid* used the water to wash the Qur'an, and tried to stitch the Qur'an together with the flour he was to supposed to make bread with to eat. The report states that the *mujahid* said that after the incident, the color of the Qur'an had been turning increasingly red with each passing day, and that the words were disappearing. The *mujahid* stated that he was sure that Allah will destroy the U.S. and Northern Alliance troops soon.

Sadly, in light of the revelations at the Abu Ghraib prison in the spring of 2004, this description is not as implausible as it should have been.

Clearly this tradition of martyrologies is an important one for radical Islam, and it is striking how similar the themes between classical and contemporary Muslim jihad literature are. In all cases, the motifs of assistance from heaven, seeing visions of paradise and *houris*, and receiving unexpected aid are prominent. It is extremely important that the bodies of the martyrs reflect the nobility of their death and be treated respectfully, while it is equally important that the bodies of their enemies demonstrate outwardly their torment in hell. Moreover, the stories of the martyrs are usually detailed in such a way as to "prove" that every time a *mujahid* is martyred, his children will follow in his footsteps. The stories of the martyrs are, according to my analysis, responsive to their environments: some emphasize the miraculous, others the piety of the fighters or their bravery, and yet others the role of women in the fighting. In all cases they serve to prove to the Muslim audience that God is supporting the *mujahidin*.

Since this is true, we must ask: what is the final vision of the jihad?

APOCALYPTIC AND MESSIANIC VISION

The apocalyptic and/or messianic vision of the jihad is of obvious importance to the fighters. Without an explanation of its purpose, the

process of jihad becomes less meaningful. Apocalyptic explanations justify to the believer the trials and tests of this world. Usually these events
are explained as preparation for Paradise, separating the righteous from
the sinners. This is in close accord with several verses from the Qur'an:

> Such are the times; we alternate them among the people, so that Allah
> may know who are the believers and choose martyrs from among you.
> Allah does not like the evildoers! And that Allah might purify the believ-
> ers and annihilate the unbelievers. Or did you suppose that you will
> enter Paradise, before Allah has known who were those of you who
> have struggled, and those who are steadfast? (3:140–42)

This process of separation is integral to the apocalyptic outlook and an
important part of radical Islam.[46] Therefore, it is equally important to
construct an apocalyptic interpretation of events and to fit them into the
eternal process of separation so that "true" Muslims will not lose hope
(although ultimately an apocalyptist rationalizes losses on the part of
the faithful by maintaining that they were never "truly" faithful).

Radical Muslims start their apocalyptic vision by citing *hadith*s to
prove that jihad is a salvific action that will continue until the time of the
Day of Resurrection. We have already noted most of these traditions.
What distinguishes the saved from the damned is the willingness to fight
for the sake of Islam. All other criteria are of lesser value—even worth-
less—according to this interpretation. During the course of this apocalyptic future, dramatic and cataclysmic events are expected to occur—
indeed, the believers should *want* them to occur because they herald the
passing of the old non-Muslim order and the beginning of the new.

There are two categories of apocalyptic signs: the lesser and the
greater signs of the Hour. Lesser signs of the Hour are largely moral or
social in nature, although some are political, natural (earthquakes and
plagues), or cosmic. For the most part, radical Muslim apocalyptic writers agree that these events have already taken place or are too indistinct
to ascertain. The greater signs of the Hour are the appearance of the
Dajjal (the Muslim Antichrist), who will tempt the entire world to follow him in direct opposition to God; the appearance of Jesus, who will
return from heaven in order to slay the Dajjal; and the appearance of the
Mahdi, the Muslim messianic figure. There are other signs, but these are
the ones that are the most important for our purposes.

As one might surmise from the number of conspiracy theories in the
Muslim world, the Dajjal is a major figure in Muslim religious culture.
Books and pamphlets about him regularly appear in the markets, and

there are many websites on the Internet that discuss his identity. For many radical Muslims, the Dajjal is closely identified with the "world Jewish conspiracy," which is especially convenient since in the classical sources the Dajjal is said to be a Jew. To make the leap that the Dajjal is a social force or an anti-Muslim idea—such as the West, the "global Jewish conspiracy" or even the United Nations—is not difficult. The following tradition is most useful in this regard:

> A group of my [Muhammad's] community will continue, fighting for the truth, victorious over those who oppose them, until the last of them fights the Antichrist.[47]

As far as globalist radical Muslims are concerned, they are fulfilling this tradition in its entirety.

With regard to specific events signaling the apocalypse, many radical Muslims invoke the traditions published during the early Muslim conquests. For the Muslims of that time, the foremost enemy was the Byzantine Empire, with its capital at Constantinople. There are a plethora of traditions detailing the ultimate conquest of the Byzantines and their capital, which took place in 1453. However, these traditions can be reinterpreted to mean "Christians" overall (such as either the United States as a Christian country, or the West collectively as a direct descendant of the Christian society of the pre-Enlightenment period). A number of these traditions indicate that the "Byzantines" *(Rum)* will work together with the Muslims fighting a common enemy in the East. After this enemy is defeated, there will be a dispute between the two groups as to whose God was responsible for the victory—the "Byzantines" will ascribe credit to the Cross, while the Muslims will promote the unity of God. This is a typical apocalyptic showdown based upon religious differences and designed to demonstrate the superiority of Islam (cited by the Iraqi radical Muslims led by Abu Musa'b al-Zasqawī).

Today these traditions can be easily reinterpreted. The "Byzantines" (or the United States) and radical Muslims did work together to defeat a third party, the Soviet Union, in Afghanistan between 1979 and 1989. The differences that have appeared since that time can easily be ascribed to conflicting religious beliefs (or in Manichean terms, the "clash of civilizations"), making this group of apocalyptic traditions an interpretative framework for present-day events. The apocalypse then goes on to detail a massive "Byzantine" invasion of Muslim lands—again, a very easily reinterpreted event—and the defeat of the Muslims. Only after the Muslims are purged of unreliable elements and place their trust wholly in God, will He personally intervene in the battle to favor the Muslims and defeat the infidels, and then the Muslims go on to conquer the entire world. This line of apocalyptic thinking emphasizes the continuity of the Muslim community as a fighting community. As the Egyptian apocalyptic writer Sa'id Ayyub, in his 1987 best-seller, *al-Masih al-Dajjal (The Antichrist)*, put it:

> The scholars of the Jews and Christians say concerning the camp of belief [the Muslims], the camp of the Faithful, the True that we [the Muslims] will confront first the Western coalition and then the Eastern coalition [the Communist bloc]. This is our fate! This is our fate that we face off with the heavily armed. We will break his [the Antichrist's] nose in the great apocalyptic war, the Day of God, who is able to do everything. This is our fate, we will face the heavily armed Antichrist and he will shed most of our blood, and then we will drown him in it. This is our fate from the Day of Badr [624] to the Day of the Antichrist. It is our fate that we would have battle-chants upon the Yarmuk [636] from the first, and that we would have battle-chants in Rome at the end of time. It was our fate that we would hear the Crusaders singing and finish them off twice. This is because the Muslims are troops in the service of God, utensils in a community calling to the right and enjoining the good, and forbidding the evil. A community living simply in the understanding of right and wrong.[48]

The conquest scenario that starts with the earliest conquests then finishes with the apocalyptic conquest of Rome and Europe. Since the original Crusaders are equated with contemporary Europeans and Americans (as Usama b. Ladin writes in the appendix), history has an apocalyptic cyclicality to it.

This is one trend in beliefs about the future. Another could be characterized as the messianic trend. The Muslim messianic figure, the Mahdi, has been the focus of expectation for Muslims for hundreds of years, and many dynasties have risen to power because of messianic slogans or claims to be the Mahdi. There are two basic frameworks for the appearance of the Mahdi: either he will appear in Mecca at the time of the *hajj* and lead a large number of Muslims to conquer the core lands of Islam and purify them, or else he will appear in Khurasan, the area that today includes parts of Iran, Central Asia, and Afghanistan.

The latter scenario is very convenient for globalist radical Muslims— or at least it was during the interval when the Taliban controlled Afghanistan. Since the Taliban's principal claim was that they imposed the *shari'a* in its entirety—a claim that radical Muslims supported and acclaimed—devoted themselves to the waging of jihad, and gave sanctuary to globalist radical Muslims such as Usama b. Ladin (in 1996), there was some substance to this idea. In 1996 Mulla 'Umar Muhammad Mujahid, the leader of the Taliban, took the title of *amir al-mu'minin,* a caliphal title. Since the abolition of the caliphate in 1924, many Muslims, including radical Muslims, have been seeking a manner by which a caliph could be elected. Thus there was a messianic component to the title, even though it was never accepted by the majority of Muslims.

However, beyond all doubt the primary messianic aspect of the Taliban state was the perpetuation of jihad. This dovetailed nicely with the radical Muslim critique of Muslim societies: they have lost their Islam, have been humiliated by the West (and the rest of the world), and occupy a subordinate position because they abandoned jihad. Since Afghanistan, as Khurasan, has powerful resonance with many Muslims because of the messianic expectations focused on that region, this gave the globalist radical Muslims associated with al-Qa'ida under the leadership of Bin Ladin additional moral authority to proclaim jihad and call for the purification of the present Muslim governments and elites.

In the end, the globalist radical Muslim vision of jihad is world domination (see appendix). Islam must come to dominate the world in its entirety, in accordance with the radical Muslim interpretation of Qur'an 8:39, "And fight them, so that sedition [temptation] might end and the only religion will be that of Allah." Clearly this absolute vision does not speak for all Muslims, but it does have a resonance for many.

AFTERWORD

There is no lack of evidence concerning the Muslim practice of jihad. The classical and modern works on the subject are voluminous, and they are documented by an examination of Muslim actions as recorded by historians. There can be no reasonable doubt that jihad is a major theme running through the entirety of Muslim civilization and is at least one of the major factors in the astounding success of the faith of Islam. However, despite the centrality of the theme of jihad, there have been numerous and sometimes complicated developments in its interpretation and practice. From the initially straightforward conquest of Mecca by the Prophet Muhammad, to the multifaceted Islamic conquests of the following century, to the defensive jihads against the Crusaders and the Mongols, to the revivalist and defensive jihads of the nineteenth century, there are considerable twists.

Today the scholar must ask whether the word *jihad* has been degraded or has lost all coherence due to the multiple tasks for which the Muslim community has used it during the past fourteen centuries. Is jihad still a grand religiously based form of warfare, designed to raise the Word of Allah to the highest? Or has the fact that any political and religious malcontent, such as Usama b. Ladin, can label his struggle *jihad* caused the term to lose all meaning? This question is closely linked with another that many Muslims raise with regard to antigovernmental and globalist radical jihads: are these types of fighting related to the classical concept of jihad at all? This is not an easy question to answer, and some of the answer must be connected to the degree to which the answerer is willing to accept or reject apologetic or negative tendencies in either Islam itself or in radical Islam. In other words, Muslims have themselves raised the question of whether radical Islam, descended from Wahhabism, has remained within the parameters of classical Islam.[1] Whether radical Islam is part of Islam as a whole has never been resolved conclusively by Muslims (for example, by declaring it to be apostasy), and until this happens the reasonable outsider must conclude that it is indeed a legitimate expression of Islam.

From an outsider's point of view, after surveying the evidence from classical until contemporary times, one must conclude that today's jihad movements are as legitimate as any that have ever existed in classical Islam, with the exception of the fact that they disregard the necessity of established authority—that a legitimate authority such as a caliph or an *imam* could declare jihad.[2] Other than this one major difference, contemporary jihad groups fall within the confines of classical definitions of jihad. That this is true can be seen by their careful regard for classical and contemporary law, their heavy emphasis on the spiritual rewards of jihad, and their frequently voiced claim to be fighting for the sake of Islam. However, both antigovernmental and globalist radical groups are guilty of taking exceptions listed in the classical texts and making them the rule—for example, with regard to killing innocents. In short, although the actions of many of these groups may disgust many Muslims, as far as their conduct of jihad, they fall within the limits set by classical and contemporary Muslim law. It can only be added that no Muslim—to the best of my knowledge—working from the classical materials on the subject of jihad and using the traditional Muslim definitions of jihad, has ever succeeded in seriously refuting the claim to be legitimate heirs to the legacy of jihad.

Does the waging of militant jihad have a future as a major theme in Islam? I think that it does not. As appealing as fighting and taking revenge for actual and perceived wrongs inflicted upon the Muslim community over the past centuries might be, the reality is that jihad during the past two centuries has been a dismal failure, with the possible exception of the expulsion of the Soviet Union from Afghanistan (and that was achieved only with extensive aid from the United States). It is difficult to see situations in the world at the present time where jihad is likely to gain the Muslim community anything. The world is simply too interconnected, despite the best efforts of Samuel Huntington to prove otherwise,[3] for jihad to separate Muslims from non-Muslims. From the growth of Muslim minorities in non-Muslim countries to the growth of non-Muslim minorities in Muslim countries, as well as the ongoing process of globalization, the evidence suggests that this process will continue to expand in the coming years. Jihad cannot stop it, at least not in its present form, even with the aid of martyrdom operations.

The era of jihad being an effective tool for conversion has passed as well, and the evidence for its usefulness in transforming Muslim societies is weak. In societies such as Algeria, Egypt, Afghanistan, and Iran where radical Muslim groups have either tried or succeeded in gaining control, generally there has been a strong backlash against their version of Islam and sometimes, as in Iran, against Islam overall (at least among the student and intellectual population). This pendulum effect, so common in all aspects of human society, is fundamentally unacceptable to radical Muslims. They see the truth as immutable; the idea that their actions could produce a reaction against them can only, for them, be explained in terms of a satanic plot or deviation.

Thus, while I do not think that jihad has a future in the larger Muslim world, I also do not think that there is any doubt that it will continue among marginalized groups, and it may even gain power in certain Muslim states of third-tier importance, especially those close to the boundary between Muslim and non-Muslim states and those with substantial non-Muslim minorities. The ideology of jihad will always be an attractant, especially as more and more marginal and syncretistic Muslims from Africa and Indonesia-Malaysia learn Arabic and are able to read the classical sources. Militant Jihad will not die out entirely, simply because it is too well attested in the Arabic Muslim sources, and constitutes to Muslims—because of the conquests—one of the most important proofs of the truth of Islam. Any Muslim reflecting on Islam's days of glory during the seventh and eighth centuries will inevitably be drawn, at least to some extent, by the subject of jihad because of the intertwined relationship between the historical events and the religious beliefs that motivated them.

Yet the fact that the majority of contemporary Muslims do not actively participate in militant jihad demonstrates a decisive rejection of which the radical Muslims are keenly aware. In chapter 2 I cast doubt on the reality of the "greater jihad" for reasons that I consider to be historically sound. In reading Muslim literature—both contemporary and classical—one can see that the evidence for the primacy of spiritual jihad is negligible. Today it is certain that no Muslim, writing in a non-Western language (such as Arabic, Persian, Urdu), would ever make claims that jihad is primarily nonviolent or has been superseded by the spiritual jihad. Such claims are made solely by Western scholars, primarily those who study Sufism and/or work in interfaith dialogue, and by Muslim apologists who are trying to present Islam in the most innocuous manner possible. Presentations along these lines are ideological in tone and should be discounted for their bias and deliberate ignorance of the Muslim sources and attitudes toward the subject. It is no longer acceptable for Western scholars or Muslim apologists writing in non-Muslim languages to make flat, unsupported statements concerning the prevalence—either from a historical point of view or within contemporary Islam—of the spiritual jihad. Thus far these writers have offered no evidence as to whether the spiritual jihad was actually the primary expression of jihad. It is incumbent upon them, therefore, first to prove that this doctrine had some type of reality outside of the Sufi textbooks and second to demonstrate that either a substantial minority or a majority of Muslims historically believed and acted upon it or that the spiritual jihad actually superseded the militant jihad. Thus far no scholar has accomplished this.

However, the motives of the Western scholars and (in some cases) of the Muslim apologists who make these claims are good ones. The most charitable among them would like to see Islam transform itself from a religion rooted in and emphasizing domination and violence to the more peaceful and tolerant style of the internal jihad. Other religions such as Judaism and Christianity have violent pasts (and in certain cases violent attitudes and trends still persist), and have gradually been transformed in this manner, with offensive texts (such as Joshua 10) either reinterpreted or repudiated. This has yet to be accomplished in Islam, despite the hopeful outlook of Western scholars and Muslim apologists. It is important not to exchange wishful thinking for reality. If and when this change happens, it will probably happen along the lines of a definition of jihad that will exclude violence and embrace true religious diversity and tolerance, and it may very well start with emphasizing the spiritual jihad. However, this redirection of jihad would require a complete separation between militant and spiritual jihad that is not present as yet in contemporary Islam.

As can be seen in the discussions in chapters 5 and 6, the primary factors that keep militant jihad from becoming part of Islam's past are the close relationship between Islam and power,[4] exemplified by the *shari'a,* and the historical interpretation and religious significance of the Islamic conquests. Since the *shari'a* is basically the manner by which Muslim domination is expressed through law, calls for its implementation—aside from the legal problem of defining what precisely the *shari'a* means—are essentially calls for the renewal of Muslim domination. Since Muslims are no longer politically or militarily in the world, all implementation of the *shari'a* will ultimately collide with the non-Muslim world's norms (human rights). This can easily be seen by examining the few states that attempt to implement the *shari'a*—Saudi Arabia, Afghanistan during the rule of the Taliban, and the Muslim regions of Nigeria. In all of these regions the domination that the *shari'a* assumes constantly comes under critical surveillance or is rendered impotent. For Muslims this will lead to a sense that the situation is fundamentally wrong and must be rectified by jihad in order to reassert Islamic power.

The other factor that keeps militant jihad from disappearing is the historical recollection of the conquests and their religious significance. As was noted in chapter 5, this issue is far from being irrelevant because of the centrality of the conquests to the propagation of Islam. Although non-Muslims were not converted forcibly to Islam—in most cases—the conquests laid the preconditions for their eventual conversion. In addition to this fact, the conquests were seen from the beginning as one of the incontrovertible proofs of Islam. To disavow them or to examine them critically—which has yet to happen in the Muslim world—will be very painful for Muslims, especially Arabic-speaking Muslims. At every point, as noted above, when Muslims have tried to abandon militant jihad for the internal, spiritual jihad or translate fighting into proselytizing—both of which are completely logical and understandable reinterpretations of jihad—the memory of the conquests and the need to rationalize them have defeated this effort. The problem may lie in the unwillingness to confront the fact that the conquests were basically unjustified. They were not a "liberation" and they were not desired by the non-Muslim peoples;[5] they were endured and finally accepted.[6]

Unwillingness to compare the Islamic conquests with the European colonial conquests—a comparison that to an outside observer seems quite natural and obvious—leads to extensive rationalization of the conquests and in the end opens the door to those, such as radical Muslims and most especially globalist radical Muslims, who embrace the conquests and seek to continue them. At every point rationalization of the conquests also denies Muslims an objective definition of aggression in warfare. Since the "mission" that the first Muslims proclaimed through their conquests was right and just—according to this rationalization— on what basis could one say that European imperialism and colonialism were unjust? The latter also had a powerful vision of civilization for the world, although today it is rejected by its former colonies and largely regretted by the countries that produced it. A sense of self-judgment and an accurate historical acceptance of the Islamic conquests and their effects on the conquered and the colonized would eventually liberate Muslims from the need to defend the conquests and would enable them to join in adopting global norms concerning violence and aggression.

As can be seen in chapters 5 and 6, jihad also represents a danger to Muslims. It is all too easy to turn this weapon against Muslims, as has been done in the recent past. Moving beyond the use of militant jihad would dampen the appeal of radical groups, although it would not cause it to disappear altogether. But it would serve to isolate them from the larger Muslim community and enable the community to confront the danger they represent more clearly and distance itself from it, something that has clearly not yet happened.

APPENDIX

SOME TRANSLATED DOCUMENTS

1
COMMUNIQUÉ FROM THE ARMED ISLAMIC GROUP (ALGERIA)
September 8, 1995[1]

"Might belongs to Allah, His Apostle, and the believers but the hypocrites do not know" [63:8] and in the same manner: "Whoever wishes glory, it is to Allah that glory utterly belongs" [35:10]. The believer who believes in Allah alone and disbelieves in all of the unjust rulers *(tawaghit)*, lords, gods, and rivals will not [fully] realize his belief until he declares all of these to be infidels. Following that [process] he will discover the glory Allah most high described, and none but the one who inclines towards them [the rulers], who flatters them, believes in them—who denies Allah and is a hypocrite with regard to Allah's religion—can ever take it away from him, as it is said: "And do not incline toward the wrongdoers, lest the Fire touch you. You have no supporters apart from Allah, and you will not be helped" [11:113].

The Armed Islamic Group—the only recognized and unified legal flag in these parts—calls all of those infidels. Its call is to repeat that of Abraham which has come to us: "You have had a good example in Abraham and those with him, when they said to their people: 'We are quit of you and what you worship apart from Allah. We disbelieve in you. Enmity and hatred have arisen between you and us forever, till you believe in Allah alone'" [60:4]. This is the religion of Abraham, what is said: "And who would forsake the religion of Abraham except one who makes a fool of himself?" [2:130], and so calling the unjust rulers infidels necessitates being quit of their followers, their worshippers and denying them and their religion just as Abraham and those with him said in the previous verse.

This is the dominating Group, the believing faction, and the victorious sect—with the permission of Allah, all of this will come about—and just as it calls all the unjust rulers infidels, it also calls all their families, their followers, and any who render them aid or owe them allegiance infidels. For this reason you will find it following those who owe the apostates allegiance in the cities, the villages, and the deserts in order to extirpate them completely, and to annihilate their green gardens, to loot their possessions, and to take their women captive in order to make them taste their own evil. The explosions in their homes and their protected cities are because of the unjust rulers; also the repeated slaughters and the blood that flows in every place that has robbed them of their sleep. Let not even one of them close his eyes without expecting his head to be cut off from his body, for his possessions to be looted and his women taken captive. This is Allah's bounty; He gives it to whomever He wishes.

This is the distinction that [has been granted] to the Armed Islamic Group in that they are victorious over every enemy and do not concern themselves with numbers or with provisions, for they know with absolute certainty that control is in the hands of Allah, and that Allah helps those who help Him and defeats those who deny Him; thus the Prophet said: "Be mindful of Allah and He will be mindful of you. When you are mindful of Allah you will find Him turning toward you. Know that if the community was united to aid you, it would never aid you in anything that Allah had not preordained for you, and if it was united to hurt you, it would never hurt you in anything that Allah had not preordained for you, so that the pens are lifted and the papers are dried."[2] Allah has promised to aid His servants, and we are certain of this aid, as He said: "O believers, if you support Allah, He will support you and steady your footsteps" [47:7] and "It was incumbent upon Us to give the believers support" [30:47].

Since our religion and our manner are blameless, everything after that is easy—praise be to Allah, first and last. For this reason the infidelity of this hypocritical people that has turned away from helping the *mujahidin* and owing loyalty to them, and its apostasy will not cause us to turn away from our resolve, and will never hurt us in the slightest; it will only cause our resolve to strengthen and our reward in Allah's eyes.

The Prophet said in one of the traditions concerning the victorious sect that "Allah will turn hearts of people toward them, and cause them to gain sustenance from them"[3] so this is only a gain of reward and sustenance.

At this junction I will turn to the decomposing corpse of France and its uncleanliness—the polytheist enemy of Allah—and say: We do not forget, nor will we ever forget, the aid you have rendered to fight us in our war against those apostates, the enemies of the religion, and we will not flag nor neglect to fight you—we will remain with the covenant of our brothers [in the French-Algerian War, 1958–62] who robbed you of your sleep and caused you and your homosexuals to drink bitterness like the bitterness of the colocynth or worse than that. Woe to you; destruction and defeat is coming not far off, as Allah said: "Indeed, the unbelievers spend their wealth to bar [people] from Allah's path. They will continue to spend it, but it will be a source of anguish for them; then they will be vanquished. And those who disbelieve shall be gathered in Hell" [8:36].

I will not pass up this opportunity to warn what is called the [United] Nations—at its head the Banu Qurayza (the cursed Jews), America, and its homosexual allies, may Allah make them ugly and blind their eyes from the end into which France, the mother of perversions, and its parties have fallen. Watch out that you do not squeeze yourselves into what they have squeezed themselves, lest what strikes them will strike you. We will have no pity or mercy upon you, as Allah said: "Did they not travel in the land and see what was the fate of those who preceded them? Allah brought utter destruction upon them; and the like of this awaits the unbelievers" [47:10].

The entire world should know that we do not fear any created creature; we only fear Allah, the One, "So fear not men, but fear Me" [5:44], and "Surely you ought to fear Allah more, if you are real believers" [9:13]. If you all came, men and jinn, and the trees and the rocks came with you, we would fight you all for the sake of this religion and not fear any condemnation in the sight of Allah.

Know that any affection from you is like dirt, and that your machinations are like farts that leave a bad smell but do not stay once the wind is gone, and it is as if they never were—that is all the trace your machinations leave—and a penis in all your women and daughters. Everyone should know that the killing, massacring, slaughtering, expulsion, burning, and taking of captives that we do, these are sacrifices for the sake of Allah.

We will inform you that because of our creed and our way, **there is no dialogue, no cease-fire and no compromise!** with those filthy, unclean apostates in accordance with the way the righteous forbears acted and our earlier brothers [from 1958–62]. Everyone should know that the penalty for those who call for dialogue or a cease-fire with apostates or claims of compromise is the same as the penalty for apostates, exactly. There is no ambiguity in this matter. We ask Allah that He grant us power over them so that we can cut off their heads and make an example of them, and the same with other innovators, hypocrites, and tempters. We are not afraid of death or killing, since it is one of the two good things—either martyrdom with absolute certainty or victory and power, and we will ambush them so that Allah will strike them with torment either from Him or from us, so that the rage will be removed from our hearts and our hearts will be healed [paraphrase of 9:14–15].

The Messenger of Allah said: "This religion will continue as long as a group fights for it until the Hour [of Judgment] appears"[4] and we are that group, with Allah's permission, and we will kill and slaughter and never cease "so that sedition [temptation] might end and that the only religion will be that of Allah" [8:39]. We will continue like this until this religion is victorious, and the Word of Allah is raised while all others perish.

We say to all the enemies of Allah: suck the clitorises of your mothers and sisters in the same way as Abu Bakr said to ʿUrwa b. Masʿud al-Thaqafi on the Day of Hudaybiyya[5] when he said to the Messenger of Allah: "I am not seeing nobles, but a rabble; a group that would flee or leave you," and then Abu Bakr said to him: "Go suck the clitoris of [the goddess] al-Lat; we would never flee from him or leave him."

We ask Allah to strengthen us in our religion, to aid us against our enemy, to give us power in the land, to perform the prayers, to give the charity, and to enjoin the right and forbid the wrong, or to take us to Him when He is pleased with us so that we can meet our beloved ones, Muhammad and his Companions. The Messenger of Allah said, when he was still in Mecca, oppressed with his Companions before emigrating, to the infidels of Quraysh, "O Quraysh, I have come to you in order to slaughter you,"[6] and no one either east or west feared him. But we have a good example [see 33:21] in them—and woe, woe to all of the enemies of Allah.

Blood, blood, destruction, destruction

"We shall support Our messengers and the believers in the present life and on the day the witnesses shall arise" [40:51].

2

WORLD ISLAMIC FRONT FOR JIHAD AGAINST
ZIONISTS AND CRUSADERS: DECLARATION OF WAR

From al-Quds al-ʿArabi, *February 23, 1998*

Praise be to Allah, mover of the clouds, defeater of the Confederates, and who stated in his law-giving Book: "Then, when the sacred months are over, kill the idolaters wherever you find them, take them [as captives], besiege them, and lie in wait for them at every point of observation" [9:5], and prayers and peace upon His Prophet Muhammad b. ʿAbdallah, who stated: "I was sent with a sword just before the Hour [of Judgment], so that they would worship Allah alone, and my daily sustenance was placed beneath the shadow of my spear, and humiliation and contempt were placed upon those who resist my message."[7]

Since the time when Allah spread the Arabian Peninsula [see 79:30], created within it its deserts and surrounded it with its seas, it has never been crushed and overcome [see 12:7] as by these Crusader hordes that have spread over it like locusts, pressing upon its land, devouring its wealth, and annihilating its greenery. All of this is happening at the same time as "the nations are quarreling with each other over the Muslims, just as starving people quarrel over a bowl [of food]."[8] The seriousness of the times and the minimum [number] of helpers compel us, and also you, to make a stand concerning current concealed events, just as it obligates us to agree on a course of action.

No one today will argue concerning three truths that are backed up by abundant proofs concerning which all fair-minded people will agree. We will list them to remind those who can be reminded, to destroy those who will be destroyed by clarity, and to embarrass those who are embarrassed by clarity, and they are:

1. For [a period of time] going on seven years, America has been occupying the lands of Islam, the holiest of its places, the Arabian Peninsula, stealing its produce, dictating to its rulers, humiliating its people, and frightening its neighbors. It has turned its bases on the peninsula into a spearhead with which to fight the adjoining Islamic peoples. Possibly in the past there were some who would argue the fact of the occupation, but now all of the people of the peninsula would acknowledge it. I will not even note the continual American aggression against the Iraqi people, using the peninsula, despite the refusal of the rulers to permit this, since they are overpowered.

2. Despite the great destruction which has occurred among the Iraqi people at the hands of the Crusader-Zionist alliance, and despite the frightening number of killed—close to a million— despite all of this, the Americans are trying once again to return to these terrible slaughters, as if they were not satisfied with the long siege after the violent war, and not even with ripping apart or destruction. Now they come once again to annihilate what is left of this people and to humiliate their Muslim neighbors.

3. Since the motivations of the Americans behind these wars is religious and economic, and also to serve the interests of the minuscule Jewish state in order to remove eyes from its occupation of Jerusalem and its killing of Muslims there [so, too, the Muslims should respond with a religious and economic war]. The best demonstration of this is their desire to destroy Iraq, the strongest of the adjoining Arab nations, and their aspiration to dissolve the states of the region into paper statelets, such as Iraq, Saudi Arabia, Egypt, and the Sudan. Through their fragmentation and weakness the continuation of Israel will be ensured, as well as the continual brutal Crusader occupation of the peninsula.

All of these crimes and calamities from the Americans are an open declaration of war upon Allah and His Messenger, and upon the Muslims. All the religious leadership—past and present—has had through the Islamic age a consensus that jihad is an individual obligation if an enemy destroys the lands of the Muslims. Among those who have related this are the Imam Ibn Qudama [d. 1223] in his *Mughni*, the Imam al-Kasani [d. 1191] in his *Bada'i'*, al-Qurtubi [d. 1273] in his *Tafsir,* Shaykh al-Islam [Ibn Taymiyya] [d. 1348] in his *Ikhtiyarat,* where he stated: "As for defensive fighting, the most important of the types [of fighting] is to repel an invader from the sanctity and the religion is an obligation according to consensus. There is nothing more obligatory—other than actually believing [in Islam]—than repelling an attacking invader who corrupts the religion and this world."

So, building upon all of this, and taking the command of Allah as our example, we give the following opinion to all Muslims:

The ruling of killing Americans and their allies—whether civilians or military—is incumbent upon every Muslim who is able and in whichever country is easiest for him, in order to liberate the Mosque of al-Aqsa and the Holy Mosque [in Mecca] from their grip, and until their armies leave the lands of Islam, punished according to the law, broken and unable to threaten any Muslim. This is in accordance with the Word of Allah: "Fight them until there is no sedition [temptation] and the religion becomes that of Allah" [2:193]; and His Word: "And why don't you fight for the cause of Allah and for the down-trodden, men, women and children, who say: 'Lord, bring us out of this city whose inhabitants are unjust and grant us, from You, a protector, and grant us, from You, a supporter'" [4:75].

So, with Allah's permission, we call every Muslim who believes in Allah and desires a reward to take as his example the order of Allah to kill Americans and to steal their possessions in everyplace they are to be found, and during every time possible. We also call upon the religious leadership of the Muslims, their leaders, their youth, and their armies to initiate attacks upon the American devil, and upon those allies of Satan who have allied themselves with them, in order to frighten them away from behind them [the Americans], so that they may [re]consider.

"O believers, respond to Allah and to the Apostle if He calls you to that which will give you life; and know that Allah stands between a man and his heart, and that unto Him you shall be gathered" [8:24]; and His Word: "O believers, what is the matter with you? If you are told: 'March forth in the way of Allah,' you simply cling heavily to the ground. Are you satisfied with the present life rather than the Hereafter? Yet the pleasures of the present life are very small compared with those of the Hereafter. If you do not march forth, He will inflict a very painful punishment on you and replace you by another people, and you will not harm Him in the least; for Allah has power over everything" [9:38–39]; and also "Do not be faint-hearted and do not grieve; you will have the upper hand, if you are believers" [3:139].

Shaykh Usama b. Muhammad b. Ladin
Ayman al-Zawahiri, amir of the Gama'at al-Islamiyya (Egypt)
Rifa'i Ahmad Taha, of the Gama'at al-Islamiyya (Egypt)
Mir Hamza, Jami'at al-'Ulama'-i Pakistan (Pakistan)
Fazlur Rahman, amir of the Haraka al-Jihadiyya (Bangladesh)

3

A COMMUNIQUÉ FROM QA'IDAT AL-JIHAD CONCERNING THE TESTAMENTS OF THE HEROES AND THE LEGALITY OF THE WASHINGTON AND NEW YORK OPERATIONS

April 24, 2002

In the Name of God, the Merciful, the Compassionate.

Praise be to the Lord of Worlds, who stated in His Book, "Fight those among the People of the Book who do not believe in Allah and the Last Day, do not forbid what Allah and His Apostle have forbidden, and do not profess the true religion, till they pay the poll-tax out of hand and submissively" [9:29], and prayers and peace upon the Imam of the *Mujahidin*, the Commander of the best of the best, Muhammad b. ʿAbdallah, who stated to those who were infidels "I have come to you in order to slaughter you."[9]

Allah granted to a troop of youths of Islam by His favor and generosity—and the purity of His success and grace—to give back to the community some of its rightful due, and to cause the Crusader enemy to drink from the cup from which we have drunk for a long time. The heroes who put themselves forward in order to demolish the fortresses of the enemy did not put themselves forward because of an earthly reward that they would receive or an ephemeral position or a fleeting lust, but they put forth their spirits as a ransom for the religion of Allah, in order to protect the Muslims, who taught the American hands a lesson through them—by different types of torment and different kinds of supremacy and domination in every place. Thus, in order to support the way of jihad, self-sacrifice, and martyrdom in this community, we bring forth the first of the testaments of the heroes of the Washington and New York raids as part of a series of all of their testaments that they recorded previous to their journey to the land of the enemy beginning with the hero Ahmad al-Ghamidi, may Allah's mercy be upon him.

We are not presenting this series for any reason other than to clarify to the community that the sole motivating factor for these youths was to protect the religion of Allah, and their honor and their sanctities. This was not as a service to any human or taking sides with any philosophy— either East or West—but in service to Islam, and as protection of its people by the purity of their desire—obedient, uncompelled. We also present this as a message to all the enemies of the community [as an example of] that which can be learned from this, that we will strike with an iron hand the heads of our enemies despite their strength and despite our weakness. Our presentation of [the testaments] at this particular time is a confirmation to the community that is living in [a time of] troubles in every place that the only way to salvation from this humiliation is through the sword, as the enemy does not know any other language than it. [The document then discusses whether it is wise to publish the statement because the material contained in it might be used against al-Qaʿida.]

Through this document we are sending a message to America and to the entire world that we—despite what America is doing—are coming and that it will never be safe from the wrath of the Muslims, since [the United States] has started the war and will eventually lose it. Because of the awesomeness of these events [September 11] that have changed the face of history and the enormity of what was accomplished in the community, there have appeared—to our great sorrow— those who accuse those who perpetrated the September Operation. But those who disapprove have not spoken on the basis of [Islamic] legal proofs, or in accordance with logic, but with the tongues of their masters and the concepts of the enemy of this community. Everyone should know that those who carried out these operations and gave themselves up were heroes, and we should never despise those who give themselves up, especially the Muslims among them. For this reason we are compelled to present the issue according to the legal proofs from all sides, without preferring one side over the other, and without ignoring the matter. After research and mutual consultation, we have found that these types of operations are those that will return glory to the community and persuade the unjust enemy of the rights of the Muslim community.

Therefore, we will review the proofs for allowing these types of operations without detail or explanation so that this will be a legal message toward those who have clothed their political attentions in the misery of the legal opinion, and for this also to be a call to fear Allah, to repent and return to the legal proof for those who opposed and accused [us] because of these operations. Even if they are too cowardly to help the fighters (mujahidin) they should at least be quiet. So we will summarize the proofs according to what follows:

America is exactly the same as the Jews in the Muslims' view, and both of them are "people of war." What is permitted with regard to the one who occupies the land of Palestine is permitted with regard to its likeness [the United States] that helps and aids it [Israel]. If this is astonishing, then one should be astonished by those who permitted (legally) the martyrdom operations, in which civilians fall victim in Palestine, as one of the highest forms of jihad; then they say that martyrdom operations in America are forbidden because they kill civilians. This contradiction is astonishing; how is it possible to permit the killing of the branch and not the killing of the root and the support? Everyone who has permitted martyrdom operations in Palestine against the Jews must permit them in America, unless this contradiction is some type of game-playing with legal opinions.

America has never been a land that is protected by a covenant [with Muslims] and never will be; even if we were to grant to the opponent that it is a land protected by a covenant, we would have to say that it has become a nation at war [with the Muslims] because of its breaking of the covenant, its support of the Jews for more than fifty years in occupying Palestine, the expulsion of its people and killing of them. Thus it is a nation of war, that has broken its covenant from the day that it bombed and besieged Iraq, bombed and besieged the Sudan, and bombed and besieged Afghanistan, and it has attacked the Muslims in every place for the past decades. Some who do not know the meaning of legal proofs have disapproved, saying that the operations in America claimed women, elderly people and children as victims, and those are people whose blood is forbidden in Islam, so how can the operations be permitted from a legal standpoint?

We say: the sanctity of the blood of women, young children, and elderly infidels is not absolute. There are cases under which it is permitted to kill them, if they are part of a nation of war. Those situations are during the course of special circumstances, and we believe that a number of those innocents fell victim in the September operations, but they are not placed completely outside the boundaries under certain circumstances during the course of which killing them is permitted, and we will describe them in summary. The opponent may suffice by affirming that if only one of these circumstances holds true, then he must permit the operations because the circumstances are not conditional upon fulfilling all of them, but only one will suffice. These are the circumstances:

a) Muslims are permitted to kill infidel innocents reciprocally; if the infidels are targeting the women, the young children and the elderly Muslims, then it is permissible for the Muslims to act reciprocally, and kill just as they were killed. Allah said: "Thus, whoever commits aggression against you, retaliate against him in the same way" [2:194] and other proofs. An operation of extermination is under way today against the Muslim peoples under the blessing of America, and even with its active participation, even with its actions. The best witness of this is what happened before the eyes and ears of the world in Palestine, in Jenin, Nablus, Ramallah, and other places. Everyone every day followed cruel massacres with American support during the course of which children, women, and the elderly were the targets. Is it not permitted for the Muslims to treat them reciprocally, and kill them in the same way as the Muslims were killed? Indeed, by Allah, it is the *right* of the Muslims.

b) Muslims are permitted to kill innocent infidels in the event of the former being attacked because it is impossible to separate the innocent infidels from the fighters, or in fortresses it is permitted to kill them if they were following but not intentionally. This is in accordance with the word of the Messenger when he was asked about the families of the polytheists who were sleeping, whether they could target women and families. He said, "They are the same." This proves that it is permitted to kill women and young children who are following their fathers when there is no possibility of telling them apart.

c) Muslims are permitted to kill innocent infidels if the innocents aid in the fighting whether by action, word, opinion, or in any form of aid, according to the order of the Prophet to kill Durayd b. al-Simma who joined Hawazin, even though he was 120 years old. He joined them to advise them, and they [the Muslims] treated him just as they treated the fighters. He moved from being protected to being permitted [to kill him] because of his advice against them [the Muslims] in that he advised fighting Islam. How much more then, with regard to one who supported with his vote the election of an unjust criminal government with regard to Islam and the Muslims, would he not deserve killing so that he be denied the possibility of voting for such a government? Judgment is according to probability.

d) Muslims are permitted to kill innocent infidels if it is necessary to burn the fortresses or fields of the enemy in order to weaken his strength with the objective of taking the fortress or causing the state to fall even if innocents fall victim to this, as the Prophet did with Banu al-Nadir.

e) Muslims are permitted to kill innocent infidels if it is necessary to cast heavy projectiles against them which are unable to differentiate between fighter and innocent, just as the Prophet did when he bombarded al-Ta'if with mangonels.

f) Muslims are permitted to kill innocent infidels if the enemy uses their own women and children as shields and it is not possible to kill the fighters and stop their evil from the lands of Islam without killing the "shield"; this is permitted by general consensus.

g) Muslims are permitted to kill innocent infidels when the people with whom there is a covenant break the covenant, so the imam must kill innocents in order to teach the others a lesson, as the Prophet did with Banu Qurayza.

Many will say: but what about the proofs of the permissibility of killing Muslims who were in the World Trade Center, if there really were [any]? We will grant that innocent infidels fit into one of the categories above, but what about the Muslims who died in these operations from what was done there? The answer to this question is in seven aspects, of which the opponent only has to affirm that one of them is true in order to be compelled to permit [the operation].

a) The justifications of the perpetrator if he is a Muslim must be known, and if the justifications are equivalent to that of an emergency then this action is permitted; if there is no emergency to the justifications, then we will answer following.

b) The probability is that in the targets that were hit there were only infidels, and action according to probability in the matter of *shari'* is what binds the legally culpable.

c) Al-Shafi'i [d. 820] and al-Jassas [d. 982] of the Hanafi [school] permit the burning, drowning, or destruction of the lands of hostile foes, even if there are Muslims in these lands who will die because of these actions. Cessation [of conducting warfare] in the lands of war because of the Muslims who live in them would bring about the obstruction of jihad, so al-Jassas answered with the verse "Had it not been for some believing men [and some believing women], whom you did not know, lest you should trample them and earn thereby the guilt unwittingly, that Allah might thereby admit into His mercy whomever He wishes. Had they stood apart, We would have inflicted on those of them who disbelieved a painful punishment]" [48:25] that it does not indicate a complete ban, but in these cases the initiator of the operation is permitted to complete this action.

d) Use of the previous verse and generalizing legal rulings from it would lead to the obstruction of the focus[10] of jihad from all the warring nations, because there is no nation today which does not have large numbers of Muslims in it. Wars today kill large numbers of people; thus use of the law of the verse is null, because it would obstruct the focus of jihad or block it without reason.

e) The most that can be imposed upon the one who mistakenly kills Muslims intermixed with hostile foes as in this case is that they pay one half of the blood price of the one who was killed as Muhammad judged with regard to the Muslims of Khath'am who were living among the warring people of their tribe and were killed. The Prophet paid half of their blood money from the central treasury but did not declare their killer infidel, nor punish him, curse him, or disassociate himself from his action, but disassociated himself from those who lived among [infidels].

f) It is permitted to treat a Muslim who helps the infidels and strengthens them so that he is to be numbered among them according to earthly law. In heavenly terms, he will be raised according to his intention, just as Allah caused the army that was attacking the Ka'ba to be swallowed up by the earth when there were among them those who were not [guilty]. . . .

The previous traditions permitting the martyrdom operations in attacking New York and Washington are derived from the book *Haqiqat al-harb al-Salibiyya al-jadida [The Truth of the New Crusader War]*; whoever wants an extended version of the proofs and discussion of the issue should consult this complete book.

4

'ALI AL-'ALIYANI, "THE IMPORTANCE OF JIHAD, ON THE GOALS OF JIHAD"

From www.alneda.com (May 1, 2002)[11]

The primary goal is to make certain that people worship Allah and to remove them from the worship of creatures to the worship of the Lord of the creatures, to remove all unjust rulers from the entire world, and to make the world free from corruption. This is because the primary cause for corruption from the generations following Noah until the present day has been the submission of humanity to humans who are like them, and the dedication of types of service to them, whether in prayer, oath-taking, slaughter, glorification, law-making, or ruling. This is a deviation from the natural disposition as Allah created it to monotheism, as "I [God] created my servants pure *(hunafa')*, all of them, but demons came to them and tempted them from their religion, forbidding what I permitted for them and commanding them to associate [other deities] with Me—that upon which I did not designate rule."[12] Therefore, the greatest goal of Islamic jihad is to return humanity to the original state that is the primal monotheism (*hanifiyya*) that will cause them to be submissive to the Lord of Worlds, and to make them derive their worldly way of life from Him, and to worship Him, since Allah commanded that they should not worship anyone other than Him. This submission to Allah will enable them to realize felicity and success in this world and the next. . . .

There are other goals and laws for jihad that follow from the primary goal that we have stated just now. Among them are the following:

1) To repel the aggression of those who attack the Muslims

The Most High stated, "And fight for the cause of Allah those who fight you, but do not be aggressive. Surely Allah does not like the aggressors" [2:190]. "Will you not fight a people who broke their oaths and intended to drive the Apostle out, seeing that they attacked you first? Do you fear them? Surely, you ought to fear Allah more, if you are real believers?" [9:13].

2) Removal of temptation from the people so that they can pay attention to the proofs of monotheism without impediment, and so that they will see the system of Islam in its totality so as to know the justice and righteousness for humanity in it, and its exaltedness in all manners. Temptation is of three types:

a) The type that the infidels practice by types of torment and restriction upon the Muslims to cause them to apostatize from their religion. Allah has authorized Muslims to wage jihad in order to liberate the oppressed (*mustada'fin*) when He stated, "And why don't you fight for the cause of Allah and for the down-trodden, men, women, and children who say: 'Lord bring us out of this city whose inhabitants are unjust and grant us, from You, a protector, and grant us, from You, a supporter'" [4:75].

b) These are the circumstances and polytheistic organizations, and the corruption that they produce in different walks of life. By their very existence they serve to tempt the Muslim from his religion, and for that reason removal of them is a primary goal of jihad, as was previously mentioned. Most of the forefathers interpreted the word "temptation" in the verse "so that sedition [temptation] might end and the only religion will be that of Allah" [8:39] as polytheism. There are those who interpret "temptation" as that which the infidels practice in order to cause the Muslim to turn away from his religion, through different types of torment. There is no inconsistency between the verse and the first group [of interpreters], since removal of polytheism is the goal. But removal of temptation from the Muslims, as well as the liberation of the oppressed, is also a goal, since the Book [the Qur'an], the Sunna, and the consensus of the scholars of the community have agreed upon these two matters.

The subjection of the people paying the *jizya* to the laws of Islam, together with forbidding them from openly proclaiming their religions and forbidding them from involving themselves with interest, fornication, or other things also comes under this heading. These circumstances by their very nature tempt the Muslim from his religion, so Allah has commanded the Muslims to wage jihad until the temptation be removed. [A historical example of the Christians of Najran is adduced.] One of the ways in which temptation is removed from the Muslims is the redemption of their prisoners. The infidels will try to tempt the prisoners from their religion; for this reason the jurisprudents have said that redemption of prisoners is an individual obligation upon every Muslim, and have specified jihad for them [the Muslims] until all of the Muslim prisoners have been liberated.

Removal of temptation from the Muslims and their glorification, together with the humiliation of the infidels is a goal of the jihad . . . the verse "till they pay the poll-tax out of hand and submissively" [9:39] is proof that one of the goals of Islamic jihad is that the infidels must be compelled to be humiliated and submissive. In the same way, glorification of the Muslims, and lifting disgrace from them [is a goal].

c) The temptation of the infidels themselves, and their deviance from paying attention to the truth and accepting it; this is because polytheistic organizations and governments constitute a barrier between the people and paying attention to the truth and accepting it. [They accomplish this] because of their destruction of the natural state of the people through their procedural legislation for them in different walks of life. When the natural state and mind of the people are corrupted, they rarely respond to the guidance [Islam], and when a generation has been raised according to humiliation, subjection, and worship of the creation rather than the Creator, and raised in addition to drugs, wallowing in the mire of sex and freedom from the higher qualities, then it is rare to be lifted up to the level of the human soul which knows right from wrong, loves good and hates evil, except when Allah in His compassion reaches out and seizes the person from this state.

For this reason one of the goals of the jihad is the removal of temptation from the infidels themselves, in addition to removal of it from the Muslims according to the earlier point (2). When temptation is removed from the infidels, who are ruled by unjust rulers who pretend to be gods and legislate that which corrupts the natural human disposition in order to arrogate for themselves the worship [due to God], then there is the hope of their conversion to Islam and their [positive] response to the call of true guidance, especially when they live in an Islamic society which is submissive to the legislation of Allah. . . . This is part of Godly wisdom in that He legislated the payment of the *jizya* upon the People of the Book in order to give them the chance to right their natural dispositions by applying the general laws of Islam, by mixing with Muslims, and knowledge of its ennoblement of the human soul, its lifting [people] up from the ugly qualities to the noble ones, and its [turning] from the worship of the creation and Satan toward the guidance of the worship of the Living One, the Self-Existent One, contained in the religion of Islam.

3) Protection of the Islamic state from the evil of the infidels . . . al-Bukhari said in his chapter on the merits of one day standing in readiness in jihad, and the verse, "O believers, forbear and vie in forbearance and steadfastness, and fear Allah so that you may prosper" [3:200]. The Messenger of Allah said: "One day standing in readiness in jihad is better than the world and all that is in it." Clear proofs exist in these previous citations that protection of the Islamic state is one of the great goals of jihad. But one should be aware that the Islamic state is not a territory on the earth that has specific boundaries to be guarded, but it is everywhere in which Islam has penetrated and removed the polytheistic organizations—this has become part of the Islamic state. The Muslims must guard it and urge the ruler of Islam to push forward toward those lands adjacent [to those of the Muslims] in order to expand the area of the Islamic state, because Islam seeks [to dominate] the entire earth in order to subject it to the laws of Allah and His Messenger. Thus the religion of Allah is not connected to a given land or merely one of the races.

4) Killing the infidels, annihilating them, and exterminating them. This is because infidelity is like cancer or even worse, so when an infidel does not convert to Islam or is not submissive to the laws of Islam then it is necessary to extirpate him so that the society in which he exists is not corrupted. The Most High said, "So, when you meet the unbelievers, strike their necks till you have bloodied them, then fasten the shackles. [Thereupon, release them freely or for a ransom, till the war is over" (47:4).] Further He said: "Fight them, Allah will punish them at your

hands, will disgrace them, give you victory over them, and heal the hearts of a believing people" [9:14], and "Strike them upon the necks and strike every fingertip of theirs" [8:12]. "Kill them wherever you find them and drive them out from wherever they drove you out. Sedition [or temptation, *fitna*] is worse than slaughter" [2:191]. "Allah, however, willed the Truth to triumph in accordance with His word and to cut off the remnants of the unbelievers" [8:7]. "It is not up to any prophet to take captives except after too much blood is shed in the land" [8:67]. "That He may cut off a group of the unbelievers or humiliate them, so that they may turn away completely baffled" [3:127]. One of the Messenger of Allah's statements encouraging the killing of infidels is, "An infidel and his killer will never be together in Hell."[13] . . . The Qur'an was revealed in order to incite [people] to this goal, which is killing the leaders of infidelity until the bloodshed on the earth is excessive, as the Most High said: "It is not up to any prophet to take captives except after too much blood is shed in the land. You desire the fleeting goods of this world, but Allah desires the Hereafter, and Allah is Mighty, Wise. But for a prior ordinance of Allah, you would have been afflicted on account of what you have taken by a terrible punishment" [8:67–68].

5) Terrorizing the infidels, shaming them, humiliating them, foiling their tricks, and enraging them. "And make ready for them whatever you can of fighting men and horses to terrify thereby the enemies of Allah and your enemy" [8:59]. "Fight them, Allah will punish them at your hands, will disgrace them, give you victory over them, and heal the hearts of a believing people. And He will remove the rage from their hearts. Allah shows mercy to whomever He pleases, and Allah is All-Knowing, Wise" [9:14–15]. "So that Allah might foil the machinations of the unbelievers" [8:18]. Proof that frightening the enemy is one of the goals of the jihad is from the tradition: "The best of people during the time of tribulation is one who withdraws, taking his possessions with him, to worship his Lord and fulfill his due, and a man who leads his horse by the head in the way of Allah terrifying them.". . . .

Jihad has elevated goals, noble benefits, and many uses. It realizes for the Muslims what is inside themselves when they practice jihad. For example,

a) It exposes hypocrites. When the Muslims are in a state of comfort and plenty, many are joined to them who desire the worldly goods and do not want to lift the Word of Allah above the word of infidelity [see 9:41]. They achieve salvation but conceal their real [motives] from the rest of the Muslims. The best way to expose them is jihad, because jihad is fought for the sake of something more expensive than what a man can own other than his creed, which is his spirit. But the hypocrite does not want to put forth other than to save his spirit and to increase the pleasures of his soul. So when the call of jihad is made, which could expose him to losing his spirit, his hypocrisy is exposed to the people. The Most High said, "Allah will not leave the faithful in the state in which you are, until He separates the vile from the decent" [3:179], "but when a sound *sura* is sent down and fighting is mentioned therein, you will see those in whose hearts is a sickness look at you like one who has fainted in the throes of death" [47:20].

For the Muslims to know the hypocrites would bring unnumbered benefits, for the latter are the internal enemy, and the danger they constitute oftentimes is greater than that of the external enemy. If they were known, then they could be prevented from going on raids with the Muslims, and the believers would not have to pay attention to the false rumors or delays they initiate, nor to their words dressed in the clothes of good counsel and improvement. The believer would be able to fight them according to what Allah commanded them, "O Prophet, fight the unbelievers and the hypocrites and be stern with them" [9:73].

b) Purification of the believers from their sins. The Muslim fighter, when his intention is pure toward Allah, during the course of the battle when he kills the infidels, gains a great reward, just as is described in the tradition, "the infidel and his killer will not be together in Hell." If the dust and fear in the path of Allah are combined in his heart, then his sins fall away. If the infidels kill him then that is the great victory, the like of which nothing else is the equal: martyrdom. What will tell you what is "martyrdom"? [Muhammad] said, "There is no one who enters Paradise who wants to return to this world—despite everything that he owned on it—other than the martyr, who ardently desires to return and be killed ten times because of the nobility in it [the rank of martyr]."[14]

Martyrdom in the path of Allah and forgiveness of sins is a lofty goal and a great benefit that comes to the Muslims in their jihad. The Most High said, "Such are the times; We alternate them among the people, so that Allah may know who are the believers and choose martyrs from among you. Allah does not like the evildoers! And that Allah might purify the believers and annihilate the unbelievers. Or did you suppose that you will enter Paradise, before Allah has known who were those of you who have struggled, and those who are steadfast." [3:140–42]. . . .

c) Education of the Muslims toward perseverance, steadfastness, obedience, self-sacrifice, and other educational benefits. Reliance upon prosperity, gentleness, and lack of the pursuit of hardships and difficulties breeds humiliation, weakness, and [a desire] to cling to the goods of this world, while entering into battles, struggling against enemies, and offering [oneself] the possibility of gaining the favor of Allah in areas of tumult refines the soul, instructs it, causes it to be reminded of its fate, and necessitates preparation for the journey [death]. Pursuit of jihad then becomes a habit that is desirable, just as the meek desire rest and prosperity. Jihad educates in the human soul many qualities, such as the quality of bravery, courage, perseverance, brotherhood, clemency, and other praiseworthy qualities, while removing from the soul the equivalent negative qualities, such as the quality of cowardice, stinginess, selfishness, and others.

d) Obtaining spoils and captives, since this has a place in the human soul. For this reason [Muhammad] would give the booty of the dead person to the killer and take part of the spoils to the other members of the army when just one person was fighting. . . . One should note that the goal of spoils is one of the subsidiary goals of jihad and not one of the basic ones. For this reason someone is not to fight for the sole sake of spoils lest no good [reward] be counted to their jihad. The basic goal of the jihad is to raise the Word of Allah, to diminish the word of the tyrant, to extend the rule of Allah upon the earth. If the Muslim intends to accomplish this with his jihad, and then his soul desires gaining spoils from the infidels after breaking their power and dominating over them, then there is no sin in that if Allah wills it.

Since these are the greatest of the goals of the jihad, what is the ultimate goal and when will jihad cease?

The ultimate goal, at which time jihad will cease, is conversion of the entire world to the creed of Islam, other than those of the People of the Book [Jews and Christians] and the Zoroastrians. As for the People of the Book and the Zoroastrians, when they pay the *jizya* they are bound by the laws of Islam that mandate their existence in a state of humiliation and submissiveness, and the Muslims will cease their jihad against them, leave them alone and protect them from their enemies. But the Islamic jihad will never cease during the duration of life because Satan will continue to lead humanity astray, and so the struggle between right and wrong as a godly way will not cease as long as humanity is in existence on this earth . . . the Prophet said: "Now fighting comes, and a group of my community will continue, victorious over the people—and Allah will continue to lift people's hearts up who will fight them, and Allah will sustain them [the Muslims] through them [their enemies] until the decree of Allah comes while they are in the process of doing that. But the homeland of the believers is Syria, and the horse, entangled in its mane, is the good until the Day of Resurrection."[15] "For whoever Allah desires good, He causes him to be learned in religion; a band of Muslims will continue fighting for the Truth, victorious over those who oppose them until the Day of Resurrection."[16]. . .

It is clear with this that jihad will continue until the Hour of Judgment, and that waging jihad against the infidels does not cease until they have converted to Islam, or submitted to the laws of Islam and paid the *jizya* as a condition of their existence, clothed in humiliation and submissiveness. Was there any difference of opinion between the scholars as to which [ones] can pay the *jizya?* The predominant opinion is the word of al-Shafi'i that from polytheists only Islam or the sword can be accepted, but as to the People of the Book, the Jews and the Christians both whether they are Arabs or non-Arabs, the *jizya* can be received from them, and likewise the Zoroastrians—even if they are polytheists because of the special proofs that apply only to them. This is not the place to cover this question in-depth.

Finally we ask Allah to make the fighters constant, to give them the victory and the capacity, just as we ask Him to seal us and them with His seal of goodness and felicity, and to make our deaths a testimony (or martyrdom) on His path solely for His noble face. And that He would receive those martyrs who have died from among the fighters, to grant them the highest levels of Paradise, and to place them with the Prince of Martyrs, Hamza b. 'Abd al-Muttalib.[17]

O Allah, collect us and them in the shadow of Your Throne on the Day that there will be no other shadow besides Yours, give us to drink a salubrious drink from the hand of Your Prophet Muhammad after which we will never thirst. O Allah, we ask you as You are the Mighty, the Glorious, You are the Omnipotent, the Avenger, to annihilate the enemies of the religion, that Your anger would descend upon them, the suffering of Your punishment, the harshness of Your torment which will not be repelled from those criminals, that You would destroy the hypocrites and deceive them entirely! O Allah, destroy the Jews, the Christians, and the polytheists, and whoever has befriended them or helped them in any way against your servants the believers. Prayers and peace upon Muhammad and all of his family.

5

SULAYMAN ABU GHAYTH,
UNDER THE SHADOW OF THE SPEARS

Part I

From the pen of Sulayman Abu Ghayth:[18] It seems that the community has expected that one of the al-Qaʻida organization would come out to it and put the dots on the letters and explain many of the questioning and wondering signs that accompany each communiqué, message, picture, or scene so as to know the truth, the motives, and the goals behind the struggle with the "[pagan god] Hubal of this age" despite its voracity, viciousness, and savagery!! The community deserves the truth that should be known, if it desires the path of true change, of which there is no other path: that is the path of the prophets, the messengers, and those who followed them in purity until the Day of Resurrection.

So I will start with the permission of Allah Most High to explain the issue, describe the event, and lay forth the coming way through my *Under the Shadow of the Spears.*

For what reason do we fight America?

Why is the world surprised and astonished?! For what reason were millions of people baffled by what happened to America on September 11, 2001; did the world really think that something other than this [would happen] or did the world expect something less than that? What happened to America constituted a natural matter and an expected event for a nation that has pursued a manner of terror, a policy of aggrandizement, and the law of force against nations and peoples, and imposed a single way, thought, and manner of life as if all people were employed in its government bureaus or were serving its companies and its economic establishments.

Those who were surprised, astonished, and did not expect [the September 11 attack], those simply do not know the reality of humanity and human nature or the effect of tyranny and oppression upon its feelings, sensations, and perceptions. They apparently thought that tyranny breeds submission, that force yields resignation, that injustice leaves nothing but passivity and subjection. Probably they also thought that this environment would guarantee that manhood would die, that the will would be broken, and that nobility would be wrenched from the person. Those people have missed the mark twice. Once because they are ignorant of reality of derision toward a person, and another time because they do not know the ability of a person to achieve victory. This is any person, let alone to one who believes in Allah as Lord, in Islam as a religion, and in Muhammad as Prophet and Messenger. [He] knows that his religion refuses lowliness and does not permit humiliation for him, and rejects degradation. How could it, when he knows that his community [Islam] was brought forth to be at the center of leadership and trail-blazing, at the center of hegemony and domination, at the center of giving and receiving? How could it, when he knows that the basis of governing the earth belongs to Allah—not to either east or west, not to a philosophy or a way other than the way of Allah "And fight them, so that sedition [temptation] might end and the only religion will be that of Allah" [8:39]?

As long as the Muslim knows these truths and believes in this way, he will not stop even for one second in his hasty rush to arrive at them and act in accordance with realizing them, since his spirit, as well as his time, wealth, and children, obligate him to do this. "Say: If your fathers, your sons, your brothers, your spouses, your relatives, the wealth you have gained, a trade you fear might slacken, and the dwellings you love are dearer to you than Allah and His Apostle or than fighting in His way, then wait until Allah fulfills His decree. Allah does not guide the sinful people" [9:24]. These justifications are incidental and natural, and were spoken by any child sitting before the television screens on that blessed day, to say in all innocence and spontaneity "Would America have expected anything less than this!" As for the factual and legal justifications, they will be the subject of the second part.

Part II

As for the justifications from which we, as an organization, proceed and build our activities, plan out our direction and our manner of operation, these are operational and factual justifications that take into account happenings and readings of events. These are also knowledge-based and legal justifications that give us feelings of assurance and certainty that what we are doing is for the aid of our religion and community. It is not my purpose to record these justifications merely in order to justify what happened, but also to place them before you as a token of assurance that we will continue to strike the Americans and the Jews and to target them, whether as human targets or as institutions. What will come upon the Americans will not be less than what has already come, so let America expect and prepare. It should take steps to prepare and tighten its seatbelts because we will come to it from a place they do not expect ". . . while we await for you that Allah will smite you with a punishment, either from Him, or at our hands. So, wait and watch, we are waiting and watching with you" [9:52].

As for our operational and factual justifications, they are many, above counting. I will suffice here with just mentioning a few, and leave the reader the freedom to consider the other matters. America is the head of infidelity in our present-day world, the leader of the infidel democratic system that is based upon the principle of division between religion and state, and that the people govern the people through making laws that collide with the way of Allah and allow that which Allah has forbidden. It [America] compels other nations to govern by means of these laws and ways, and considers any country that rebels against these laws as one that is outside the world community and its law. It uses this as a pretext to punish them [outlaw nations] and besiege them, and then cut them off. Thus, it [America] desires that religion on this earth belong to someone other than Allah, but Allah rejects [the idea that] the religion be anything other than His [8:39].

America, in partnership with the Jews, is the head of corruption and decay, whether this is moral, conceptual, political, or economic corruption, and it intends to propagate depravity and iniquity between people by means of the trash media and base methods of education. America is the reason for every injustice, wrong, and oppression to befall the Muslims. It is behind all of the disasters that have happened and continue to happen to the Muslims. It is drenched in the blood of the Muslims and cannot conceal or hide this.

In Palestine for more than fifty years the Jews, with the blessing, aid, support, and standing behind them in international fora of the Americans, have pursued the cruelest forms of killing, force, maltreatment, and expulsion—and the events of Jenin are the best witness of this. The Jews have expelled close to five million Palestinians, killed close to 260,000, wounded close to 180,000, and detained close to 160,000. In Iraq because of the American bombardment and siege, more than 1.2 million Muslims have been killed, and during the past ten years more than a million children have died because of the siege, or approximately 83,333 children per month or 2777 children each day. In the al-ʿAmiriyya shelter, 5000 Iraqis were killed.

In Afghanistan, America has killed during its war with the Taliban and al-Qaʿida 12,000 Afghani civilians and 350 Arab fighters—among them women and children so that entire families of Arab fighters were finished off in their cars after being bombed by American planes [using] R.P.G.s so that no remains other than scattered fragments were found. In Somalia, America killed more than 13,000 Somalians and performed types of sexual assaults upon young boys and women. As for America's support of world Christians against the Muslims . . . in the Sudan, the Philippines, Indonesia, Kashmir, Macedonia, Bosnia, and other places, there are sorrowful things that are a disgrace. As for the sieges that America imposes upon Muslim countries as a punishment against them because of their rebellion against its laws, they exceed the ability to measure. Muslims suffer economic disasters beyond imagination because of them.

Beyond all of that, is it not the right of prey when it is bound and being dragged to the slaughter to try to liberate itself? As it is being sacrificed, is it not its right to kick the leg [of its oppressor]? Is it not its right, after it is slaughtered, to spray its slaughterer with its blood??

After all of this, some still shed crocodile tears over what happened to the nation of infidelity and try to exonerate Islam (like idiots) from what has happened to it, and beg for its sympathy and benevolence in its dealings with the Muslims. They send messengers and messages to the fighters in the hope that they will desist from butting Hubal; is this what they think of us??

No, by Allah! we are attracted to the Americans and they to us. We will not be saved if they are; there is no good in us if our firing ceases, and no power or nobility if we do not take vengeance for our brothers in Palestine, Iraq, Afghanistan, and every place. Nay, we praise Allah who made the head of this alliance the Americans so that Allah can distinguish between the disgusting and the good. "Allah will not leave the faithful in the state in which you are, until He separates the vile from the decent" [3:179], and we praise Allah a second time that it [the United States] announced that it was a Crusader war, as this [announcement] made the standard clear: there is none other than the trench of belief and the trench of infidelity. And we praise Allah a third time that He made the infidel world and those apostates with it distinguish [friend from foe] so that the truth will be manifest to the community, the picture will be clarified, and censure will be lifted.

Part III

Thus the justifications from which we begin our jihad against the Americans, and that fill us with certainty and assurance in that we are aiding our religion, our creed, and our community, are many, and this is not the place to enumerate them, since they are spread throughout the writings of the people of knowledge. No one can argue with these justifications or refute them except the one who lives in the bureau of fear whose axis is "We fear that a misfortune will befall us" [5:52] or the one who slips into pleasures thinking that he can repel evil or gain some benefit, or the one who is an opportunist ". . . and if a victory is accorded to you from Allah, they will say: Were we not on your side?; and if the unbelievers have a share [in victory], they will say: Did we not subdue you, and thus protect you from the believers?" [4:141] thinking that he will take pleasure at the highest levels of cleverness and political enlightenment. Or the one who prostrates himself before the threshold of the doors of tyrants hoping for a position, promotion, gift, or present!

These [diversions] have never diverted us even for one day from continuing on our path, our jihad, our design, and our important issue, and they will never divert us. In this article I will present one justification that will suffice for jihad against the Americans and the Jews, and any who act like them in preventing it from being realized—and that legal justification is that according to their actions there should be reciprocity. The Most High said, "Thus, whoever commits aggression against you, retaliate against him in the same way" [2:194], "The reward of an evil is an evil like it" [42:40], "If you punish, then let your punishment be proportionate to the wrong done to you" [16:126].

The words of the learned ('ulama') are clear with regard to these verses. Ibn Taymiyya in *al-Ikhtiyarat* and *al-Fatawa*, Ibn Qayyim [al-Jawziyya] in *I'lam al-mawqi'in* and in *al-Hashiya,* al-Qurtubi in his

Tafsir, al-Nawawi in *al-Muhadhdhab,* al-Shawkani in *Nayl al-awtar,* and others. Whoever looks at these citations will come to the conclusion that they all agreed that the punishment of reciprocity that is found in these verses does not merely apply to the individual instance referred to in the text, but it is a general legal principle with regard to blood-revenge, the laws of Allah *(al-hudud),* treatment of infidels, iniquitous Muslims, and tyrants. When it is permitted to take revenge upon a Muslim for his crime, then it is self-evident that the hostile infidel deserves to be treated in the same manner in which he treated the Muslims.

After the numbers of Muslims that we have mentioned in the previous section that were annihilated at the hands of the Americans either openly or with their aid, support and backing—according to this, we are still at the beginning of the road. The Americans have not tasted from us what we have tasted from them. The number killed in the World Trade Center and the Pentagon does not even reach the number killed in the 'Amiriyya shelter in Iraq, and this is only a tiny number of those killed in Palestine, Somalia, the Sudan, the Philippines, Bosnia, Kashmir, Chechnya, and Afghanistan. We have not arrived at equivalency with them; thus, we have the right to kill four million Americans, among them one million children, expel twice that number, wound and incapacitate hundreds of thousands. No, it is our right that we fight them with chemical and biological weapons, to cause them to catch lethal, strange, and bizarre diseases that have struck the Muslims because of their [the Americans'] use of chemical and biological weapons.

America does not know any other language than the language of power as a means of stopping it and lifting its hands from the Muslims and their affairs. America does not know the language of dialogue! Nor the language of living together in peace! Nor appeals, destruction, or disapproval. Nothing but blood will reach America: "Fight them, Allah will punish them at your hands, will disgrace them, give you victory over them, and heal the hearts of a believing people" [9:14]. Yes, He will heal the hearts of a believing people, He will heal the heart of a mother who has lost her child, He will heal the heart of a wife who has lost her husband, He will heal the hearts of the children who are orphans, the women who are widows, and the demented old men, and He will heal the hearts of those expelled from their homes unjustly.

Lastly, I say to our oppressed brothers in every place that we have sworn an oath to Allah to aid His religion and His oppressed servants. We will not leave you in the darkness of tyranny, tyrants, force, and degradation, but we will aid you with everything that we have. We know well what the slanderers and defeatists do not know, what the governmental clergy do not know, what the fickle, the vacillating, and the chameleons do not know, what the opportunists do not know, what the hypocritical and uninformed missionaries do not know, what the tradition of the Prophet says: "There is no one who leaves a Muslim in the lurch in anyplace from whence his honor is being besmirched, or his sanctity is being destroyed without Allah leaving that person in the lurch someplace; there is no one who helps a Muslim in someplace from whence his honor is being besmirched, or his sanctity is being destroyed without Allah helping him in someplace in which he wants."[19]

We know well what Uways al-Qarni said, bearing what has come to us: "O you of Murad,[20] the believer's fulfilling the ordinance of Allah will leave him friendless, but by Allah, we will enjoin the right and forbid the wrong, so that they will take us as enemies, finding iniquitous people to support them, so that by Allah, they will accuse us of terrible things. This, however, will not prevent me from speaking the truth."[21] Nothing will prevent us from speaking the truth and continuing in the truth and acting to fulfill the truth.

6
TRANSLATION OF "THE LAST NIGHT"
From reproduction in New York Times[22]

The Last Night[23]

He said: One of the Companions said: The Messenger of God ordered us to recite it previous to a raid, and we recited it, took booty and were safe.[24]

1. Mutual swearing of the oath unto death and renewal of [one's] intention. *Shave excess hair from the body and apply cologne. Shower.

2. Knowing the plan well—all the angles, together with the [likely] reaction and opposition from the enemy.

3. Reading/recitation of *suras* al-Tawba [9] and al-Anfal [8], and considering their meanings together with Paradise that God has promised to the believers, especially to the martyrs.

4. Reminding the soul of hearing and obedience[25] that night [the "Last Night"] for you will be faced with what will cause it to be less than 100 percent in its hearing and obedience, so spiri-

tually exercise its purification [the soul], understand it, subordinate it, and incite it [to good works] at that time. The Most High said: "And obey God[26] and His Apostle and do not quarrel among yourselves lest you lose heart and your strength dissipates. And stand fast, for God is on the side of those who stand fast." [8:46]

5. Staying the night [praying], pressing onward in prayer, divination (jafr), strengthening [oneself], [obtaining a] clear victory,[27] and ease of heart that you might not betray us.

6. Much remembrance [of God], and know that the best way of remembrance is to read/recite the Noble Qur'an—according to the consensus of the knowledgeable people so far as I know. It is sufficient that it is the Word of the Creator of heaven and earth—to whom you are going.

7. Purify your heart[28] and cleanse it from all uncleanliness. Forget and become oblivious to that thing called "this world." The time for play is over and the appointed time for seriousness has come. How much of our lives we have wasted! Is it not [right] that we should occupy ourselves during these hours with advancing in acts pleasing to God and obedience?

8. Let your breast be open, tranquil to the bounty of God because it is only a few minutes before the happy, satisfying life and the eternal Paradise begins in the company of the prophets, the upright people, the martyrs, and the righteous, may God have mercy on all of them. We ask God of His bounty. Be optimistic, because [Muhammad] "loved optimism (fa'ı) in everything he did."[29]

9. You should consider how—if you fall into temptation—you will be able to resist, remain steadfast, and recover. You know that whatever happens to you would never detract from [your spiritual level] and whatever would detract from you would never happen to you. This is nothing but God's test in order to raise the level [of your martyrdom] and to expiate your sins. You can be certain there are only minutes left until the merit will be clear—with God's permission—of that great reward from God. The Most High said: "Or did you suppose that you will enter Paradise, before God has known who were those of you who have struggled, and those who were steadfast" [3:142].

10. Remember the Word of God Most High: "You were yearning for death before you actually met it. Now you have seen it and you are beholding it." [3:143] And also remember: "How many a small band has defeated a large one by God's leave. [God is with the steadfast]."[30] [2:249] And His Word Most High: "If God supports you, no one will overcome you; but if He forsakes you, then who will be able to support you after Him? And in God let the believers put their trust!" [3:160]

11. Remind yourself of the prayers—and [those] of your brothers—and contemplate their meanings (morning and evening devotionals, [the devotional of entering] the town, the devotional of traveling, and the devotional of meeting the enemy [in battle]).[31]

12. The expectoration (from the soul, into a siphon;[32] and the clothes, the knife, your personal belongings, your ID, your passport, and all of your papers).

13. Check your weapon before you leave and again before you leave. "Sharpen your knives so as not to cause pain to your sacrifice."[33]

14. Tighten your clothing tightly around you. This is the way of the pious forefathers. They would tighten their clothing around them prior to a battle. Tighten your shoes well. Wear socks so that your feet will fit in the shoes and not come out. All of these things are circumstances of this present [world]. God suffices for us, and what a Guardian!

15. Pray the morning [prayer] in a group, and meditate on its merit. Repeat the devotionals after it [the prayer], and do not leave your apartment without performing the ritual ablutions.

Continue to pray [. . .][34] Read His Word: "Did you, then, think that We created you in vain and that unto Us you will not be returned?" [23:115] *surat al-mu'minin.*[35]

Then you begin the Second Phase
When the taxi is taking you to the a[irport], then recite the devotional of travel, the devotional of [entering a] town, the devotional of praise, and other devotionals.

When you have arrived and you see the a[irport] and have gotten out of the taxi, then say the prayer of shelter; every place you go say the prayer of shelter in it. Smile and be tranquil, for this is pleasing to the believers. Make sure that no one of whom you are unaware is following you. Then say the prayer: "God, make me strong through your entire creation," and say: "O God, make me sufficient for what You wish," and say: "O God, we place You on their [the enemies'] throats, and we take refuge in You from their evil,"[36] and say: "O God, make for us a barrier before them and one behind them, and then fool them when they are not looking," and say: "God suffices for us; He is the best Guardian" in accordance with His Word Most High: "Those to whom the people said: 'The people have been arrayed against you; so fear them.' But this increased their faith and so they said: 'God is sufficient for us. He is the best Guardian.'" [3:173][37]

Then when you have said it, you will find matters straightened; and [God's] protection will be around you; no power can penetrate that. [God] has promised His faithful servants who say this prayer that which follows:

1. [They will] return with grace [from God] and His bounty
2. Evil will not touch them
3. [They will be in] accordance with the grace of God

The Most High said: "Thus they came back with a grace and bounty from God. No harm touched them; and they complied with God's good pleasure. God's bounty is great." [3:174] All of their devices, their [security] gates[38] and their technology will not save them nor harm [anyone] without God's permission.

The believers will not fear it [death]; only the followers of Satan will fear it—those who at the core are fearful of Satan and have become his followers. The servitude belongs to God, for fear is mighty servitude toward God, [making certain that one is] turned only toward God—praised is He and Most High—and He alone is worthy of it. Those who said—fearing to perish—the verses: "That indeed is the Devil frightening his followers . . ." [3:175] [those] who are impressed by the civilization of the West, those who have drunk of hell; it has given them to drink together with cold water [?],[39] and they have feared its weak and perishing abilities: ". . . but do not fear them and fear Me; if you are true believers!" [3:175] Fear is inside of God's followers, but the believers do not look other than to God, the One and Only, who has everything in His hand and the power of the people.[40] The most certain form of belief is that God will overturn the guile of those unbelievers, for the Most

High said: "That was done so that God might foil the machinations of the unbelievers" [8:18]. Then you must remember the most important of all the [possible] remembrances, and that is that it must not be lost upon you to remember the statement "there is no god but God."[41] For if you said it a thousand times none would be able outdo it—even if you were silent[ly praying] or if you were remembering God [out loud]. Of the greatest [remembrances] are the words of [Muhammad] "Whoever says: 'There is no god but God' truly in his heart will enter paradise."[42] Or as he said with the same meaning: "If the seven heavens and the seven earths were placed in one palm and 'there is no god but God' in another palm then 'there is no god but God' would outweigh them all."[43] You should be able to consider the awesomeness of this statement when you fight the "Confederates" *(al-ahzab).*[44]

The one who considers it will find that there are no pointed letters— this is a sign of perfection and completeness, as the pointed words or letters lessen its power. This is made perfect by the repetition of the word of the unity [of God] with which you affirm to your Lord through fighting under its banner as did the Messenger of God. It is incumbent upon Him to raise them [to Paradise] on the Day of Judgment.

And additionally, do not show outward signs of embarrassment or nervousness, but be joyful and happy, open of heart and calm because you are going toward God's welcome and His favor; then this will be a day— with the permission of God—that you will finish with the *houris* [women] in Paradise:

> Smiling towards the face of the perished one [dead]: O youth
> You are coming to the Gardens of Eternity

In other words, you are going toward it [Paradise], and saying: "We are coming toward you!" with remembrance and prayer: "God is with His servants, the believers, to protect [them], ease [their way], guide [them], and to make certain of the victory in everything."

The Third Phase
When you board the p[lane], the first step you take as you enter should be to give the prayer and the supplications. Visualize that this is "going out in the morning" in the path of [God] as [Muhammad] said: "Going out in the morning and coming back in the evening in the path of God are better than this world and all that is in it,"[45] or whatever he would say. When you place your foot into the p[lane] and take your seat, then say the devotionals, and give the prayers as a good deed to God as we

have mentioned previously. Then stay occupied with the remembrance of God—maximizing it. The Most High said: "O believers, if you encounter an enemy host, stand fast and remember God frequently, that perchance you may prosper" [8:45]. Then when the p[lane] starts to move toward liftoff, and it begins to advance f[orward?], say the prayer of the traveler, because you are traveling toward God Most High—and how blessed is this journey!

Then you will find it stop and then take off.[46] This is the time of the meeting of the two groups,[47] and so pray to God Most High as the Most High mentioned in His Book: "Lord, fill us with forbearance, enable us to stand fast, and help us against the unbelievers" [2:250],[48] and His Word: "Their only words were: 'Lord, forgive us our sins and our excess in our affairs. Make firm our feet and grant us victory over the unbelieving people'" [3:147], and the word of His Prophet: "O God, Revealer of the Book, Mover of the clouds, defeater of the Confederates (ahzab); defeat them and grant us victory over them. O God, defeat them and shake them!"[49] Pray for victory for yourself and all of your brothers, and that they might strike their targets. Do not be afraid to ask God that He would grant you [the rank of] martyr, as you advance without retreating, patient and hoping for God's reward.

Then each one of you should prepare to fulfill his part together with the one with whom God is satisfied, and to clench his teeth just as the pious forefathers did prior to entering into battle.[50]

At the beginning of the confrontation, strike in the manner of champions who are not desirous of returning to this world, and shout: *Allahu akbar!* [God is great!], for this shout causes fear to enter into the hearts of the unbelievers. The Most High said: "[And when your Lord revealed to the angels: 'I am with you; so support those who believe. I will cast terror into the hearts of those who disbelieve.'] So strike upon the necks and strike every fingertip of theirs." [8:12] You should know that the Gardens [of Paradise] have been decorated for you in the most beautiful way, and that the *houri*s are calling to you: "O friend of God, come," after dressing in their most beautiful clothing.

When God requires one of you to slaughter, go to it as if [the order] came from their father and mother for it is necessary for you. Do not dispute, but listen and obey. When you have slaughtered, loot those whom you have killed—for this is one of the Ways *(sunna)* of the Chosen One [Muhammad]. But he made this conditional upon being certain that no one would be occupied with looting, and consequently abandon that which was more important: watching the enemy—whether [they are occupied with] trickery or attack—this danger is much greater. And if it is thus that they are led according to the necessity of action, and if the group does the opposite to the action of the individual, then forbid him because the action [. . .][51] the Way [of the Prophet Muhammad] *(sunna)*—and necessity overrides the Way.

Do not take vengeance for yourself, but strike every blow for God Most High. This is in accordance with 'Ali b. Abi Talib[52] who fought one of the unbelievers in [a spirit of] vengeance against the unbeliever and the latter pressed upon 'Ali, and he brandished his sword, and then struck him and then struck [again]. When the battle finished, the Companions [of the Prophet] asked him about this action—why was it that he had not struck [back at] this unbeliever, who had struck him and struck him again. 'Ali said: "This was because I was afraid that I would strike him in vengeance for myself, so I lifted my sword [only in defense]," or whatever he said.[53] Then when he had summoned [correct] intention, he went and struck him [the unbeliever], killing him. "All of this was my religion[54] in the hands of God, seeking to do well to myself before God, so that this action would be for the sake of God alone."

Then follow the law regarding prisoners and pay very close attention to them, fighting them as the Most High said: "It is not up to any prophet to take captives except after too much blood is shed in the land. You desire the fleeting goods of this world, but God desires the Hereafter, and God is Mighty, Wise." [8:67]

When everything is finished according to what is planned complete that which you have begun, striking whoever resists in the c[ockpit][55] or in the p[lane] and the c[abin], remembering that this action is for God, Exalted and Lifted Up. The brothers should not become gloomy because of what is imposed upon them, but proclaim good news to them, calm them, remind them [of God], and give them courage. How beautiful that the man should read/recite verses from the Qur'an! According to the Word of the Most High: "So let those who sell the present life for the life to come fight in the way of God. [Whoever fights in the way of God and is killed or conquers, We shall accord him a great reward]" [4:74] and His Word Most High: "And do not think those who have been killed in the way of God as dead; [they are rather living with their Lord, well-provided for]" [3:169] and others that are similar, or declaim them just as the pious forefathers would compose poetry in the midst of battles to calm their brothers and to cause tranquility and joy to enter their hearts.

Do not forget to bring a little portion [of food?], a coffee cup, or a glass of water for yourself and your brothers to drink so that it is easier for you, as now the True Promise is near and the hour of victory comes.

Open your heart and part your breast as a greeting to death in the path of God; be always remembering [God], and renew your prayer so that it will be easier to follow just before the [sight of the] goal causes one to waver and let your last words be: "There is no god but God and Muhammad is His Messenger."

After that—if God wills—there will be the meeting [with God] and the opening into the mercy of God. When you see the masses of the unbelievers, remember the Confederates *(al-ahzab)*, whose numbers were approximately ten thousand thousand fighters[56] and how God gave victory to His servants the believers [Muslims].[57] The Most High said: "When the believers saw the Confederates, they said: 'This is what God and His Apostle have promised us, and God and His Apostle are truthful.' And it only increased them in faith and submission." [33:22][58]

Prayers and peace be upon Muhammad

7

"MOMENTS BEFORE THE CRASH, BY THE LORD OF THE 19"
BY LOUIS ATIYAT ALLAH

Published at www.jehad.net (January 22, 2003)[59]

Before I started to write this article, I had considered many different false words and thoughts privately that I had decided to pour out in it. The earlier idea had been to discuss which direction events were taking and what the future of the battle between the *mujahidin* and America will be. Naturally, discussion of the future is a stimulating and exciting topic, especially since we have now passed a year since the blessed [September 11] raid, and I had thought to discuss this issue in order to dispel the anxiety that has afflicted many and to clarify that the victory of *mujahidin* is certain and undeniable, if God wills. Their victory will fulfill many cosmic [Prophetic] ways, and multiple laws in the texts of the Divine Law (the *shari'a*), and the affairs of humanity and [all of] history point to the fact that these ways cannot be delayed:

> When Moses comes and throws down his staff,
> then magic and the magician are null and void.

Usama and the *mujahidin* have come and have thrown four "staffs" at America, and they have nullified what they [Americans] have done, since what America has done is nothing but the deception of a magician. A magician will never succeed when he comes.

But then this morning every desire except that to weep has disappeared. Do not think that this was the weeping of sadness and anxiety, but the weeping of one who is ecstatic with pride at courage, when one sees it embodied in front of one, as a human being, speaking. [It was] the shaykh 'Abd al-'Aziz al-'Umari, may God have mercy upon him, giving the community of Islam his final testament before departing to fight in the path of God. May God's peace and His mercy be upon you, O 'Abd al-'Aziz!

I saw visions of mountains of courage, stars of masculinity, and galaxies of merit. I saw visions of the Nineteen Men, great—and everything else in this world became smaller in my eyes, as I lamented, and tears filled my eyes as I repeated in secret emotional pain a voice I would like for them to hear this moment:

> Do you hear my pain, and the world's pain, in my chest, O you who travel from this life and are tranquil? O you who travel to the Gardens of Eternity—the highest of places, I see that you have hastened, but I have not. Would it hurt if in your appointment you included me? Saying to me "Come to the land of eternity or return." I saw the vision of the heroes, who won the apocalyptic war, the contemporary Battle of Badr.

I saw the vision of 'Abd al-'Aziz al-'Umari, Wa'il and Walid al-Shehri, Muhammad 'Ata', and Satam al-Suqami . . . I saw the picture and fell into a lengthy meditation about the vision of them. Those radiant faces, one of which is worth a million of the "scum" of the Arabs . . .

During the final moments before the crash of the first plane, I imagine them reciting the Qur'an in their hearts, repeating that: "God has bought from the believers their lives and their property in return for Paradise" [9:111]. Here Muhammad 'Ata' sits in front of the steering wheel, with Satam beside him, each one of them fortifying the other . . . both of them seeing the distance lessen with terrifying speed that cannot strengthen any other human hearts than those filled with the love of Allah . . . with the love of meeting Allah, and with deep desire to meet the beloved ones, Muhammad and the Companions.

The moments are dominated by the strain and the anxiety that accompany the beginning [of an operation] . . . the operation succeeded in gaining control of the plane, subduing the infidels *('uluj)*, and the *mujahidin* held the upper hand and controlled the plane, and then Allah caused His calm to descend upon them and showered them with clothes of tranquility, steadfastness, satisfaction, and happiness because of the closeness of the final destination. The plane closed in with frightening speed toward the Tower, while Muhammad ʿAtaʿ and Satam gaze at it with tranquility and calm, repeating internally . . . "O Allah, take our blood until You are satisfied; do not make a grave for us. O Allah, we have only gone out to fight in Your path, and seeking Your favor. O Allah, receive our souls as a small gift for Your sake, as 'we have rejoiced in the bargain that we have made' [9:111]."

In tranquility and calm they repeat this prayer internally, while they urge the plane onward, just as ʿUmayr b. al-Hammam one day urged [himself] onward saying: "O Messenger of Allah, is there nothing between myself and Paradise other than these dates? By Allah, what for a long life!"[60] So Muhammad ʿAtaʿ and Satam repeat: "By Allah, there is nothing between us and Paradise except for this air that separates us from the first building. By Allah, what for a long life!" Thus, they urge the plane forward, as if to remove with their hands the time, the distance and all the worldly separation so as to arrive immediately in Paradise. O Allah, make them arrive in Paradise!

In the back Waʿil, Walid, and al-ʿUmari . . . every one of them looking at the other ones with smiles, and the eyes of each one tell the others: "We have cut loose from this life in order to come to this moment . . . the moment in which we will leave this world to Paradise, the breadth of which is [the size of] the heavens and the earth . . . O Lord, when will this moment end and when will we arrive in Paradise??" The tranquility encompasses the place, and there is no sound other than the roar of the engines . . . so these three knights look toward the faces of the frightened, terrified Americans, looking at them with a gaze of pity, since they are now on the way to Hell—the Hell that "leaves nothing or spares nothing, scorching mankind. Upon it stand nineteen . . ." [74:29–30]. ʿAbd al-ʿAziz al-ʿUmari looks at those infidels, and wishes that they would only say "There is no god but Allah" so that they would be saved from the torment, saying to them: "Say: There is no god but Allah; this is the word that will intercede for you."

But the faces of those infidels do not understand "There is no god but Allah" and do not want to understand, and think that the government of the United States of America will save them from destiny. They do not know that when the Day of Allah comes, the Day of Bush is null and void. When the commander of the detachment, Muhammad ʿAtaʿ, sees that there is no more than several hundred meters between him and the building, he says to Satam: "Tell the youths to come here; praise to Allah that we are on the verge of entering our dwellings!" Satam hurries and calls the youths, Walid, Waʿil, and ʿAbd al-ʿAziz, "Come here, immediately!" So they come in and lock the cockpit door behind them.

These are the impressions of martyrdom according to the new martyrdom operation method in the contemporary world. We Muslims invented it, and we will be leaders of humanity in it. We will seek martyrdom together, holding fast with our hands, embracing each other, singing the tune of eternity and repeating it while we face death:

> In the path of Allah we continue, desiring the uplifting of the standard, so that we will return glory to the religion, so that we will return might to the religion. Blood will flow from us, blood will flow from us.

Nothing but a few moments remain—very few moments. At a few meters, Muhammad ʿAtaʿ leaves the controls, takes the youths—each one embracing the other, laughing and crying, and each one saying good-bye to the others. Satam shouts: "We will meet in Paradise, O youths!" and Waʿil says: "O Lord, bring us together in Paradise with our brothers whom we have left in Afghanistan. O Lord, bring us together with them in Paradise!" Tears of joy are mixed with tears of farewell, as they remember the others who cannot join them.

And they remember the Shaykh Usama as feelings of gratefulness flash from their eyes to this man who guided them upon this path, and Walid looks before him one last time as he says: "O Allah, collect us together in Paradise with the Shaykh Usama!" Then their voices rise, while they are joined together, each one with their hand on the shoulder of the other, standing in a line, united with Allah, the Lord of Worlds. "This is the moment of closing into the beginning of the journey towards Paradise, and so let us all form a line, joined together, intent upon praying, praising, saying *Allahu akbar* [God is greater], and *al-Hamdu li-llah* [Praise be to God]. Let us all stand in a line, joined together, as Allah described for the believers: 'Allah loves those who fight in His cause arrayed in battle, as though they were a compact structure' [61:4], facing forward, not backward. There is no god but Allah, and Muhammad is the Messenger of Allah."

These are the last words that the Muslim hero, going forward to Allah, not going backwards, should say, who holds death in his heart, asking Allah for forgiveness. These ones did not fear death, they went out seeking death, and death is that which they value. It is sad that it was necessary for it to meet them—if it were possible for them to seek life, then the community would be ashamed in the face of these heroes! But the decree of Allah is irresistible, and they sought to meet Allah.

Thus, the Sword of Islam, Usama b. Ladin, the Supreme Commander of the Armed Muslim Forces began. This is the first battle in contemporary Muslim history, and it is as if the Shaykh Usama stands on the edge of the galaxy, clothing the community in war, saying to his knights: "When you see my signal, go forward" and then they see his signal and the first detachment goes forward, and crashes into the first tower. Then the Shaykh Usama says *Allahu akbar!* and the Muslims say *Allahu akbar* in all directions with him. Then the shaykh gives the signal and the second detachment goes forward in the second plane.

Marwan al-Shehhi, Faʿiz al-Qadi, Ahmad al-Ghamidi, Hamza al-Ghamidi and Muhannad al-Shehri . . . this second detachment encounters some difficulty, but detachments of Muslims do not acknowledge difficulties, and do not know the word "impossible." Marwan and the youths swear by Allah that the army of Allah are those who overcome [see 37:173], and they fervently pray while they are piloting this plane: "O Lord, O Lord, O Lord, grant us our places as You granted to those of the first detachment!" They entreat Allah not to allow them to deviate, and Allah grants them mercy, smoothing the route for them and preparing the way of god-fearers for them. Allah inspires them: if they pilot the plane in just such a way, so as to hit the corner of the building, then it will be too late for the people inside to respond to the evacuation procedures. Thus, there will be no time for mutual congratulations and no benedictions close to the arrival in Paradise. There are no glances of joy and felicity, or repetitions of *Allahu akbar*—there is simply not time for this, since there was barely time after taking control of this recalcitrant plane. This is not important, since their desire was more for Paradise than to stay for a few extra minutes.

Praise be to Allah, praise be to Allah, the plane completes its way and demolishes the second fortress. The heroes take rest having reached their places, and made the world wonder after them, with some of the weak-minded repeating: "Impossible, impossible, impossible that people would do something like this piloting a plane." They did not know that it was Allah who ordained it in this manner. "The second detachment succeeded, by the Lord of the Kaʿba; yes! By the Lord of the Kaʿba!" and the Shaykh Usama says *Allahu akbar,* and the Muslims in every direction follow him. Then he orders the third detachment: they must go to the abode of Satan, the collection point of the forces of world infidelity, and demolish it in such a way that perhaps Allah will ease our struggle in Palestine, and so we will destroy what is exalted above us, completely.

They shook the foundations of infidelity, and attacked in the manner of heroes and persevered. The arrows of Satan and the knights of Allah have met in the first confrontation with the head of infidelity, America, but it was a confrontation that the *mujahidin* had made and planned with new weapons—infidelity stood aghast, not moving, and its stronghold was utterly destroyed. But as for the fourth detachment, it was delayed slightly, and infidelity was roused from its drunkenness and from the terror of what had struck it, and downed it with one of its planes.[61] Then the Muslims praised their Lord, and the Shaykh Usama fell to the earth bowing, while the Nineteen heroes fly up to Paradise, looking down to earth and asking: "O Lord, when will our brothers join us?"

Thus ended the greatest battle in the history of contemporary Islam in a complete victory. This is what I saw as I considered the faces of these knights. Each one of them tells a story of bravery. I saw their faces and I wept—I wept because they have traveled the path of jihad and martyrdom, while we sit here . . . and I knew that those knights did not attain Paradise and martyrdom because they "committed suicide." They knew that they were not crazy people who found planes to hijack, but they came as soldiers who opened an aperture in the walls of the enemy. They came because they were an avant-garde who were not burning themselves like the anonymous Japanese who covered himself in gasoline so that he could gain the sympathy of people, but were burning themselves at a high price so as to smash the foundations of the tyrant and to demolish the idol of this age, America.

And they came at the word of their shaykh, who called them from the silly [rulers] of Ibn Saʿud, and Husni [Mubarak], and all the other retards who falsely call themselves "those in authority" [see 4:59]—they are nothing but tentacles of the octopus upon you, with the head of the octopus [being] in New York and Washington, D.C. They came because they wanted to take the world from one state into another: a state in which the Muslims bow their heads, and the people do not know of anything other than America, the great nation, to a state in which the Muslim will have self-confidence, his own identity, and will be able to say: "We are just like that: a great state which is exemplified by Usama." They came because they represented a terrifying historical leap which will cover the stages of social change and extricate the Muslims in one fell swoop from humiliation, dependency, and servility. They also came because they had finished numerous [planning] sessions that had taken up long months that were blessed by Allah, who took away from them the eyes and sight [of the enemy] . . . He could only bless them by granting success, and so take joy!

They also knew without a shadow of a doubt that what they were doing was right, but they only wished that they could both attain martyrdom and see the destruction of the might of the enemies of Allah they accomplished by their bravery. But since there was no way to have both of them, it was necessary that they realize the former.

I considered this scene and was reminded of the Shaykh Usama, since he was overcome when he blessed them and blessed their actions. I knew that this man would not hold back his tears when he blessed them, blessing his sons who lived with him for many months organizing them, training them and educating them.

O Allah, just as You allowed them to demolish the fortresses of the enemy, extricate the Muslims from their weakness and humiliation! Just as You closed the eyes and vision [of the enemy] and allowed them to arrive at their goals, O Allah, grant to our Shaykh Usama what he has desired from You as a gift: the destruction of America! Thus, history will write that he and his men were the second generation after that of the Prophet's Companions to destroy two empires in a few short years. O Allah, just as You granted to them and ennobled them with martyrdom, and gave them great fame in this world, allow us to reach what they reached. Take from our blood as You took from theirs. O Allah, our sins are many and our guilt is large; there is no salvation for us except through martyrdom that will purify us from our guilt. We come forward, not backward, O Allah, make the path easy for us to join with our brothers, the mujahidin.

TIMELINE

610	Approximate beginning of revelations to Muhammad
622	The *hijra* from Mecca to Medina; year one of the Muslim calendar (*anno hijira*)
630	The conquest of Mecca
632	Death of Muhammad
637	The conquest of Syria-Palestine
732	Battle of Tours; high-point of Muslim conquests in western Europe
1099	Crusader conquest of Jerusalem
1187	Salah al-Din (Saladin) defeats the Crusaders at the Horns of Hattin
1258	Mongol destruction of Baghdad
1260	Mongols defeated at ʿAyn Jalut; high-point of Mongol conquests in the Muslim world
1291	Expulsion of the Crusaders from Syria-Palestine
1453	Constantinople and the Byzantine Empire are conquered by the Ottoman Turks
1683	Ottomans defeated at Vienna; high-point of Muslim conquests in eastern Europe
1707	The death of Aurengzeb, the last effective Moghul Muslim ruler of India

1817	The death of Usaman Dan Fodio, the *mujaddid* of Nigeria
1882–85	The Mahdist movement in the Sudan
1914–18	World War I
1924	The end of the Ottoman caliphate
1947–49	The foundation of the state of Israel
1967	The Six-Day War between Israel and the neighboring Arab states of Egypt, Syria, and Jordan
1973	The October War between Israel and Egypt and Syria
1979	Peace accord between Israel and Egypt; the Soviet Union invades Afghanistan
1987	Beginning of the First Intifada among the Palestinians of the West Bank and Gaza
1993	The Oslo negotiations between Israel and the Palestine Liberation Organization
2000	The failure of the Oslo negotiations; beginning of the Second Intifada
2001	The September 11 attacks; United States' invasion of Afghanistan

GLOSSARY

AHZAB	The "Confederates" against whom the Muslims fought in 627 C.E.
ALLAHU AKBAR!	God is greater!
AL-AMR BI-L-MA'RUF WA-L-NAHY 'AN AL-MUNKAR	"To enjoin the good and forbid the evil"; the basis of the Muslim social order
BIDA'	Blameworthy innovations
DA'WA	Communication or missionization
FATWA	A legal ruling solicited from a mufti
HADITH	The tradition literature ascribed to the Prophet Muhammad and his Companions
JIHAD	Religiously mandated warfare
JIZYA	The poll tax required of non-Muslims in order to live under the *shari'a*
MAMLUK	White slave-soldiers
MUHAJIRUN	Immigrants
MUJAHID/MUJAHIDIN	Fighters in the jihad
MUTTATAWWI'A	Volunteer fighters, often Sufis
RIBAT/MURABIT	A border post/ one who fights or is stationed at a border post
SHAHID/SHAHADA	Martyr, martyrdom, or the Islamic confession of faith
SHARI'A	The divine law of Islam
SURA	A "chapter" of the Qur'an

TAKFIR	To label someone a non-Muslim
TAWHID	The declaration of the absolute unity of God
WAHDAT AL-WUJUD	The unity of being (all of creation is part of God)

NOTES

Several of the radical Muslim websites cited below have recently been sup-pressed or have disappeared. Those that are no longer available are marked by an asterisk.

INTRODUCTION

1. *Encyclopedia of Islam,* new ed., *s.v.* "Djihad" (E. Tayan). The more com-monly used transliteration of the term is adopted herein. For exhaustive discus-sions of jihad, see Albrecht Noth, *Heiliger Kreig und heiliger Kampf in Islam und Christentum* (Bonn, 1966), pp. 22–25, 42–57; and Alfred Morabia, *Le gihad dans l'Islam médiéval* (Paris, 1993), pp. 119–75. I am indebted to these two great scholars for their fundamental studies of jihad to a much greater degree than can be acknowledged in the notes.

2. For examples, see my "Suicide Attacks or 'Martyrdom Operations' in Contemporary *Jihad* Literature," *Nova Religio* 6 (2002), p. 37 n. 21.

3. For a discussion of whether these conquests were actually jihad or the dynasty's after-the-fact rationalization, see Linda Darling, "Contested Territory: Ottoman Holy War in Comparative Context," *Studia Islamica* 91 (2000), pp. 133–63, esp. 137f

4. See Noth, *Heiliger Krieg,* pp. 47f.

5. For a thorough discussion of this theme, see John Kelsay and James Turner Johnson, eds., *Just War and Jihad* (Westport, Conn., 1991); and James Turner Johnson, *The Holy War Idea in Western and Islamic Traditions* (Uni-versity Park, Penn., 1997) , esp. pp. 1–27.

ONE: QUR'AN AND CONQUEST

1. See al-Waqidi, *Maghazi* (Beirut, 1984 repr.), I, p. 27; Muslim, *Sahih* (Beirut, n.d.), V, pp. 199–200; 'Abd al-Razzaq, *Musannaf* (Beirut, 1983), V, pp. 294–95 (nos. 9659–60); the full list in Ibn al-Nahhas al-Dumyati, *Mashari' al-ashwaq* (Beirut, 2002), II, pp. 896–908; and the clarification of J. M. B. Jones, "The Chronology of the *Maghazi*—A Textual Survey," *Bulletin of the School of Oriental and African Studies* 19 (1957), pp. 245–80 (detailing a total of eighty-six).

2. For example, al-Waqidi; Ibn Hisham also refers to this period as *al-mag-hazi.*

3. Uri Rubin, "*Bara'a*: A Study of Some Qur'anic Passages," *Jerusalem Studies in Arabic and Islam* 5 (1984), pp. 113–32; however, Reuven Firestone has questioned the relationship between historical events and certain jihad verses, pointing out that there is a far greater unity in Qur'anic teaching with regard to the subject than previously thought: see his "Disparity and Resolution in the Qur'anic Teachings on War: A Reevaluation of a Traditional Problem," *Journal of Near Eastern Studies* 56 (1997), pp. 1–19.

4. Surveys of the conquests include Marius Canard, "Les expeditions des Arabes contre Constantinople dans l'histoire et dans la legende," *Journal Asiatique* 208 (1926), pp. 61–121; S. A. Hasan's three-part "A Survey of the Expansion of Islam into Central Asia during the Umayyad Caliphate," *Islamic Culture* 44 (1970), pp. 165–76; 45 (1971), pp. 95–113, 47 (1973), pp. 1–13; and 48 (1974), pp. 177–86; Fred Donner, *The Early Islamic Conquests* (Princeton, 1981), chaps. 2–4; Khalid Yahya Blankinship, *The End of the Jihad State* (Albany, 1993), chaps. 6–9; and Elizabeth Savage, *A Gateway to Hell, a Gateway to Paradise: The North African Response to the Arab Conquest* (Princeton, 1997), chaps. 4 and 6.

5. Donald Hill, "The Role of the Camel and the Horse in the Early Arab Conquests," in V. J. Parry and M. E. Yapp, eds., *War, Technology, and Society in the Middle East* (Oxford, 1975), pp. 32–43.

6. Isaac Hasson, "Les *mawali* dans l'armée musulmane sous les premiers umayyades," *Jerusalem Studies in Arabic and Islam* 14 (1991), pp. 176–213; Khalil 'Athamina, "Non-Arab Regiments and Private Militias during the Umayyad Period," *Arabica* 45 (1998), pp. 347–78.

7. Ibn Hisham, *Sira* (Beirut, n.d.), III, pp. 234–35.

8. Ibid., p. 235; and note the concept of *hijra* implied by this tradition, for which see Patricia Crone, "The First-Century Concept of *Hijra*," *Arabica* 41 (1994), pp. 352–87.

9. Ibn al-Mubarak, *Kitab al-jihad* (Beirut, 1971), pp. 30–31 (no. 7); al-Tabarani, *Musnad* (Beirut, 1987), II, pp. 116–17 (no. 1023); Ibn Hanbal, *Musnad* (Beirut, n.d.), IV, pp. 185–86; and al-Bayhaqi, *Sunan* (Beirut, 2001), IX, p. 164; al-Bayhaqi, *Shu'ab al-iman* (Beirut, 2001), IV, p. 29 (no. 4262); see also Blankinship, *End of the Jihad State*, pp. 11–18.

10. Ibn al-Mubarak, *Jihad*, p. 30 (no. 6).

11. Ibid., p. 112 (no. 137).

12. Ibid., pp. 104–5 (no. 125).

13. Al-Awza'i, *Sunan* (Beirut, 1993), p. 387 (no. 1252); and see M. J. Kister, "Do Not Assimilate Yourselves . . ." *Jerusalem Studies in Arabic and Islam* 13 (1989), pp. 321-44.

14. Al-Bukhari, *Sahih* (Beirut, 1991), III, pp. 269 (no. 2903), 272 (no. 2811), 274 (no. 2816), 284 (no. 2853); Abu Da'ud, *Sunan* (Beirut, 1998), III, pp. 15-16 (nos. 2523-24).

15. Al-Bukhari, *Sahih*, III, pp. 265 (no. 2788), 291-93 (nos. 2875-83); Muslim, *Sahih* (Beirut, n.d.), V, pp. 196-99; Abu Da'ud, *Sunan*, III, pp. 17-18 (no. 2531).

16. E.g., al-Nasa'i, *Sunan* (Beirut, n.d.), VI, pp. 3-4; and the examples cited in my "Muslim Apocalyptic and *Jihad*," *Jerusalem Studies in Arabic and Islam* 20 (1996), pp. 99-100, n. 120.

17. Al-Bukhari, *Sahih*, IV, pp. 15-16 (nos. 2977-78).

18. Note how much poetry is cited concerning jihad in Muslim, *Sahih*, V, pp. 168, 186-89, 191-92, and 194-95.

19. Khalil 'Athamina, "The Black Banners and the Socio-Political Significance of Flags and Banners," *Arabica* 36 (1989), pp. 307-26.

20. Al-Bukhari, *Sahih*, III, p. 307 (no. 2933); Muslim, *Sahih*, V, p. 143.

21. See Michael Bonner, "Ja'a'il and Holy War in Early Islam," *Der Islam* 68 (1991), pp. 45-64.

22. Muslim, *Sahih*, V, p. 158; Abu Da'ud, *Sunan*, III, pp. 31-2 (nos. 2586-87).

23. Abu Da'ud, *Sunan*, III, p. 13 (no. 2513); Ibn Maja, *Sunan* (Beirut, n.d.), II, p. 924 (no. 2811); al-Tirmidhi, *Sunan* (Beirut, n.d.), III, p. 95 (no. 1687).

24. Ibn Abi 'Asim, *Jihad* (Medina, 1986), I, pp. 140-41 (no. 11); and see al-Hindi, *Kanz* (Beirut, 1989), IV, p. 282 (no. 10,500): "I was sent as a mercy and as a fighter, not as a merchant or as a farmer; the worst people of this community are the merchants and the farmers, other than those who take their religion seriously," ignoring the fact that Muhammad was a merchant for most of his life.

25. Abu Da'ud, *Sunan*, III, pp. 37-38 (no. 2612); compare Muslim, *Sahih*, V, p. 140; and usually cited by Muslim jurists at the beginning of their discussions on jihad; e.g., al-Sarakhsi, *al-Mabsut*, V (section 10), p. 6.

26. Other Shafi'i jurists such as al-Mawardi (d. 1058) go further than Shafi'i in detailing the specific laws governing combat, however, and we will cover them in more detail in chapter 4.

27. See Mathias von Bredow, *Der Heilige Kreig (ğihad) aus der Sicht der malikitischen Rechtsschule* (Beirut, 1994).

28. Al-Hakim al-Tirmidhi, *al-Munhiyat*, pp. 246, 253-54.

29. Al-Haythami, *al-Zawajir an iktiraf al-kaba'ir*, II, pp. 325-59 (sins 390-408).

30. See my "Survey of Muslim Material on Comets and Meteors," *Journal for the History of Astronomy* 30 (1999), pp. 131-60.

31. Ibn. al-Mubarak, *Jihad*, pp. 89-90 (no. 105); compare al-Awza'i, *Sunan*, p. 360 (no. 1165); and Ibn Abi Shayba, *Musannaf*, IV, p. 218 (no. 19,394); and the discussion in Ibn Rajab, *al-Hukm al-jadira bi-l-idha'a min qawl al-nabi* "*bu'ithtu bi-l-sayf bayna yaday al-sa'a*" (Riyadh, 2002).

32. Most are summarized by Suliman Bashear, "Muslim Apocalypses and the Hour: A Case-Study in Traditional Interpretation," *Israel Oriental Studies* 13 (1993), pp. 75–99.

33. Abu Da'ud, *Sunan*, III, p. 18 (no. 2532); al-Bukhari, *Sahih*, III, p. 284 (no. 2852).

34. Abu Da'ud, *Sunan*, III, p. 4 (no. 2484); and see the discussion in al-Ghimari, *al-Ajwiba al-sarifa li-ishkal al-hadith al-ta'ifa* (Beirut, 2002) (with all of the variants).

35. E.g., Ibn Batta al-'Ukbari's *al-Ibana 'an shari'at al-firqa al-najiya* (Beirut, 2002); and Abu al-Muzaffar al-Isfara'ini's *al-Tabsir fi al-din wa-tamyiz al-firqa al-najiya 'an al-firaq al-halikin* (Cairo, 1999).

36. This material is taken from my book, *Studies in Muslim Apocalyptic* (Princeton, 2002), chaps. 1–3.

37. Abu Da'ud, *Sunan*, III, pp. 44–45 (no. 2640); al-Nasa'i, *Sunan*, VI, pp. 4–7; see M. J. Kister, *"illa bi-haqqihi . . ." Jerusalem Studies in Arabic and Islam* 5 (1984), pp. 33–52, for many variants.

38. Cited in "Muslim Apocalyptic and *Jihad*," p. 93 (from al-Sulami's *al-'Iqd al-durar fi akhbar al-muntazar* [Maktabat al-Manar, 1993], pp. 260–61 [no. 303]).

39. Al-Bukhari, *Sahih*, III, p. 272 (no. 2710); and see Ibn Maja, *Sunan*, II, p. 931 (no. 2783).

40. See Mahmoud Ayoub, "Martyrdom in Christianity and Islam," in Richard Antoun and Mary Elaine Hegland, eds., *Religious Resurgence: Contemporary Cases in Islam, Christianity and Judaism* (Syracuse, 1987), pp. 67–77; also Etan Kohlberg, "Martyrdom and Self-Sacrifice in Classical Islam," *Pe'emim* 75 (1998), pp. 5–26 (Hebrew); idem, "Medieval Muslim Views on Martyrdom," *Mededelingen der Koninklijke Nederlandse Akademie van Wetenschappen* 60 (1997), pp. 281–307; also A. J. Wensinck, "The Oriental Doctrine of the Martyrs," *Mededelingen der Koninklijke Akkademie van Wetenschappen, Afdeeling Letterkunde* 53 (1921), pp. 147–74.

41. Ibn al-Mubarak, *Jihad*, pp. 110–11 (no. 135); and see the prayers in al-Wasiti, *Fada'il al-Bayt al-Maqdis* (Jerusalem, 1979), p. 23 (no. 29); Abu Da'ud, *Sunan*, III, p. 21 (no. 2541); al-Tabarani, *Kitab al-du'a* (Beirut, 1987), III, p. 1703 (no. 2015); al-Tirmidhi, *Sunan*, III, p. 103 (no. 1704).

42. Ibn al-Mubarak, *Jihad*, pp. 63–64 (no. 68); also al-Bukhari, *Sahih*, III, p. 278 (nos. 2829–30).

43. See Jalal al-Din al-Suyuti, *Abwab al-sa'ada fi asbab al-shahada* (Cairo, 1987), *passim*.

44. Abu Da'ud, *Sunan*, III, p. 14 (no. 2517).

45. Ibn al-Mubarak, *Jihad*, p. 37 (no. 20); also Ibn Maja, *Sunan* (Beirut, n.d.), II, p. 935 (no. 2798); Ibn Hanbal, *Musnad* (Beirut, n.d.), II, pp. 297, 427.

46. Ibn al-Mubarak, *Jihad*, p. 38 (no. 22); and see also pp. 117–18 (no. 143), 124–25 (no. 150), where fighters just before going into battle would tell stories of the *hur al-'in* or even say that they were "married" to them; also Ibn Abi Zaminayn, *Qudwat al-ghazi* (Beirut, 1989), p. 242 (no. 111); Ibn al-Nahhas al-Dumyati, *Mashari' al-ashwaq* (Beirut, 2002), II, pp. 771–78.

47. Most of these are described very graphically by Hunnad b. al-Sari, *Kitab*

al-zuhd, (Kuwait, 1985) I, pp. 59–60, 86–88; al-Suyuti, *al-Budur al-safira fi ahwal al-akhira* (Beirut, 1996), pp. 554–73.

48. E.g., Ibn Abi Zaminayn, *Qudwat al-ghazi* (Beirut, 1989), pp. 243–45 (no. 112) (a near-death experience coupled with a tour of heaven and a sampling of its sexual pleasures).

49. Abu Da'ud, *Sunan*, III, p. 15 (no. 2522); and compare Ibn Abi Zaminayn, *Qudwat al-ghazi* (Beirut, 1989), p. 236 (no. 104); and al-Bayhaqi, *Shu'ab al-iman* (Beirut, 2000), IV, p. 25 (no. 4254), for a full list of the benefits conferred on a martyr.

TWO: THE "GREATER JIHAD" AND THE "LESSER JIHAD"

1. Cf. al-Nasa'i, *Sunan* (Beirut, n.d.), VI, p. 6.

2. Michael Bonner, "Some Observations concerning the Early Development of *Jihad* on the Arab-Byzantine Frontier," *Studia Islamica* 75 (1992), pp. 5–32; Bonner, *Aristocratic Violence* (New Haven, 1994) chapter 4; and my "Muslim Apocalyptic and *Jihad*," *Jerusalem Studies in Arabic and Islam* 20 (1996), pp. 99f.

3. Ibn al-Mubarak, *Kitab al-jihad* (Beirut, 1971), p. 36 (no. 16).

4. Al-Awza'i, *Sunan* (Beirut, 1993), p. 368 (no. 1186); compare al-Bukhari, *Sahih* (Beirut 1998), III, p. 264 (no. 2786); and Nu'aym, *Kitab al-fitan* (Beirut 1993), pp. 78f.

5. Abu Da'ud, *Sunan* (Beirut 1988), IV, p. 122 (no. 4344); al-Ghazali, *Ihya* (Beirut, n.d.), II, pp. 284–85; and see Wensinck, ed., *Concordance et indices de la tradition musulmane* (Leiden, 1936–64), *s.v.* "Sultan," for numerous references; as well as Jalal al-Din al-Suyuti (d. 1505), *Ma rawahu al-asatin 'an 'adam maji' al-salatin* (Beirut 1992), pp. 31f.

6. See on this subject, Michael Cook, *Commanding the Right and Forbidding the Wrong* (Cambridge, 2000).

7. Al-Darimi, *Sunan* (Damascus 1996), II, p. 659 (no. 2341); and see Ibn Hanbal, *Musnad* (Beirut, n.d.), III, pp. 456, 460, VI, p. 387.

8. Ibn al-Mubarak, *Jihad*, p. 143 (no. 175); idem, *Kitab al-zuhd* (Beirut, n.d.) (*Istidrak* of Nu'aym b. Hammad), p. 36 (no. 141); Ibn Abi al-Dunya, *Muhasibat al-nafs wa-l-izra' 'alayha* (Beirut, 1986), p. 102 (no. 64); and al-Bayhaqi, *Zuhd* (Beirut, n.d.), p. 163 (no. 369), and see the sources cited by the editor.

9. Al-Bayhaqi, *Zuhd*, p. 165 (no. 373); compare the saying attributed to 'Umar II in al-Mubarrad, *al-Kamil fi al-lugha wa-l-adab* (Beirut 1997), I, p. 120: "[When asked which type of jihad was the best], he said: 'Fighting your passions.'" Much of my discussion below is indebted to John Renard, "*Al-Jihad al-akbar*: Notes on a Theme in Islamic Spirituality," *Muslim World* 78 (1988), pp. 225–42.

10. Al-Tirmidhi, *Sunan* (Beirut, n.d.), III, p. 89 (no. 1671); even so, he cites this tradition in the context of the reward of the *murabit* (one who guards the frontier), so it is not entirely without military implications.

11. For example, al-Jarrahi, *Kashf al-khifa' wa-muzil al-ilbas* (Cairo, n.d.), pp. 424–25 (no. 1361), cites the "greater jihad" tradition as a popular proverb and not as an authentic *hadith*.

12. Al-Muhasibi, *Adab al-nufus* (Beirut, 1991), pp. 54–57.
13. For example, Ibn Abi al-Dunya, *Muhasibat al-nafs* (Beirut, 1986), pp. 96–97; also al-Qasim b. Ibrahim (d. 861), *al-ʿAlim wa-l-wafid* (Sanaʿa, 2001), pp. 436–39 (in his *Majmuʿ kutub wa-rasaʾil al-Imam al-Qasim b. Ibrahim* [Sanaʿa, 2001], II), where he speaks of "fighting the soul," does not cite the tradition of the "greater jihad."
14. Al-Hindi, *Kanz al-ʿummal* (Beirut, 1989), IV, p. 431 (no. 11,263); citing Abu Hilal al-ʿAskari.
15. Al-Ghazali, *Ihya ʿulum al-din* (Beirut, n.d.), III, pp. 7–8ff.
16. E.g., *Ihya*, III, pp. 72f, 261f.
17. Al-Ghazali, *Ihya*, II, pp. 314–15, also 285; cited by Ibn al-Nahhas al-Dumyati, *Mashariʿ al-ashwaq* (Beirut, 2001), I, p. 557 (no. 957).
18. Ibn al-ʿArabi, *Futuhat al-Makkiyya* (Beirut, 1991), II, p. 275; note that in his commentary on this verse (*Tafsir Ibn al-ʿArabi* [Beirut, 1987], I, p. 223), he does not discuss the identity of the subject.
19. See chapter 1, note 32, for references.
20. Ibn al-ʿArabi, *Futuhat*, I, p. 496; other examples of famous jihad traditions cited by Ibn al-ʿArabi can be found as well: e.g., I, pp. 475, 493; III, p. 180; VIII, p. 294.
21. William Chittick, *The Sufi Path of Knowledge* (Albany, 1998), p. 211. For Chittick's understanding of Muslim warfare, see his "Theological Roots of Peace and War According to Islam," *Islamic Quarterly* 34 (1990), pp. 145–63.
22. Chittick, *The Self-Disclosure of God*, pp. 171–72.
23. Ibn al-ʿArabi, *Futuhat*, VI, p. 270.
24. Hamid Algar, trans., *Islam and Revolution: Writings and Declarations of Imam Khomeini (1941–80)* (Berkeley, 1981), pp. 387–88 (the tradition of the "greater jihad" is cited on p. 385); see also the Arabic version, *Jihad al-nafs aw al-Jihad al-akbar*, pp. 48–49.
25. Alfred Morabia, *Le gihad dans l'Islam médiéval* (Paris, 1993), pp. 330–44.
26. Ahmed Rashid, *Jihad: The Rise of Militant Islam in Central Asia* (New Haven, 2002), pp. 1–2.
27. See Linda Darling, "Contested Territory: Ottoman Holy War in Comparative Context," *Studia Islamica* 91 (2000), pp. 133–63.
28. Carole Hillenbrand, *The Crusades: Islamic Perspectives* (Edinburgh, 1999), p. 97.
29. John Esposito, *The Islamic Threat: Myth or Reality?* (New York 1999), p. 30; repeated in *Unholy War: Terror in the Name of Islam* (Oxford, 2002), pp. 27–28.
30. Esposito, *Islamic Threat*, p. 31.
31. Robert Crane, "Hirabah versus Jihad," at www.cuii.org/hirabah.htm (February 9, 2003); for a serious discussion of *hiraba*, see Sherman Jackson, "Domestic Terrorism in the Islamic Legal Tradition," *Muslim World* 91 (2001), pp. 293–310.
32. E.g., Abdul Razaq Kilani, "*Jihad*: A Misunderstood Aspect of Islam," *Islamic Culture* 70 (1996), pp. 35–46; A. G. Noorani, *Islam and Jihad: Prejudice versus Reality* (New York, 2002), pp. 45–60; and many examples from the Internet, e.g., "Jihad" and "Jihad Explained," at *www.unn.ac.uk/societies/Islamic/

jargon/jihad1.htm (June 26, 2003); "Jihad in Islam and Its Real Meaning," at www.dislam.org/jihad/meaning.html (June 13, 2004).

33. See the serious discussions of Abdallah Schleifer, "Understanding Jihad: Definition and Methodology," *Islamic Quarterly* 27 (1983), pp. 118–31, "Jihad and Traditional Muslim Consciousness," *Islamic Quarterly* 27 (1983), pp. 173–203, "Jihad: Modernist Apologists, Modern Apologetics," *Islamic Quarterly* 31 (1984), pp. 25–46, "Jihad: Sacred Struggle in Islam (IV)," *Islamic Quarterly* 31 (1984), pp. 87–102.

34. See Deborah Tor, "From Holy Warriors to Chivalric Order: The ʿAyyars in the Eastern Islamic World, A.D. 800–1055," PhD diss., Harvard University, 2003, chap. 2.

35. Abu Nuʿaym al-Isfahani, *Hilyat al-awliyaʾ* (Beirut, 1997), VIII, pp. 299–301 (no. 12,274); Ibn al-Jawzi, *Sifat al-safwa* (Beirut, 2001), IV, pp. 478–79 (no. 797).

36. Steven Runciman, *A History of the Crusades* (Cambridge, 1988), II, p. 460; and see Ibn Kathir, *al-Bidaya wa-l-nihaya* (Beirut, 1990), XII, pp. 321–22.

37. Al-Munawi, *al-Kawakib al-durriyya fi tarajim al-sadat al-Sufiyya* (Beirut, 1999), II, pp. 435–36.

38. Al-Munawi, II, p. 260.

39. ʿAbd al-Qadir al-Jilani, *al-Fath al-rabbani wa-l-fayd al-rahmani* (Cairo, 1988), p. 83.

40. Simon Digby, *Sufis and Soldiers in Awrangzeb's Deccan* (New York, 2001), pp. 69–70; other interesting citations can be found on pp. 83–84, 122–23, 216 (where Sufi *murid*s are common soldiers in the army).

41. Humphrey Fisher, "Prayer and Military Activity in the History of Muslim Africa South of the Sahara," *Journal of African History* 12 (1971), pp. 391–406.

42. See B. G. Martin, *Muslim Brotherhoods in Nineteenth-Century Africa* (Cambridge, 1976).

43. There were, of course, those who practiced purely internal struggle and never participated in any conquests: the philosophers. On their jihad, see Joel Kraemer, "The *Jihad* of the *Falasifa*," *Jerusalem Studies in Arabic and Islam* 10 (1987), pp. 372–90.

44. The editor of al-ʿIzz b. ʿAbd al-Salam al-Sulami, *Ahkam al-jihad wa-fadaʾilihi* (Beirut, 1996), pp. 9–18, lists fifty-nine books, booklets, and pamphlets written solely on the subject of jihad since the eighth century; while the editor of Ibn al-Nahhas al-Dumyati, *Mashariʿ al-ashwaq* (Beirut, 2002), I, pp. 39–47, lists sixty-eight. This, of course, is only a tiny selection of the number in which jihad is described.

45. Eric Geoffroy, *Jihād et contemplation* (Beirut, 2003), pp. 9–14.

46. See my translation in "Suicide Attacks," pp. 29–35, reproduced in the appendix.

THREE: THE CRYSTALLIZATION OF JIHAD THEORY: CRUSADE AND COUNTER-CRUSADE

1. See Kees Versteegh, "The Arab Presence in France and Switzerland in the Tenth Century," *Arabica* 37 (1990), pp. 359–88; and Manfred Wenner, "The

220 / NOTES TO PAGES 49-56

Arab Muslim Presence in Medieval Central Europe," *International Journal of Middle Eastern Studies* 12 (1980), pp. 59–79.

2. For a discussion of the Sicilian Muslims and jihad, see William Granara, "*Jihad* and Cross-Cultural Encounter in Muslim Sicily," *Harvard Middle Eastern and Islamic Review* 3 (1996), pp. 42–61.

3. See Luis Molina, "Las campañas de al-Manzor," *al-Qantara* 2 (1981), pp. 204–64.

4. Mirabel Fierro, "Christian Success and Muslim Fear in Andalusian Writings during the Almoravid and Almohad Periods," *Israel Oriental Studies* 17 (1997), pp. 155–78; also Manuela Marin, "Crusaders in the Muslim West: The View of Arab Writers," *Maghreb Review* 17 (1992), pp. 95–101.

5. For a graphic picture of the desperate last days of the state of Grenada, see the anonymous *Akhir ayyam Gharnata: nubdhat al-'asr fi akhbar muluk Bani Nasr* (Beirut, 2002).

6. The best comparative treatment of jihad and the Crusades is that of Albrecht Noth, *Heiliger Kreig und heiliger Kampf in Islam und Christentum* (Bonn, 1966).

7. Joseph Drory, "Early Muslim Reflections on the Crusaders," *Jerusalem Studies in Arabic and Islam* 25 (2001), pp. 92–101; Carole Hillenbrand, *The Crusades: Islamic Perspectives* (Edinburgh, 1999), pp. 103–112, notes that the first real indications of a revival of the spirit of jihad came after the fall of Edessa in 1144; see also Noth, "Heiliger Kampf *(Ğihad)* gegen die Franken: Zur position der Kreuzzüge im Rahmen der Islamgeschichte," *Saeculum* 37 (1986), pp. 240–58.

8. Reading through the memoirs of Usama b. Munqidh (of the ruling family of the town of Shayzar), *Kitab al-I'tibar* (Beirut, 1999), one sees the level of symbiosis between the two groups at this time.

9. Reuven Amitai-Priess, *Mongols and Mamluks* (Cambridge, 1995), pp. 8–9.

10. Ibid, pp. 26–48.

11. See Jere Bacharach, "African Military Slaves in the Medieval Middle East," *International Journal of Middle Eastern Studies* 13 (1981), pp. 471–95.

12. For details, see David Ayalon, "Mamluk Military Aristocracy: A Non-Hereditary Nobility," *Jerusalem Studies in Arabic and Islam* 10 (1987), pp. 205–10; "The Military Reforms of Caliph al-Mu'tasim," in *Islam and the Abode of War* (no. 1), pp. 1–39; and see Daniel Pipes, *Slave Soldiers and Islam: The Genesis of a Military System (*New Haven, 1981), pp. 140–58.

13. This title, translated as *The Ways of Thorns to the Struggle-places of Lovers,* conveys little of the contents of the work. Consequently, references to it (such as Dierk Lange, *A Sudanic Chronicle: The Borno Expeditions of Idris Alauma (1564-1576)* [Wiesbaden, 1987], p. 103) have frequently confused it with a romantic treatise of almost the same name.

14. Ibn Hisham, *Sira* (Beirut, n.d.), IV, p. 128.

15. Ibn al-Nahhas al-Dumyati, *Mashari' al-ashwaq* (Beirut, 2002), II, p. 1024.

16. Ibn Abi Zaminayn, *Quduat al-ghazi* (Beirut, 1989), p. 172.

17. Ibn al-Nahhas, I, p. 98 (no. 29).

18. Ibid., p. 129 (no. 60).

19. Hadia Dajani-Shakeel, "*Jihad* in Twelfth-Century Arabic Poetry," *Muslim World* 66 (1976), pp. 96–113.

20. See ʿAbd al-Haqq al-Marini, *Shiʿr al-jihad fi al-adab al-Maghribi* (Rabat, 1989), I, pp. 65–85.

21. Al-Suyuti, *Abwab al-saʿada fi asbab al-shahada* (Cairo, 1987), *passim;* note that al-Subki, *Fatawa al-Subki* (Beirut, 1992), II, pp. 339–54, writing slightly earlier than al-Suyuti, also spends a good deal of time trying to define what constitutes a martyr in Islam (significantly, the questioner was writing from an area stricken by plague, probably the Black Death, in 1349).

22. Ibn Hazm, *al-Muhalla* (Beirut, 2002), V, p. 348 (no. 928); for a complete discussion of this subject, see Khalid Abou El Fadl, "The Rules of Killing at War: An Inquiry into Classical Sources," *Muslim World* 89 (1999), pp. 144–57, especially pp. 150f.

23. Ibn Hazm, *al-Muhalla,* V, p. 352 (nos. 929–30).

24. Ibn al-ʿArabi, *Ahkam al-Qurʾan* (Beirut, 1987), II, pp. 901–2.

25. Mark Cohen, "What Was the Pact of ʿUmar? A Literary-Historical Study," *Jerusalem Studies in Arabic and Islam* 23 (1999), pp. 100–151.

26. Ibn al-ʿArabi, *Ahkam al-Qurʾan,* II, pp. 922–23.

27. Al-Kasani, *Badaʾiʿ al-sanaʾiʿ fi tartib al-sharaʾiʿ* (Beirut, 2000), VI, p. 57.

28. Ibid., p. 63.

29. Ibn Qudama, *al-Mughni* (Beirut, n.d.), X, pp. 366–67.

30. Ibid., pp. 372–75.

31. Ibid., p. 385.

32. Ibid., p. 400.

33. Examples are al-Burzuli, *Fatawa al-Burzuli* (Beirut, 2002), II, pp. 24, 27, 28, 29, 30, 40.

34. Al-Wansharisi, *al-Miʿyar al-mughrib* (Beirut, 1991), II, pp. 112–16; also P. S. van Koningsveld, "Muslim Slaves and Captives in Western Europe during the Late Middle Ages," *Islam and Christian-Muslim Relations* 6 (1995), pp. 1–23, for the fate of those Muslims who were taken prisoner.

35. Al-Wansharisi, *al-Miʿyar al-mughrib,* II, pp. 137–40.

36. Most of this material is collected in *al-Jihad li-Shaykh al-Islam Ahmad b. Taymiyya* (Beirut 1991) (section 1), and is simply culled from his *fatawa;* for the significance of his work, see Alfred Morabia, "Ibn Taymiyya: Dernier grand théoreticien du *Ǧihad* medieval," *Bulletin d'études orientales* 30 (1978), pp. 85–100.

37. Ibn Taymiyya, *Majmuʾa Fatawa* (Cairo, n.d.), XXVIII, pp. 240–41.

38. Ibid., pp. 410–67, especially pp. 413–16, and pp. 501–8, 589–90.

39. Ibid., pp. 462–64.

40. Johannes Jansen, "Ibn Taymiyyah and the Thirteenth Century: A Formative Period of Modern Muslim Radicalism," *Quadreni di Studi Arabi* 5–6 (1987–88), pp. 391–96.

41. See Donald Hill, "The Role of the Camel and the Horse in the Early Arab Conquests," in V. J. Parry and M. E. Yapp, eds., *War, Technology and Society in the Middle East* (Oxford, 1975), pp. 32–44.

42. Shatzmiller, "The Crusades and Islamic Warfare—A Re-evaluation," *Der Islam* 69 (1992), p. 277, states that the reason for this was that horse warfare did not require tactics but relied solely upon the charge or the feigned retreat; for the best discussion of warfare during this time, see Hillenbrand, *Crusades*, chap. 7.

43. See J. D. Latham, "The Archers of the Middle East: The Turco-Iranian Background," *Iran* 8 (1970), pp. 97–103; and E. McEwen, "Persian Archery Texts: Chapter Eleven of Fakhr-i Mudabbir's *Adab al-harb* (Early Thirteenth Century)," *Islamic Quarterly* 18 (1974), pp. 76–99. Ibn al-Nahhas (Beirut, 2002), I, pp. 461–90, is a manual on how to shoot accurately.

44. Al-Tartushi, *Siraj al-muluk* (Beirut, 1995), p. 415.

45. On the mangonel, see Ibn Arnabagh al-Zardakush, *al-Aniq fi al-majaniq* (Aleppo, 1985); other important military treatises are Mubarakshah (fl. ca. 1169), *Adab al-harb* (Dushanbe, 1987); al-Taʿsusi (d. 1357), *Tuhfat al-turk* (Damascus, 1997); Ibn Manjli (d. 1376), *al-Adilla al-rasmiyya fi taʿabi al-harbiyya* (Baghdad, 1988); Abu Saʿid al-Harthami, *al-Mukhtasar fi al-harb* (Damascus, 1995); al-Rashidi, *Tafrij al-kurub fi tadbir al-hurub* (Damascus, 1995); and Khuttali, *ʿAwn ahl al-jihad* (Damascus 1996).

46. For a standard account of its history, see Halil Inalcik, *The Ottoman Empire: The Classical Age, 1300–1600* (London, 1995); for an account of the warfare, see Murphy Rhoads, *Ottoman Warfare 1500–1700* (New Brunswick, N.J., 1999).

47. Accounts of Mahmud's raids are discussed by A. Alami, "Les conquêtes de Mahmud al-Ghaznawi d'après le *Kitab al-Yamini* d'ʿUtbi," PhD diss., University of Paris, 1989; for accounts of his desecrations of Hindu temples, see Richard Eaton, "Temple Desecration and Indo-Muslim States," *Journal of Islamic Studies* 11 (2000), pp. 283–319.

48. Ellison Findly, "Jahangir's Vow of Non-Violence," *Journal of the American Oriental Society* 107 (1987), pp. 245–56.

49. See *Encyclopedia of Islam* (new edition), s.v. "Awrangzib" (W. Irvine and Mohammad Habib).

50. Nizam, *al-Fatawa al-Hindiyya* (Beirut, 2000), II, p. 209.

51. See Dierk Lange, ed. and trans., *A Sudanic Chronicle: The Borno Expeditions of Idris Alauma (1564–1576)* (Wiesbaden, 1987); also P. M. Holt, *The Sudan of the Three Niles: The Funj Chronicles 910–1288/1504–1871* (Leiden, 1999); H. de Castries, ed., "La conquête du Soudan," *Hesperis* 3 (1923), pp. 433–88; and Muhammad Bello, *Infaq al-maysur fi taʾrikh bilad al-Takrur* (Ribat, 1996).

52. For Muslim attacks on Ethiopia prior to the sixteenth century, see B. G. Martin, "Mahdism and Holy War in Ethiopia before 1600," *Proceedings of the Seminar for Arabian Studies* 3 (1973), pp. 106–17.

53. ʿArabfaqih, *Futuh al-Habasha* (Cairo, 1974), p. 2.

FOUR: JIHAD DURING THE NINETEENTH CENTURY: RENEWAL AND RESISTANCE

1. Hamid Algar, *Wahhabism: A Critical Essay* (Oneonta, N.Y., 2002), pp. 3–4. Although Algar is very critical of Wahhabism and does not conceal his par-

tisan point of view, his basic analysis seems to me to be historically correct. See the contemporary radical Saudi leader Sulayman al-ʿUlwan's edition of Ibn ʿAbd al-Wahhab's *al-Tibyan fi sharh nawaqid al-Islam*, pp. 20–24, where the second "nullifier" of Islam is using or believing in any intermediary between the believer and God.

2. As Sulayman b. ʿAbd al-Wahhab, *al-Sawaʿiq al-ilahiyya fi al-radd ʿala al-Wahhabiyya* (Damascus, 2000), pp. 14ff, notes, giving numerous examples (Sulayman was Muhammad b. ʿAbd al-Wahhab's brother and most cogent opponent); and see Samira Haj, "Reordering Islamic Orthodoxy: Muhammad ibn ʿAbdul Wahhab," *Muslim World* 92 (2002), pp. 333–70; and Samer Traboulsi, "An Early Refutation of Muhammad Ibn ʿAbd al-Wahhab's Reformist Views," *Die Welt des Islams* 42 (2002), pp. 384–87.

3. See Ivor Wilks, Nehemia Levtzion, and Bruce Haight, eds., *Chronicles from Gonja* (Cambridge, 1986), pp. 1–17.

4. For these connections, see Bernard Lewis, *Race and Slavery in the Middle East* (Oxford, 1990), chaps. 8–10; for the expansion of Islam in the area, J. P. Charnay, "Expansion de l'Islam en afrique occidentale," *Arabica* 27 (1980), pp. 140–53.

5. I am using his name as it is vocalized in the region; in Arabic texts he is referred to as ʿUthman b. Fuda.

6. Michael Hiskett, "*Kitab al-farq*: A Work on the Habe Kingdom Attributed to ʿUthman Dan Fodio," *Bulletin of the School of Oriental and African Studies* 23 (1960), pp. 558–79.

7. Patricia Crone, "The First-Century Concept of *Hijra*," *Arabica* 41 (1994), pp. 352–87; and for Dan Fodio's thought on the subject, A. M. Kani, *The Intellectual Origins of the Sokoto Jihad*, pp. 6–14; and Muhammad Khalid Masud, "Shehu Usuman Dan Fodio's Restatement of the Doctrine of Hijrah," *Islamic Studies* 25 (1986), pp. 59–77.

8. Shawqi ʿAtaʾallah al-Jamal, "ʿUthman b. Fuda wa-siyasatuhu al-jihad al-Islami al-lati ittabaʿaha," *al-Bahith al-ʾIlmi* 26 (1976), pp. 41–68.

9. See F. H. el-Masri, ed. and trans., *Bayan wujub al-hijra* (Khartoum, 1977), chaps. 1, 4–5, 12–13, 16–17, 22–24.

10. John Willis, "*al-Jihad fi sabil Allah*—Its Doctrinal Basis in Islam and Some Aspects of Its Evolution in Nineteenth-Century Africa," *Journal for African History* 8 (1967), pp. 395–415, especially pp. 402f.

11. Translated by Hiskett, *The Sword of Truth* (Evanston, 1994), p. 66 (with minor modifications), from *Wird ʿUthman b. Fudi*.

12. Using the list of Ismail Balogun, "The Life and Work of the Mujaddid of West Africa, ʿUthman b. Fudi Popularly Known as Usumanu Dan Fodio," *Islamic Studies* 12 (1973), pp. 271–92, at pp. 282–86.

13. See Hiskett, *Sword of Truth*, pp. 92, 105f.

14. Starting out with the resistance to the Portuguese in the early sixteenth century: see K. M. Mohamed, "A Critical Study of *Tahrid ahl al-iman ʿala jihad ʿabdat al-sulban*," *Islamic Culture* 64 (1990), pp. 121–30.

15. See Taufiq Ahmad Nizami, "Muslim Political Thought and Activity in India during the First Half of the Nineteenth Century," *Studies in Islam* 4 (1967), p. 147; and see also Siddiq Hasan Khan al-Qanuji, *al-ʾIbra bi-ma jaʾa fi al-ghazw wa-l-shahada wa-l-hijra* (Beirut, 1998), pp. 237f., where he discusses

this issue. The proclamation is given in Rajabi, *Rasa'il va-fatava-yi jihadiyya* (Teheran, n.d.), p. 21.

16. Nizami, "Muslim Political Thought," p. 147. It is Nizami's conclusion that he was exposed to Wahhabism; I do not know whether visiting Mecca in 1821 would *necessarily* mean that Ahmad Shahid was exposed to Wahhabism, however, since at that time the city was going through a reaction *against* Wahhabism.

17. A. S. Bazmee Ansari, "Sayyid Ahmad Shahid in the Light of His Letters," *Islamic Studies* 15 (1976), pp. 231-45.

18. For example, Quraishi's *Cry for Freedom: Proclamations of Muslim Revolutionaries of 1857* (Lahore, 1996) summarized below; this subject is covered by Schleifer, "Jihad: Modernist Apologists, Modern Apologetics" *Islamic Quarterly* 31 (1984), pp. 25-46, at pp. 26-34.

19. Obviously this name was bestowed by the British, and from an imperialist perspective. I use it for the sake of convenience.

20. Quraishi, *Cry for Freedom*, p. viii.

21. Ibid, pp. 26-28, are magical incantations for protection.

22. Ibid, pp. 81-83.

23. Ibid, pp. 89-90 (I have modified the English translation); other versions pp. 91-92, 96-99.

24. Khan, *Al-'Ibra mi-ma ja'a fi al-ghazw wa-l-shahada wa-l-hijra* (Beirut, 1988), pp. 11f.

25. Ibid, pp. 231-56.

26. See my *Studies in Muslim Apocalyptic* (Princeton, 2002), p. 67 n. 136, citing the tradition (from Ibn Abi Shayba): "If you are offered [the opportunity] to raid, do not choose Armenia, because it has one of the punishments of the grave."

27. I am indebted to Moshe Gammer, *Muslim Resistance to the Tsar: Shamil and the Conquest of Chechnia and Daghestan* for most of my material on Shamil and the jihad against the Russians in the Caucasus; see also Michael Kemper, "Khalidiyya Networks in Daghestan and the Question of *Jihad*," *Die Welt des Islams* 42 (2002), pp. 41-71, for material on Daghestan.

28. This is Gammer's conclusion, *Muslim Resistance to the Tsar: Shamil and the Conquest of Chechnia and Daghestan* (London, 1994) pp. 292-93, illustrated by numerous examples.

29. Russians are merely referred to as *mala'in* (cursed ones): Sharafutdinovoi, *Araboia azychneye dokumenty epohki Shamiliaa* (Moscow, 2001) pp. 42, 43, 45, 77, or as Russians, pp. 57, 72, 88, 99 (letters dating from 1843 to 1858).

30. See Johan de Bakker, "The *Jihad* Waged by the First 'Alawi Sultans of Morocco (1660-1727): A Major Contribution to Their Legitimacy," typescript; and his "Slaves, Arms, and Holy War: Moroccan Policy vis-à-vis the Dutch Republic during the Establishment of the 'Alawi Dynasty 1660-1727," PhD diss., University of Amsterdam, 1991.

31. Amira Bennison, *Jihad and Its Interpretations in Pre-Colonial Morocco* (New York, 2002), chaps. 3-6, is the basis for my account of 'Abd al-Qadir.

32. Pessah Shinar, "'Abd al-Qadir and 'Abd al-Krim: Religious Influences on Their Thought and Action," *Studies in Islam* 6 (1969), pp. 135-64, at pp. 136f.

33. *Ajwibat al-Tusulli ʿan masaʾil al-Amir ʿAbd al-Qadir fi al-jihad* (Beirut, 1996), pp. 107f.

34. Ibid., questions 1:d, e, f, 2:c, 3, 4:c, 5.

35. Ibid., questions 1:b, c.

36. Ibid., questions 2:a, b.

37. Ibid., questions 4:b, d; Shinar, "ʿAbd al-Qadir and ʿAbd al-Krim," p. 146, notes that ʿAbd al-Qadir insisted upon the necessity of emigration in his truce of 1837. On the issue of peace agreements, see Wilson Bishai, "Negotiations and Peace Agreements between Muslims and Non-Muslims in Islamic History," in Sami Hanna, ed., *Medieval and Middle Eastern Studies in Honor of Aziz Suryal Atiya* (Leiden, 1972), pp. 50–61.

38. This is Shinar's conclusion as well: "ʿAbd al-Qadir and ʿAbd al-Krim," pp. 143–45.

39. See John Voll, "The Mahdi's Concept and Use of 'Hijrah,'" *Islamic Studies* 26 (1987), pp. 31–42.

40. P. M. Holt, *The Mahdist State in the Sudan 1881–98* (Oxford, 1958), pp. 156f.

41. The "Pole" or "Axis" is the highest rank of the Sufi hierarchy.

42. *Al-Athar al-kamila li-l-Imam al-Mahdi* (Khartoum, 1991), I, pp. 94–95 (number 21), dated 1298/1881; see also Muhammad Ibrahim Abu Salim, *Manshurat al-Mahdi* (Beirut, 1979), pp. 18–21.

43. Holt, *Mahdist State,* pp. 208f.

44. I accept the comments of Abdi Sheik-Abdi, *Divine Madness: Mohammed Abdulle Hassan (1856–1920)* (London, 1993), pp. x, 1–10, 43–45, that the term "mad Mullah" cannot be used to describe Mohammed Abdulle Hassan other than to reference him in the manner that he is best known to the outside world. He was clearly no more "mad" than any other person described in this book. My entire account of the mullah and his activities is based upon Sheik-Abdi.

45. See Sheik-Abdi, *Divine Madness,* pp. 201–12 for discussion, pp. 52–53, 68–80 for translations of his proclamations; also Robert Hess, "The 'Mad Mullah' and Northern Somalia," *Journal of African History* 5 (1964), pp. 415–33.

46. With the exception of the pamphlet by the al-Shawkani (d. 1850) titled *al-Dawʾ al-ʿajil fi dafʾ al-ʿaduww al-saʾil* in his *Thalathat rasaʾil ila ʿulamaʾ al-Yaman* (Kuwait, 1985), which was apparently written in response to the British occupation of Aden in the Yemen. It is significant, though, that al-Shawkani did not write such a pamphlet against the 1798–1801 French occupation of Egypt.

47. Etan Kohlberg, "The Development of the Imami Shiʿi Doctrine of Jihad," *Zeitschrift der Deutschen Morgenlandischen Gesellschaft* 126 (1976), pp. 64–86; see also Ann Lambton, "A Nineteenth-Century View of *Jihad*," *Studia Islamica* 32 (1970), pp. 181–92.

48. Reproduced in Muhammad Hasan Rajabi, *Rasaʾil va-fatava-yi Jihadiyya* (Teheran, n.d.), pp. 27–54; see also versions in Muhammad Hasan Iraqi and Nasrallah Salihi, *Jihadiyya* (Teheran, 1977), pp. 39f.

49. Rajabi, *Rasaʾil va-fatava-yi Jihadiyya* (Teheran, n.d.), pp. 55–82, at p. 57.

50. Quoted from Rudoph Peters, *Islam and Colonialism: The Doctrine of Jihad in Modern History* (The Hague, 1979), pp. 90–91; the original and a

German translation appear in *Der Islam* 5 (1914), pp. 391–93; a total of fifty-three Ottoman, Persian, and Arab *fatawa* on jihad during World War I are assembled by Rajabi, *Rasa'il va-fatava*, pp. 269–335.

FIVE: RADICAL ISLAM AND CONTEMPORARY JIHAD THEORY

1. Yohanan Friedmann summarizes the traditions enjoining this in "Islam Is Superior," *Jerusalem Quarterly* 11 (1979), pp. 36–42.

2. Rashid Rida, *Fatawa* (Beirut, 1970), III, pp. 1152–53.

3. Ibid., pp. 1155–56.

4. Ibid., p. 1156.

5. Muhammad ʿAbduh and Rashid Rida, *Tafsir al-Manar* (Beirut, 1999), X, pp. 160–62 (commentary to 9:5); Khaled Abou el-Fadl, "The Rules of Killing at War: An Inquiry into Classical Sources," *Muslim World* 89 (1999), pp. 144–57, at p. 150, notes that Ibn Rushd (d. 1198) had also exempted these two groups from being attacked.

6. ʿAbduh and Rida, *Tafsir al-Manar*, XI, pp. 38–39.

7. Ibid., II, pp. 251–53; X, pp. 188f.

8. *Majmuʿat Rasaʾil al Shahid Hasan al-Banna'* (Beirut and Cairo, n.d.), p. 297.

9. Mawdudi, *al-Jihad fi al-Islam* (Damascus, 1984), pp. 9–10; on his thought during the time when Mawdudi wrote his pamphlet on jihad, see Seyyed Vali Reza Nasr, *Mawdudi and the Making of Islamic Revivalism* (Oxford, 1996), pp. 23, 99.

10. Mawdudi, *al-Jihad fi al-Islam*, p. 25.

11. Ibid., pp. 50–51.

12. Ibid., p. 54.

13. The Egyptian modernist Mahmud Shaltut, as translated by Rudolph Peters, *Jihad in Medieval and Modern Islam* (Princeton, 1996), pp. 26f., continues these arguments.

14. Qutb, *Maʿalim* (Riyadh, n.d.), pp. 56–57; for analyses of Qutb's thought, see Ibrahim Abu Rabiʿ, "Sayyid Qutb: From Religious Realism to Radical Social Criticism," *Islamic Quarterly* 28 (1984), pp. 126; idem, "Discourse, Power and Ideology in Modern Islamic Revivalist Thought: The Case of Sayyid Qutb," *Islamic Culture* 65 (1991), pp. 84–102; and William Shepard, "What Is 'Islamic Fundamentalism'?" *Studies in Religion* 17 (1988), pp. 5–26.

15. *Maʿalim*, p. 66; see ʿUkasha ʿAbd al-Manan al-Tibi, *al-Shahada wa-l-istishhad fi Zilal al-Qurʾan li-Shaykh Sayyid Qutb* (Cairo, 1994), pp. 19–34.

16. Qutb, *Maʿalim*, p. 59, trans. Badrul Hasan, *Milestones*, pp. 113–14 (translation amended).

17. Ibid., p. 80 (my translation).

18. Ibid., pp. 64–55, 77f.; trans., pp. 120–22, 141.

19. For example, Ahmad Shalbi, *al-Jihad wa-l-nazm al-ʿaskari fi al-tafkir al-Islami* (Cairo, 1974); Muhammad Darwaza, *al-Jihad fi sabil Allah fi al-Qurʾan wa-l-hadith* (Damascus, 1975); Muhammad Shadid, *al-Jihad fi al-Islam* (Beirut, 1982); and ʿAfif al-Bazri, *al-Jihad fi al-Islam* (Damascus, 1984). All of these are

serious studies of militant jihad, for the most part with the emphasis on fighting Israel.

20. Farag, *al-Farida al-gha'iba* (Amman, n.d.), p. 28; trans. Johannes Jansen, *The Neglected Duty* (New York, 1986), p. 192.

21. Ibid., p. 26; trans., p. 190.

22. Ibid., pp. 38–39; trans., pp. 205f.

23. Etan Kohlberg, "The Development of the Imami Shi'i Doctrine of *Jihad*," *Zeitschrift der Deutschen Morgenländischen Gesellschaft* 126 (1976), pp. 64–86.

24. Algar, *Islam and Revolution* (Berkeley, 1981), pp. 116, 132, 148, 261; for similar more traditional Shi'ite doctrines of jihad, see al-Shaykh al-Rikabi, *al-Jihad fi al-Islam* (Damascus, 1997).

25. Algar, *Islam and Revolution*, p. 303.

26. See, e.g., the lecture of Ayatullah Morteza Mutahhari, *Jihad*, translated by Mohammed Salman Tawhidi as *Jihad: The Holy War of Islam and Its Legitimacy in the Qur'an* (Qumm, 1985).

27. See, for example, *al-'Amaliyyat al-istishhadiyya: Watha'iq wa-suwar al-muqawama al-wataniyya al-Lubnaniyya 1982–85* (Damascus, 1985); and Sa'd Abu Diya, *Dirasa tahliliyya fi al-'amaliyyat al-istishhadiyya fi janub Lubnan;* Bernard Freamon, "Martyrdom, Suicide and the Islamic Law of War," *Fordham International Law Journal* 27 (2003), pp. 338–57, gives a very good overview of the Shi'ite developments.

28. See *Masa'il jihadiyya wa-hukm al-'amaliyyat al-istishhadiyya* (a collection of *fatawa*) (Beirut, 2002), pp. 37–38; see, for the other Shi'ite leaders, pp. 27–29; and for Shaykh Hasan Nasrallah's recent comments, "Sanuqatil ayy muhtill" at www.intiqad.com (November 25, 2002).

29. Islamic Jihad communiqués were formerly available at *www .aljihadonline.org; see those of October 23, 1987, and their important proclamation of December 11, 1987.

30. His collected works were published by Rifa'at Sayyid Ahmad, ed., *Rihlat al-damm al-lati hazamahu al-sayf: al-a'mal al-kamila li-l-shahid al-duktur Fathi al-Shiqaqi* (Cairo, 1997) (4 vols.).

31. See *al-Haqiqa al-gha'iba* (Gaza, 1987) (undoubtedly a play off 'Abd al-Salam Farag's book *al-Farida al- gha'iba*); and see Jabara, *Dawr al-Harakat al-Islamiyya fi al-Intifada al-Mubaraka* (Amman, 1992), for a more apologetic account.

32. On this subject see Basheer Nafi, "Shaykh 'Izz al-Din al-Qassam: A Reformist and a Rebel Leader," *Journal of Islamic Studies* 8 (1997), pp. 185–215; and Bassam al-'Asayli, *Thawrat al-Shaykh 'Izz al-Din al-Qassam* (Tunis, 1991), esp. pp. 106f.

33. See on this subject, Muhammad Khalid Masud, "*Hadit* and Violence," *Oriente Moderno* 22 (2002), pp. 5–18 (with regard to the Algerian Front Islamique de Salut [FIS] and GIA, but the article is also true for other radical Muslim groups).

34. Shaul Mishal and Reuven Aharoni, *Speaking Stones: Communiqués from the Intifada Underground* (Syracuse, 1994), pp. 201–3, 210, 212, 213, 216–17, 224f.

35. See *Fada'il al-Shahid Yahya 'Ayyash,* referring to the initiator of the Palestinian martyrdom operation, assassinated in 1996.

36. See "A Palestinian Communiqué against Martyrdom Operations," at www. memri.org, special dispatch no. 393 (June 25, 2002).

37. For example, see Mohammed Masood Azhar, *The Virtues of Jihad* (London, n.d. [2000]) (containing forty traditions on the subject); *Fundamentalism* (London, n.d.) (despite its title, this work is exclusively about jihad); and his two articles "Guardians of Deen [Religion] and Country" and "I Have a Question." A great deal of the material concerning the Kashmiri jihad from a Pakistani perspective is published in Muhammad Habiballah Mukhtar, *Jihad* (Karachi, 1989) (in Urdu).

38. See Yoginder Sikand, "The Changing Course of the Kashmiri Struggle: From National Liberation to Islamist Jihad?" *Muslim World* 91 (2001), pp. 229–56.

39. 'Abd al-Rahman Makki, "A Call to the Jihad in Kashmir" (trans. Abu Sayf Muwahhid) at *maktabah.net/articles (December 15, 2001). Note the refutation by Haydar Faruq Mawdudi (son of Abu al-'Ala Mawdudi) "There Is No Case for *Jihad* in Kashmir" at www.jammu-kashmir.com (January 5, 2002).

40. Note the foundational treatise published by Abu 'Abd al-Fattah Bin Hajj (leader of the FIS), *Ghayat al-murad fi qadaya al-jihad* (Algiers, 1994), on legal issues connected with jihad.

41. Communiqué no. 1, 25 Jumada I, 1419 (September 7, 1998).

42. See their response, *Nusrat Abi Sa'id al-'Amili* (at *www.salafiyya.com); others also responded to this *fatwa,* see Abu Hamza al-Masri, *Khawaarij and Jihad* (Birmingham, n.d.), pp. 134f, in which one of the leaders of radical Islam in Great Britain dissects their position.

43. Al-Buti, *Al-Jihad fi al-Islam* (Beirut, 1997), p. 93 (Absi, trans., p. 90).

44. Ibid., pp. 123–24 (Absi trans., p. 120; translation amended).

45. For example, in the third edition, pp. 266–67, al-Buti answers one of his critics who asks how Islam spread entirely peacefully from Spain to China. To this al-Buti says that any Muslim knows that this *entire* process was accomplished as a peaceful proclamation—which strains credulity and ignores Islamic history.

46. Ibid., pp. 238–40 (note).

47. Ibid., p. 271.

48. Ibid.

49. Al-Ghunaymi, *Waqafat ma' al-Dukhtur al-Buti fi kitabihi 'an al-jihad* (Beirut, 1999), e.g., pp. 78–81, 158–59, 175; see also his *Marahil tashri' al-jihad* (Beirut, 1999), pp. 89–100.

50. Al-Qadiri, *al-Jihad fi sabil Allah* (Jiddah, 1992), II, pp. 413f.

51. Muhammad Khayr Haykal, *Al-Jihad wa-l-qital fi al-siyasa al-shara'iyya* (Beirut, 1993), I, p. 518.

52. Ibid., I, pp. 597–602.

53. Ibid., I, p. 820.

54. Ibid., II, pp. 1352–59, at p. 1353. The logic of this discussion is extended considerably by Shaykh Nasir b. Hamd al-Fahd in his controversial "Fatwa concerning the Use of Weapons of Mass Destruction" (2003) at *http://groups .yahoo.com/group/abubanan2/message/221.

SIX: GLOBALIST RADICAL ISLAM AND
MARTYRDOM OPERATIONS

1. They were to be found at *www.azzamjihad.com.

2. ʿAbdallah ʿAzzam, "Martyrs: The Building Blocks of Nations," at *www.azzam.com (November 30, 2001). I have modified the English translation slightly; see Ibn Baz's *fatwa* about Afghanistan, in *Fatawa wa-tanbihat wa-nasaʾih* (Beirut, 1991), p. 601.

3. Ibid. (translation amended).

4. Contemporary globalist radical Muslims, such as Ayman al-Zawahiri, continue this tendency; see the latter's "al-Tariq ila al-Quds ʿabira bi-l-Qahira," at *www.aloswa.org (December 2002).

5. ʿAzzam, "The Will of ʿAbdallah Yusuf ʿAzzam, Who Is Poor unto His Lord" (dictated April 20, 1986), at *www.alribat.com (September 27, 2001). I have modified the English translation slightly.

6. Ibid.

7. For this period in Bin Ladin's life, see "Bin Ladin's Life in the Sudan," at www.fas.org/irp/world/para/ladin-sudan.htm (July 27, 2002).

8. "Seven Misconceptions in Fighting the Apostate Ruler and His Regime," at *www.azzam.com (December 30, 2001).

9. See communiqués 6, 7, 8, and 9, at *www.ummmah.org.uk/talaaiegypt (September 5, 2002).

10. For full details, see Tracey German, *Russia's Chechen War* (New York, 2003), and the more journalistic account of Anatol Lieven, *Chechnya: Tombstone of Russian Power* (New Haven, 1999).

11. A number of hagiographic details concerning his life came out after his death in 2002; see www.qawafilashshuhada.com, *www.jeeran.com, and *www.qoqaz.com.

12. For the Central Asian radical Muslim movements, see Ahmed Rashid, *Jihad: The Rise of Militant Islam in Central Asia* (New Haven, 2002), pp. 137–86; and for documents, Martha Brill Olcott and Bakhtiyar Babajanov, "Notes of a Terrorist," *Foreign Policy* (March–April 2003), pp. 30–42.

13. See appendix, no. 2 for the 1998 *fatwa* to kill Zionists and Americans; previously, in August 1996, Bin Ladin had issued the "Declaration of War against the Americans Occupying the Land of the Two Holy Places" (available on many websites in Arabic and English, and translated in *The Declaration of War*).

14. Abu Daʾud, *Sunan* (Beirut, 1988), IV, p. 108 (no. 4297); a complete list of classical citations is given by al-Silfi, *al-Fawaʾid al-hisan min hadith Thawban* (Casablanca, 2001), pp. 7–10; also see its citation by Farag, *al-Farida al-ghaʾiba* (Alexandria 1997), pp. 37–38; trans., pp. 205–7. It is regularly to be found in radical Muslim writings, e.g., Muhammad al-Zuhayli, "al-Wahn Wabaʿ Khatir wa-mard qatil," at *www.aloswa.org (May 10, 2002).

15. Mohammed Masood Azhar, *The Virtues of Jihad* (London, n.d. [2000]), pp. 132–33.

16. See appendix, no. 3 (ʿAli al-ʿAliyani, "The Goals of the Jihad").

17. See, e.g., appendix, no. 1; Abu Baseer, *Qawaʾid al-takfir;* al-Anbari, *Ruling by Other Than What Allah Revealed: The Fundamentals of Takfir*

(Detroit 1999); ʿUmar ʿAbd al-Rahman, *The Present Rulers and Islam: Are They Muslims or Not?* (London, 1990), with discussions by Abu Hamza al-Masri, *Khawaarij and Jihad* (Birmingham, n.d.), pp. 134f.; and refutations by al-Damadi (d. 1873), *Hukm al-takfir al-muʿayyin* (Riyadh, 2001), and al-Akhdar, *In Defense of Islam in Light of the Events of September 11* (Toronto, 2001).

18. Among the many radical Muslims who have written about the subject of *al-Walaʾ wa-l-baraʾ*, see Muhammad Saeed al-Qahtani, *al-Walaʾ wa-l-baraʾ According to the Aqeedah of the Salaf* (3 vols.) (Ipswich, 1996); Hamud b. ʿUqla al-Shuʿaybi, "al-Walaʾ wa-l-Baraʾ," at *www.aloqla.com (April 18, 2002); Shaikh Saalih bin Fouzan al-Fouzan, *al-Walaaʾ wal-Baraaʾ*; and Ayman al-Zawahiri, *al-Walaʾ wa-l-baraʾ* (written December 2002), available at www.e-prism.com. See also ʿAbd al-ʿAziz b. Faysal al-Rajihi, *Qudum kataʾib al-jihad li-ghazw al-zanadiqa wa-l-ilhad*.

19. A large percentage of the radical and globalist radical Muslim literary output deals with this issue; see, e.g., "Tamyiz saff rahmatan li-l-muʾminin wa-ʿadhab ʿala al-munafiqin," at *www.alemarh.com (July 19, 2002); ʿAbd al-ʿAziz Kamil, "Jihad al-munafiqin," at *www.aloswa.org (May 9, 2002); and the discussion at www.memri.org, special dispatch no. 333, from an article by the Tunisian liberal ʿAfif al-Akhadar in *al-Hayat* (January 13, 2002).

20. Franz Rosenthal, "On Suicide in Islam," *Journal of the American Oriental Society* 66 (1946), pp. 239–59.

21. "The Islamic Ruling on the Permissibility of Martyrdom Operations" (authored by a "Council of Scholars from the Arabian Peninsula" for the Chechens), p. 1; for a full discussion of this issue, see my "Suicide Attacks or 'Martyrdom Operations' in Contemporary *Jihad* Literature," *Nova Religio* 6 (2002), pp. 7–44, and my "Implications of Martyrdom Operations for Contemporary Islam," *Journal of Religious Ethics* 23 (2004), pp. 129–51.

22. "The Islamic Ruling on the Permissibility of Martyrdom Operations" (I have modified some of the translation to make it more readable).

23. Ibid; most of the definitions are given also by Nawwaf al-Takruri, *al-ʿAmaliyyat al-istishhadiyya fi al-mizan al-fiqhi*, pp. 47–57; and Muhammad Ghayba, *al-ʿAmaliyyat al-istishhadiyya wa-araʾ al-fuqahaʾ fiha*, pp. 72–74.

24. For a listing of the various *fatawa*, see *Masaʾil jihadiyya wa-hukm al-ʿamaliyyat al-istishhadiyya*, pp. 26–42; and see "Debating the Religious, Political and Moral Legitimacy of Suicide Bombings," wwwmemri.org, inquiry and analyses nos. 53, 54, 65, and 66 (respectively May 2 and 3, 2001, July 26 and 27, 2001), and my "Implications of Martyrdom Operations."

25. E.g., "Leading Egyptian Government Cleric Calls for 'Martyrdom Attacks That Strike Horror into the Hearts of the Enemies of Allah,'" www.memri.org, special dispatch no. 363 (April 7, 2002); however, al-Tantawi has changed his views several times and most recently has said that there is no Islamic basis for martyrdom operations ("Cleric Condemns Suicide Attacks" at www.bbc.com [July 11, 2003]), so it is difficult to know what he truly believes.

26. See www.memri.org, special dispatch no. 580 (October. 1, 2003) where ʿAli Gumaʿa, the new mufti of Egypt, tries to make this distinction. It is one that al-Qaʿida and its allies find ludicrous: see ʿAbdallah b. Nasr al-Rushayd, *Intiqad al-iʿtirad ʿala tafjirat al-Riyad*, pp. 5–22.

27. Most are listed by ʿAbd al-Ghani al-Maqdisi, *Manaqib al-nisaʾ al-sahabiyyat;* and ʿIlliya Mustafa Mubarak, *Sahabiyyat mujahidat;* see my article "Women Fighters in Islam," forthcoming.

28. *www.kataeb-ezzeldeen.com/fatwa (no. 3) (November 10, 2002); for the legality of women conducting "martyrdom operations," see al-Takruri, *ʿAmaliyyat al-istishhadiyya* (Damascus, 1997), pp. 208–23.

29. See my "Poetry by Globalist Radical Muslims," forthcoming.

30. "Videotape of Usama b. Ladin" (released December 13, 2001), CNN transcript, p. 3.

31. Abu Ayman al-Hilali, "Wasiyat al-Shahid bayna maqass al-Jazira wa-takhadhul al-ikhwan" at *www.muslimeen.co.uk/maqa/haznawi/htm (March 9, 2003).

32. See "A Bin Laden Special on al-Jazeera Two Months before Sept. 11" (aired July 10, 2001) at www.memri.org, special dispatch no. 319 (December 21, 2001): a discussion between al-Hatim ʿAdlan and ʿAbd al-Bari ʿAtwan, the editor of *al-Quds al-ʿArabi.* John Esposito, *Unholy Warfare* (Oxford, 2002), pp. 23–25, disagrees with this accusation.

33. This issue is dealt with in detail by the anonymous book *Haqiqat al-harb al-salibiyya al-jadida,* from which appendix no. 3 is an excerpt.

34. For example, see "The Islamic Ruling on the Permissibility of Executing Prisoners of War," at *www.azzam.com (authored by a "Council of Scholars from the Arabian Peninsula"). Study no. 2 of this opinion considers the issue of the rejection of international treaties such as the Geneva Convention.

35. www.memri.org, special report no. 8 (September 8, 2002) "The Sept. 11 Attacks Were Perpetrated by the Jews."

36. "Videotape of Usama b. Ladin" (released December 13, 2001), CNN transcript.

37. See my "Recovery of Radical Islam after the Defeat of the Taliban," *Terrorism and Political Violence* 16 (2003), pp. 31–56.

38. ʿAbdallah ʿAzzam, *ʿIbar wa-basaʾir li-jihad al-hadir* (Peshawar, 1999), pp. 19–39; see also his *Ayat al-Rahman fi jihad al-Afghan;* for an English summary, "Signs of ar-Rahman" at *www.almansurah.com/articles/2003/jan/140103b.htm (March 9, 2003); also "Why the Difference?" at *www.khurasaan.com (May 1, 2002), which explores the question of why the bodies of *mujahidin* do not decay but smell sweet after their deaths (as distinct from those of their enemies).

39. Also attested by the Palestinian fighters: "Angels Fight along with *Mujahidin* in Palestine" at *www.khurasaan.com (April 9, 2002); ʿUmar, *al-Jihad fi sabil Allah* (Damascus, 1998), pp. 224–31, discusses the role angels play in jihad.

40. "In the Hearts of Green Birds, side B" at *www.almansurah.com/jihad/2003 (March 9, 2003); many other martyr stories are available at *www.saaid.net/Doat/hamad (a collection of sixty-eight martyrdom stories from the Bosnian, Chechen, and Afghani wars).

41. "In the Hearts of Green Birds."

42. Clark McCauley, "Psychological Issues in Understanding Terrorism and the Response to Terrorism," in Christopher Stout, ed., *The Psychology of Terrorism* (Westport, Conn., 2002), pp. 3–29, at p. 11.

43. All of the news citations are taken from *www.azzam.com for the day marked.

44. See, for example, Nasir b. Hamd al-Fahd, *al-Tibyan fi kufr man a'ana al-Amrikan.*

45. See my "Recovery of Radical Islam in the Wake of the Defeat of the Taliban," *Terrorism and Political Violence* 15 (2003), pp. 31–56, at pp. 40–43, for this theme.

46. See Sayf al-Din al-Ansari, "Wa-yattakhidh minkum shuhada'," at *www.aloswa.org (May 17, 2002).

47. Found in many collections; see my "Muslim Apocalyptic and *Jihad,*" *Jerusalem Studies in Arabic and Islam* 20 (1996), pp. 66–102, at pp. 71–74; and cited in Ibn Taymiyya, *Fatawa* (Beirut, 1991), vol. 37, p. 416; "The Excuses and Pretexts We Put Forward in Order to Avoid *Jihad,*" at *www.taliban-news.com (April 25, 2002); "Thawabit 'ala darb al-jihad," at *www.jehad.net (February 19, 2002), p. 2; Abu Sa'id al-'Amili, "Lan Tughniya 'ankum fitnatukum sha'an wa-law kathurat," at *www.aloswa.org (May 9, 2002), p. 2, among many examples.

48. Sa'id Ayyub, *al-Masih al-Dajjal,* p. 241.

AFTERWORD

1. For example, Hamid Algar, *Wahhabism: A Critical Essay* (Oneonta, N.Y., 2002), pp. 2–5, 31–37, makes this case.

2. See Shaikh Taalib ur-Rehmaan Shah, *Jihaad: Fardh ayn or fardh kifaayah: A Refutation of the Takfeeree Jihaadee Groups* (Maktabat Ashab al-Hadeeth, n.d.), which is a summary of Nasir al-Din al-Albani's discussions with radical Muslims, *Fatawa al-Shaykh al-Albani,* pp. 294–310, also included in his *Fitnat al-takfir.*

3. See Samuel Huntington, "The Clash of Civilizations?" *Foreign Affairs* 72 (1993), pp. 22–49; for a thoughtful discussion of this, see Immanuel Wallerstein, "Islam, the West and the World," *Journal of Islamic Studies* 10 (1999), pp. 109–25.

4. For examples, see Yohanan Friedmann, "Islam Is Superior," *Jerusalem Quarterly* 11 (1979), pp. 36–42.

5. See John Moorhead, "The Monophysite Response to the Arab Invasions," *Byzantion* 51 (1981), pp. 579–91; and the comprehensive discussion of Robert Hoyland, *Seeing Islam as Others Saw It,* especially chaps. 12–14.

6. Mervyn Hiskett, *The Sword of Truth: The Life and Times of Shehu Usaman Dan Fodio* (Evanston, 1994), pp. viii–xviii, has detailed how a similar problem has continually derailed efforts of Muslim-Christian dialogue in Nigeria: the continual need to justify the jihad of Usamana Dan Fodio (see chapter 5).

APPENDIX: SOME TRANSLATED DOCUMENTS

1. Text from Abu Hamza al-Masri, *Khawaarij and Jihad* (Birmingham, n.d.), appendix.

2. Al-Tirmidhi, *Sahih* (Cairo, 1986), IV, p. 76 (no. 2635).

3. See my "Muslim Apocalyptic and *Jihad*," *Jerusalem Studies in Arabic and Islam* 20 (1996), pp. 66–102, at p. 73.

4. Ibid, pp. 71–73.

5. In 628 C.E.

6. Ibn Hisham, *Al-Sira al-nabawiyya* (Beirut, n.d), I, p. 309; Ibn Hanbal, *Musnad* (Beirut, n.d.), II, p. 218; al-Ghazali, *Ihya* (Beirut, n.d.), II, p. 314; cited by Farag, *al-Farida al-gha'iba* (Amman, n.d.), p. 6, trans. Jansen, *The Neglected Duty* (New York, 1986), p. 161.

7. See, e.g., Ibn al-Mubarak, *Kitab al-jihad* (Beirut, 1971) pp. 89–90 (no. 105); and numerous citations in my "Muslim Apocalyptic and *Jihad*," *Jerusalem Studies in Arabic and Islam* 20 (1996), pp. 66–102, at p. 75, n. 32.

8. The *hadith* of Thawban, described in chapter 6.

9. See note 6.

10. Literally "bead" such as in "the line of fire."

11. Compare "Mashru'iyyat al-Jihad al-Jama'i," at www.salafi.net/books/hbook43.html (August 20, 2002); and Hafiz Abdul Salam Bin Muhammad, "Jihad in the Present Time," at *www.jamatdawa.org (February 22, 2003).

12. Muslim, *Sahih* (Beirut, 1991), VIII, p. 159; Ahmad b. Hanbal, *Musnad* (Beirut, n.d.), IV, p. 162.

13. Abu Da'ud, *Sunan* (Beirut, 1998), III, p. 7 (no. 2495).

14. See al-Bukhari, *Sahih* (Beirut, 1991), III, pp. 267 (no. 2795), 274 (no. 2817).

15. Al-Nasa'i, *Sunan* (Beirut, n.d.), VI, pp. 241–15.

16. Al-Bukhari, *Sahih,* I, p. 30 (no. 71).

17. The reference is to the Prophet Muhammad's uncle, who was killed at the Battle of Uhud (625).

18. The spokesman for al-Qa'ida.

19. Abu Da'ud, *Sunan,* IV, p. 272 (no. 4884).

20. An Arab tribe at the time of Muhammad.

21. See Ibn Hajar, *Isaba* (Beirut, 1998), I, pp. 115–17 (no. 500).

22. This text is translated by the author from the reproduction in the *New York Times* (September 28–29, 2001) at www.nytimes.com/library/national/092801letter.htm. I would like to thank Carolynne White for her invaluable help in reproducing this document.

23. As there is no *basmala* ("In the Name of God, the Merciful, the Compassionate"), most probably this is not the beginning of the document.

24. This tradition is a paraphrase of Ibn Hanbal, *Musnad,* V, pp. 248–49, 255, 258.

25. See Qur'an 2:285.

26. Minor modifications have been made to Fakhry's translation of the Qur'an cited throughout this translation of "The Last Night." He prefers to use the name "Allah" for "God"; for the sake of consistency I have used "God" throughout.

27. See Qur'an 48:1.

28. This is the first verb in the command form; all the previous points are introduced by verbal nouns.

29. See Ibn Hanbal, *Musnad*, II, p. 332. The word *fa'l*, here translated as "optimism" (the way the writer is using it) meant "an omen for good" during the Prophet's time (which was divined by various methods).

30. Verse material in brackets is supplied because the text indicates that the citation was abbreviated, but that the rest of the verse is also meant.

31. All of these devotional prayers are listed in small prayer-books well known to Muslims.

32. For this process, see Wensinck, *Concordance, s.v., nafth*. This expectoration is designed to rid the believer of the devil's influence.

33. Muslim, *Sahih*, VI, p. 72; Ibn Hanbal, *Musnad*, IV, p. 123.

34. Another line, partially cut off in the reproduction, presumably dealt with transportation to the airport.

35. It is curious that the writer of this document would identify this verse as from *surat al-mu'minin* (23), as none of the other verses in the text are identified.

36. The devotional for when one fears someone.

37. This verse was cited by Sulayman Abu Ghayth in the statement of October 7, 2001, who added "this is a creedal statement among us and a certainty we carry in our hearts."

38. This is the section designed for passing through the security devices of the airport.

39. This line is very difficult to read and the translation is conjectural. Apparently the sense is that they (those who are impressed by the West) think that they are drinking cold water, but are really drinking hellfire. This idea appears in al-Bukhari, *Sahih*, IV, p. 173 (no. 3450), where we are told that the Antichrist will induce his followers to drink hellfire thinking that they are drinking cold water.

40. Compare Qur'an 4:76.

41. The first half of the *shahada*.

42. See multiple versions in al-Hindi, *Kanz* (Beirut, 1991), I, pp. 48f.

43. I could not find this precise tradition in this version, but the formula is clear and others of its type exist (see al-Isfahani, *Hilyat al-awliya'* [Beirut, 1997], VIII, p. 368 [no. 12529]; Ibn Hanbal, *Musnad*, I, p. 258; and al-Hindi, *Kanz*, VI, p. 133 [no. 15,144]).

44. The euphemism for the enemy (Americans).

45. The quotation slightly amends the passage's phrasing in Al-Bukhari, *Sahih*, III, p. 266 (no. 2792).

46. Probably what is meant by this statement is the brief stop that an airplane often makes just prior to takeoff.

47. Perhaps this means those hijackers who were the leaders (and ultimately flew the planes) and those who were there for "muscle" (see the "Videotape of Usama b. Ladin," released December 13, 2001, from the CNN transcript), or perhaps the two sides, meaning the hijackers and their enemies.

48. It is significant that this prayer in the Qur'an is uttered by those Israelites who fought with David against Goliath. One cannot help but notice the parallels with the perceptions of the hijackers fighting against a superior enemy in a hopeless battle.

49. Al-Bukhari, *Sahih*, III, p. 307 (no. 2933).

50. I cannot find any mention of this practice.

51. Two words are too blurred to read. The context seems to imply that if an action taken by a lone individual departs from the necessity of the larger group, that action should not be allowed according to the Sunna of the Prophet Muhammad.

52. The cousin, son-in-law, and fourth successor to the Prophet Muhammad (d. 661).

53. See Ibn Kathir, *Bidaya* (Beirut, 1990), IV, pp. 106–7 (an account of the Battle of the Khandaq).

54. It is difficult to know whether to read this as *din* (religion) or as *dayn* (loan); either one would make sense.

55. This is conjecture.

56. A considerable exaggeration.

57. Cf. Qur'an 33. This event took place in 626 C.E. during the second siege of Medina by the infidel Quraysh.

58. This verse was cited by Ayman al-Zawahiri in his statement of October 7, 2001.

59. This website has since been suppressed. Regarding the reference to "19" in the title: Aside from 19 being the number of the September 11, 2001, hijackers, this number also appears in Qur'an 74:30, which has caused some gematrical speculation; and note the manner in which this writer employs the verse below.

60. At the Battle of Badr (624 C.E.).

61. Note how the author denies any possibility of heroism on the part of the Americans.

BIBLIOGRAPHY

Websites cited in chapters 2, 5, and 6 and the appendix are not included in this bibliography, as full details are available in the notes. Those websites cited here that have recently been suppressed or have disappeared are marked by an asterisk.

ʿAbd al-ʿAziz, Jumʿah Amin. *Al-Farida al-muftara ʿalayha: al-Jihad fi sabil Allah*. Alexandria: Dar al-Daʿwah, 1997.

ʿAbd al-Rahman, ʿUmar Ahmad. *The Present Rulers and Islam: Are They Muslims or Not?* Trans. Umar Johnstone. London: al-Firdous, 1990.

Abou al-Fadl, Khaled. "The Rules of Killing at War: An Inquiry into Classical Sources." *Muslim World* 89 (1999), pp. 144–57.

Abu Basir, ʿAbd al-Munʿim Mustafa Halima. *Qawaʾid fi al-takfir*. n.p., n.d.

Abu Faris, Muhammad ʿAbd al-Qadir. *Al-Jihad fi al-Kitab wa-l-Sunna*. Amman: Dar al-Furqan, 1998.

Abu Rabiʿ, Ibrahim. "Discourse, Power and Ideology in Modern Islamic Revivalist Thought: The Case of Sayyid Qutb." *Islamic Culture* 65 (1991), pp. 84–102.

———. "Sayyid Qutb: From Religious Realism to Radical Social Criticism." *Islamic Quarterly* 28 (1984), pp. 103–26.

Abu Salim, Muhammad Ibrahim. *Manshurat al-Mahdiyya*. Beirut: Dar al-Jil, 1979.

Ahmad, Rifaʿat Sayyid, ed. *Rihlat al-damm al-lati hazamahu al-sayf: Al-aʿmal al-kamila li-l-shahid al-duktur Fathi al-Shiqaqi*. Cairo: Markaz Yafa li-Dirasat wa-Abhath, 1997.

Ajayi, J. F. A., and Michael Crowder, eds. *History of West Africa*. New York: Columbia University Press, 1976.

Al-Akhdar, Abu al-Hasan Malik. *In Defense of Islam in Light of the Events of September 11th.* Toronto: TROID Publications, 2002.

Akhir ayyam Gharnata: Nubdhat al-'asr fi akhbar muluk Bani Nasr. Beirut: Dar al-Fikr al-Mu'asir, 2002.

Alami, A. "Les conquêtes de Mahmud al-Ghaznawi d'après le *Kitab al-Yamini* d'*Utbi*." PhD diss., University of Paris, 1989.

Algar, Hamid, trans. *Islam and Revolution: Writings and Declarations of Imam Khomeini.* Berkeley: Mizan Press, 1981.

———. *Wahhabism: A Critical Essay.* Oneonta, N.Y.: Islamic Publications International, 2002.

Al-'Amaliyat al-istishhadiyya: Watha'iq wa-suwar al-muqawama al-wataniyya al-Lubnaniyya 1982–85. Damascus: al-Markaz al-'Arabi, 1985.

Amitai-Priess, Reuven. *Mongols and Mamluks: The Mamluk-Ilkhanid War, 1260–1281.* Cambridge: Cambridge University Press, 1995.

Al-Anbari, Khalid b. Muhammad. *Ruling by Other Than What Allah Has Revealed: The Fundamentals of Takfir.* Detroit: al-Qur'an wa-l-Sunnah Society of North America, 1999.

Ansari, A. S. Bazmee. "Sayyid Ahmad Shahid in the Light of His Letters." *Islamic Studies* 15 (1976), pp. 231–45.

Al-'Aql, Nasr. *Imitation of the Kufaar.* Detroit: al-Qur'an wa-l-Sunnah Society of North America, 1996.

'Arabfaqih, Shihab al-Din Ahmad (d. ca. sixteenth century). *Tuhfat al-zaman aw Futuh al-habasha.* Cairo: al-Ha'iya al-Misriyya al-'Amma, 1974.

Arini, 'Abdallah b. Salih. *Shi'r jihad al-Rum.* Riyadh: Jami'at al-Imam Muhammad b. Sa'ud al-Islamiyya, 2002.

Al-'Asayli, Bassam. *Thawrat al-shaykh 'Izz al-Din al-Qassam.* Tunis: Dar al-Baraq, 1991.

'Athamina, Khalil. "The Black Banners and the Socio-Political Significance of Flags and Slogans." *Arabica* 36 (1989), pp. 307–26.

———. "Non-Arab Regiments and Private Militias during the Umayyad Period." *Arabica* 45 (1998), pp. 347–78.

Al-Athar al-kamila li-l-Imam al-Mahdi. Khartoum: Khartoum University Press, 1991–96.

Al-Awza'i, 'Abd al-Rahman (d. 774). *Sunan al-Awza'i.* Beirut: Dar al-Nafa'is, 1993.

Ayalon, David. "Mamluk Military Aristocracy: A Non-Hereditary Nobility." *Jerusalem Studies in Arabic and Islam* 10 (1987), pp. 205–10.

———. "The Military Reforms of Caliph al-Mu'tasim." In *Islam and the Abode of War: Military Slaves and Islamic Adversaries.* Aldershot: Variorum Reprints, 1994 (#1).

Ayoub, Mahmoud. "Martyrdom in Christianity and Islam." In Richard Antoun and Mary Elaine Hegland, eds., *Religious Resurgence: Contemporary Cases in Islam, Christianity and Judaism*, pp. 67–77. Syracuse: Syracuse University Press, 1987.

Ayyub, Hasan. *Fiqh al-jihad fi al-Islam.* Cairo: Dar al-Salam, 2002.

Ayyub, Sa'id. *Al-Masih al-Dajjal.* Cairo: Al-Fath li-l-A'lam al-'Arabi, 1987.

Azhar, Moulana Mohammed Masood. *Fundamentalism.* London: Ahle Sunna wal Jama'at, n.d.

———. *The Virtues of Jihad*. London: Ahle Sunna wa-l-Jamaʿa, n.d. [2000].

ʿAzzam, ʿAbdallah. *Bashaʾir al-nasr*. Peshawar: Markaz al-Shahid ʿAzzam al-Iʿlami, 1989.

———. *ʿIbar wa-basaʾir li-l-jihad fi al-ʿasr al-hadir*. Peshawar: n.p., 1986.

———. *Ilhaq bi-l-qafila*. Peshawar: Muʾassasat Maswadi, 1987.

Bacharach, Jere. "African Military Slaves in the Medieval Middle East." *International Journal of Middle Eastern Studies* 13 (1981), pp. 471–95.

Baddeley, John. *The Russian Conquest of the Caucasus*. New York, Bombay, and Calcutta: Longman's, 1908.

Bakker, Johan de. "The *Jihad* Waged by the First Alawi Sultans of Morocco (1660–1727): A Major Contribution to Their Legitimacy." Typescript.

———. "Slaves, Arms, and Holy War: Moroccan Policy vis-à-vis the Dutch Republic during the Establishment of the ʿAlawi Dynasty 1660–1727." PhD diss., University of Amsterdam, 1991.

Balogun, Ismaʿil. "The Life and Work of the Mujaddid of West Africa, ʿUthman b. Fudi, Popularly Known as Usumanu Dan Fodio." *Islamic Studies* 12 (1973), pp. 271–92.

Al-Bannaʾ, al-Hasan. *Majmuʿat rasaʾil al-Imam al-Shahid Hasan al-Bannaʾ*. Beirut: al-Muʾassasa al-Islamiyya li-l-Tibaʿa wa-l-Sahafa wa-l-Nashr, n.d.; Cairo: al-Maktaba al-Tawfiqiyya, n.d.

Bashear, Suleiman. "Early Muslim Apocalyptic Materials." *Journal of the Royal Asiatic Society* 1991, pp. 173–207.

Al-Bayhaqi, Ahmad b. al-Husayn (d. 1066). *Shuʿab al-iman*. Beirut: Dar al-Kutub al-ʿIlmiyya, 2000.

———. *Sunan al-kubra*. Riyadh: Maktabat al-Maʿarif, n.d.

Al-Bazri, al-Fariq ʿAfif. *Al-Jihad fi al-Islam*. Damascus: al-Karmil, 1984.

Bello, Muhammad (d. 1837). *Infaq al-maysur fi taʾrikh bilad al-Takrur*. Ribat: Maʿhad Dirasat Ifriqiyya, 1996.

Bennison, Amira. *Jihad and Its Interpretations in Pre-Colonial Morocco*. New York: Routledge, 2002.

Bessaih, Boualem. *De l'emir Abdelkadir à l'imam Chamyl: Les heros des tchétchènes et du Caucase*. Algiers: ENAG, 2001.

Bin Hajj, Abu ʿAbd al-Fattah. *Ghayat al-murad fi qadaya al-jihad*. Algiers: al-Jabha al-Islamiyya li-l-Inqadh, 1994.

Bin Humaid, Abdallah b. Muhammad. *Jihad in the Qurʾan and Sunna*. Riyadh: Maktabat Dar al-Salam, 1995.

Bin Ladin, Usama. *Declaration of War*. London: Khurasan Press, n.d.

Bishai, Wilson. "Negotiations and Peace Agreements between Muslims and Non-Muslims in Islamic History." In Sami Hanna, ed., *Medieval and Middle Eastern Studies in Honor of Aziz Suryal Atiya*, pp. 50–61. Leiden: E. J. Brill, 1972.

Blankinship, Khalid Yahya. *The End of the Jihad State*. Albany: SUNY Press, 1993.

Bonner, Michael. *Aristocratic Violence*. New Haven, Conn.: American Oriental Society Publications, 1996.

———. "*Jaʿaʾil* and Holy War in Early Islam." *Der Islam* 68 (1991), pp. 45–64.

———. "Some Observations Concerning the Early Development of Jihad on the Arab-Byzantine Frontier." *Studia Islamica* 75 (1992), pp. 5–32.

Bredow, Mathias von. *Der Heilige Kreig (ǧihad) aus der Sicht der malikitischen Rechtsschule.* Beirut: In Kommission bei Franz Steiner, 1994.

Al-Bukhari, Muhammad b. Isma'il (d. 256/870). *Sahih.* Beirut: Dar al-Fikr, 1991.

Al-Burzuli, Abu al-Qasim (d. 1438). *Fatawa al-Burzuli, Jami' masa'l al-ahkam.* Beirut: Dar al-Gharb al-Islami, 2002.

Al-Buti, Muhammad Sa'id Ramadan. *Al-Jihad fi al-Islam.* Beirut: Dar al-Fikr al-Mu'asir, 1997. Trans. Munzer Absi, *Jihad in Islam: How to Understand It and Practice It.* Beirut: Dar al-Fikr al-Mu'asir, 1995.

Canard, Marius. "Les expeditions des Arabes contre Constantinople dans l'histoire et dans la legende." *Journal Asiatique* 208 (1926), pp. 61–121.

Castries, H. de. "La conquête du Soudan." *Hesperis* 3 (1923), pp. 433–88.

Charnay, J. P. "Expansion de l'Islam en afrique occidentale." *Arabica* 27 (1980), pp. 140–53.

Chittick, William. *The Self-Disclosure of God: Principles of Ibn al-'Arabi's Cosmology.* Albany: SUNY Press, 1998.

———. *The Sufi Path of Knowledge: Ibn al-'Arabi's Metaphysics of Imagination.* Albany: SUNY Press, 1989.

———. "The Theological Roots of Peace and War According to Islam." *Islamic Quarterly* 34 (1990), pp. 145–63.

Cohen, Mark. "What Was the Pact of 'Umar? A Literary-Historical Study." *Jerusalem Studies in Arabic and Islam* 23 (1999), pp. 100–151.

Colvin, Lucie Gallistel. "Islam and the State of Kajoor: A Case of Successful Resistance to Jihad." *Journal of African History* 15 (1974), pp. 587–606.

Cook, David. "The Implications of Martyrdom Operations for Contemporary Islam." *Journal for Religious Ethics* 23 (2004), pp. 129–51.

———. "Muslim Apocalyptic and *Jihad.*" *Jerusalem Studies in Arabic and Islam* 20 (1996), pp. 66–102.

———. "Poetry by Globalist Radical Muslims." Forthcoming.

———. "The Recovery of Radical Islam in the Wake of the Defeat of the Taliban." *Terrorism and Political Violence* 15 (2003), pp. 31–56.

———. *Studies in Muslim Apocalyptic.* Princeton: Darwin Press, 2002.

———. "Suicide Attacks or 'Martyrdom Operations' in Contemporary *Jihad* Literature." *Nova Religio* 6 (2002), pp. 7–44.

———. "A Survey of Muslim Materials on Comets and Meteors." *Journal for the History of Astronomy* 30 (1999), pp. 131–60.

———. "Women Fighters in Classical and Contemporary Islam." Forthcoming.

Cook, Michael. *Commanding Right and Forbidding Wrong in Islamic Thought.* Cambridge: Cambridge University Press, 2000.

Crone, Patricia. "The First-Century Concept of *Hijra.*" *Arabica* 41 (1994), pp. 352–87.

Curtin, Philip. "Jihad in West Africa: Early Phases and Inter-Relations in Mauretania and Senegal." *Journal of African History* 12 (1971), pp. 11–24.

Dajani-Shakeel, Hadia. "*Jihad* in Twelfth-Century Arabic Poetry." *Muslim World* 66 (1976), pp. 96–113.

Al-Damadi, al-Husayn b. Ahmad b. 'Abdallah 'Akish (d. 1873/74). *Hukm takfir al-mu'ayyin.* Riyadh: al-Dibaji, 2001.

Al-Daqas, Kamil Salama. *Al-Jihad fi sabil Allah*. Damascus: Mu'assasat 'Ulum al-Qur'an, 1988.

Al-Darimi, 'Abdallah b. 'Abd al-Rahman (d. 869). *Sunan al-Darimi*. Damascus: Dar al-Qalam, 1996.

Darling, Linda. "Contested Territory: Ottoman Holy War in Comparative Context." *Studia Islamica* 91 (2000), pp. 133–63.

Darwaza, Muhammad 'Izzat. *al-Jihad fi sabil Allah*. Damascus: Dar al-Yaqza al-'Arabiyya, 1975.

Doi, A. R. I. "The Political Role of Islam in West Africa with Special Reference to 'Uthman Dan Fodio's *Jihad*." *Islamic Quarterly* 12 (1968), pp. 235–42.

———. "Shehu Uthman Dan Fodio, 1754–1817." *Studies in Islam* 7 (1970), pp. 111–22.

Donner, Fred. *The Early Islamic Conquests*. Princeton: Princeton University Press, 1981.

Drory, Joseph. "Early Muslim Reflections on the Crusaders." *Jerusalem Studies in Arabic and Islam* 25 (2001), pp. 92–101.

Eaton, Richard. "Temple Desecration and Indo-Muslim States." *Journal of Islamic Studies* 11 (2000), pp. 283–319.

Encyclopedia of Islam, new edition. Leiden: E. J. Brill, 1960–2003.

Esposito, John. *The Islamic Threat: Myth or Reality?* New York: Oxford University Press, 1999.

———. *Unholy War: Terror in the Name of Islam*. Oxford: Oxford University Press, 2002.

Fahd, Nasir b. Hamd. *Al-Tibyan fi kufr man a'ana al-Amirikan*. n.p., 2002.

Fakhry, Majid, trans. *The Qur'an: A Modern English Version*. London: Garnett Press, 1997.

Farag, Muhammad 'Abd al-Salam. *al-Farida al-gha'iba*. Amman: n.p., n.d. Trans. Johannes Jansen, *The Neglected Duty*. New York: Macmillan, 1986 *(see below)*. Also trans. Abu Umama, *The Absent Obligation*. Birmingham: Maktabat al-Ansar, 2000.

Fierro, Maribel. "Christian Success and Muslim Fear in Andalusi Writings during the Almoravid and Almohad Periods." *Israel Oriental Studies* 17 (1997), pp. 155–78.

Findly, Ellison. "Jahangir's Vow of Non-Violence." *Journal of the American Oriental Society* 107 (1987), pp. 245–56.

Firestone, Reuven. "Disparity and Resolution in the Qur'anic Teachings on War: A Reconsideration." *Journal of Near Eastern Studies* 56 (1997), pp. 1–20.

Fisher, Humphrey. "Prayer and Military Activity in the History of Muslim Africa South of the Sahara." *Journal of African History* 12 (1971), pp. 391–406.

Al-Fawzan, Salih b. Fawzan b. 'Abdallah. *Al-Wala' wa-l-Bara'a*. Ipswich: Jami'at Ihya Minhaj al-Sunna, 1996.

Freamon, Bernard. "Martyrdom, Suicide, and the Islamic Law of War: A Short Legal History." *Fordham International Law Journal* 27 (2003), pp. 299–369.

Friedmann, Yohanan. "Islam Is Superior." *Jerusalem Quarterly* 11 (1979), pp. 36–42.

Gammer, Moshe. "The Beginnings of the Naqshbandiyya in Daghestan and the Russian Conquest of the Caucasus." *Die Welt des Islams* 34 (1994), pp. 204–17.

———. *Muslim Resistance to the Tsar: Shamil and the Conquest of Chechnia and Daghestan.* London: Frank Cass, 1994.

Gauss, J. "Tolerranz und Intolerranz zwischen Christen und Muslimen in der Zeit vor den Kreuzzügen." *Saeculum* 19 (1969), pp. 362–89.

Geoffroy, Eric. *Jihâd et contemplation.* Beirut: Albouraq, 2003.

German, Tracey. *Russia's Chechen War.* New York: Routledge, 2003.

Ghayba, Muhammad Saʿid. *Al-ʿAmaliyyat al-istishhadiyya wa-araʾ al-fuqahaʿ fiha.* Damascus: Dar al-Maktabi, 2001.

Al-Ghazali, Muhammad (d. 1111). *Ihya ʾulum al-din.* Beirut: Dar al-Qalam, n.d. (5 vols).

Al-Ghimari, ʿAbdallah b. Muhammad (d. 1960). *A-Ajwiba al-sarifa li-ishkal al-hadith al-taʾifa.* Beirut: Dar al-Kutub al-ʿIlmiyya, 2002.

Al-Ghunaymi, ʿAbd al-Akhir Hammad. *Marahil tashriʿ al-jihad.* Beirut: Dar al-Barayiq, 1999.

———. *Wafaqat maʿ al-Duktur al-Buti fi kitabihi ʾan al-jihad.* Beirut: Dar al-Barayiq, 1999.

Granara, William. "*Jihad* and Cross-Cultural Encounter in Muslim Sicily." *Harvard Middle Eastern and Islamic Review* 3 (1996), pp. 42–61.

Haj, Samira. "Reordering Islamic Orthodoxy: Muhammad Ibn ʿAbdul Wahhab." *Muslim World* 92 (2002), pp. 333–70.

Al-Hajj, Muhammad. "The Fulani Concept of Jihad—Shehu Uthman Dan Fodio." *ODU* 1 (1964), pp. 45–58.

Al-Haqiqa al-ghaʾiba. Gaza: Sawt al-Haqq wa-l-Quwwa wa-l-Hurriyya, 1987.

Haqiqat al-harb al-salibiyya al-jadida. Available at *www.alneda.com

Harthami, Abu al-Saʿid (d. fifteenth century). *Mukhtasar fi siyasat al-harb.* Damascus: Dar Kanan, 1995.

Hasan, S. A. "A Survey of the Expansion of Islam into Central Asia during the Umayyad Caliphate." *Islamic Culture* 44 (1970), pp. 165–76, 45 (1971), pp. 95–113, 47 (1973), pp. 1–13, 48 (1974), pp. 177–86.

Hasson, Isaac. "Les *mawali* dans l'armée musulmane sous les premiers umayyades." *Jerusalem Studies in Arabic and Islam* 14 (1991), pp. 176–213.

Haykal, Muhammad Khayr. *Al-Jihad wa-l-qital fi al-siyasa al-sharaʿiyya.* Beirut: Dar al-Barayiq, 1993.

Al-Haythami, Ibn Hajar (d. 1565). *Al-Zawajir ʿan iktiraf al-kabaʾir.* Beirut: Dar al-Maʿrifa, 1998.

Hess, Robert L. "The 'Mad Mullah' and Northern Somalia." *Journal of African History* 5 (1964), pp. 415–33.

Hill, Donald. "The Role of the Camel and the Horse in the Early Arab Conquests." In V. J. Parry and M. E. Yapp, eds., *War, Technology and Society in the Middle East*, pp. 32–43. Oxford: Oxford University Press, 1975.

Hillenbrand, Carole. *The Crusades: Islamic Perspectives.* Edinburgh: Edinburgh University Press, 1999.

Al-Hindi, al-Muttaqi (d. 1567/68). *Kanz al-ʿummal.* Beirut: Muʾassasat al-Risala, 1989.

Hiskett, Mervyn. "*Kitab al-farq:* A Work on the Habe Kingdom Attributed to 'Uthman Dan Fodio." *Bulletin of the School of Oriental and African Studies* 23 (1960), pp. 558–79.

_____. *The Sword of Truth: The Life and Times of Shehu Usaman Dan Fodio.* Evanston: Northwestern University Press, 1994.

Holt, Peter Malcolm. *The Mahdist State in the Sudan 1881–1898.* Oxford: Oxford University Press, 1958.

_____. *The Sudan of the Three Niles: The Funj Chronicles 910–1266/1504–1871.* Leiden: E. J. Brill, 1999.

Al-Hunnad b. al-Sari (d. 857). *Kitab al-zuhd.* Kuwait: Dar al-Khulafa, 1985.

Huntington, Samuel P. "The Clash of Civilizations?" *Foreign Affairs* 72 (1993), pp. 22–49.

Ibn 'Abd al-'Aziz, 'Abd al-Qadir. *Risalat al-'umda li-l-jihad fi sabil Allah.* Available at *www.tawhed.com.

Ibn 'Abd al-Wahhab, Sulayman (d. 1818). *Al-Sawa'iq al-ilahiyya fi al-radd 'ala al-Wahhabiyya.* Damascus: Dar Hira', 2000.

Ibn Abi al-'Asim, Ahmad b. 'Amr (d. 900). *Kitab al-jihad.* Medina: Maktabat al-'Ulum wa-l-Hikam, 1986.

Ibn Abi al-Dunya, 'Abdallah b. Muhammad (d. 894/95). *Muhasibat al-nafs wa-l-izra' 'alayha.* Beirut: Dar al-Kutub al-'Ilmiyya, 1986.

Ibn Abi Shayba, 'Abdallah b. Muhammad (d. 850). *Kitab al-musannaf.* Beirut: Dar al-Kutub al-'Ilmiyya, 1995.

Ibn Abi Zaminayn, Muhammad b. 'Abdallah (d. 1008/9). *Qudwat al-ghazi.* Beirut: Dar al-Gharb al-Islami, 1989.

Ibn al-'Arabi al-Ma'afiri, Muhammad b. 'Abdallah (d. 1148/49). *Ahkam al-Qur'an.* Beirut: Dar al-Jil, 1987.

Ibn al-'Arabi, Muhi al-Din (d. 1240/41). *Al-Futuhat al-Makkiyya.* Beirut: Dar al-Kutub al-'Ilmiyya, 1999.

Ibn Arnabagh al-Zardakush (d. 1462). *Al-Aniq fi al-majaniq.* Aleppo: Jami'at Halab, 1985.

Ibn Batta al-'Ukbari, 'Ubaydallah (d. 997). *Al-Ibana 'an shari'at al-firqa al-najiya.* Beirut: Dar al-Kutub al-'Ilmiyya, 2002.

———. *Kitab al-jihad.* Cairo: Maktabat al-Qur'an, 1989.

Ibn Baz, 'Abd al-'Aziz. *Fatawa wa-tanbihat wa-nasa'ih.* Beirut: Dar al-Jil, 1991.

Ibn Fuda, 'Uthman *(also Dan Fodio, Usaman). Kitab bayan wujub al-hijra 'ala al-'ibad wa-bayan nasb al-Imam wa-iqamat al-jihad,* ed. F. Al-Masry. Khartoum: Khartoum University Press, 1977.

Ibn Hanbal al-Shaybani, Ahmad (d. 855). *Musnad.* Beirut: Dar al-Fikr, n.d.

Ibn Hazm al-Andalusi, 'Ali b. Ahmad (d. 1064). *Al-Muhalla bi-l-athar.* Beirut: Dar al-Fikr, 2001.

Ibn Hisham, 'Abd al-Malik (d. 833). *Al-Sira al-nabawiyya.* Beirut: Dar al-Fikr, n.d.

Ibn al-Jawzi, Abu al-Faraj 'Abd al-Rahman (d. 1200). *Sifat al-safwa.* Beirut: Dar al-Ma'rifa, 2001.

Ibn Kathir, Abu al-Fida' (d. 1378). *Al-Bidaya wa-l-nihaya.* Beirut: Maktabat al-Ma'arif, 1990.

Ibn Maja al-Qazwini, Muhammad b. Yazid (d. 888/89). *Sunan*. Beirut: Dar al-Fikr, n.d.

Ibn Manjli, Muhammad (d. 1376). *Al-Adilla al-rasmiyya fi al-ta'abi al-harbiyya*. Baghdad: Matba'at al-Majma' al-'Ilmi al-'Iraqi, 1988.

———. *Al-Hiyal fi al-hurub*. Riyad: S. al-Ruhayli, 1998.

Ibn Mansur al-Khurasani, Sa'id (d. 842). *Sunan*. Beirut: Dar al-Kutub al-'Ilmiyya, n.d.

Ibn al-Mubarak, 'Abdallah (d. 797). *Kitab al-jihad*. Beirut: Dar al-Nur, 1971.

———. *Kitab al-zuhd wa-l-raqa'iq*. Beirut: Muhammad 'Afif al-Zu'bi, n.d.

Ibn Munqidh, Usama (d. 1188). *Kitab al-i'tibar*. Beirut: Dar al-Kutub al-'Ilmiyya, 1999.

Ibn al-Nahhas, Ahmad b. Ibrahim al-Dumyati (d. 1411). *Mashari' al-ashwaq ila masari' al-'ushshaq wa-muthir al-gharam ila dar al-salam (fi al-jihad wa-fada'ilihi)*. Beirut: Dar al-Basha'ir al-Islamiyya, 2002.

Ibn Nubata al-Fariqi, 'Abd al-Rahman b. Muhammad (d. 984). *Diwan khutab minbariyya*. Beirut: al-Maktab al-Sha'biyya, n.d.

Ibn Qudama al-Maqdisi, 'Abdallah b. Muhammad (d. 1223). *Al-Mughni wa-yalihi al-sharh al-kabir*. Beirut: Dar al-Kitab al-'Arabi, n.d.

Ibn Rajab al-Hanbali, 'Abd al-Rahman b. Ahmad (d. 1392/93). *Al-Hukm al-jadira bi-l-idha'a min qawl al-nabi "bu'ithtu bi-l-sayf bayna yaday al-sa'a."* Riyadh: Dar al-Warraq, 2002.

Ibn Taymiyya, Taqi al-Din Ahmad (d. 1328). *Al-Jihad*. Beirut: Dar al-Jil, 1991.

———. *Majmu'at Fatawa*. Cairo: n.p., n.d. (37 vols).

Inalcik, Halil. *The Ottoman Empire: The Classical Age, 1300–1600*. London: Phoenix, 1994.

Iraqi, Muhammad Hasan, and Nasrallah Salihi, eds. *Jihadiyya*. Tehran: Idarah-yi Intishar-i Asnad, 1997.

Al-Isfahani, Abu Nu'aym Ahmad b. 'Abdallah (d. 1038/39). *Hilyat al-awliya'*. Beirut: Dar al-Kutub al-'Ilmiyya, 1997.

Al-Isfara'ini, Abu al-Muzaffar (d. 1078/79). *Al-Tabsir fi al-din wa-tamyiz al-firqa al-najiya 'an al-firaq al-halikin*. Cairo: al-Maktaba al-Azhariyya, 1999.

Jabara, Taysir. *Dawr al-Harakat al-Islamiyya fi al-Intifada al-Mubaraka*. Amman: Dar al-Furqan, 1992.

Jackson, Sherman. "Domestic Terrorism in the Islamic Legal Tradition." *Muslim World* 91 (2001), pp. 293–310.

Al-Jamal, Shawqi 'Ata'allah. "'Uthman b. Fuda wa-siyasatuhu al-jihad al-Islami al-lati ittaba'aha." *Al-Bahith al-'Ilmi* 26 (1976), pp. 41–68.

Jandora, John. *Militarism in Arab Society*. Westport, Conn.: Greenwood Press, 1997.

Jansen, Johannes. "Ibn Taymiyyah and the Thirteenth Century: A Formative Period of Modern Muslim Radicalism." *Quadreni di Studi Arabi* 5–6 (1987–88), pp. 391–96.

_____, trans. *The Neglected Duty*. New York: Macmillan, 1986 (*see also* Farag, Muhammad 'Abd al-Salam).

Al-Jarrahi al-'Ajluni, Isma'il b. Muhammad (d. 1749). *Kashf al-khifa' wa-muzil al-ilbas 'an al-ahadith al-lati ishtahara 'ala alsinat al-nas*. Cairo: Dar al-Zahid al-Qudsi, n.d.

The Jihad Fixation. Delhi: Wordsmiths, 2001.

Al-Jihad wa-khisal al-muhajidin fi al-Islam. Beirut: Markaz Baqiyat Allah al-A'zam, 1999.

Al-Jilani, 'Abd al-Qadir (d. 1166). *Al-Fath al-rabbani wa-l-fayd al-rahman.* Cairo: Dar al-Riyan li-l-Turath, 1988.

Johnson, James Turner. *The Holy War Idea in Western and Islamic Traditions.* University Park: Pennsylvania State University Press, 1997.

Jones, J. M. B. "The Chronology of the *Maghazi*." *Bulletin of the School of Oriental and African Studies* 19 (1957), pp. 245–80.

Kani, A. M. *The Intellectual Origins of the Sokoto Jihad.* Ibadan: Imam Publications, 1405/1984.

Al-Kasani al-Hanafi, Abu Bakr b. Mas'ud (d. 1191). *Bada'i' al-sana'i' fi tartib al-shar'i'.* Beirut: Mu'assasat al-Ta'rikh al-'Arabi, 2000.

Kelsay, John. *Islam and War: A Study in Comparative Ethics.* Louisville, Ky.: John Knox Press, 1993.

Kelsay, John, and James Turner Johnson, eds. *Just War and Jihad: Historical and Theoretical Perspectives on War and Peace in Western and Islamic Traditions.* Westport, Conn.: Greenwood Press, 1991.

Kemper, Michael. "Khalidiyya Networks in Daghestan and the Question of Jihad." *Die Welt des Islams* 42 (2002), pp. 41–71.

Khadduri, Majid. *War and Peace in the Law of Islam.* Baltimore: Johns Hopkins University Press, 1955.

Al-Khumayni, Ruhallah. *Jihad al-nafs aw al-jihad al-akbar.* n.p., n.d.

Khuttali, Muhammad b. Ya'qub. *'Awn ahl al-jihad min al-umara wa-l-ajnad.* Damascus: Dar Kanan, 1996.

Kilani, Abdul Razaq. "*Jihad:* A Misunderstood Aspect of Islam." *Islamic Culture* 70 (1996), pp. 35–46.

Kister, M. J. "Do Not Assimilate Yourselves": *La tashabbahu;* with an appendix by M. Kister." *Jerusalem Studies in Arabic and Islam* 12 (1989), pp. 321–71.

———. "*illa bi-haqqihi . . .*" *Jerusalem Studies in Arabic and Islam* 5 (1984), pp. 33–52.

———. "Land, Property, and *Jihad.*" *Journal of the Economic and Social History of the Orient* 34 (1991), pp. 270–311.

Kohlberg, Etan. "The Development of the Imami Shi'i Doctrine of *Jihad.*" *Zeitschrift der Deutschen Morgenländischen Gesellschaft* 126 (1976), pp. 64–86.

———. "Martyrdom and Self-Sacrifice in Classical Islam." *Pe'amim* 75 (1998), pp. 5–26 (in Hebrew).

———. "Medieval Muslim Views on Martyrdom." *Mededelingen der Koninklijke Nederlandse Akademie van Wetenschappen* 60 (1997), pp. 281–307.

van Koningsveld, P. S. "Muslim Slaves and Captives in Western Europe during the Late Middle Ages." *Islam and Christian-Muslim Relations* 6 (1995), pp. 1–23.

Kraemer, Joel. "Apostates, Rebels and Brigands." *Israel Oriental Studies* 10 (1980), pp. 34–73.

———. "The *Jihad* of the *Falasifa.*" *Jerusalem Studies in Arabic and Islam* 10 (1987), pp. 372–90.

Kruse, Hans. "*Takfir* und *Ğihad* bei den Zaiditen des Jemen." *Die Welt des Islams* 23–24 (1984), pp. 424–57.

Lambton, Ann. "A Nineteenth-Century View of *Jihad*." *Studia Islamica* 32 (1970), pp. 181–92.

Lange, Dierk, ed. and trans. *A Sudanic Chronicle: The Borno Expeditions of Idris Alauma (1564–1576)*. Wiesbaden: Franz Steiner, 1987.

Latham, J. D. "The Archers of the Middle East: The Turco-Iranian Background." *Iran* 8 (1970), pp. 97–104.

Lewis, Bernard. *Race and Slavery in the Middle East*. Oxford: Oxford University Press, 1990.

Lieven, Anatoly. *Chechnya: Tombstone of Russian Power*. New Haven: Yale University Press, 1999.

Mahmud, 'Ali 'Abd al-Halim. *Rukn al-jihad*. Cairo: Dar al-Tawzi', 1995.

Maqdisi, Muhammad, trans. "Charter of the Islamic Resistance Movement *(Hamas)* of Palestine." *Journal of Palestine Studies* 22 (1993), pp. 122–34.

Marin, Manuela. "Crusaders in the Muslim West: The View of Arab Writers." *Maghreb Review* 17 (1992), pp. 95–101.

Al-Marini, 'Abd al-Haqq. *Shi'r al-jihad fi al-adab al-Maghribi*. Rabat: Wizarat al-Awqaf wa-l-Shu'un al-Islamiyya, 1989.

Martin, Bradford G. "Mahdism and Holy War in Ethiopia before 1600." *Proceedings of the Seminar for Arabian Studies* 3 (1973), pp. 106–17.

———. "Mahdism, Muslim Clerics, and Holy Wars in Ethiopia, 1300–1600." In Harold Marcus, ed., *Proceedings of the First United States Conference on Ethiopian Studies, Michigan State University, 2–5 May 1973*, pp. 91–100. East Lansing, Michigan, 1975.

———. *Muslim Brotherhoods in Nineteenth-Century Africa*. Cambridge: Cambridge University Press, 1976.

Masa'il jihadiyya wa-hukm al-'amaliyyat al-istishhadiyya. Beirut: al-Wahda al-Islamiyya, 2002.

Al-Masri, Abu Hamza. *Khawaarij and Jihad*. Birmingham: Maktabat al-Ansar, n.d.

Masud, Muhammad Khalid. "*Hadit* and Violence." *Oriente Moderno* 21 (n.s.) (2002), pp. 5–18.

———. "Shehu Usuman Dan Fodio's Restatement of the Doctrine of Hijrah." *Islamic Studies* 25 (1986), pp. 59–77.

McCauley, Clark. "Psychological Issues in Understanding Terrorism and the Response to Terrorism." In Christopher Stout, ed., *The Psychology of Terrorism*, pp. 3–29. Westport, Conn.: Praeger Publishers, 2002.

McEwen, E. "Persian Archery Texts: Chapter Eleven of Fakhr-i Mudabbir's *Adab al-Harb* (Early Thirteenth Century)." *Islamic Quarterly* 18 (1974), pp. 76–99.

Mercer, Patricia. "Palace and Jihad in the Early 'Alawi State in Morocco." *Journal of African History* 18 (1977), pp. 531–53.

Mohamed, K. M. "A Critical Study of *Tahrid ahl al-iman 'ala jihad 'abdat al-sulban*." *Islamic Culture* 64 (1990), pp. 121–30.

Molina, Luis. "Las campañas de al-Manzor." *Al-Qantara* 2 (1981), pp. 204–64.

Moorhead, John. "The Monophysite Response to the Arab Invasions." *Byzantion* 51 (1981), pp. 579–91.

Morabia, Alfred. *Le gihad dans l'Islam médiéval.* Paris: Albin Michel, 1993.
———. "Ibn Taymiyya: Dernier grand théoreticien du *gihad* médiéval." *Bulletin d'études orientales* 30 (1978), pp. 85–100.
Mubarakshah, Muhammad b. Mansur (fl. 1169). *Adab al-harb wa-l-shuja'a,* ed. S. N. Babadzhanov. Dushanbe: Tadzhikshii vyshii yoennyi kolledzh, 1997.
Al-Mubarrad, Muhammad b. Yazid (d. 899). *Al-Kamil fi al-lugha wa-l-adab.* Beirut: al-Maktaba al-'Asriyya, 1997.
Al-Muhasibi, al-Harith b. Asad (d. 857). *Adab al-nufus (wa-yalihi Kitab al-tawahhum).* Beirut: Mu'assasat al-Kutub al-Thaqafiyya, 1991.
Mukhtar, Muhammad Habibullah. *Jihad.* Karachi: Dar al-Tasnif, Jami'at 'Ulum Islamiyya, 1989.
Al-Munawi, 'Abd al-Ra'uf (d. 1612/13). *Al-Kawakib al-durriyya fi tarajim al-sadat al-Sufiyya.* Beirut: Dar Sadir, 1999.
Mu'nis, Husayn. *Watha'iq 'an al-Mahdi.* Cairo: Hawliyyat Kulliyyat al-Adab bi-Jami'at Ibrahim, 1953.
Murad, Barakat Muhammad. *Al-Amir 'Abd al-Qadir al-Jaza'iri: al-Mujahid al-Sufi.* Cairo: al-Sadr li-Khidmat al-Tiba'a, 1990.
Muslim: *see* al-Qushayri, Muslim b. al-Hajjaj.
Mutahhari, Ayatullah Morteza. *Jihad.* Tehran: Intisharat-i Sadra, 2001. *Jihad: The Holy War of Islam and its Legitimacy in the Qur'an.* Trans. Mohammad Salman Tawhidi. Qumm: Islamic Propagation Society, 1985.
Nafi, Basheer. "Shaykh 'Izz al-Din al-Qassam: A Reformist and a Rebel Leader." *Journal of Islamic Studies* 8 (1997), pp. 185–215.
Al-Nasa'i, Ahmad b. Shu'ayb (d. 915/16). *Sunan* (with commentary of Jalal al-Din al-Suyuti). Beirut: Dar al-Fikr, n.d.
Nasr, Seyyed Vali Reza. *Mawdudi and the Making of Islamic Revivalism.* Oxford: Oxford University Press, 1996.
Nizam. *Al-Fatawa al-Hindiyya al-ma'rufa bi-l-fatawa al-'Alamgiriyya fi madhhab al-Imam al-A'zam Abi Hanifa Nu'man.* Beirut: Dar al-Kutub al-'Ilmiyya, 2000.
Nizami, Tawfiq Ahmad. "Muslim Political Thought and Activity in India during the First Half of the Nineteenth Century." *Studies in Islam* 4 (1967), pp. 139–62.
Noorani, A. G. *Islam and Jihad: Prejudice versus Reality.* New York: Palgrave, 2002.
Noth, Albrecht. "Heiliger Kampf *(Ğihad)* gegen die Franken: Zur Position der Kreuzzüge im Rahmen der Islamgeschichte." *Saeculum* 37 (1986), pp. 240–58.
———. *Heiliger Krieg und heiliger Kampf in Islam und Christentum: Beiträge zur Vorgeschichte und Geschichte der Kreuzzüge.* Bonn: Röhrscheid, 1966.
Nu'aym b. Hammad al-Marwazi (d. 844). *Kitab al-fitan.* Beirut: Dar al-Fikr, 1993.
Olcott, Martha Brill, and Bakhtiyar Babajanov. "Notes of a Terrorist." *Foreign Policy,* March–April 2003, pp. 30–42.
Pipes, Daniel. *Slave Soldiers and Islam: The Genesis of a Military System.* New Haven: Yale University Press, 1981.
Al-Qadiri, 'Abdallah b. Ahmad. *Al-Jihad fi sabil Allah.* Jidda: Dar al-Manara, 1992.

Al-Qahtani, Muhammad. *Al-Wala' wa-l-bara'a*. London: al-Firdous, 2000.

Al-Qanuji al-Bukhari, Siddiq Hasan Khan (d. 1890). *Al-'Ibra mi-ma ja'a fi al-ghazw wa-l-shahada wa-l-hijra*. Beirut: Dar al-Kutub al-'Ilmiyya, 1988.

Al-Qarrab, Ishaq b. Abi al-Ishaq (d. 1037/38). *Fada'il al-rami fi sabil Allah*. In *Majmu'at ajza' hadithiyya*, ed. Abu 'Ubayda Mashhur b. Hasan Al Salman. Beirut: Dar Ibn Hazm, 2001, vol. 1, pp. 265–305.

Al-Qasim b. Ibrahim (d. 860/61). *Majmu' kutub wa-rasa'il al-Imam al-Qasim b. Ibrahim al-Ra'is*. Sana'a: Dar al-Hikma al-Yunaniyya, 2001.

Al-Qasimi, Zafir. *Al-Jihad wa-l-huquq al-duwwaliyya fi al-Islam*. Damascus: Dar al-'Ilm li-l-Malayyin, 1982.

Al-Qayrawani, 'Abdallah b. Abi Zayd (d. 997). *Al-Nawadir wa-l-ziyadat 'ala ma fi al-mudawwina min ghayriha min al-ummahat*. Beirut: Dar al-Gharb al-Islami, 1999.

Al-Quraishi, Salim al-Din. *Cry for Freedom: Proclamations of Muslim Revolutionaries of 1857*. Lahore: Sang-e-Meel Publications, 1996.

Al-Qushayri al-Naysaburi, Muslim b. Hajjaj (d. 875). *Sahih*. Beirut: Dar Jil, n.d.

Qutub, Sayyid. *Ma'alim fi al-tariq*. Riyadh: al-Ittihad al-Islami al-'Alami li-Munazzamat al-Tullabiyya, n.d. Trans. S. Badrul Hasan, *Milestones*. Karachi: International Islamic Publishers, 1981.

Rajabi, Muhammad Hasan. *Rasa'il va-fatava-yi Jihadiyya*. Teheran: Wizarat-i Farhang va-Irshad-i Islami, n.d.

Rajihi, 'Abd al-'Aziz b. Faysal. *Qudum Ahl al-jihad li-ghazw al-zanadiqa wa-l-ilhad*. Riyad: Dar al-Sumay'i, 1998.

Ramadan, 'Abd al-Baqi. *al-Jihad sabiluna*. Beirut: Mu'assasat al-Risala, 1990.

Rashid, Ahmed. *Jihad: The Rise of Militant Islam in Central Asia*. New Haven: Yale University Press, 2002.

Rashidi, Muhammad b. Muhammad. *Tafrij al-kurub fi tadbir al-hurub*. Damascus: Dar Kanan, 1995. Trans. George Scanlon, *A Muslim Manual of War, Being* Tafrij al-karub fi tadbir al-hurub. Cairo: American University in Cairo Press, 1961.

Renard, John. "*Al-Jihad al-akbar*: Notes on a Theme in Islamic Spirituality." *Muslim World* 78 (1988), pp. 225–42.

Rhoads, Murphy. *Ottoman Warfare, 1500–1700*. New Brunswick, N.J.: Rutgers University Press, 1999.

Rida, Muhammad Rashid. *Fatawa Rashid Rida*. Beirut: Dar al-Kitab al-Jadid, 1970.

———. *Tafsir al-Qur'an al-hakim al-mashhur bi-Tafsir al-Manar*. Beirut: Dar al-Kutub al-'Ilmiyya, 1999.

Al-Rikabi, al-Shaykh. *Al-Jihad fi al-Islam*. Damascus: Dar al-Fikr, 1997.

Rosenthal, Franz. "On Suicide in Islam." *Journal of the American Oriental Society* 66 (1946), pp. 239–59.

Rubin, Uri. "Bara'a: A Study of Some Qur'anic Passages." *Jerusalem Studies in Arabic and Islam* 5 (1984), pp. 113–32.

Runciman, Steven. *A History of the Crusades*. Cambridge: Cambridge University Press, 1988.

Al-Rushayd, 'Abdallah b. Nasir. *Intiqad al-i'tirad 'ala tafjirat al-Riyad*. At *www.alfarouq.com (A.H. 5/23/1424).

Sabahuddin, S. "Conduct of Strategy and Tactics of War during the Muslim Rule of India" *Islamic Culture* 20 (1946), pp. 154–64, 291–96, 345–52, 21; (1947), pp. 7–15, 123–34.

Sachedina, Abdulaziz. "The Development of *Jihad* in Islamic Revelation and History." In James Turner Johnson and John Kelsay, eds., *Cross, Crescent and Sword*, pp. 35–50. New York: Greenwood, 1990.

Al-San'ani, 'Abd al-Razzaq b. Hammam (d. 826). *Al-Musannaf.* Beirut: 'Alam al-Kutub, 1983.

Al-Sarakhsi, Abu Bakr Muhammad b. Ahmad (d. ca. eleventh century). *Kitab al-mabsut.* Beirut: Dar al-Fikr, 2000.

Savage, Elizabeth. *A Gateway to Hell, a Gateway to Paradise: The North African Response to the Arab Conquest.* Princeton: Darwin Press, 1997.

Schleifer, S. Abdullah. "Jihad: Modernist Apologists, Modern Apologetics." *Islamic Quarterly* 31 (1984), pp. 25–46.

———. "Jihad: Sacred Struggle in Islam (IV)." *Islamic Quarterly* 31 (1984), pp. 87–102.

———. "Jihad and Traditional Islamic Consciousness." *Islamic Quarterly* 27 (1983), pp. 173–203.

———. "Understanding Jihad: Definitions and Methodology." *Islamic Quarterly* 27 (1983), pp. 118–31.

Shadid, Muhammad. *Al-Jihad fi al-Islam.* Beirut: Mu'assasat al-Risala, 1982.

Al-Shafi'i, Muhammad b. Idris (d. 820). *Kitab al-umm.* Al-Mansura: Dar al-Wafa' li-l-Tiba'a wa-l-Nashr, 2001.

Shah, Taalib ur-Rahman. *Jihaad: fardh ayn or fardh kifaayah?* Maktabat Ashab al-Hadeeth, n.d.

Shaked, Haim. *Life of the Sudanese Mahdi.* New Brunswick, N.J.: Transaction Books, 1978.

Shalbi, Ahmad. *Al-Jihad wa-l-nizam al-'askari fi al-tafkir al-Islami.* Cairo: Maktabat al-Nahda al-Misriyya, 1974.

Shaltut, Mahmud. *al-Qur'an wa-l-qital.* Beirut: Dar al-Fath, 1983.

Sharafutdinovoi, R. Sh. *Araboia azychneye dokumenty epokhi Shamiliaa.* Moscow: Vostochnaia Literatura RAM, 2001.

Sha'rawi, Muhammad Mutawalli. *Al-Jihad fi al-Islam.* Cairo: Maktabat al-Turath al-Islami, 1998.

Shatzmiller, Maya. "The Crusades and Islamic Warfare—A Re-Evaluation." *Der Islam* 69 (1992), pp. 247–88.

Al-Shawkani, Muhammad b. 'Ali (d. 1850). *al-Daw' al-'ajil fi daf' al-'aduww al-sa'il* in *Thalathat rasa'il ila 'ulama al-Yaman.* Al-Kuwayt: Dar al-Arqam, 1985.

Sheik-Abdi, Abdi. *Divine Madness: Mohammed Abdulle Hassan (1856–1920).* London and Atlantic Highlands, N.J.: Zed Books, 1993.

Shepard, William. "What Is 'Islamic Fundamentalism'?" *Studies in Religion* 17 (1988), pp. 5–26.

Sherwani, Haroon Khan. "Incursions of the Muslims into France, Piedmont, and Switzerland." *Islamic Culture* 4 (1930), pp. 397–424, 588–624; 5 (1931), pp. 71–112, 472–95.

Shinar, Pessah. "'Abd al-Qadir and 'Abd al-Krim: Religious Influences on Their Thought and Action." *Studies in Islam* 6 (1969), pp. 135–64.

Sikand, Yoginder. "The Changing Course of the Kashmiri Struggle: From National Liberation to Islamist Jihad?" *Muslim World* 91 (2001), pp. 229–56.

Al-Sijistani, Abu Da'ud, Sulayman b. al-Asha'th (d. 888/89). *Sunan.* Beirut: Dar al-Jil, 1988.

Al-Silfi, Salim b. 'Abd al-Hilali. *Al-Fawa'id al-hisan min hadith Thawban (tada'i al-umam).* Casablanca: Dar Ibn 'Affan, 2001.

Simon, Robert. "Muhammad and the *Jihad.*" *Acta Orientalia [Academiae Scientiarum Hungaricae]* 52 (1999), pp. 235–42.

Al-Subki, 'Ali b. 'Abd al-Kafi (d. 1355). *Fatawa al-Subki.* Beirut: Dar al-Jil, 1992.

Al-Sulami, 'Izz al-Din 'Abd al-'Aziz b. 'Abd al-Salam (d. 1262). *Ahkam al-jihad wa-fada'ilihi.* Beirut: Dar al-Fikr al-Mu'asir, 1996.

Al-Sulami, Yusuf b. Yahya (d. 1261/62). *'Iqd al-durar fi al-Mahdi al-muntazar.* Al-Zarqa': Maktabat al-Manar, 1993.

Al-Suyuti, Jalal al-Din (d. 1505). *Abwab al-sa'ada fi asbab al-shahada.* Cairo: al-Maktaba al-Qiyama, 1987.

———. *Arba'un hadithan fi fadl al-jihad.* Cairo: Dar al-Fadila, n.d.

———. *Al-Budur al-safira fi ahwal al-akhira.* Beirut: Dar al-Kutub al-'Ilmiyya, 1996.

———. *Ma rawahu al-asatin 'an 'adam maji' al-salatin.* Beirut: Dar Ibn Hazm, 1992.

Al-Tabarani, Sulayman b. Ahmad (d. 971). *Kitab al-du'a.* Beirut: Dar al-Basha'ir al-Islamiyya, 1987.

———. *Musnad al-Shamiyyin.* Beirut: Mu'assasat al-Risala, 1996.

Taha, Rifa'i Ahmad. *Imatat al-litham 'an ba'd ahkam dhurwat sinam al-Islam.* *www.tawhed.com.

Takruri, Nawwaf. *Al-'Amaliyyat al-istishhadiyya fi al-mizan al-fiqhi.* Damascus: Nawwaf al-Takruri, 1997 (2002 re-edition).

Al-Tarsusi, Najm al-Din (d. 1357). *Kitab Tuhfat al-Turk.* Damascus: Institut Français de Damas, 1997.

Al-Tartushi, Muhammad b. al-Walid b. Khalaf (d. 1126). *Siraj al-muluk.* Beirut: Dar Sadir, 1995.

Thalatha rasa'il fi al-jihad (Sayyid Qutb, Abu al-'Ala al-Mawdudi, Hasan al-Banna'). Amman: Dar 'Ammar, 1991.

Al-Tibi, 'Ukasha 'Abd al-Manan. *Al-Shahada wa-l-istishhad Fi Zilal al-Qur'an li-Shaykh Sayyid Qutb.* Cairo: Maktabat al-Turath al-Islami, 1994.

Al-Tirmidhi, Muhammad b. 'Ali al-Hakim (d. 930). *Al-Manhiyat.* Cairo: Maktabat al-Qur'an, 1986.

Al-Tirmidhi, Muhammad b. 'Isa (d. 892). *Al-Jami' al-sahih.* Beirut: Dar al-Fikr, n.d.

Tor, Deborah. "From Holy Warriors to Chivalric Order: The 'Ayyars in the Eastern Islamic World, A.D. 800–1055." PhD diss., Harvard University, 2003.

Traboulsi, Samer. "An Early Refutation of Muhammad ibn 'Abd al-Wahhab's Reformist Views." *Die Welt des Islams* 42 (2002), pp. 373–415.

Al-Tusulli, al-Imam 'Ali b. 'Abd al-Salam (d. 1842/43). *Ajwibat al-Tusulli 'an masa'il al-Amir 'Abd al-Qadir fi al-jihad.* Beirut: Dar al-Gharb al-Islami, 1996.

Umar, Umar Ahmad. *Al-Jihad fi sabil Allah*. Damascus: Dar al-Maktabi, 1999.

Versteegh, Kees. "The Arab Presence in France and Switzerland in the Tenth Century." *Arabica* 37 (1990), pp. 359–88.

Vikør, Knut. "*Jihad, 'ilm,* and *tasawwuf*—Two Justifications of Action from the Idrisi Tradition." *Studia Islamica* 46 (2000), pp. 153–76.

Voll, John. "The Mahdi's Concept and Use of 'Hijrah.'" *Islamic Studies* 26 (1987), pp. 31–42.

Waldman, Marilyn Robinson. "The Fulani *Jihad:* A Reassessment." *Journal of African History* 6 (1965), pp. 333–55.

Wallerstein, Immanuel. "Islam, the West, and the World." *Journal of Islamic Studies* 10 (1999), pp. 109–25.

Al-Wansharisi, Ahmad b. Yahya (d. 1508/9). *al-Mi'yar al-mughrib*. Beirut: Dar al-Gharb al-Islami, 1981.

Al-Waqidi, Muhammad b. 'Umar (d. 822). *Kitab al-maghazi*. Beirut: 'Alam al-Kutub, 1984 (reprint).

Al-Wasiti, Muhammad b. Ahmad (d. ca. eleventh century). *Fada'il al-Bayt al-Maqdis*. Jerusalem: Magnes Press, 1979.

Wenner, Manfred. "The Arab Muslim Presence in Medieval Central Europe." *International Journal of Middle Eastern Studies* 12 (1980), pp. 59–79.

Wensinck, A. J., ed. *Concordance et indices de la tradition musulmane*. Leiden: E. J. Brill, 1936–64.

———. "The Oriental Doctrine of the Martyrs." *Mededeelingen der Koninklijke Akkademie van Wetenschappen, Afdeeling Letterkunde* 53 (1921), pp. 147–74.

Wilks, Ivor, Nehemia Levtzion, and Bruce Haight. *Chronicles from Gonja*. Cambridge: Cambridge University Press, 1986.

Willis, John Ralph. "*Al-Jihad fi sabil Allah*—Its Doctrinal Basis in Islam and Some Aspects of Its Evolution in Nineteenth-Century West Africa." *Journal for African History* 8 (1967), pp. 395–415.

Zajackowski, Ananiasz. *Le traité iranien de l'art militaire: Adab al-Harb wa-sh-Shagha'a du XIIIe siècle*. Warsaw: Panstawowe Wydawn, 1969.

INDEX

ʿAbd al-Nasir, Gamal, 102
ʿAbd al-Qadir, 85–86, 123, 225n37
ʿAbd al-Rahman, Sultan Mawlay, 86
ʿAbd al-Razzaq, 16
ʿAbdallah b. al-Mubarak, 14–16, 35, 44, 55, 66, 132, 155
ʿAbdallah b. Ubayy, 9
ʿAbdallahi, Khalifa, 88
ʿAbduh, Muhammad, 94, 97, 110, 201
Abu Bakr, 172
Abu al-Darda', 30
Abu Ghayth, Sulayman, 189
Abu Ghraib, 157
Abu Hurayra, 13
Abu Sufyan, 7
Abu Zayd, Nasr, 139
Afghanistan, 70, 136, 141, 148, 191
Africa, 16; East, 72, 87–90; North, 21, 85; West, 21, 71, 74, 75–78
Aharoni, Reuven, 116
ahzab, 9, 65, 66
Akbar, 70
Akhulgoh, 83
ʿAlam, Jalal, 137
Alexander the Great, 12
Alexandria, 55
Alexios I Komnenos, 51
Alfonso VI of Leon, 50
Algar, Hamid, 74, 75, 232n1
Algeria, 73, 84–87, 119, 139
Allahu akbar, 18, 154, 200, 205–6
Almohads (al-Muwahhidun), 50

Alp Arslan, 55, 67
Americans, 174–75, 191–92, 194, 202
amir al-muʾminin, 136, 161
Antichrist, 24, 158, 160
apocalypse, 157–58, 203; apologetics, 2, 126; literature of, 8; mahdi and, 24, 25; Muslim, 43, 101, 122, 124; predictions of, see hadith
Apostate. See Muslims
al-Aqsa Martyrs Brigade, 117
ʿArabfaqih (Mir Shihab al-Din), 46, 71, 72
Arabian Peninsula, 11, 24, 75, 76, 136, 173
Arabic language, 12, 43, 47, 102, 165
Arabs, 82, 105
Arafat, Yasser, 116
Aramaic, 12
Armed Islamic Group (GIA), 120, 121, 132, 169–70
asceticism (rahbaniyya), 33, 44; jihad, 33–35
ʿAta', Muhammad, 203–5
Atiyyatallah, Louis, 202
Awrangzeb, 46, 69, 70; jihad, 79
ʿAws, 5
al-Awzaʿi, 15–16
ʿAyn Jalut, 53, 65
Ayyub, Saʿid, 160
al-Ayyubi, Salah al-Din, 45, 52
Azhar, Mohammed Masood, 118
al-Azhar University, 144
ʿAzzam, ʿAbdallah, 128, 131, 141, 149

Badakhshan, 135
al-Banna', Hasan, 97, 102
Banu al-Nadir, 6, 179
Banu Qaynuqa, 6, 180
Banu Qurayza, 171
Battle of Badr, 6–8, 27, 203
Battle of Lepanto, 69
Battle of Manzikert, 51, 55
Battle of Horns of Hittin, 45
Battle of Hunayn, 6
Battle of Khandaq, 6
Battle of Mecca, 6
Battle of Uhud, 6, 46
battles, 6; thematic, 7
Bedouin, 66
Begin, Menachem, 107
Beirut, 112
Bek, Hamza, 83
Ben-al-Shibh, Ramzi, 140
Berbers, 11
bida' (innovations), 76, 77
al-Bikali, Nawf, 26
Bin Ladin. See Ladin, Usama b.
al-Birjundi, Muhammad Hadi, 94, 95
blood, 15, 17, 137, 139, 160, 185, 191,
    208
blood price, 181
booty, 25, 187
Bosnia, 134, 137, 192
British East India Company, 80
British government, 87
British people, 7, 84, 88, 90, 115
Buddhists, 70
al-Bukhari, 10, 16, 17
al-Burzuli, 62, 63
al-Buti, 122, 228n45
Byzantine Empire, 12, 23, 49, 52
Byzantines, 6, 11, 12, 24, 30, 54, 61, 68,
    159

caliph, 93, 164; 'Abbasid, 53; amir al-
    mu'minin, 136, 161; imam, 22, 61,
    83, 125, 132, 164
caliphates: 'Abbasid, 52; Sokoto, 76
Caucasus, 11, 46, 82–84
Caucasus Mountains, 82, 134
Center for Understanding Islam, 43
Chechnya, 82, 84, 134–35; Muslims in,
    135
children, 178–79
Chittick, William, 38
Christians, 3, 10, 12, 25, 61, 64, 65, 94;
    imperialist rule of, 88
colonialism, 167
colonization, 102
communism, 107
communists, 135, 154

companions of the Prophet Muhammad,
    172, 201, 208
Confederates, 18, 65, 199–200, 202
conquest, 76, 102, 168
Constantinople, 11, 22, 24, 68, 159
Covenant of 'Umar, 59
Crane, Robert, 43
Crete, 49
Crimean War, 84
Crone, Patricia, 23
Crusades, 40, 51–52, 56, 61, 116, 160,
    163, 173, 176, 193
Cyprus, 55

Daghestan, 82, 84
Dajjal, 158–59
Damascus University, 122
Dan Fodio, Shehu Usaman, 72, 75, 77,
    78, 87, 89, 90
Dar al-Harb, 20, 64, 79, 81
Dar al-Islam, 20, 64
Dar al-Kufr, 123
Dar al-Sulh, 20
David and Goliath, 144, 156
Da'wa, 147
Day of Hudaybiyya, 172
Day of Judgment, 199
Day of Resurrection, 13, 23, 25, 158, 188
Dayton Peace Accord of 1995, 134
de Lusignan, Guy, 45
Decisive Word, The (al-Qawl al-Qati'),
    132
Devil, 198
dhimmis, 125
Digby, Simon, 46
Dihlawi, Shah 'Abd al-'Aziz, 79
Distinction concerning Religions, Here-
    sies, and Sects, The (al-Fasl fi al-
    milal wa-l-ahwa' wa-l-nihal), 58
Divine Law. See shari'a
Dove's Neck-Ring, The (Tawq al-
    hamama), 58
Dozy, Reinhart, 41
Durayd b. al-Simma', 179
dynasties: 'Alawi, 85; Moghul, 79;
    Ottoman Turkish, 54

East Timor, 137
Egypt, 51, 52, 53, 64, 87, 98, 106, 113,
    136, 139
Eritrea, 88
Esposito, John, 41
Ethiopia, 24, 71, 72
Ethiopians, 97
Euphrates River, 53
Europe, 24
European Union, 134

Fadlallah, Ayatullah Muhammad Husayn, 112
Farag, 'Abd al-Salam, 107, 110, 121
al-Farida al-gha'iba (The Neglected Duty), 107, 109
al-Fasl fi al-milal wa-l-ahwa' wa-l-nihal (The Distinction concerning Religions, Heresies, and Sects), 58
fatawa, 62, 91, 92, 144
Fatawa al-Hindiyya, 70–71
Ferdinand of Aragon, 50
Fertile Cresent, 11
Fi Zilal al-Qur'an (In the Shadow of the Qur'an), 102
fighters, 17, 38, 43, 138, 177; see also *mujahidin*
Firestone, Reuven, 214n3
fitna, 185
five pillars of Islam, 14, 130
Food of Hearts, The (Qut al-qulub), 36
France, 11, 84, 87, 92, 119, 120; national pride, 87

Gama'at al-Islamiyya, 132, 134, 136, 148
Ganges River Valley, 80
Geneva Convention, 149
Geoffroy, Eric, 47
al-Ghamidi, Ahmad, 176
Ghana, 75
al-Ghazali, Abu Hamid, 37, 42
Ghazi Muhammad, 83
ghazw (raiding), 36
al-Ghunaymi, 123
GIA (al-Jama'a al-Islamiyya al-Musallaha; Armed Islamic Group), 120, 121, 132, 169–70
Gihad dans l'Islam medieval, Le, 40
Golden Horde, 52, 69
Gordon, General Charles, 87, 88
Grabbe, Pavel, 83
Grañ, Ahmad b. Ibrahim, 71
Granada, 63
Great Britain, 92; *see also* British government; British people
Gujarat, 70
Gulf War, 119

Habe kingdoms, 76
hadith, 10, 12–15, 17, 20, 21, 28, 30, 47, 59, 86, 145, 158
hajj, 160
Hamas (Harakat al-Muqawama al-Islamiyya), 114, 115, 116, 117, 146
al-Hamdani, Husayn Nuri, 112
Hamza b. Abd Muttalib, 188
Hanafi, 21, 180
Hanbali legal school, 21

Hanifiyya, 182
Harakat al-Mujahidin, 118
Harakat al-Muqawama al-Islamiyya. *See* Hamas
Hassan, Mohammed Abdulle, 89–90, 225n44
Haykal, Muhammad Khayr, 124, 126, 142
al-Haythami, 22
Heaven. *See* Paradise
hegemony, 190
Hell, 157, 185–86, 204
heresiography, 24
Herzegovina, 134
hijra, 5, 63, 76, 77
Hillenbrand, Carole, 41, 220n7
al-Hindi, al-Muttaqi, 215n24
Hindus, 70, 80, 82, 118
Hiskett, Mervyn, 77, 232n6
Hitler, Adolf, 12
Hizbullah, 112, 113
Hohenzollern German Empire, 3
Holding the Soul Accountable and Blaming It (Muhasibat al-nafs wa-l-izra' 'alayha), 36
houris, 28–29, 155, 157, 199–200
Huntington, Samuel, 164
Husayn, 75
hypocrites, 9, 185–86

Iberian Peninsula, 49, 85
Ibn Abi al-Dunya, Ibn Abi, 36
Ibn Abi Shayba, 16
Ibn Abi Zaminayn, 56
Ibn al-'Arabi, Muhyi al-Din, 38, 39, 59, 218n18
Ibn Arnabagh al-Zardakush, 68
Ibn Hazm, 58, 59, 61
Ibn al-Jawzi, 44
Ibn Kathir, 125
Ibn al-Mubarak. *See* 'Abdallah b. al-Mubarak
Ibn al-Nahhas, 55, 56
Ibn Qayyim al-Jawziyya, 193
Ibn Qudama, 61–62
Ibn Sa'ud, 207
Ibn Taymiyya, 63–66, 106, 108, 109, 131, 174, 193
Ibrahim Pasha, 75
Ihya 'ulum al-din (Revival of the Religious Sciences), 37
imam, 22, 61, 83, 125, 132, 164
immigrants *(muhajirun)*, 19
In the Shadow of the Qur'an (Fi Zilal al-Qur'an), 102
India, 11, 45, 52, 78–82, 118; British, 102

Indian Ocean, 72
Indonesia, 73, 192
Indus River Valley, 11
infidels, 139,169–70, 178, 180, 183–84, 203
innovations (bida'), 76, 77
Intifada, 116, 117
Iran, 53, 93, 110, 111
Iran-Iraq war, 111
Iraq, 53, 178, 192
Isabel of Leon-Castile, 50
al-Isfahani, Abu Nu'aym, 44
Islam: definition of, 141; globalist radical, 137, 147, 152; Isma'ilism, 142; radical, 113, 132, 135, 146, 150–51, 164; Sunni, 24, 64, 129; "true," 109. See also Muslims; Qu'ran
Islamic feminism, 145
Islamic period, middle, 57
Islamic National Salvation Front, 119
Islamic polity, 20
Islamic Ruling on Permissibility of Martyrdom Operations, The, 142
Islamic Salvation Front, 120
Isma'ili Assassins, 53
Israel, 106
al-Istambuli, Khalid, 107
'Izz al-Din al-Qassam, 115

al-Jabha al-Islamiyya li-l-Inqadh, 119
Jahangir, 70
Jahiliyya, 103
al-Jama'a al-Islamiyya al-Musallaha. See Armed Islamic Group (GIA)
al-Jama'a al-Salafiyya li-Da'wa wa-l-Qital (Salafiyaa Group for Proclamation and Fighting), 120
Janissaries, 54
al-Jassas, 180
Jaysh-i Muhammad, 118
al-Jazeera, 148
Jazira, 51
Jesus, 158
Jews, 10, 25, 94, 191
jihad, 1, 85, 163; defense of, 94; defensive, 95, 101, 122; definition of, 2, 32, 42, 71, 93, 99; goals of 182, 184–85; greater, 32–48, 95, 106, 109, 123, 165; in hadith, 12; "holy war," 3, 99; internal, 48, 95, 106, 111, 166; Islamic, 114; lesser, 32–48; literature, 18, 143, 213n1; offensive, 101, 105; redefinition, 94; spiritual aspects of, 2, 123, 165–67; theory of, 93; wars of, 2; women and, 17
al-Jilani, Abd al-Qadir, 42, 45, 48, 77–78
jizya, 21, 59, 60, 122, 183, 188

Jordan, 106, 113
jurisprudence/jurists, 19, 27, 54; Muslim, 62, 63

Ka'ba, 181, 207
al-Kasani, Abu Bakr, 60
Kashmir, 134, 192; Valley of, 118
Kazakhstan, 135
Khalil, Fazl al-Rahman, 118
al-Khamenei, 112
Khan Ghazan, 65
Khan Ghenghis, 12, 53
Khan Kublai, 53
Khan Siddiq Hassan, 81, 86
Khan Sir Sayyid Ahmad
Khandaq, 9, 12, 18
Khartoum, 87
Khazraj, 5
al-Khumayni, Ayatullah Ruhallah, 39, 111, 112
khums, 20
Khurasan, 61, 160
Khwarazm-Shah, 53
Kipling, Rudyard, 98
Kister, M. J., 25
Kitab al-jihad, 14, 15, 28, 33, 155
Kitab al-zuhd wa-l-raqa'iq, 43
Kohlberg, Etan, 91
Kurdish PKK, 112

Ladin, Usama b., 4, 131–32, 135–36, 139, 147–48, 160–61, 206
al-Lankarani, Muhammad Fadil, 112
Lashkar-i Tayba, 118, 119
Last Night, The, 195–202, 233n26
law, Muslim, 164
Lebanon, 110, 112, 113
Lessons and Insights for Present-day Jihad, 153
liberation, from colonialism, 102, 167
Libya, 46
Luxor, 133

Ma'alim fi al-tariq (Milestones along the Way), 102, 104, 105, 106
al-Mabsut, 21
Macedonia, 192
"Mad" Mullah, the (Mohammed Abdulle Hassan), 89–90, 225n44
madhahib (Islamic schools of legal thought), 21
al-Maghazi, 6
Maghrib, 13
Mahdi, 87, 158, 160
Mahmud of Ghazna, 69, 79
Makki, 'Abd al-Rahman, 119
Malfuzat-i Naqshbandiyya, 46
Mali, 75

Malik b. Anas, 15
Maliki legal school, 21
Mamluk period, 55, 68
mamluk system, 54–55
Mamluks, 53, 55, 65
Manicheans, 12, 54, 159
al-Mansur b. Abi al-ʿAmir, 50, 67
Mardin, 64
Martel, Charles, 11
martyrologies, 153–55, 157
martyrs, 17, 27, 28, 31; definition of, 26;
    martyrdom operations of, 26, 97,
    110, 112, 128, 142, 144–45, 205;
    Muslim, 26; reward for, 27; women,
    17, 146, 156
Mascara, 85, 86
*Mashari ʿal-ashwaq ila masari ʿal-
    ʿushshaq,* 55
Masʿud, Ahmed Shah, 135
al-Mawdudi, Abu al-ʿAla, 99, 103, 105,
    124
Mecca, 5, 75, 172
Medina, 7, 75
Menelik II of Ethiopia, 89
messianic prophecies, 81
*Milestones along the Way (Maʿalim fi al-
    tariq),* 102, 104, 105, 106
miracle stories, 153–57
Mishal, Shaul, 116
misogyny, 56
Mongols, 53, 64, 108
monotheism, 181–82
Morabia, Alfred, 40
Morocco, 63, 73, 84–87, 93
Moses, 13
Mount Uhud, 8
Muʿawiya al-Aswad, 44
Mubarak, Husni, 132–33, 207
Mudawwina of Sakhnun, 21
Mughni, 174
muhajirun (immigrants), 19
Muhammad, the Prophet, 4, 5, 9, 13, 22,
    29, 55, 65, 75, 82, 92, 95, 106, 124,
    126, 145, 152, 163, 201; biography
    of, 66; visitation from, 89
Muhammad ʿAli Pasha, 75
Muhammad, Mullah Umar Mujahid,
    136, 161
*Muhasibat al-nafs wa-l-izraʾ ʿalayha
    (Holding the Soul Accountable and
    Blaming It),* 36
al-Muhasibi, 35, 36, 44
mujahidin (fighters), 38, 43, 74, 89, 130,
    135, 148, 151–53, 157, 202–3,
    207
al-Mujammaʿ al-Islamiyya. *See* Hamas
Murabitun, 45, 50
Muslim Brotherhood, 97, 102, 115

Muslims: African, 50; apologists, 46;
    Arabic-speaking, 113, 115; armies
    of, 17; conquests by, 12, 30, 102;
    false, 138, 146; globalist radical
    136, 139, 149, 167 (*see also* al-
    Qaʾida); history of, 20; imperialism
    by, 102; Indian, 81; literature of, 21;
    lukewarm, 138; martyrs (*see* mar-
    tyrs); radical, 138; Shiʿite, 53; Span-
    ish, 40, 49, 50, 64, 85; Sunni, 53,
    54, 65, 93, 110, 112, 144; Syrian,
    16, 123. *See also* Islam
al-Muwahhidun (Almohads), 50

Napoleon, 12
Naqshbandiyya Sufi order, 83
al-Nawadir wa-l-ziyadat, 21
al-Nawawi, 194
*Neglected Duty, The (al-Farida al-
    ghaʾiba),* 107, 109
New York, 176, 181; *see also* World
    Trade Center
Nigeria, 75–78, 137, 167
Nile Valley, 87
Noah, 181
Nokrashy Pasha, 98
non-Muslims, 101, 104, 121–22, 139,
    141, 143, 167
Northern Alliance, 152, 157
Nubia, 11, 71

Ottoman Empire, 3, 40, 68, 75, 84, 90,
    93

Pact of ʿUmar, 94
Pahlavi, Shah Reza, 111
Pakistan, 11, 46, 118, 139
Palangposh, Baba, 46
Palestine Liberation Organization (PLO),
    113, 114, 115, 128
Palestinian National Authority (PNA),
    116, 117
Palestinians, 113, 192
pantheistic monism *(wahdat al-wujud),*
    38
Paradise, 9, 28, 186–7, 196, 199, 203,
    205, 207
Path of Allah, the, 15
People of the Book, 176, 184
Persia, 30, 91; and call for jihad, 91; lan-
    guage of, 47
Persian Achmenaeid Empire, 12
Philippines, 137
Plague of Justinian, 23
PLO (Palestine Liberation Organization),
    113, 114, 115, 128
PNA (Palestinian National Authority),
    116, 117

poetry, 17
Poitiers, 22
polemics, 2, 99; Christian, 102; Muslim, 101; theological, 24
polytheists, 34, 97, 183–84
Portuguese, 71
prayer, 197–99
purification, 186

Qadiris, 46
Qadiriyya Sufi order, 45, 77, 85
al-Qaʿida, 4, 67, 134, 144, 147–48, 152, 176, 189, 192; see also Islam, globalist radical
al-Qaradawi, 144
al-Qawl al-Qatiʿ (The Decisive Word), 132
Qayrawani, 21
al-Quds al-ʿArabi, 173
Qurʾan, 1, 17, 57, 58, 63, 100, 138, 147; see also suras of Qurʾan
Quraysh, 5, 7, 66, 172
al-Qurtubi, 193
al-Qushayri, 36
Qut al-qulub (The Food of Hearts), 36
Qutb, Sayyid, 102, 103, 104, 121, 139

radical Islam. See Islam, radical
raiding (ghazw), 36
Rashid, Ahmad, 40
reconquista, 51, 58, 85
Red Sea, 87
Revival of the Religious Sciences (Ihya ʿulum al-din), 37
Ridaʾ, Rashid, 94, 95, 96, 97, 110
Rome, 24
Russia, 92, 135
Russians, 84

Sabeans, 25
al-Sadat, Anwar, 107
Safavids, 45
Saladin. See al-Ayyubi, Salah al-Din
Salafiyya Group for Proclamation and Fighting (al-Jamaʾa al-Salafiyya li-Daʾwa wa-l-Qital,), 120
al-Sarakhsi, 21, 22
Sasanian Empire, 12, 23
Satan, 42, 198
Saudi Arabia, 132
self-sacrifice. See martyrologies; sub martyrs
September 11, 2001, 1, 48, 139, 147, 150, 153, 155, 176, 177, 181, 189–90
al-ShafiʿI, 21, 22, 180
Shah, Firoz, 80

shahada (martyrdom), 97; see also martyrologies; sub martyrs
shahid. See martyr
Shahid, Sayyid Ahmad, 79, 224n16
Shamil, Imam, 83, 84, 85
shariʿa (Divine Law), 19, 20, 70, 76, 108, 126, 139, 160, 167, 202
Shatzmiller, Maya, 222n42
al-Shawkani, 194, 225n46
Sheik-Abdi, Abdi, 225n44
al-Shirazi, Nasir Makarim, 112
Shiʿites, 53; clerics, 111; religious culture of, 110; teachings on jihad of, 91
Sicily, 49
Sikhs, 79
Six Day War, 106, 107, 113
Slave Dynasty of Delhi, 69
socialism, 107
Somalia, 87, 89, 90
Songhai, 75
Soviet Union. See Russia; U.S.S.R.
Spain, 40, 49, 96, 123
Sudan, 87–90, 178, 192
Sufis, 29, 39, 97, 135; Naqshbandiyya, 83; Qadiriyya, 45, 77, 85
suicide, 142–43
al-Sulami, al-ʿIzz b. ʿAbd al-Salam, 36
al-Suqami, Satam, 203–4
suras of Qurʾan: eight, 7, 195; forty-eight, 9; nine, 9–10, 96, 131, 195; three, 8
al-Suyuti, Jalal al-Din, 57, 221n21
"Sword of Truth," 77
syncretism, 165
Syria, 11, 16, 106, 113
Syrian Social Nationalist Party, 112

Tabaristan, 30
Tabaʿtabaʿi, Aga Sayyid ʿAli, 91
al-Taʾif, 6, 66
Takfir, 139
Tajikstan, 135
Talib, ʿAli b. Abi, 91
Taliban, 135–36, 153, 156, 160–61, 167, 192
al-Tantawi, 144, 230n25
al-Tartushi, 67
Tawq al-hamama (The Dove's Neck-Ring), 58
Tehran, 111
Temple of Hatshepsut, 133
terror, 17, 189, 200
terrorism, 42, 185
al-Thaqafi, ʿUrwa b. Masʿud, 172
Tijanis, 46
al-Tirmidhi, 16, 22, 34, 36, 217n10
Toledo, 50
Transoxiana, 13

Tunisia, 93
Turkey, 92
Turkmenistan, 135
Turks, 55, 97; Seljuq, 52
al-Tusulli, ʿAli b. ʿAbd al-Salam, 85

ulama, 56, 108, 193
Umar b. al-Khattab, 13, 95, 134
al-Umari, ʿAbd al-ʿAziz, 203–5
Umayyad caliphate, 49, 50
Umayyad dynasty, 11
umma (community), 129, 149, 163, 177, 183, 193
United Nations, 134
United States, 92, 134, 139, 149, 152, 155, 159, 177, 193, 204
Urdu language, 47, 102
Usama b. Zayd, 6
U.S.S.R., 134, 141, 156, 159; see also Russia
Uthman, 13
Uzbekistan, 40

"Verse of the Sword," 10; see also suras of the Qu'ran, nine
Vilayat-i Faqih, 111
von der Goltz, Rudiger, 92

wahdat al-wujud (pantheistic monism), 38
Wahhabism, 74, 98, 164, 224n16
al-walaʾwa-l-baraʾ, 141–42
Wali, Shah Niʾmat Allah, 81
al-Wansharisi, 62, 63
warfare, 3, 14, 19, 167; social, economic aspects of, 18; spiritual, 124; see also jihad
Washington, D.C., 176, 181
West Bank, 113, 114
women, 178–79; of Paradise, see houris
World Trade Center, 149, 150, 180, 194; see also September 11, 2001
World War I, 69

Xianjaing, 137

Yazdi, Shaykh Muhammad, 112
Yazid b. Shajara, 28
yenicheri, 54

Zangi, 51
Zangid-Ayyubid period, 55
al-Zawahiri, Ayman, 133, 134, 235n58
Zionist movement, 174
Zoroastrians, 12, 61, 188

Compositor:	Sheridan Books, Inc.
Text:	10/13 Sabon
Display:	Franklin Gothic
Printer and binder:	Sheridan Books, Inc.